The first new religion in the Caribbean since Rastafari, the Earth People draw on local strategies of resistance and on West African sources to assert a renascent African identity and celebrate female creativity. They argue that Black people are the guardians of a natural environment, which is constantly under threat from European science. Roland Littlewood, who is both a psychiatrist and a social anthropologist, criticises received ideas about pathology and creativity, and on the development of religions. While the founder's ideas emerged in her experience of cerebral disease, Dr Littlewood shows how the Earth People appropriate such radical personal experiences to build a community. Naturalistic and personalistic interpretations of human life are both valid and necessary. Neither can be reduced to the other.

Cambridge Studies in Social and Cultural Anthropology

Editors: Ernest Gellner, Jack Goody, Stephen Gudeman, Michael Herzfeld, Jonathan Parry

90

PATHOLOGY AND IDENTITY

A list of books in the series will be found at the end of the volume

PATHOLOGY AND IDENTITY

The work of Mother Earth in Trinidad

ROLAND LITTLEWOOD

University College London

CAMBRIDGE
UNIVERSITY PRESS

Published by the Press Syndicate of the University of Cambridge
The Pitt Building, Trumpington Street, Cambridge CB2 1RP
40 West 20th Street, New York, NY 10011–4211, USA
10 Stamford Road, Oakleigh, Melbourne 3166, Australia

First published 1993

Printed in Great Britain at the University Press, Cambridge

A catalogue record for this book is available from the British Library

Library of Congress cataloguing in publication data
Littlewood, Roland.
Pathology and identity: the work of Mother Earth in Trinidad /
Roland Littlewood.
  p.   cm. – (Cambridge studies in social and cultural anthropology)
Includes bibliographical references and index.
ISBN 0 521 38427 3
1. Earth People (Cult). 2. Mother Earth – Mental health.
3. Mentally ill – Religious life – Case studies. 4. Genius and mental
illness – Case studies. 5. Psychology, Religious – Trinidad.
I. Title. II. Series.
BL2566.T7L58 1992
299'.67–dc20   92–18251   CIP

ISBN 0 521 38427 3 hardback

WD

'How can we know the dancer from the dance?'

W. B. Yeats, *Collected Poems*, Macmillan, New York, 1950

Contents

Plates

Preface

The Pinnacle villagers had warned me about the Earth People. Dangerous and unpredictable strangers to the coast, they were certainly no friends to a White. When I arrived in the fishing village to study local knowledge of health and sickness I had been told about the community established some nine miles away in Hell Valley. A week afterwards I saw three of them bartering ground provision for cutlasses in one of the village stores; they looked at me with surprise (I was the only White along the coast except for the two Irish Dominicans at Toco) and then ignored me. A few months later I took the opportunity of joining the villagers on a government forestry expedition into the bush near the Earth People, both to obtain medicinal plants, but also, it was evident, to visit the Valley.

One of the foresters had met Mother Earth on her march to town in the previous year and offered to take me. Leading away from the abandoned *ajoupa* (bush hut) which had served as our base camp for two days, the now disused track followed the headland, covered in fallen vegetation, coconut fronds, leaf mulch, forest debris. We forded a stream, overhung by a decayed footbridge, occasionally glimpsing through the overgrown scrub the remains of the wooden houses which twenty years before had comprised small hamlets along the shore, and climbed to a small plateau facing the sea, backed by the mountains which descended to behind the settlement and then on either side dropped down to a rocky bay some thirty feet below. Out at sea pelicans floated on the tide, occasionally taking ungainly flight to dive for fish, only to have them contested by the wheeling frigate birds.

The most outstanding characteristic of the valley was surely its neatness and precision. The lower slopes of the mountains were cleanly cut into well-tended terraces, planted with banana, plantain, and ground provisions – yam, tannia, dasheen and cassava. Along the cliff edge the forest was cut back. Between piles of slowly burning scrub remained breadfruit, orange and avocado trees, coffee and cocoa. Nearer the house, pumpkins and coconut palms framed the first lawn I had seen since leaving Port-of-Spain, the grass cropped short by two goats.

The lawn stretches between the house and the track at the edge of the cliff, down which a slippery path twists along the rock face, down to a carved canoe and two rafts pulled up on the shingle. A shallow ravine passes along the side of the house and then across the lawn which nearer the house is paved with rocky stones. The house itself is the only remaining building of a once thriving village: a small wooden house with an attic, boards unpainted apart from the words 'HELL VALLEY, THE DEVIL LIVE HERE' facing the sea; window and door spaces open, fronted on one side by a silk cotton sapling and joined on the other to a large open-sided and simply carved extension, the bottom of which comprises open baskets woven into support posts and piled with harvested fruit and provision, scented with woodsmoke and the damp earth. Unlike other isolated country huts, there was no rubbish, no rusting tins or discarded tools lying about, no fragments of clothing, old calendars or fading copies of the farmer's almanac. The work here was wooden, roughly carved and polished through use, giving a precise sense of permanence, of place. The house seemed to exist for itself, no longer an echo of a society located somewhere else – in town, in Britain or in the United States.

The sound of timber being cut with axes came from behind the house. Chickens picked underneath; like all those in rural Trinidad, it is raised up on short stilts. In the space where a door had once hung stood a middle-aged woman of African ancestry, of medium stature, naked, her hair in short dreadlocks. Two small children played around her on the threshold. She greeted us with friendly reserve and discreetly avoided shaking hands, but briskly admonished my companion who had stuck our cutlasses into the ground as we neared the hut: 'The Earth is The Mother, all of we is She.' He was ill at ease, refused her invitation to stay and wandered off, saying he would return to collect me later. I entered the house, sat on the ground and accepted some coconut water in a calabash with a local cigar, to be told that my visit had been anticipated in a dream the previous night. I stayed on and off for over a year.

In the following pages I offer a story of this small community. Whilst attempting to evoke the Earth People's ideals and their way of life, and their relationship to the wider society, I am concerned also with their origin in the visionary experience of their founder. Mother Earth, as she is known by them, is regarded locally as insane and twice has been taken to the St Ann's psychiatric hospital in Port-of-Spain.

Medical anthropologists often examine popular knowledge of those experiences we call 'mental illness'; how these are experienced, shaped, received and amplified in different societies against the background of other local institutions. Understandings of madness, its origins and consequences, illuminate local psychological knowledge which may otherwise pass without explicit comment – a distinction between the moral and the physical, the limits of intentionality or empathy, or indeed the way in which people usually expect to identify external objects accurately. I am concerned here with another and different question, indeed the converse: can the extreme personal experiences of what medicine terms psychosis, when taken in part as some random, 'natural' event, give shape to society? May such arbitrary intrusions actually have a place in social innovation, sometimes serving as the charter for new departures?

The origins of severe 'mental illness' are not simply cultural and conventional; such illnesses do appear similar in different societies, often directly associated with those biological changes we term 'diseases', and independently of any necessary social awareness of such disease itself. This is not to deny that the eventual expression of 'psychopathology' can only occur through social institutions – which therefore may be said to have some determining role – but such expression may be comparatively invariant and may, like other representations of a world 'out there', provide the ground for local understanding of human life, of our motivations, causalities and values.

My account thus takes a rather different approach to the question of 'madness and creativity' from the well-known psychoanalytic argument. Psychoanalysis, I argue here, assumes a quantitative gradient between sanity and madness, ascribing an innovatory role to 'psychosis' only through employing it as a figuring for everyday and universal human dilemmas. Instead I suggest that there is perhaps nothing so very distinctive about the innovatory possibilities of mental illness and, although some psychological assumptions are inevitable, I have generally avoided psychodynamic interpretations. This is not an essay in psychobiography. I place comparatively little determining power on the actual processes of psychopathology themselves and merely suggest that, like any other cognitive innovation, they can serve to provide new variants of everyday values and conventional symbolisms which may or may not 'gel' with a given – or potential – set of social concerns at a particular time. I am not concerned with establishing psychopathology as a common mode of innovation, let alone the major one, but with arguing its very possibility, together with examining some of its characteristics and limitations. Nor do I engage in any detail with the social psychology of why particular individuals join the new movement, but more with interpreting the how of innovation and

congruence: Mother Earth's experiences and their translation into a set of
shared beliefs make a good deal of sense to many people, myself included.

I have often been asked, in Britain as well as in Trinidad – do I too believe
in Mother Earth's teaching? The notion of 'belief' is not perhaps appropriate –
one fit rather for the drastic doctrines of Christian eschatology or for its
successor, the rationalist theory of knowledge – and certainly not one
appropriate to the workings of the Earth People themselves. Something like
'acceptance'? Then perhaps yes. 'Resonance' certainly. Yes, if I accept that
humankind is part of the natural order of things; that we can never try to obtain
any privileged knowledge or control over the non-human without thereby
radically altering ourselves; that what we know as 'power' is often the attempt
to do this through denying such knowledge and control to others; that such
denials on the basis of gender and of race often have much in common; and
that alternative voices to those of the dominant order may well be generated
especially from the ranks of women, from Black people and those we call
mentally ill. If sometimes we may wonder why international markets are taken
as natural phenomena, why government pacification becomes arbitrary terror,
why welfare agencies may perpetuate poverty, and technological development
leads to famine, then indeed we may consider, along with the Earth People,
whether our implicit order of knowledge has not indeed got some things
upsided down. Mother Earth's notion of scientific knowledge as an ultimately
flawed attempt to mimic our origins seems to me no less reasonable than that
of science as a privileged epistemology.

I start by introducing her community, and then examine the extent to which
some recognised and now medically segregated domain of 'madness' may be
taken up by societies as a source of contributions to shared and generally
accepted notions within which it may offer new perspectives: a rather different
idea from the social scientist's perception of rapid social change as itself
'dysfunctional' or 'pathological'. Later I turn to the preconditions for this sort
of innovation, emphasising in particular the communal response rather than the
personality and intentions of the innovator. Local Trinidadian understanding of
madness is given some place, as the context within which Mother Earth's own
experiences are to be understood, and I consider how these experiences can be
represented in biomedicine with a conventional clinical assessment. I place
particular emphasis on a locally recognised experience we may gloss for the
moment as 'depression': *tabanka* articulates two linked sets of opposed but
complementary sensibilities with which Mother Earth's teachings are
particularly concerned, those associated with gender, and those associated with
ethnicity and class in the West Indies. The following chapters deal at greater
length with these understandings and how they are transformed through her

personal experiences into a new and relatively structured set of ideas. Comparison here between her different images involves an interplay between different types of interpretation – textual but also historical, symbolic, biomedical, and (parenthetically) psychological.

There is no single reading of the Earth People, nor do I attempt it. The cool-headed reductionist will be disappointed; I neither attempt to reduce natural facts to social facts, nor the reverse. To attempt to know what happens, and to describe how we make sense of it whether as a place or as a procedure – each seem to me to be inescapable and to be equally valid, the one constituting the other in a continuing dialectic within Western thought: whether couched in the idiom of explanation versus meaning, arbitrary but causal necessity versus human agency, the contingent versus the necessary, the natural sciences versus the humanities, the empirical versus the structured, the technical versus the aesthetic, or whatever. Attempts to fuse them into a single system – whether it be through psychoanalysis or sociobiology – work by a sleight of hand whose illusive simplicity palls after a few passes as they collapse into either the one or the other. Madness is not merely a literary trope, nor can human society be predicated on neurophysiology alone. To paraphrase Engels (or indeed Mother Earth) we are made by nature and yet we make nature. Inclusion here of the biological perspective does not assume some causal sequence of brain states to psychological events and thence to social institutions; but rather that certain physiologies may be said to constrain and also make possible the meanings which societies as active agents then ascribe back to them. Going one way we have the biologist's determinism; going the other we follow the humanist's voluntarism. Neither is false, nor true.

I argue that Mother Earth's ideas appeal to other members of her group with an interpretation of the community's organisation as constituted through individuals, each of whom resonates as an individual with the personal meaning of her ideas, whilst these ideas simultaneously generate the whole community as a family developed around Mother Earth herself. I end by considering the limits and facilitations of psychopathology as a likely vehicle of social and cognitive change. While psychopathology reflects those events we may term biological more than recent historians of madness may wish to accept, the social meanings which constitute the outsider can at times transform the whole, centre and margin alike.

My own role as writer and participant has some place here, and how I myself became incorporated into her unfolding cosmogony. It will be evident that my involvement with the Earth People precluded (whether or not I had wished it so) any pretence at ethnographic neutrality. Fanon and Foucault have argued that the European's 'Other' is constituted through the dominant order. But only in part. For men, Whites, psychiatrists and anthropologists (and sons) are in turn constituted through our Other; my own gender, race, profession (and childhood) are hardly autonomous constructions. This account is not however one of personal self-discovery. Others have their authentic biographies, their struggles, their appropriations of our classification. Though these are entwined with the dominant order, and reflect it, their lives are hardly cyphers of the dominant code: lived through it indeed, but not by it. Works not texts. If I have attempted here some glosses on Mother Earth's work, glosses which for me are significant, it is not to render that work plausible and reasonable. Indeed it is powerfully unreasonable, both in its origins and in its critique of our conventional knowledge.

It is easy to talk of a 'dialectic' here but how do we actually proceed? Are our two procedures, and hence the domains which they generate, mutually constitutive? Let me take an example which I have used elsewhere:

(a)   Why do lesbians wear ear-rings?
(b)   Who is asking question (a), and why?

One of these questions is likely to prove more congenial to us than the other; indeed the other is likely to evoke strong personal feelings. And the juxta-position of the two seems discordant, even distasteful, for each argues for a conventionalised way of proceeding which allows no validity to the other. Taking question (a), our likely path may follow something like this: a broad cultural materialism, reproductive fitness, mating behaviours, sexually arousing signals, the evolutionary biology of homosexuality and its contemporary interpersonal formations, perhaps to social rereading of the persistence of 'natural symbols' through symbolic inversion in new situations of dominance. Question (b) will lead us through the history and politics of contemporary scientific discourse, the hardly disinterested choice of its 'Other', and the pay-offs in a male and heterosexual discourse for practitioners, and hence their desires, perhaps physiologies, of power. Anthropology, like psychiatry, tends to veer from one starting point to the other depending on whether it sees itself as scientific or humanistic. Psychiatry has usually chosen the former approach, even managing to transform 'phenomenology' into an objectified discourse (as I myself do in Chapter 5).

If we recognise that neither question is without interest, it is by no means obvious what we do next. A hermeneutic elision, say reading science as narrative (Margolis 1989), or just asserting they are really the same (Bateson 1979), or emergent stages (Hegel's *Phenomenology of Spirit*, or indeed Mother

Earth herself), all fail to do justice to the first perspective as practised knowledge. I am not concerned here with reviewing the various theoretical solutions which have been offered since the seventeenth century or with attempting a new privileged foundation but with trying to do justice to each in their own terms. And yet, a closer look at each schema suggests that they are perhaps not really so distinct after all, and that they are dealing with the 'same' question howbeit from different ends as it were. There is an essential unity in that each is dependent on the other. We can thus try to integrate them together in a discursive account which will end up asn a pluralistic paste-book or else a muddy middle ground (a psychology), or we can offer some sort of dialogic ebb and flow in which each understanding overextends itself into the other and constrains it, or we can just place the two down together in an ironic simultaneity. Where we draw the line or halt our chain depends on our accepted sense of disciplinary boundaries and of the 'fitness' of the argument. In Chapters 2 and 3 I suggest how certain social understandings allow certain biological understandings: in Chapters 4 and 10 the reverse. I make no apologies for what might seem at times a return to Kantian antinomy for this seems inevitable if we are to do justice to each knowledge as a conventional procedure. In approaching Mother Earth, I have used here both the 'ironic' and the 'ebb and flow' without claiming an eventual reconciliation; but informally not programmatically, for here the object of a naturalistic discourse like (a) is the active agent who asks me something like question (b) – and answers it. As I argue later, my text then is not just an external interpretation (and it is that) but simultaneously an action elaborated by Mother Earth herself in which she and I may come to constitute each other. It is common for the writer to end a preface by claiming full responsibility. Not here.

Acknowledgements

Part of my argument has previously appeared in The Imitation of Madness: The Influence of Psychopathology Upon Culture (*Social Science and Medicine*, 1984, 19: 705–15); An Indigenous Conceptualisation of Reactive Depression in Trinidad (*Psychological Medicine*, 1985, 15: 275–81); From Vice to Madness: The Semantics of Naturalistic and Personalistic Understandings in Trinidadian Local Medicine (*Social Science and Medicine*, 1988, 27: 129–48); Putting Out The Life (in *Anthropology and Autobiography*, eds. Judith Okely and Helen Callaway, Routledge, 1992); History, Memory and Appropriation: Some Problems in the Analysis of Origins (in *Rastafari and Other African-Caribbean Worldviews*, ed. Barry Chevannes, in press).

I am grateful to the Social Science Research Council for a Post-Doctoral Fellowship to undertake part of my work in Trinidad. I owe a strong personal debt to Godfrey Lienhardt for encouraging me to pursue what from Oxford must have seemed to be rather idiosyncratic notions, and also to Maurice Lipsedge and Ioan Lewis for their continuing support. Bernard Wasserstein and the Tauber Institute provided a welcome opportunity for discussions with American colleagues. The departments of psychiatry at Guy's Hospital, Birmingham University and University College London have generously provided time for writing in a critical but not unsympathetic atmosphere. Among the numerous colleagues, friends and others who have commented most usefully on earlier drafts or conference papers are Chimen Abramsky, David Armstrong, Shango Baku, Michael Beaubrun, Joseph Berke, Philip Burnham, Morris Carstairs, Barry Chevannes, Georges Devereux, Horacio Fabrega, Clifford Geertz, Patricia Gillan, Maurice Greenberg, Ezra Griffith, David Harrison, Cecil Helman, Ladislav Holy, Bruce Kapferer, Arthur Kleinman, Britt Krause, Jessica Kuper, Murray Last, Takie Lebra, Gilbert Lewis, Maurice Lipsedge, Jenny Littlewood, David Lowenthal, Carol

MacCormack, David McLagan, Danny Miller, H. B. M. Murphy, Rodney Needham, John Orley, Robin Price, Raymond Prince, Peter Rivière, Bernard Rosen, William Sargant, M. G. Smith, James Watson, William Wedenoja, Anthony Williams, Roy Willis, Carole Yawney; and colleagues from St Ann's Hospital, Port-of-Spain, and the University of the West Indies; the Institute of Social Anthropology at Oxford; the Institute of Social Studies in the Hague; Beijing Medical School; the British Medical Anthropology Society; the Society for Caribbean Studies, and the participants at various seminars.

Parts of this book were read to members of Mother Earth's family in Never Dirty and Arima in 1991: I am grateful to Shurland, Keith, Martin, Vicky, Laurel and Maureen for their comments then, and also to Breadfruit, Coconut, Cane, Cassava, PawPaw and Pepper for our debate during a return visit to the Valley. Michael Beaubrun offered generous encouragement and academic facilities in Trinidad during 1980–2 and again in 1988 and 1991. The University of the West Indies office at the General Hospital in Port-of-Spain and the UWI Library staff at the St Augustine's campus were particularly helpful. Josephine Milne-Holme provided advice on Creole and Trinidad English, and Robin Bruce was generous both with his time and in lending me recording equipment. John Neehall and his staff at St Ann's Hospital and the Port-of-Spain General Hospital allowed me access to patients and to clinical records. Among the many people who offered extensive hospitality I can name only Jack and Peggy Downer, the Sisters of L'Hospice, the Dominican Fathers Joseph Kavanaugh and Steven Doyle, and Geoffrey Frankson. Jorsling Peters and the Spiritual Baptist groups in Chaguanas, Grande Rivière and elsewhere, numerous Rastas in Port-of-Spain, neighbours and patients were generous with time and patience. Patrick Joseph introduced me to the village which I have called here Pinnacle, where I received much kindness. My hosts there, Athanase and Carmen Salvary, were the models of sensitive and critical encouragement. For many people in Trinidad my interest in Mother Earth was the occasion for initial dismay and embarrassment but this never precluded sympathetic interest and frequently enthusiasm. My wife Jenny and our daughter Leti came to the Valley of Decision for part of my time there, and their ungrudging resilience did much to encourage us all.

Mother Earth died two years after my initial stay in the Valley. Since her death the Earth People have divided into four separate groups. Although I spent time with three of these in 1988 and 1991, this account is generally composed in the present tense, here referring to the period 1980–2. While the Earth People and I engaged in various joint projects (and still do), the text remains the personal account of an outsider, one at times intensively involved but nonetheless hardly to be considered as a committed adherent.

More (and less) than a dedication

This is an interpretation of my experiences of one particular person, Mother Earth, and of her experiences of me. Her initial invitation, and that of the Earth People, to stay with them, to share the Beginning of the End, and to write about them in my own way, overcome my initial reluctance to intrude on a millennial community. That the practice of medicine and academic research of any type are fundamentally antithetical to their ideals says much for their tolerance. As Mother Earth put it:

I know Science has to search me out, to fight me, to check me out. You got to put it down as it come to your own senses.

A note on idiom

The ethnography of an essentially English speaking community whose local idiom does not have a recognised orthography presents problems when quoting direct speech. I have generally rendered speech in international English with the ubiquitous Trinidad *eh* ('ain't', 'isn't', 'doesn't') as *ai*. For simplicity my transcriptions omit pitch distinctions which can sometimes serve as different lexical items, affixes or even syntactical structures. This inevitably makes some misleading assumptions about the underlying grammar (thus *now now* may indicate both precision and pluralisation); and in reported conversation with me, informants often essayed the acrolect in what linguists term hypercorrection. Additionally, what may strike readers as deliberate metaphor (*cut eye*) may also be calquing from French Creole, Yoruba or other languages. Local Creole words are italicised here unless they are used frequently in the text or in direct speech. I have referred to both human personage and divinity as 'Mother Earth' but for the latter I have usually capitalised pronouns. Specific expressions used by the Earth People (glossed on page 244) are either capitalised when they have a novel ideological significance (Social = Son) or italicised when they are employed in a sense shared with other Trinidadians (*social* = snobbish). At times this will be clumsy but much of their ideas involves a subtle transformation of everyday English, and the difference needs to be borne in mind. A particular problem is posed by the homophone Son/Sun which is nearly a conceptual unity; I use either Son or Sun depending on immediate context. 'Caribbean' connotes here the whole Caribbean basin, and 'West Indies' the non-Hispanic, principally ex-British and French, islands together with Guyana and Belize. 'Afro-Caribbean' and 'African-Caribbean' refer to those West Indians who recognised themselves as partly or wholly descended from Africans and who in Trinidad refer to themselves as *Africans* or *Negroes*. The term 'Black' is used variously to refer to the local Afro-Caribbean population, or to all local non-Europeans (following recent changes in local usage); the context should make clear which I am following.

1

The coming of the Earth People

The earthly paradise

Few people in the West Indian island of Trinidad have not heard of the Earth People. Their community lies between the forested mountains of the Northern Range and the rock-strewn coast, above the rough seas where the Atlantic meets the Caribbean, and a few miles from where Columbus is locally said to have obtained a landing in 1498 and whose native Caribs he identified as living in 'the Earthly Paradise'. It is situated not far from the headland where in the sixteenth century the last remnants of one Carib group leapt to their deaths rather than face Spanish slavery, and where, some three hundred years later, the American anthropologists Melville and Frances Herskovits were to describe their African successors in the first ethnography of the English-speaking Caribbean.[1]

For a country long familiar with the religious charisma of the Spiritual Baptists – the Shouters – frequently gathered by the roadside in their brightly coloured robes, intoning lugubrious 'Sankey and Moody' hymns and enthusiastically ringing their handbells, and also with the newer Rastafari movement introduced from Jamaica in the 1970s, the Earth People remain an enigma. Their appearance in the villages or in the capital Port-of-Spain causes public outrage, for they go about naked. Local opinion favours the view that these taciturn young men, carrying staves and cutlasses, and with the long matted dreadlocks of the Rastas, are probably crazy: if not the whole group then certainly their leader Mother Earth, for it is she whose visions gave birth to the movement and who leads their annual marches to town. Alternatively, argue some, they are just a new and particularly dangerous variant of Rastafari.

Every year the group comes from the coast to Port-of-Spain to Put Out The Life: to gather new recruits from the poorer shanty towns around the capital, decaying areas which the country's new-found oil wealth seems to have passed

by. Communication is hampered by the Earth People's provocative language,
their deliberate and studied use of obscenities, and Mother Earth's striking
teachings. Trinidadians, a largely devout if not exactly church-going population, are outraged to hear that while God does not exist, she is the biblical
Devil, the Mother of Africa and India, Nature herself.

Her island is the most southerly of the Lesser Antilles. Some thirty-seven
miles across by fifty long, it lies in the Orinoco delta, eight miles away from
the South American Main. A Spanish possession until its capture by the British
in 1797, it was ignored by the Spaniards after they had exterminated most of
the native Caribs and Arawaks. For a time it served simply as the base for
expeditions into the continental hinterland in search of the fabled El Dorado.
Spain did eventually encourage colonisation by French Catholic planters from
other islands, together with their slaves who grew sugar in the lower areas to
the west along the Caroni River.

Apart from a French cultural identity (which necessitated extended Crown
Colony status) and the influence of the once powerful local Catholic Church,
Trinidad's later history is typical of the British Caribbean: the development of
sugar plantations and the emancipation of the slaves in 1838, followed by the
introduction of indentured labourers from India together with some free
African immigrants from the middle of the nineteenth century; conflict
between colonial officials and the local plantocracy; the collapse of the price of
cane sugar after the loss of colonial preference and competition with European
beet sugar; economic stagnation and imperial neglect; the collapse of the other
main exports, cocoa and coffee; the development of Creole nationalism;
universal adult suffrage in 1946; increasing local participation in the
Legislative Council progressing to internal self-government in the nineteen-
fifties, and independence in 1962 as a single parliamentary state with the
neighbouring island of Tobago. The governing party since 1956, the People's
National Movement (PNM), has been committed to a mixed economy and
a welfare state.[2] It derived its support predominantly from the African[3]
population and comfortably maintained power until 1986 through direct and
indirect patronage and regular parliamentary elections, apart from racial
tensions preceding independence and a brief hiccup in 1970 when an army
mutiny sparked a short-lived Black Power rebellion.[4]

Trinidad differs from other West Indian islands in its relative wealth from oil
and its low population density (with continued immigration during the nineteenth and twentieth centuries from the smaller islands), and also the presence
of substantial numbers of free Black Creoles in the period of slavery. The
White *French Creoles* only stopped speaking French at the beginning of
this century, while the last Spanish courts were abolished as late as 1879.

Compared with the rest of the Caribbean, relations between African and European may be said to be relaxed if not altogether harmonious, although discriminatory legislation continued until the Second World War, and practical social segregation based on colour lasted well after independence. Colour, class and wealth still run together.

Black family life in Trinidad and Tobago resembles that of other parts of the English-speaking West Indies: relatively flexible cognatic kin relations, with shallow 'lineages' of *title* (surname) through the father if parents are married. Personal economic ties are developed through acquired dyadic relationships rather than through kinship or even residence. Although scholarly debate continues as to the legitimacy of the African heritage, the consensus is that contemporary working-class patterns of life owe more to the continuing relationship between Black and White, between island and metropolitan country, than to any African 'survivals': one element of the Western working class, a 'rural proletariat' as Sidney Mintz has termed them.

Trinidad's oil resources (off-shore wells and a refining industry) have been intensively exploited since independence. Together with natural gas deposits in the south-east and the world's largest pitch lake near the western town of San Fernando, they are the basis for the national economy through taxation on the international corporations and partial nationalisation. Tourism has not developed, perhaps because of the scarcity of beaches, but also because it is regarded as politically demeaning. The local standard of living is high, reputedly the third highest in the Americas after the United States and Canada; there is one motor vehicle for every 10 of the island's 1.2 million population and, a few rural areas excepted, concrete houses, electricity, television, health clinics, piped water and metalled roads are taken for granted. Secondary education is compulsory and the oil revenues have allowed the building of a steel works, construction and other industries. These are grouped together with the major conurbations of Port-of-Spain and San Fernando in the west and centre of the country. The labour intensive agricultural cultivation of sugar, coffee, cocoa and ground provisions has been effectively abandoned and in 1981 Trinidad became a net importer of sugar.[5] Meat, dairy products and flour have always been imported but now the foreign exchange surplus allows the bulk of 'local' food to be brought in from abroad, rice from Guyana and ground provisions from the smaller and poorer islands of the Lesser Antilles.

In the north-east of Trinidad, the mountains of the northern range, the geological continuation of the South American Cordillera, rise from the sea to over 3,000 feet. The terrain, shallow soils and heavy rainfall prevented the establishment of cane plantations and the area was only to be settled in the late nineteenth century by isolated families who established small estates of coffee and cocoa in the lower reaches of the mountains, growing coconuts and provision along the narrow littoral. These families were predominantly Creole or Spanish speakers from Tobago and the Spanish Main. The occasional White or Chinese established a store and acquired land, often through the failure of the smallholders to pay their store bills, but the general pattern of landholding was a peasantry of small local family groups working their own land. Cocoa and coffee were harvested, dried and picked up by the steamer which passed along the coast to land domestic goods every few weeks. With the collapse of the price of cocoa after the First World War, the rural north-east became relatively depopulated (now less than fifty people per square kilometre) as young adults moved to the cities and oil-fields or emigrated to the United States and Canada. No Whites remain. The distinctive Creole peasant culture is becoming urbanised and its language, Patois, is now seldom spoken outside a few villages and only by the *older heads*.[6]

The commune of the Earth People straddles a faint coastal track, known by the name of a long projected but never completed road, the Turnpike. The nearest village, Pinnacle, 9 miles away, is probably the remotest in Trinidad from Port-of-Spain and only reached by a winding coastal road, the Turnpike proper.[7] The smallholdings of coffee and cocoa have returned to forest; their owners either left the area for good or retreated back to the village. The mountains, never settled and seldom crossed, remain part of the island's extensive forest reserves, exploited for wood only on their southern side where they meet the Caroni plateau.

The Turnpike track follows the coast, occasionally passing over headlands and allowing a glimpse of the sea but usually winding through the dense bush of secondary forest, hidden from the sun, occasionally dipping down to ford small rivers and mangrove swamps. Through the tangled foliage of overgrown coffee and cocoa and the tall spreading immortelle trees planted eighty years ago to give them shade, the occasional traveller can glimpse the remains of abandoned cocoa houses and rotten wooden huts. The track ends after 20 miles at Petite Rivière, another fishing village usually reached by the road from the other side which passes through a gap in the Northern Range. The Turnpike is cleared once a year by the Pinnacle villagers as a *ten days* – temporary work allocated by the government public works department; for the rest of the year few pass along it – some forestry workers conducting a survey or occasional groups of hiking schoolchildren. The villagers who still gather copra from the palms along the coast prefer to visit their coconut groves by *canot*, the small high-prowed boat they use for fishing.

This coast is regarded by urban Trinidadians as the most desolate part of the island, 'behind God's back', a fitting retreat for the handful of Black Power mutineers who briefly established themselves there in 1972 after blowing up the Pinnacle Village police station. They were tracked down and shot by the Regiment, Trinidad's modest army.

Mother Earth in the Valley of Decision

A year after the 'guerillas' were killed, Jeanette Baptiste, a 39-year-old woman from Port-of-Spain, came to live on the coast, together with six of her twelve children and her partner Cyprian. After spending two years on various estates near Petite Rivière, the family settled among the remains of one of the deserted hamlets midway along the Turnpike, where on one side the track overlooks a small rocky bay and on the other a long curving beach bisected by the Madamas River which, laden with mangroves, slowly enters the sea as a modest delta. The family were initially paid by an overseer to collect copra but after an argument they continued to squat on the land by tacit agreement. They grew ground provisions, selling the surplus to the villagers.

Both Jeanette and her husband had been Spiritual Baptists and they continued to 'pick along in the Bible', fasting in Lent and interpreting the visionary import of their dreams. From 1975, after the birth of twins in their wooden hut, until 1976, Jeanette experienced a series of revelations which became the foundation of the Earth People. She came to understand that the Christian teaching of God the Father as creator was false and that the world was the work of a primordial Mother, whom she identified with Nature and with the Earth. Nature gave birth to a race of Black people, but the rebellious Son (God) re-entered his Mother's womb to gain Her power of generation and succeeded by producing (or forcing Her to create) White people. The Whites, the Race of the Son, enslaved the Blacks and have continued to exploit them. The Way of the Son is that of Science – of cities, clothes, schools, factories and wage labour. The Way of The Mother is the Way of Nature – a return to the simplicity of the Beginning, a simplicity of nakedness, cultivation of the land by hand and with respect, and of gentle and non-exploiting human relationships.

The Son, in a continued quest for the power of generation, has recently entered into a new phase. He has now succeeded in establishing himself in Africans and Indians and is also on the point of replacing humankind altogether with computers and robots. Nature, who has borne all this out of love for the whole of Her creation, has finally lost patience. The current order of the Son will end in a catastrophic drought and famine, or a nuclear war, a destruction of the Son's work through his own agency, after which the original state of Nature will once again prevail.

Jeanette herself is a partial manifestation of The Mother who will fully enter into her only at the End. Her task now is to facilitate the return to Nature by organising the community known as Hell Valley, the Valley of Decision, to prepare for the return to the Beginning and to 'put out the life' to her people, the Black Nation, The Mother's Children. She has to combat the false doctrines of existing religions which place the Son over the Mother and to correct the distorted teaching of the Bible where she is represented as the Devil. She stands for Life and Nature, in opposition to the Christian God who is really the Son, the principle of Science and Death. As the Devil she is opposed to churches and prisons, education and money, contemporary morals and fashionable opinions. Because God is 'right' Mother Earth teaches the Left, and the Earth People interchange various conventional oppositions: 'left' for 'right'; 'evil' or 'bad' for 'good'. Seeming obscenities are only Natural words for She Herself is the Cunt, the origin of all life.

The exact timing of the End is uncertain but it will come in Jeanette's physical lifetime. Then Time will end, Sickness will be healed and the Nation will speak one language. The Son will be exiled to his planet, the Sun, really the Planet of Ice which is currently hidden by Fire placed there by The Mother – Fire which will eventually return to where it belongs, back to the heart of the nurturant Earth.

Since her revelations which initiated the Beginning of the End, Mother Earth's immediate family have been joined by numbers of Trinidadians, usually young men who bring their partners and children. The community has a high turnover and, while over fifty people have been associated with the Earth People, when I lived with them there were twenty-two staying in the valley with perhaps forty committed sympathisers in town. About once a year the group march into town, camp out in the Laventille area and present their message in the central streets and parks, particularly in Woodford Square, the popular site for political demonstrations, next to the parliament. After a few weeks of Putting Out The Life and visits to friends and relatives, they return to the valley to continue to Plant for the Nation.

The response

The nearby Pinnacle villagers were the first to become aware of the new community and their response was typical of subsequent Trinidadian reaction. A young married woman told me how she had seen them when they passed through in 1977 on their first trip to town: 'Man come up and he say people down there coming up naked. I think he joking but he ai'. I go and look and, man, I so ashame'. For months after I thinking "My God, what happen?"' An old villager, Tante Marie, whose sister lives in town and who herself frequently complains about the benighted state of the village, had been 'walking down the street and I hear something behind me and I turn – O my Lord! – I see these savages. I start to run so they won't attack me and I run till I reach [home].'

Many women in Pinnacle expressed sympathy for the only girl in the group at that time, Mother Earth's own daughter, who seemed embarrassed by the watching villagers and had covered her breasts with one hand, the other across her hips. Mother Earth reproached the girl, stopped and parted her own legs, pointed between them and called out, to general outrage, 'Here is where you all come from!' The group consisted largely of young men, and the village girls, while publicly expressing disgust, hid to peep, for 'If I go talk with them now my mother she got to throw me out.'

Apart from these marches to town the Earth People occasionally stop in the village to exchange their crops for salt and agricultural cutlasses at the two stores. On these occasions they now wear a short kilt of sacking (*bag*) which is discarded when outside the village. Conversation stops as these solemn young dreadlocks stand silently over their staves outside the shop, cutlasses laid discreetly on the ground, whilst one of them makes the purchases. Their departure is the sign for an animated conversation to break out, indignation blended with derision; if they have bought sacks then 'bag people come to get a new suit there!' Few village women venture outside into the *cocoa* but the men occasionally meet the Earth People passing on the foot-trodden *traces* which criss-cross the nearby bush, and the fishermen can see the community's huts from their boats when they pull up their turtle nets in the early morning; slogans roughly painted on the hut overlook the Turnpike track and the sea below – 'Hell Valley', 'the Devil live here', 'Fock God'.

Popular interpretations of what is going on in Hell Valley follow the usual topics of Pinnacle conversation – religion, sex and sickness. Perhaps the group are just a collection of rather odd Rastas come up from town? No one believes Mother Earth is really the Devil but many feel there may be a close relation; she is at least some type of *lajabless*, the rather folkloric female power who entices men into the bush, there to entrance them and strip them naked, sometimes to rape them. Alternatively the whole thing is an excuse for everybody to have sex with Mother Earth – 'Why else they naked? You jus' tell me that now!' Many feel that Mother Earth is mad or indeed the whole group has gone crazy through smoking too much *ganja*.[8] In private some villagers express a belief that Mother Earth is really 'very clever', that she has got the young men growing food for her and that she is selling vast quantities of ganja in town, stashing the money away ready to leave suddenly and then buy a large house somewhere in Port-of-Spain to enjoy the comforts of the urban life she affects to despise – 'How they work so?'

Part of the land used by the Earth People belongs to a Pinnacle family and some years ago arguments over the ownership of its produce led to an incident in which a villager set a pipegun[9] in the bush near the settlement, but was found out and his dog killed in a scuffle. For the villagers, the contract to clear the Turnpike as a *ten days* is an important part of their cash income; many of them once lived near the track and still own the land on either side. Soon after the establishment of the Valley, the Earth People (at that time more inclined than later to solicit official support) applied for the contract, failed, but nevertheless cleared the track for some miles. When the villagers arrived to do the job along with the public works foreman, a violent confrontation was only just averted, but the villagers later made half-hearted plans to use their guns to drive the Earth People away. For the present they are content to grumble about the theft of their land and hint to the local police that the government should do something. Anxious lest rumours of these plots should reach the Valley they make a point of saying publicly that they will not trouble the Earth People: 'I ai' go there again. We ai' enemies but I don't like the way they move.'[10]

Many of the older Creole-speaking inhabitants of Pinnacle, particularly the men who used to live along the Turnpike, regret the depopulation of the coast and the passing of traditional rural life: 'Now little boy is drinking with big man, son drink with father, son beating father on wapi [gambling] table. What!' While valuing the benefits of piped water and pensions, they criticise the young men's expectations of an easy life: 'It come so all they want is fêting. They can' take hard work again.' They cite the recent collapse of the village agricultural and fishing co-operatives, and deplore the reliance of Pinnacle on the regular public works programmes rather than on mutual assistance. Villagers accord grudging respect to the return to agricultural life in the Valley, all the more so as the Earth People themselves come from the town. Their opinions about Trinidad's future often echo those of the Earth People: that the removal of the oil, the blood of the soil, is slowly turning the land into a *cripsy*,[11] an unproductive arid desert. They too are suspicious of the newer farming techniques advocated by the government agricultural officers and, refusing pesticides or fertilisers, continue to plant and harvest according to the phases of the moon. The oil wealth, they say, is temporary; it will disappear, leaving Trinidadians now unable to plant, starving in their once fertile but now 'unbalanced' land. But still, as Jobie, one of the fishermen, mused: 'If you can' buy rice, you just pick a plantain. The earth is the mother for true!'

Their disagreement is less with Mother Earth's novel ideas than with her nudity. No adult Trinidadian has gone naked since the African slaves came to the Caribbean. 'They must be evil, God tell all of we wear clothes.' Villagers quote the expulsion from Eden – 'Even the trees and beasts carry clothes, God make them with bark and hair and feathers.' Few take the 'devil worship' seriously for 'that is just to fright we away' but to live without any modern technology at all is a mistake, and they cite the instance of one of the Earth People who died in childbirth.

A number of the younger village men demonstrate an allegiance to Rastafari through wearing dreadlocks and have some knowledge of Jamaican Rasta ideas (Plate 1). They have remained behind in the village to pursue a *natural* life and they express considerable sympathy for the Earth People.[12] Two of them told me they would actually join if it were not for the nudity and Mother Earth's reputation for making everyone work so hard. Some of them meet the Earth People in the bush, smoke a little ganja with them and offer the fish they have caught in exchange for provision. Through them and other friends in the village who knew Mother Earth before she went naked, the Earth People are kept well informed of any village gossip against them.

Trinidadians who have never met Mother Earth immediately volunteer two facts about her: she used to be a school teacher and she has had incestuous relations with her son. The incest clearly refers to her teaching about the return of the Son into Nature's womb. The suggestion that she was once a teacher is a tribute to Jeanette's startling eloquence. Her mother was a domestic servant and until 1973 she had an impoverished life in town; with only a rudimentary

1   Rastas in Pinnacle: two of them had just cut off their dreadlocks following a rumour that the police were arresting locksmen for selling ganja.

primary education she continues to read with difficulty. As she is frequently unwell another persistent tale is that she has just died, a rumour of much annoyance to the Earth People when they return to town to visit their families and friends. Many local people predict that the commune will end in murder, and cite the Peoples Temple in Guyana, or Trinidad's own Michael X in Arima, a town not so distant from the coast.[13]

In 1976, on hearing the first stories of a family going naked, the *Trinidad Express*, the more popular of the two national newspapers, sent a reporter to visit Hell Valley. This account was typical of later reports in its emphasis on the dangers of snakes and the unhygienic conditions for young children whose education was being neglected. Since then the community has been raided frequently by the police who on one occasion, assisted by social workers, removed the children to an orphanage and a convent boarding school. Members have been arrested for possession of ganja both in the Valley and outside, and the local police regard the group simply as a variant of 'Rastafarianism'; when the Earth People were arrested on marching through Arima, they had their dreadlocks cut off in a waiting police van.

The presence of a community apparently proclaiming adherence to pan-African ideals in this remote area is a matter of some concern to the authorities with their memories of the Black Power guerrillas who hid in the nearby forests. Even before Jeanette's revelations, the Regiment had raided the estate, apparently with orders to kill the gunmen hiding there. (According to Jeanette only the sound of her baby crying prevented the hut being riddled with bullets.) Now, as Mother Earth, she causes particular embarrassment to the government through her use of the balisier plant as a standard when 'going down town to free up the nation'. The balisier (plate 3, p. 185) was chosen by Eric Williams, prime minister from 1956 until he died in 1981, as the emblem for the party he founded, the People's National Movement. Superficially resembling a plantain tree it does not bear edible fruit although its presence in the bush signifies a fertile area suitable for clearing and planting. Opponents of the PNM like to point out that rural tradition also implicates the balisier in harbouring a venomous snake, the mapapi. To Mother Earth these are identical traditions, for the mapapi, the Serpent of Africa, is the source of life, and the Earth People regard snakes as dangerous only to those who persist in wearing clothes.

Jeanette has twice been taken by the police to St Ann's, the mental hospital in Port-of-Spain: in 1977 she was arrested in Arima and in 1980 the police raided the Valley and removed her. Among the Trinidadians who have met her when 'putting out' in town, there is much sympathy for her call to return to rural life and she is regarded less as insane than eccentric: 'She come half-way mad then.' The major objection for urban Trinidadians is what both they and the Earth People regard as the most characteristic practice, nudity. After the group were fined for indecency in 1979 (the fines were paid by sympathetic bystanders the same day), they wear *bag* in town but Mother Earth and the other women in the group remain bare-breasted. When publicly criticised she ripostes with an attack on contemporary morals: 'They are too proud to take off their clothes and come in the Valley of Decision and live. They are rather go and take off the clothes in the disco! How they could take off their clothes there? If I am outside on the street with my breasts outside, they finding fault!' Older Trinidadians admit she has a point there: 'Is all sort of nonsense does go on [in clubs]. It only party, party. Is ridiculous then.'

Itinerant preachers, passing prophets and the founders of small short-lived sects find in the Earth People some justification for their own beliefs. They are disconcerted on actual contact. A local preacher who had a vision went to the Valley of Decision: 'He said "Here is Eden!" I said "You right". Then he say Armageddon going to come the next week. I say he wrong and he fuss and he carry on and he pass on' (M.E.).

Both the Rastas and the Shouter Baptists, whose practices and teaching have particular appeal for Mother Earth and who together provide the majority of her followers, are relatively sympathetic to the new community. As always, the attraction is the rejection of industrialisation and the return to nature. The details of her cosmology are debated, for there is widespread agreement that the Bible has indeed got some things 'upsided down'. Rural Catholic priests, faced with declining church attendance, privately envy the fervour and discipline in the Valley. Members of Trinidad's Indian community however remain generally unsympathetic; in spite of Mother Earth's placing of Africa and India together as the Race of the Mother, recruits to the group are all Africans. Indians regard the Earth People as a resurgence of Black Power or at best as a year-long carnival, a ludicrous parody of the creolised West Indian culture in which they are only too conscious of losing their own identity.[14]

The press maintains a fascination with the Earth People, concentrating on arrests of members and interviewing any dissidents.[15] News of my own stay with them reached town and was reported with much ironic comment.[16] Only the Rasta publications have ever printed Mother Earth's statements at any length or sympathised with her attempts to recover her children from the orphanage.[17] Newspaper reports tend to rehearse stories of snakes, ganja and group sex. While broadly accepting that adults are free to go off and do whatever they want, however odd, they constantly deplore the presence of children in the Valley. A leading article in the establishment newspaper, the *Trinidad Guardian*, expressed this view with magisterial sarcasm:

Nuisance from the Earth People

We notice that the so-called Earth People, a troupe of nude or semi-nude adults and children, have again been visiting the capital city. This time they are said to have come in furtherance of some petition of the Government for land with which to carve out a large food garden to help feed the nation. They hope to hold talks with the Prime Minister.

While we may appreciate their willingness to help the nation in this particular problem, we believe their obvious rejection of society, their lack of any serious skill or experience in farming and their disorganised and indisciplined life style would disqualify them for that kind of Government assistance.

But these are not the only matters for concern; they have numerous children it seems and these children are being brought up in the most primitive surroundings, without schooling or any kind of training that would fit them for normal life in our society.

It would seem that the first order of business on the part of the Government would be to arrange for these children to receive more orthodox care and attention. We should not permit a continuation of this nuisance.[18]

2

A certain degree of instability

The person who has attained perfection of balance in the control of his instinctive tendencies, in whom the processes of suppression and sublimation have become wholly effective, may thereby become completely adapted to his environment and attain a highly peaceful and stable existence. Such existence is not, however, the condition of exceptional accomplishment, for which there would seem to be necessary a certain degree of instability . . . It may be also that, through this instability, new strength will be given to those movements which under the most varied guise express the deep craving for religion which seems to be universal among Mankind. (Rivers 1920: 158)

Pathology as sociological abuse

In the nineteenth century the White planters of the West Indies dismissed slave uprisings against them as simple 'madness'.[1] One is hardly surprised that rebels, or the originators of novel political or religious movements, are dismissed as 'mad', particularly when their struggles appear doomed, short-lived or even just at variance with those values espoused by the powerful. For to denigrate them as insane is to deny them validity. It is to mock their followers: surely only the credulous and simple-minded could take seriously the ravings of madmen? Local citizens giving evidence during the trial of the rural pastor of a United States 'snake-handling sect' maintained that he must be mad, as did the neighbours of Mother Earth and those of Ann Lee, the Lancashire-born founder of the Shakers.[2] In Jamaica the wider society associated Rastafarianism with madness [and leaders were] taken to gaol on sedition or to the asylum for lunacy . . . The process of becoming a Rastafarian is still regarded by the wider society as one of mental deterioration and the more modern embrace of the creed by young educated high-school and University graduates is seen as an urgent matter for the psychiatrist.[3]

The insult may on occasion be returned: a nineteenth-century White clergyman in Jamaica who tried to break up a revivalist meeting of plantation workers by accusing them of insanity was promptly told 'They are not mad; they have the spirit; you must be mad yourself.'[4]

The use of terms like 'mad' or 'crazy' to imply unrestrained or unreasonable action is of course common to most, perhaps all, societies. The West Indian who describes his own culture as torn between tradition and modernity, and thus as 'schizophrenic', may be merely using a fashionable metaphor: Shiva Naipaul, a Trinidadian Indian writer, concludes that it is indeed 'madness' for the Caribbean to seek its identity in the Third World, and he describes Eric Gairy, the former Prime Minister of Grenada (famed for his speeches to the United Nations on the subject of flying saucers) as 'a street-corner eccentric, a mystical maniac'.[5] To explain the origins of the Second World War as the conspiracy of an insane dictator may be a commonplace bar-room conceit, akin to Kerensky's attribution of communism to Lenin's supposed syphilis; but how do we take the anthropologist who quite seriously proposes that Hitler had a 'hysterical phobia, conversion symptoms and classical paranoia', that St Paul, 'another vatic with inchoate ego boundaries', was epileptic, or the psychologist who confidently informs us that Tiberius and Calvin were schizophrenics and Stalin 'a paranoiac'?[6] Scholarly analysis or vulgar denigration?

'Disease' is a powerful image for politics, and we take it as such when our Trinidadian novelist tells us that the ideas behind Jim Jones' commune in Guyana were 'infected with disease'.[7] It was perhaps just a neat turn of phrase when Kroeber labelled magic as 'the pathology of culture', Seligman identified millennial movements with 'mass neuroses', or La Barre dismissed snake-handling sects as 'zany'.[8] But when academics interpret established social institutions such as shamanism as the invariable consequence of 'epilepsy, hysteria, fear neurosis, veritable idiocy', or characterise the shaman as psychotic and his religion as 'organised schizophrenia',[9] we may begin to wonder about the motivation behind such descriptions. The biblical Hebrews attempted to discredit their more embarrassing prophets by calling them insane, and the social anthropologist who talks of the 'authentic schizoid component' of the religion he is studying is hardly a potential recruit.[10]

Since the French Revolution – which was regarded by the more reactionary doctors of the time as a veritable clinical epidemic, the radicals preferring to dwell on the congenital insanity of the monarchy – the medical profession has not scrupled to use its diagnoses to interpret history.[11] The professor of medicine at Makarere University, fleeing from Idi Amin, quite seriously diagnosed his president as having: 'grandiose paranoia, hypomania, probably schizophrenia, hypomanic paranoia, possibly GPI, and the Jekyll and Hyde syndrome'.[12] American psychiatrists in a well-publicised report suggested that Senator Barry Goldwater, then a candidate for the presidency, was mentally unstable and, as a consequence, were very nearly sued.[13]

It is in their attempts to explain social change that contemporary psychiatrists, and particularly psychoanalysts, have developed interpretations couched in terms of pathology: Freud argued that organised religion is essentially a coalescence of individual neuroses, particularly evident when it is innovative.[14] While sociologists, following Durkheim's well-known dictum, have usually avoided purely psychological or psychopathological interpretations of existing religious institutions, they have near universal recourse to such arguments when describing the process of change, particularly when it seems to take a radically new form. Jarvie has suggested that it is our functionalist 'steady-state' theorists who emphasise regularities and norms, more comfortable with structure than with process, who have problems with radical innovation and rely on some idiom of irrationality which usually lies outside the social domain but which intrudes to initiate the necessary changes.[15] Failure to distinguish the normative (what people say they should do) from the statistical (what they actually seem to do and what they say privately) leaves any potential change as coming from nowhere.

Certainly, when faced with millennial movements like the Earth People, particularly those Linton has characterised as 'nativist', not only do social scientists describe them in psychological terms, but they regard them as somehow more psychological than the institutions of quieter times. Psychology seems not only a type of interpretation but a kind of stuff: there is more of it about at times of change not just in the participants' own explanation, but for the observer; individual psychological states are taken as subject to social constraints, and such constraints just appear absent at moments of transition while individual personalities and choices seem more apparent. Millennial movements, says James Beckford, are 'affectively laden' for they operate at 'high intensity'.[16] Bryan Wilson maintains that conventional organisation is hampered by this affectivity, and describes their 'affected members . . . uttering gibberish [in] outbursts of frenzy'.[17]

David Martin has argued that until recently the scholars who examined such social formations were themselves suspect, for they had crossed that 'invisible mental line' which divides the sober world of scholars from that of the chiliasts.[18] Little wonder perhaps that the denigration of frenzy serves to distance scholar from subject. The Dancing Mania of Madagascar and Papua's Vaihala Madness are 'spontaneous and stimulated frenzy';[19] either pathology or passive manipulation, in either case outside normal psychological and social functioning. The popular use of Weber's notion of 'charisma' unites the two – the disordered prophet with their suggestible flock.

Even if they do not seem to have been regarded as particularly sick by their contemporaries, millennial leaders are often described by later academics as insane: Jim Jones of the Peoples Temple; Hong Xiuquan, the leader of the Taiping rebellion; Te Ua, who founded the Maori Hauhau; Evara of the Vaihala Madness; Counselheiro, the leader of the Canudos uprising; Britain's Joanna Southcott.[20] Scholarly interpretation aside, colonial and national authorities frequently placed the leaders of new religious movements in psychiatric hospitals, often as a change from more conventional incarceration: Richard Brothers, George Turner and Sir William Courtenay, the nineteenth-century British sectarians; Ann Girling, prophet of the New Forest Shakers; Ne Loiag, a leader of Jonfrum in the New Hebrides; Rice Kamanga, founder of the Barotse Twelve Society; Alexander Bedward, the Jamaican revivalist; Leonard Howell, the Rastafarian; Father Divine, founder of the American sect which bears his name; Elijah Masinde of the Kenyan Dina ya Msambwa; Huynh Phy So, the originator of the Vietnamese Phat Giao Hoa Hoa.[21] In Canada, Doukhobors who demonstrated naked were placed in the local asylum, as were Jehovah's Witnesses in Germany in the nineteen-thirties, and Pentecostalists more recently in the Soviet Union.[22]

The legitimacy of madness
To discredit actions through the ascription of madness – and thus as meaning-less and undesirable – either in a literal ('strong') sense or as a casual metaphor, implies that we already recognise some distinct sphere of 'psychopathology', either a disorder of the individual self analogous to a physical disease or a physical disturbance of the brain itself.[23] Examining the essence of psycho-pathology as one in arbitrary individual biology alone rather than in a biosocial dialectic has restricted comparative psychiatry to considering the 'influence' of society on an already distinct, segregated and directly observable area of psychopathology. Its rather neo-Kantian schema distinguishes the biological 'determinants of a mental illness', necessary and sufficient to cause it, from those pathoplastic factors associated with individual variation.[24] Thus (to take the classic description), pathoplastic factors 'give content, colouring and contour to individual illnesses whose basic form and character have already been biologically established'.[25] Such 'content', whether individual

personality or social institutions, passively fills up appropriate spaces in the biologically determined matrix. They simply reflect social action, but they do not provide a valid representation of it.

We can, however, trace an alternative approach to madness in the West, one which while certainly accepting the existence of a separate domain of psychopathology, nevertheless refuses to divorce it from the possibility of active social meaning. For, as Roger Abrahams puts it, there are times in our history when 'those who appear to speak and act on the basis of extreme experience often seem more real to us than those involved in more mundane pursuits'.[26]

The first Western texts to ascribe meaning to psychopathology are those of Plato.[27] Historians of medicine have pictured him as an irrationalist and mystic[28] who attempted to deny the physical origins of the abnormal states of mind described by the Ionians and Hippocratics. He 'looked back rather than forward . . . [and thus] there were certain mental disturbances, obvious even to the laymen of our day, which continued to remain unrecognised'.[29] In fact Plato readily agrees that madness is a 'disease of the body caused by bodily conditions'; but he maintains that meaning can only be ascribed to it subsequent to the experience of illness and in an everyday social context: 'We only achieve [prophecy] when the power of our understanding is inhibited by sleep or when we are in an abnormal condition owing to disease or divine inspiration . . . It is not the business of any man so long as he is in an irrational state to interpret his own visions and say what good or ill they portend'[30] – a position Jarvie has perhaps surprisingly recommended for inspiration in anthropological theory[31] – less Yeats' 'excited reverie' than Wordsworth's 'emotion recollected in tranquillity'.

What we know of popular ideas in late medieval Europe suggests insanity was regarded primarily as a punishment or test, sent by God or by the Devil. Although its experience was meaningless as an experience, by struggling with the moral cause of the insanity, one could attempt to gain self-knowledge. King Lear's madness was clearly a punishment but it was also a prompting to reconsider his past actions. At the same time there existed a rather different medieval sentiment, one which found some value in the state of 'folly' (which included both foolishness, and something akin to what we might call insanity and mental retardation) through its intimations of child-like trust and innocence. If the rational world was compromised, the Incarnation could only have been an act of folly. The 'madness' of the early Christian was an enrapture by the spirit of God: perhaps Jesus himself had been mad (Mark 3; 1 Corinthians 1)?

The shift in ideological authority from the clergy to scientific medicine in the early modern period is exemplified by a new perception of one medieval figure – the witch. The nascent 'mechanical philosophy' asserted that her activities were just a disease of the brain, whose nature was arbitrary and morally neutral, although Willis and Hobbes continued to maintain something like the medieval position, that her sickness was the consequence of a loss of moral control, the product of passion, disordered fancy and lurid imagination. In the eighteenth century Swift and Pope deployed the notion that our mental states had a demonstrable biological origin as satire: eloquence in 'The Mechanical Operation of the Spirit' is no more than an orgasm which lacks prior stimulation, such that when the vapours in Louis XIV's head went up he engaged in war, while if they descended Europe was at peace. To suggest human action as 'natural', random, prior to feeling and meaning, ridiculed the action while also mocking the theory itself. A similar distinction of pathology from social meaning is found in the pamphlets of Gerrard Winstanley, the seventeenth-century Puritan radical. Winstanley criticised the clerical assumption that moral meaning was always causative of abnormal personal experience from which, rather, meaning should itself be generated: 'If the passion of joy predominates then he . . . is ripe in the expression of words . . . But if the passion of sorrow predominate, then he is heavy and mad, crying out he is damned.'[32] Ironically it was the visions of the Puritans themselves which were dismissed as 'brainsick' and 'frantic', as 'nothing but the effect of mere madness [which] arose from the stronger impulses of a warm brain'; Casaubon suggested their religious experiences were no more than 'a degree and species of epilepsy'.[33]

The development of psychiatry as a medical discipline in the nineteenth century, together with the establishment of public mental hospitals, deprived madness, now shorn of any inherent moral dimension, of the possibility of even conventional meaning. It was merely the external symptom of an underlying bodily disease. Just as Plato had reacted against a similar position, so did the Romantics: indeed for them the very 'natural' and arbitrary origin of psychopathology as independent of convention guaranteed it as an authentic communication. Like the young child or the 'primitive', the madman was asocial, elemental, and thus the source of creativity: 'The greater the genius the greater the unsoundness'.[34] So far from the physical origin of madness devaluing its manifestations, abnormal mental states, and hence inspiration, were deliberately cultivated through the use of tobacco, alcohol and other substances.[35] Those who were mad were additionally privileged through being outside everyday society altogether and thus resistant to bourgeois constraints.[36] While a few writers, like Lamb (in *The Sanity of True Genius*), deplored this necessary equation of natural madness and genius, the thesis gripped the poetic and popular imagination and is with us still.[37] Nietzsche observed that 'it seems impossible to be an artist without being diseased', for ecstatic madness gave reign to underlying feeling, to participation 'in a higher community . . . a collective release of all the symbolic powers'. In a similar vein to Plato he warned however that the meanings of madness were valid only when they were interpreted through later reflection.[38]

Lombroso introduced into medicine the Romantic equation of madness with genius – 'a system of hereditary degeneration of the epileptoid variety', as he put it.[39] Because society, as a functioning system, was naturally conservative, change could only be initiated from outside, from the natural domain through biological abnormality, random events selected by evolutionary history. Lombroso was no radical poet: while the consequences of madness could be beneficial, he distinguished 'true' (epileptoid) genius, aligned with 'the general course of evolution', from the more common 'pseudogenius' of unsuccessful revolutions. The Parisian communard was an example of the latter, and Lombroso carefully noted the evident 'stigma of degeneration: repulsiveness, an asymmetrical and enormous upper jaw, the eyes of a toad, flaccid skin'.[40] His thesis was taken up by the science of experimental psychology whose founding father, Francis Galton, confirmed an association between 'madness and creativity' in a study of eminent Britons. More recently it has been suggested that it is the relatives of the insane who are more innovative than the general population,[41] thus offering an evolutionary explanation for the persistence of what would otherwise seem to be a maladaptive genetic predisposition; madness has an active role again, not through the ascription of meaning by society but in society itself in an attenuated form.[42]

Recent reviews, such as that by Rothenberg, argue against any simple empirical association of innovation and insanity; he suggests however that both appear to share the cognitive ability of holding opposites simultaneously in mind, whether these contraries are propositions or spatial constructs. Extending his argument, it may be that insanity, like alcohol use, homosexuality or any other alterity, offers a double vision, simultaneously inside and outside immediate experience, and hence an interpretation of it. Certainly, reading the work of contemporary psychotic patients one is struck by something powerful one might gloss as 'creativity' or 'imagination'; my own view is that this is generated in part through the polythetic (loose associational) chains of psychotic thought and writing being read monothetically: the dramatic clash of successive images and fragmentary analogies are produced (and unified) through the audience's response, to give a 'higher unity' beyond the fragments and their elisions and displacements – just as we read the shifting centres of consciousness in modernist literature, structuring the apparently arbitrary, attempting to restore some 'imaginative' centre which again is necessary and inevitable.

At the same time, I would argue that there is another cultural imperative: to place together the hidden, mysterious, suspicious and unintelligible sources of novelty, whether we do so as a positive value or else in a sour *schadenfreude* – mental suffering being the nemesis for one who steps outside the normative bounds.

In 1902, in *The Varieties of Religious Experience*, William James criticised the simple equation of (biological) psychopathology with (social) innovation but wondered if the origins of religion might not indeed lie in those 'pattern setters . . . for whom religion exists not as a dull habit but as an acute fever . . . [They] frequently have nervous instability.' He quoted with approval the psychiatrist Henry Maudsley: 'What right have we to believe Nature under any obligation to do her work by means of complete minds only? She may find an incomplete mind a more suitable instrument for a particular purpose.'[43] If James admits that ultimately the meaning of radical experience is to be determined 'by its fruits' rather than by its ground, he does emphasise pathological religion as somehow 'the real thing', but appears to be talking less about what we might consider frank psychosis than 'borderline insanity, crankiness, insane temperament, loss of mental balance [and] psychopathic degeneration'.[44]

Two Romantic axioms – the natural affinity of the mad with the child, the primitive and the archaic, together with the notion of the *génie maudit* as an unbalanced prophet without recognition – reflected back to the European avant-garde an appealing image of itself. What Georg Lukács has called 'modernism's obsession with pathological and extreme states' is most evident in Surrealism's preoccupation with indeterminacy, dreams, synchronicity, 'automatic writing', and *l'acte gratuit*. André Breton's dictum that the surreal act was 'automatisme psychique . . . dictée de la pensée, en l'absence de tout contrôle exercé par la raison, en dehors de toute préoccupation esthétique ou morale'[45] celebrated the artist or poet as the one who surrendered to an untrammelled primitive core of natural creativity: the models were to be the mad, the eccentric, the mediums, the cranks, the inventors and the self-publishers. Psychiatrists sympathetic to modernism, such as Hans Prinzhorn and Ernst Kris, argued formal analogies with psychotic art, and the nucleus of Jean Dubuffet's collection of Art Brut were the drawings and paintings collected earlier this century by the large state mental hospitals of Switzerland and Germany.

Whether this is really privileging 'the Other' as such or merely seeking its reconciliation is a matter of debate. One prominent dissident from Surrealism, Antonin Artaud, spent nine years in a French asylum. He appealed to his erstwhile colleagues to rescue him: 'Heroin must be procured at all costs and it must be brought to me even at the risk of getting killed. The initiates have real instruments of torture . . . and they use them from afar to mutilate me a little more every night while I am asleep.'[46] The Surrealists who, like the anarchists, had proclaimed mental patients to be political prisoners along with criminals and conscripted soldiers,[47] failed to respond. In practice they accepted the social sequestration of lunacy. For us, it is impossible to distinguish in Artaud's work the separate reflections of psychopathology, intellectual climate and personality, and he remains our most striking recent image of the mad genius: 'Delirium' he observed, 'is as legitimate, as logical, as any other succession of human ideas or acts.'

The 'anti-psychiatrists' in Europe and the United States during the nineteen-sixties decided similarly that 'the boundary between sanity and madness is a false one'.[48] Appropriating the Romantic equation of created work and biography, they initially joined the sociological critique of psychiatry to psychoanalysis. In the writings of R. D. Laing in particular we can note a regression from the new 'deviancy theory' – the 'meaning' of the psychotic is that he is formed in the process of social ostracism and thus presents back to society a mirror of itself – to one in which he becomes again the autonomous natural hero, the privileged visionary who can offer us a critique of conventional rationality because of his resistance to indoctrination:[49] his meaning is again in the absence of meaning, for the arbitrary has its own reasons and logic. The two approaches are not altogether distinct. Deviancy theory's image of the psychotic as sacrificial victim, extruded by society and thus representing its 'Other', parodying and commenting on it, enabled the Romantic hero to remain on the stage, uncontaminated by any echoes of the Nietzschean *Übermensch* in his fascist avatar; schizophrenia provided a Dionysian ecstasy of unfettered authenticity that could not lead to fascism, for had the mentally ill not been the first victims of the Nazis?[50]

Members of the anti-psychiatric 'counterculture' who actually became insane had no more luck than Artaud. In spite of the rhetoric of Laing and Colin Wilson which, beneath a superficial Marxism, promised a unity of situation and reaction for women, ethnic and sexual minorities and the insane,[51] the counterculture failed to establish a context in which psychopathology could be perceived as meaningful in itself. In his autobiography Mark Vonnegut describes how the hippie commune members with whom he lived proved unwilling to cope with his episode of schizophrenia: after a certain amount of anguished debate they took him to the local mental hospital where he was given electroconvulsive therapy.[52] Their hesitations and guilt were identical with those of the bourgeois families so trenchantly denounced by Laing.

The sickness of the visionary leader

A number of European intellectuals at the beginning of the twentieth century attempted to reconcile Romantic irrationalism with the new positivism.[53] If in Surrealism the simple equation of insanity with authentic innovation continued unchanged, it was in Freud's psychoanalysis that it became domesticated – but at the cost of transforming and diluting the very idea of psychopathology. In practice 'madness' became a metaphor, ostensibly medical (at least at the start) but implicitly moral.

For Freud, culture was the dynamic product of our instinctual strivings and the demands of others, a conflict whose resolution could be social integration in the form of instinctual sublimation or else manifest as individual psychopathology. Psychoanalysis biologised the Romantic notion of a single natural creative ground common to children, our archaic ancestors, tribal peoples and the unconscious of the modern European; psychopathology was in part a regression back to this 'primary process' where random atemporality and contradiction ruled, for in his personal history the European recapitulated the entire history of Man.[54] Health was a balance between instinctual striving and social restraint; as culture was itself the compromise between our individual conflicts writ large, historical innovation was only possible through such conflict. For Roheim, the anthropologist who adhered most closely to an unmodified Freudian position, '[Social] change is only the discharge of suppressed emotion.'[55] While this idea was more influential in literary criticism and 'psychohistory' than in the social sciences, it was briefly contemplated by the British anthropologist W. H. R. Rivers in his book *Instinct and the Unconscious* (1920) from which I have taken the epigraph for this chapter. Derived ultimately from medicine, psychoanalysis emphasised the mechanism rather than the meaning of individual cognitions which could become represented in institutions. Or rather, the meaning *was* the mechanism.

Freud himself did not regard simple regression back to the primary process as anything to be encouraged. On the contrary, 'Where Id was, there shall Ego be.' Early psychoanalysis attempted to transcend the commonsense opposition of biological pathology to conventional meaning; in doing so it pathologised the normal at the cost of abolishing altogether the separate domain of severe psychopathology which corresponded to the popular idea of 'madness'. Assuming madness was merely conflict writ large, in practice it ignored the asylums. As a neurologist, Freud wrote little on the psychoses, and it was left to his psychiatric colleague Jung to provide a psychological theory of them. This Jung proved unable to do and he maintained throughout his work that severe psychopathology was a consequence of a discrete physical cause, a 'toxin'. Psychoanalysis has continued to be principally concerned with 'problem of living' rather than frank insanity, and the descriptive psychiatric idioms of 'paranoid' and 'manic' are employed to delineate internal states in individuals whom the lay observer would find essentially normal. In what became known as 'psychohistory', analysts examined cultural change through the individual conflict between instinct and social constraint, yet their approach was anhistorical in that institutions and their transformations themselves were merely the eternal return of the repressed, maladaptive and compulsive: the primal crime of parricide which had introduced us into history 'must have left some traces in the human soul'.[56]

While Freud's equation of child and primitive had been drawn from the Victorian evolutionary anthropologists, his influence on social anthropology was less through his historical conjectures in *Totem and Taboo* and *Moses and Monotheism* than in the method of clinical inquiry he devised – the interpretative study of the relation between symbolisation and personal experience – together with the general idea that the understanding of social institutions must always lie in the personal world. Those anthropologists influenced by psychoanalysis allocated societies (which could not as such contain any autonomous area of madness) according to a typology derived from psychiatry: Benedict implies that a paranoid illness is merely 'cultural paranoia' in its purest (individual) form.[57]

The pathologisation of whole institutions is characteristic of the psychoanalytic debate on the mental health of the millennial cult leader, but also of 'the shaman', the visionary healer in whose life history there frequently appeared a complex of personal suffering or illness followed by a vision quest, the successful resolution of which, like analysis itself, involved both personal healing and the subsequent potential to heal others.[58] Weston La Barre's book *The Ghost Dance* takes its title from the Plains Indians' movement of 1890 in which various tribes joined together under the inspiration of Wovoka, following the loss of their hunting territories to the Europeans, the virtual disappearance of the once ubiquitous buffalo and a succession of crushing military defeats, new and fatal diseases, and devastating droughts. On his recovery from an illness, in the course of which an eclipse of the sun had occurred, Wovoka preached a new dance, through the performance of which a fresh skin would spread over the earth, bearing pasture and herds, and covering up the Whites and their works. La Barre offers this Ghost Dance as the paradigm for all religions, indeed for all novel collective action. Religious innovators, he suggested, are 'culture healers' with personal visions which are essentially mental illness, asocial and idiosyncratic;[59] their 'crisis cults' are personal strategies for dealing with anxiety in times of disaster, which can then serve for other individuals, and thus they generate all forms of social change.

La Barre's general thesis is that innovation is necessarily pathological – 'culture is folie à N . . . the only difference between folie and culture is quantitative' – but 'the magnitude of the social impact is not an acceptable psychiatric criterion for psychosis [for the] genius is a psycho-social phenomenon as a shaman-messiah only if and when he is dynamically relevant to and functioning in his proper socio-cultural context'.[60] In other words there does almost seem to be (*contra* Freud) some autonomous domain of arbitrary nature which may at times gel with society. However, this domain is defined on normative psychodynamic grounds alone, perceived backwards through its shared cultural products, with the result that Plato becomes 'a Greek ghost dance[r] . . . a covert paranoid schizophrenic' and visions are described as 'psychotic' for no very clear reason.[61]

La Barre characterises every innovator as a sort of psychotic shaman; in an earlier book on the American snake-handling sects, he had marshalled the same historical parallels, the same dynamic explanations, to describe the visionary rather differently, as a moral criminal.[62] Kroeber and Linton had suggested the practising shaman might indeed be less disturbed than those people considered psychotic in the West; they offered other diagnoses, respectively 'less psychotic' and 'hysterical'. Certainly, to the contemporary descriptive psychiatrist, the 'psychotic' crisis cult leader seems hysterical at worst, for the consequences of psychosis are held to be social withdrawal and isolation, not leadership. For the psychoanalyst this happens most obviously in Western societies; in preliterate communities, society meets the madman half way, the whole community being in some measure insane, according to the primitive/ archaic/child/psychotic equation.

If commentators of a variety of schools agreed in explaining the shamanic and prophetic roles as a single pathology, the specific options they suggested include about every conceivable state known to psychiatry. To declare the visionary leader 'a deputy lunatic for his people' reflects little credit on his followers, and the psychoanalytical debate in particular was couched as a moral warning to the Western bourgeoisie, a salutary message for our own troubled time:

We now fear what we ourselves do . . . It is a time ripe for violent, mindless and blindly antiadaptive social movements [which parallel] our own existentialist [sic] predicament . . . Times of acute unrest and upheaval like our own . . . the numbed anomie, the help-less puzzlement and directionless acedia of our day.[63]

La Barre's arguments are frequently vacuous, his logic slipshod and his all-embracing wealth of exuberant detail suspect. Georges Devereux has offered a similar but rather more subtle approach in various publications which he directed against the psychiatric historian Erwin Ackernecht who had firmly attacked

the labelling of [social] phenomena with psychiatric diagnoses . . . The custom of covering moral judgements with a pseudoscientific psychopathological nomenclature is no advance at all and is equally bad for both morals and science . . . When religion is but 'organised schizophrenia' [this was Devereux's expression], then there is no room or necessity for history, sociology, etc. God's earth was, and is, but a gigantic state hospital and pathography becomes the unique and universal science.[64]

Following descriptive psychiatry's recognition of a distinct domain of bio-logical mental illness, Ackernecht proposed that this should be distinguished from the recognition of abnormality within a particular society. A messianic leader may be pathological according to Western psychiatry but normal or abnormal according to the local understanding. Ackernecht then proceeded to attack the evidence for the shaman and the prophet being invariably insane; he argued that the only possible examples of the shamanic role being routinely preceded by mental disturbance were the Siberian shamans originally described by Shierozewski and Bogoras. Other inspirational healers and all non-inspirational healers were normal in biomedical terms. As a society with concerns about witchcraft might find a niche for the paranoid individual amongst others, so the institution of shamanism might include, amongst others, the mentally ill, those recovered from mental illness, and those incipiently ill.[65] Similarly, Nadel argues that Sudanese healers cannot be mentally ill for in their non-inspirational role they engage successfully in conventional everyday activities.[66]

Devereux reposted by criticising Ackernecht for 'disregarding the existence of societies so "sick" that in order to adjust to them, one has to be very sick indeed . . . There exist societies so enmeshed in a vicious circle that everything they do to save themselves only causes them to sink deeper into the quick-sand.'[67] Devereux's examples are drawn from the reservation Indians among whom he carried out most of his fieldwork and whose Ghost Dance was the final collective insurgency against the Whites. That American anthropology, carried out on the reservations among the remnants of conquered polities, should have a particular emphasis on the isolated individual rather than on social organisation and shared representations, is understandable. That it should contain the particular level of moral denigration and psychiatric abuse that it does is perhaps puzzling. Maurice Lipsedge and I have argued that the Europeans' encounter with other societies was characterised initially by exotic description and simple force of arms, then, confronted with the threat of approaching emancipation and independence, by theories of racial superiority and manifest biological destiny, and finally in the twentieth century, by the imposition of psychiatric categories to characterise them as inadequate, co-opting them through an internalisation of their ascribed inadequacy.[68] A purely sociological theory of a subdominant group living in close association with – and opposition to – the Whites would have necessitated some sort of conflict model. The psychological, or better the psychopathological, model located the question of intergroup power solely within the attributed peculiarities of the subdominant.

In reaction against the pathologisation of some unitary shamanic or prophetic role, contemporary ethnographers, in a wide variety of studies of 'inspirational healers', have concluded that, while shamans may at times employ dissociative (hysterical) mechanisms like the rest of us, they are hardly grossly pathological. The elastic term 'shamanism' has been applied to a wide variety of rather different forms of inspirational leadership and healing (spirit mediumship and so on) and, even in a single society, these are likely to change: Jane Murphy suggests that as Inuit shamanism declined as a political institution, increasing marginal individuals came to aspire to it.[69] This may have been true of Devereux's Mohave 'shamanism', less a normative social position than an atavistic perversity. The shamanic 'election' may indeed in some instances originate in psychopathology; for while no contemporary scholar who has observed a functioning shaman in any detail claims they are psychotic, in few cases does the actual election appear to have been observed. As Ohlmarks had remarked,[70] an institution may originate in pathological individual experience which becomes 'structured' through others' responses; depending on how it engages with shared perceptions of power and productive relations, there seems no reason to deny this possibility, suggested by Bogoras' original description of a Chuckchee shaman who was periodically insane (during which time she was physically restrained) whilst practising success-fully in her lucid periods.[71]

Charisma and contagion
If millennial or revitalist leadership often seems consequent on some intense personal experience, the sociological model most applicable to the relation between prophet and follower – the reception of the message and its amplifi-cation and reworking – would appear to be that of charisma. As elaborated by Weber and his successors, charismatic authority derives not from the occu-pation of an already structured status but in the development of a highly personalised relationship between leader and follower which involves 'the social recognition of certain extrasocially sanctioned qualities imputed to the person of the leader'.[72] This seems particularly relevant to millennial

movements for, as the chronicler of 'the religions of the oppressed', Vittorio Lanternari, argues 'there is probably no known religious phenomenon in which the dialectical interpretation of relationships between personality (the individual personality of the prophet) and culture (the social personality of the group) becomes more convincing than it does in regard to messianic cults'.[73] Given psychoanalysis' presumptions of pathology (and thus idiosyncrasy) in millennial leaders, how did it envisage their influence over their followers? Largely through the postulated mechanism of 'suggestion' (later to reverse its object and become 'transference') which derived from Gustave Le Bon's studies of the crowd. Paradoxically, this argued for a loss of unique and 'higher' qualities in each individual participant to reduce the self to the lowest common denominator of the existing culture, where a single emotional tone could resonate spontaneously with that of the others; and thus we might suppose a situation of little innovation. Conceptualised primarily as a psychological mechanism, suggestion presumed a disengagement of the cognitive in favour of the affective.[74] Freud had argued that the critical passivity of the crowd was a return to archaic patterns by a leader who took the place of the developed 'superego' (parental values internalised in childhood) of each follower, but Roheim emphasised the attempt by all participants to rediscover a state of childhood bliss, a state which Devereux restricted to the 'infantilised leader' alone.

Devereux and La Barre, however, agree with Freud that the charismatic leader, devoid of moral scruples, infects his entranced followers: 'All mobs forget their inhibitions, their critical judgement and their superego controls, and borrow for a time the superego of their leader . . . The psychopathology of the mob leader that propels him to antinomian leadership in crisis now releases and mobilises the hidden psychopathology in each mob member.'[75] We have seen that La Barre identifies charisma as a contagious pathology: 'a folie à deux raised to a geometric power [in which] an authentic schizoid component in the prophet or the temporary schizophrenia of his dream speaks to passive fantasy in his faithful communicants'.[76] Devereux suggests that this sickness is already located in the prophetic moment: the charismatic leader takes power during a crisis when the usual adaptations to stress are inadequate, and society is in a 'schizophrenia-like disorientation' with individuals engaging in 'catastrophic behaviour'. But the solution then adopted is frankly irrational and can only lead to a vicious circle in which the actual situation gets increasingly out of control.[77]

Lifton and Erikson have brought a greater epistemological sophistication to bear on these 'tenuous boundaries between identity crisis, psychosis, theological innovation and individual and historical revitalisation'.[78] Erikson argues that 'the great man of history' is less a psychopathic mesmerist than one who shares and anticipates the personal dilemmas of his contemporaries and, by solving them for himself by external action in society, solves them for others; leaders then are healers who have a 'grim willingness to do the dirty work of their ages'. Rather than just labelling Hitler as a psychopathic paranoid (which he does) and leaving it at that, he proposed that the Führer allowed his own personality to 'represent what was alive in every German listener and reader'.[79] Devereux suggests rather vaguely that the charismatic leader simply represents the parent of the follower, but Erikson offers a structural model in which the relationship of father to mother stands for that of Austria to Germany, and of Bourgeois to Natural; Germany and Nature serve as potent 'superimages of a pure mother'.

The objections to the type of unitary psychological closure offered by Devereux and La Barre are those which we offer against the nineteenth-century anthropologists: an oversimplified unitary hypothesis (here conflating innovative prophets with customary shamans) based on comparative data which assumes a unilinear mode of cultural evolution and hence an inherent racism, together with ignorance of the specific contexts in which the particular institution has developed. We might add that unitary theories always have problems with anomalies, and historical 'survivals' are simply equated with pathologies, not surprisingly given the identity in psychoanalysis of the archaic, the primitive and the sick. While the analytic tradition appears super-ficially attractive in its claim not to split mechanism from meaning, thus promising a fruitful dialectic between psychopathology and society, the priority it gives to culture-bound and unitary biosocial categories reduces society itself to sickness, couched in the popular idiom of psychiatric denigration.

Given its clinical interests, for psychoanalysis there may be some slight justification for perceiving history through an idiom of pathology. Medicine's self-ascribed task of liberating Europe's witch had argued analogously that her salient characteristics – nudity, 'emotional disinhibition' and 'role reversal' – were problems of arbitrary biology not moral meaning.[80] Yet contemporary sociologists, who might be alarmed at the suggestion of any explicit affinity between themselves and psychoanalysts, share the assumption that the devel-opments of millennial groups can be explained in terms of psychology, more specifically in the satisfaction of psychological needs through the generation of certain emotional states. In his account of the sociology of the Jehovah's Witnesses, James Beckford offers three explanations, two of which are pure psychology – frustration/compensation and social solidarity, plus world view construction. Beckford cites Lofland, whose sociological studies of a chiliastic

sect led him to comment: 'It would seem that no model of human conduct
entirely escapes some concept of tension, strain, frustration, deprivation or the
like, as a factor in accounting for action.'[81] Barkun actually characterises
millennial movements as a 'regression from the social to the psychological'.[82]
As I have suggested, it may be that sociologists ignore individual (psychological) choices in established societies as apparently redundant but invariably
introduce them when considering social movements, particularly those which
appear dramatic and chiliastic. Those inclined to functionalism were concerned
with social order in 'steady-state' systems for which there could be no ultimate
cause and effect in linear time; psychological states, taken as autonomous and
biological, seeking 'release', then had to be introduced to explain the rare
change. Whitworth comments however that: 'Sects may attract the sociologist
. . . because the study of any particular sect is likely to provide an acute
depiction of the aspirations and frustrations of the members of the socio-
economic group or groups from which its adherents are primarily drawn.'[83] If
sociologists study charismatic leadership and participation in millennial
communities because they are primarily interested in normative psychology,
this is seldom so explicitly stated. What is less clear is why they tend to
concentrate on the specifically 'affective' nature only of those who seem to be
reacting *against* an established society.

Millennial groups certainly engage frequently in antinomian actions –
deliberate contraventions of conventional morality – but why should this be
seen as primarily emotional? The particularly 'affective' idiom of such groups
seems deployed to qualify them as undesirable, maladaptive and regressive –
as not 'rational' in either the Weberian or the everyday sense. As with the
evolutionary schema of psychoanalysis, the regression is both to hypothetical
infantile and to archaic patterns. Devereux had stated that such groups have
little hope of lasting success because of 'the health, maturity and potentiality of
the [wider] public'.[84] In his textbook on *Social Movements* Toch argues that
'fringe groups' must fail because they are specifically orientated to the
emotional needs of their participants rather than to any wider intellectual or
political concerns.[85] Wilson states that millennial groups are a 'deviant
religious response', doomed to impotence by their affectivity and the contra-
dictory doctrines of their disordered leaders.[86] Groups initiated by the mentally
ill are considered particularly short-lived as Cohn suggests in his account of the
seventeenth-century British Ranters.[87]

Indeed the very possibility of innovation through the mentally ill is taken as
a function of elementary technological development: 'Among the less-
advanced groups, the prophet may be a man of less than average emotional
stability who becomes the catalyst bringing a new movement on the strength of

visions.' Wilson adds that these 'spontaneous' and 'non-rational' mechanisms are usually religious for: 'The only claim that could hope to stand against constituted authority . . . was a claim to power from a transcendent source great enough to be set over against existing power structures', and it is non-European groups particularly which exhibit 'less emotional stability':

Since less developed peoples depend on local communal social organisation, the emotions are subject to much less self-control and are more easily summoned for collective behaviour . . . It is the spontaneity, emotional intensity and the sense of power engendered in such movements that stimulates collective action.

He portrays the 'affectivity' of Rastafarians as picturesque and childlike: 'Their simplicity of faith in the living God; the pictures of him; their singing of the Ethiopian national anthem; and their own hymns . . . their banners, sashes, flags – all point to uncontrolled emotional orientations.'[88] Even apparently sympathetic observers are inclined to emphasise affectivity. George Woodcock, defending the Canadian Doukhobors who set light to their homesteads in protest at conscription and compulsory state schooling, cites: 'their irresistible excitement [for] Fire had become its own end, a passion that excited some of the arsonists to the point of orgasm as they watched the deadly splendour of their handiwork burst out against the night sky'.[89]

The argument of the sociologists approaches that of Freudian *massenpsychologie*. Some social groups, sects and rabble, have regressed from, or not evolved into, rational civil society, and remain dependent for their perverse ideology and degenerate actions on the authority of certain powerful others. They 'abdicated the responsibility they would have as individuals'; their primitive mental mechanisms have burst through the existing constraints by which society is properly constituted. Down there lies something nasty:

a subterranean world, where pathological fantasies disguised as ideas are churned out by crooks and half-educated fanatics . . . There are times when that underworld emerges from the depths and suddenly fascinates, captures and dominates multitudes of usually sane and reasonable people . . . And it occasionally happens that this underworld becomes a political power and changes the course of history.[90]

By relying solely on the overt normative values of the bounded society, this sentiment precludes the possibility that a society already contains dominant and subdominant sectors, out of whose conflicts and oppositions, contradictions and latent variants are always being generated, neutralised, accommodated or at times becoming central; for the 'present' has always to be recreated in our actions. The reason for change is seen then simply through those elements which do change as a distorting impulse external to proper society (as 'stress' or 'pressure'), as is the arbitrary mechanism ('affectivity' or even 'pathology'), and the immediate consequences are regarded as maladaptive. If the movement is 'established' and its motive returns to ends–means pragmatism, then emotion is said to ebb and we return to steady-state theories of social cohesion, recruitment, management of deviance and the like.[91] We might note that even if an influential novel doctrine and practice must resonate with personal emotional experiences – what we may term 'affect' – such affects are themselves always socially constrained and are not independent of existing personal and social cognitions. Our very distinction between 'cognition' and 'affect' recalls the Cartesianism of 'head' and 'heart', or 'European' and 'primitive': the 'we think, they feel'.[92]

Societies have a culture no more than sects, sects a psychology no more than societies. Dominant ideologies, however, represent their dominance, to themselves and others, as a state of things independent of human choices: deviants and dissidents are relegated to an arbitrary under-world of personal pathology and emotion which alone can explain their futile actions. The subdominant live their lives through this ascription and thus there *is* more 'psychology' around at periods of revolt, in the experience of participants at least. And this experience becomes taken up into social theory as an explanation for how a given society (whose continued 'stability' is unproblematic and in which individual motivations and choices are apparently redundant) transforms itself: a dramatic leap into purely psychological if not psychopathological explanations to explain 'change', and then a return to the previous perspective. Sects (and societies) however continue to change, for, as Godfrey Lienhardt argues:

their coherence is not that of a logically thought out, rational scheme of ideas produced by one mind only. After the initial appeal others make their contribution to ritual and doctrine. The 'vision' of one man then becomes accepted by his followers as a source of their own distinctive collective experience.[93]

Social scientists, anthropologists as well as sociologists, have shown little interest in examining how the fortuitous experiences of individuals may become formalised in an ideology, where tenets and actions are now tacit, less able to be negotiated; in which the random becomes transformed into the customary as the frame to which successive events and experiences themselves come to be referred, and in which individuals come to see themselves in a new way. The notion of 'charisma' is not unhelpful as a typological category for certain social institutions: as a general explanation it explains nothing. An adequate sociology of the genesis of new formations must demonstrate the relationship of the existing social order and its symbolic representations to the individual experiences through which are generated both customary understandings and any novel understandings on the part of the visionary, and how these experiences are taken up and revised, employed by others and structured through active social appropriation and transformation. In the limited case to which we are addressing ourselves, innovation through abnormal brain states, we have additionally to see how this psychopathology may transform and reflect back upon personal experience to generate relatively new forms, and whether it does so in a characteristic way.

It is understandable that contemporary social anthropology, with its emphasis on a close personal relationship with its informants and a vigorous repudiation of unilinear evolutionary hypotheses with their implicit moralising and racism, should have fought shy of the whole debate leaving the occasional madman with a transitory walk-on role, as we find among *The Nuer* of Evans-Pritchard; hardly a *conditor ex machina*. The emphasis in recent medical ethnographies has been to approach madness purely as a social construct, society's perverse mirror of itself, an ideological palimpsest inscribed on an indeterminate (and indeterminant) reality. The constraints of unusual brain states themselves on their own social conceptualisation have been ignored: madness is not taken as a 'natural symbol'. Our attempts, however, to interpret psychopathology simply as a social category leave it marginal, passive and socially redundant in itself. If social facts cannot be reduced to psychopathology, neither can psychopathology be interpreted purely as a social construction. The central problem for a medical anthropology of 'abnormal' brain states remains that, unlike other bodily functionings which do not directly influence mental processes (enabling us to take them heuristically as independent natural facts 'out there' which can be variously categorised by a particular society), 'abnormal' brain states are only manifest as altered experience or action in a social field, and thus are themselves formed dialectically through their biology and their own local representations.

Elsewhere I have applied some of these arguments to Sabbatai Svi, the seventeenth-century Jewish messianic leader.[94] In this I am constrained by the usual limits of conjectural psychological history. It is necessary to take a contemporary example, preferably one amenable to a biological interpretation and then, if we can, to describe its characteristics prior to any communication, in terms acceptable to descriptive rather than psychoanalytic psychiatry; then to examine its local reception and whether there is any value in it recognised by others and how they themselves may amplify the innovator's experiences or otherwise respond to them, and how these experiences become structured to provide the charter for a new social practice.

3

Madness, vice and tabanka: popular knowledge of psychopathology in Trinidad

Before describing Mother Earth's experiences against the criteria of bio-medicine one needs to consider those existing local representations of illness which recall the psychiatrist's field of interest, for it is these ideas which reflect back upon and shape, stigmatise or amplify any personal psychopathology.

Five relatively discrete patterns are identified which we can map for the moment by not dissimilar biomedical categories: *doltishness* (broadly recalling mental handicap and senility), *malkadi* (epilepsy), *vices* (addictions and abnormal personality), *madness* (psychosis) and *tabanka* (a context-specific 'depressive' reaction). Although each may be regarded locally as akin to physical *sickness*, emphasis is placed on their ultrahuman and personalistic aetiology and on their social context, both rather different from the illnesses treated with everyday bush medicine. They cannot, however, be considered in isolation from physical sickness for there are recognised mechanisms in common, idioms which evoke significant local values, productive relations and shared history. The images of nature, power and selfhood which madness reveals make it as good a starting point as any for examining the institutions which are transformed by Mother Earth.

Bush medicine
Popular medicine in Trinidad employs *bush* – the leaves, flowers, shoots, barks and roots of a variety of plants – which can be used in conjunction with commercial oils and essences. Medicinal plants are grown in the house yards or are easily found in the forest or cocoa estates which surround the villages. Every adult in the village of Pinnacle has a working knowledge of some *bush* and most can describe the properties of between thirty and a hundred. While everyone has their favourites and there is no single overarching theory of

classification or therapeutics, some twenty common plants are recognised by every adult and are in common use.

There is little relationship between the efficacy of a bush and its shape, locality or other external characteristics. *Sickness* is physical. It has a *natural* cause and the choice of a particular bush is empirical and pragmatic, dependent on past experience and local availability. One found to be useless for the treatment of a particular complaint is soon discarded in favour of another recommended or supplied by a neighbour. It is sometimes said that 'every sickness have it own bush' although in practice the same bush may be used for different conditions, and any sickness has a variety of plant remedies. Sickness is caused by the weather and climate, conditions of work, a change in the hot–cold balance of the body or the neglect of some other health precaution, and a particular sickness can be prevented by taking small quantities of the bush normally used to treat it.

Bush medicine is valued as traditional wisdom whose ready availability in villages like Pinnacle argues one superiority of rural life over that in town. For it is preferred to medical drugs: 'Since the tablets come into being I ai' take them on. My tablets is bush. Bush is more effective. Every bush has its work. Every bush suppose to be a medicine but I don' know them all. Long time people know all. Now the older heads know a little but the younger none.' Pharmaceuticals, say most villagers, contain the same active ingredient as bush medicine but prepared in a more potent, and thus more dangerous, form. It is appropriate to use bush first, and the government doctor who visits the village every few weeks is only resorted to if bush fails. His tablets too are used empirically, inspected, tasted, tested and exchanged, and often taken concurrently with bush.

Hot and cold

Many sicknesses with their corresponding bush, and also foods, are described as either 'hot' or 'cold'. While *heat* is an intrinsic quality there is a close association between the subjective experience of heat, both bodily and environmental, and the recognition of illness. Thus many hot conditions involve inflammation, while the natural course of life gradually increases one's heat through physical labour and exercise, and also through remaining too long in the sun, sleeping, burns, cooking, eating most foods, violence, snake bites, menstruation and contact with menstrual blood, pregnancy and childbirth, and sexual activity. To relax is to *cool*, to *chill*, to *lime*, while to feel nonspecifically unwell is to be *on fire*. As sexual activity is particularly heating, as is dancing, it is not surprising that the annual Carnival is a hot time. To say that disputes, sex, music and Carnival are 'hot' is not just to speak in conscious analogy: when engaged in them, one's body is physically heated, with possible risks to health.

In view of this tendency to *catch a fire* in the course of daily work, it is advisable to take a periodic *cooling tea* – an infusion of a variety of cooling bushes. By promoting diuresis or sweating, cooling returns the body to a less heated state. It is a prophylactic rather than a treatment, and the bushes chosen may be those used generally to make the morning tea. However, if one is feeling vaguely sluggish or unwell, or otherwise *feeling a heat*, a cooling is recommended. Cooling may be backed up with a purge on the third day which helps reduce heat still further and also rids the body of other harmful substances, whether ingested from the environment or produced in the course of normal bodily functioning.

This system is not a simple 'humoral' one in which constitutional balance is retained by treating a deviation in one direction with its complement. Cooling and purges extract heat rather than going in to counteract it by opposite properties. They 'clean the blood'. An extension of the use of purges to remove heat is their employment in heavy doses to induce abortion, and purges themselves are always hot. Less commonly, hot foods are taken to treat a *head cold* but there is always the danger of passing too rapidly from hot to cold, and external applications of heating substances – *soft candle* (tallow) or rum – are preferable. A similar idiom is that of *gas* which is produced in the stomach when eating too late (or too soon) where it can be felt after a heavy meal. Gas is dangerous for it can travel about the body, causing pain, disability and paralysis or, if it rises to the head, death. It must be released by belching or breaking wind, a process which is aided by peppermint water or various aromatic local bushes which 'go about to find the gas'.

The use of bush is casual, mundane and pragmatic, an instance of what has been termed the 'according ethos' of Trinidadian society, where there are few appeals to absolute principles and where action is recognised as strategic and always dependent on the immediate circumstances:[1] norms are statistical rather than prescriptive, and conscious self-interest is legitimate. The *older heads* do maintain that, to be efficacious, some bushes have to be picked at certain phases of the moon, but this is no esoteric conjuration: although one's dreams may reveal the location of a valuable bush, recognition of sickness is always based on what we might term physical signs and symptoms. The moon, the sea and the earth (and, according to some, work capacity and the menstruation of women) are in harmony for 'the earth rule by the moon; it made for many things; it rule the planets'. Particular phases of the moon are associated with growth in plants and animals, the tides and the presence of fish, though in practice little attention is paid to the moon unless a crop of ground provision or a previously useful bush are not up to their usual quality. The efficacy of bush medicine is not influenced by an individual's state of mind or by their personality, moral attitudes or interactions with others: *pacro* (oyster) water or the bark from the *bois banday* certainly improve male sexual performance, but not by acting as a stimulant to imagination, rather by directly inducing penile erection.

The two types of sorcery, *obeah* and *high science*, are also closely related to practical needs. Both are dangerous, suspect and secret, if hardly radically evil. Obeah however is only to be opposed by counter-obeah or the use of *guards* (charms), or by the power of the Catholic priests; bush medicine is ineffective against it.[2] *Maljo*, like other variants of the evil eye or *bad talking*, is envy which may cause *blight* – a failure to thrive in children, plants or livestock. An involuntary act by the sender, maljo can, unlike obeah, be treated with bathing in an infusion of the same type of bush as that used to treat other physical diseases, but also by prayers or simply requesting the offending person to recognise and remove the blight.

Both madness and malkadi (*fits*) are usually regarded as the immediate consequence of obeah and they are manifest by inappropriate actions. Doltishness ('mental handicap', 'senility'), by contrast, is a failure to develop physically or a process of bodily decay, and while it may be the consequence of obeah, it is more usually ascribed to a fright to the pregnant woman or physical trauma. Madness and malkadi are dramatic moral ruptures in the texture of everyday life but doltishness is less distinct, and more constitutional: 'Always he distract. He ai' mature. He backwards, he bend down so. It ai' really a sickness. It ai' catching.'

Madness

Madness is called *folie* in Creole and is also variously known as *crazy, offkey, off the head, going off, loco, kinky, head ai' right, ai' right dey, ai' collective.* It is recognised through continued unintelligible behaviour which is quite meaningless:

They would do something opposite to your sense: so we style them mad people. Something unusual in madness but they selves ai' know they mad. They climb a pole; go in water; they feel they bathe when it have sun; they out of memory – they don't know what they do; they just pick up a cutlass and chop someone, or pick up a baby and dash them in road; cuss, lie down in the centre of the road; always do strange things other don't do: take he clothes and burn it up; burn house; launch boat and go out by heself.

Other mad actions commonly cited are eating plantain skin, garbage and raw food; walking around naked; touching people who pass; walking in the hot sun in the middle of the road; staring at the sun or the stars; failing to recognise people; refusing to comb one's hair, bathe or accept the help of others. One villager had been in St Ann's, the psychiatric hospital in Port-of-Spain, for many years. He was discharged home to be visited at intervals by a nurse for regular injections. Any initial sympathy for Thomas on his return was rapidly forfeited by his ungracious behaviour. His brother built him a small wooden house on family land 'but he just mash it down'. When I was in the village, he had stripped his hut of its walls for firewood for cooking, and it consisted of a leaky roof, the house posts and some floorboards. He is given old clothes at intervals but cannot always be persuaded to wear them. Thomas is seldom seen in the village, usually disappearing into the nearby bush or greeting any passerby with surly and unintelligible mutters.

The madman is described as loud, boisterous, erratic and potentially explosive. His most frequently mentioned characteristic is his violence: 'They just do anything that get in their way.' Stories circulate in Trinidad about the dangers of St Ann's and I repeatedly heard one about 'this madman a few years back take a knife and stab the boy in the next bed'. Other patterns of behaviour may superficially resemble madness: 'A child behave as if it mad but it ai' mad.' The confusion of the madman is to be distinguished from that of becoming *bazody* (dizzy), for instance in the crowds of Port-of-Spain, particularly during Carnival; or when one has frights or continued worries as when 'you don' know what you' wife doing'; or after a blow on the head. The bazody person soon recovers and the state, although it may be associated briefly with bizarre behaviour, is always intelligible through the immediate precipitants. Drunkenness is also akin to madness for 'When you runs a drunk you do similar things, you part mad.' The drunkard however can always be distinguished by his staggering gait and slurred speech: 'The mad must walk straight, they just do funny things. He has a different expression on his face – he look kind of wild. Mad person's eyes got wide and staring you, staring you; if they sit down nice, all of a sudden they want to make a sudden grip.' The madman is best avoided unless they are a relative or old friend. Talking to him is not going to help anything. Nor will he be grateful for anything you might do to help so, as you may get hurt, 'pass by a next way'. He is living in a private world of his own: 'They laugh so, just by themselves. Tell them howdy and they ai' tell you. If you carry on a conversation, they on a different [one].' Madmen say things which are manifestly not true: 'These imaginations they put on a real side. From the time it reality, you sick.'

When a villager meets Thomas, 'Thomas pass by me and he say "Right!" [the customary short greeting] and I say "Right!" but I don't go near. I keep to myself.' Madness is hardly catching – 'though some say it do rub off' – but it always carries a potential for physical aggression. If violence occurs, the police are asked to take the madman, sometimes via a magistrate, to the mental hospital. If he is feared it is for reasons of personal safety, not because of any ultrahuman influences. Pinnacle villagers maintain a robust attitude to the mystical, and Annette, an elderly widow who is half-seriously regarded as a *soucouyant* (vampire), is not publicly shunned, far less accused, although significantly she has few intimate friends.

If they do not appear violent, mad people are often treated with derision, and the nurses at St Ann's say many of their ex-patients carry a cutlass or stick to protect themselves. The assumption of violence can be used by madmen to obtain food; a patient in the hospital told me that he used to go round town saying 'I from St Ann's, I'll kill you' in a sometimes successful attempt to get food. For the madman, St Ann's is indeed a refuge from living in the streets, and staff are frequently called to see an old patient who is threatening the police: 'If you ai' take me in I gone lick you. I have my permit for St Ann's [a previous admission].'

Respectability and reputation

African-Caribbeans have been described as living by and generating two opposed local sentiments. An egalitarian working-class and male-orientated ethic of personal *reputation* is recognised and contrasted with *respectability* which is associated with church marriage, middle-class and White ideals, with education, social hierarchy and chastity; and which is represented most typically in women. *Reputation* (or *worthless behaviour* as it is usually known in Pinnacle) is represented in the footloose 'circumstance-orientated' man, pragmatic and egalitarian, drinking in the rum shop and pursuing indiscriminant sexual adventures.[3] As the calypsonian Sparrow sings:

Because a woman is a woman for me
Ah don't care how she ugly and obzocky
I'm a busy man wid no time to lose
Ah don't pass my hand, ah don't pick and choose
So any kind o' woman, one foot or one hand
Dey cannot escape from me, Mr Rake-and-Scrape[4]

It has been argued that *respectability* is the local justification of economic stratification in terms of personal moral choice, reflecting the colonial and post-colonial structurings of class and colour; *reputation* is the behavioural response to this, an active affirmation of the ascribed working-class and 'Black' characteristics.[5] Both sexes are said to move up towards respectability as they get older, wealthier or if they marry lighter skinned partners. It is a fragile and often illusive goal rather than a norm, and one which is frequently contested; less an abstract ethic than the workings of relative economic power, formalised in their justification. For the man, marriage is a move away from 'circumstance-orientated' reputation towards *tibourg* (petit bourgeois) respectability; its economic obligations may be assumed reluctantly for 'Why buy cow when I get milk free?'

Recognition of respectability is precarious, usually dependent on an adequate income, but also on who is doing the perceiving, and when. For everyone is critical of another's self-advancement and is always alert to hypocrisy and failure: 'The higher monkey climb the more he expose himself.' The pregnancy of Julia, the rather reserved daughter of a fisherman but now one of the village teachers, and who had been unwisely *friending* with a married policeman, was the occasion for unconcealed delight in the Pinnacle rum shops, for, seen from 'below', the monkey's exposure is determined by the higher standards imposed as you move up: the risks of failure are greater and the fall longer. To adopt the signs of *good training* (frequent church attendance, continued parental control over children, straightened hair, 'good English' and an apparent ignorance of patois, or an affectation of superiority) too soon or without possessing a reliable income, is pretentious – to be *social* or *béké nègre* (White Black). Peter Wilson describes this sentiment of solidarity with an ironic local expression – 'crab antics': as crabs try to climb up out of a crab barrel they are pulled down by others so the top of the barrel can be safely left off, while the single crab in an open barrel escapes. This, particularly male, value is articulated in an extensive local repertoire of *picong* (satire) represented nationally in the calypsos which offer 'a lower class viewpoint, or a Negro viewpoint, or a male viewpoint'.[6]

The madman is described as characteristically male. His attributes – poverty, disorder, semi-nudity, his preference for the bush as opposed to the house, his arbitrary actions and his potential for violence – all recall the image which respectable people offer of the *worthless* working-class man. Lawrence Fisher has noted an extraordinary salience of the madman in West Indian calypsos, tales, gossip and literature, and comments that he offers an ironical, and ultimately hopeless, internalised image, one rooted in the identity which the White has ascribed to the Black, the epitome of worthlessness. The image of the madman recalls the popular perception of the Rasta: indeed, for many middle-class West Indians, the Rasta is dismissed as 'mad'. If Rastafari can be taken as an assertion of those informal *worthless* characteristics which Whites have ascribed historically to Blacks, it is not surprising that many of the younger psychiatric patients in St Ann's have adopted dreadlocks and Rasta idiom. The adoption of Rastafari by the madman actively reappropriates an otherwise devalued self-perception. Rastas themselves have a more sympathetic attitude to madness than do other Trinidadians, at least in theory, frequently emphasising that it is simply the consequence of *social* pressure.

The roots of madness

A common but unelaborated explanation of madness is that 'some born mad because it come down in the family', either because parents or grandparents are mad and it is somehow passed down physically in the body, or because spirits sent against others may return, not to the sender but to members of his or her family in a later generation. Similarly God may punish family members other than the one with whom He is angry. Other villagers dispute this: 'You ai' born with a weak brain: it have to have something make you mad.' Although latent from birth this sort of madness does not appear until adolescence or adulthood. Its potential passes down through men or women and gradually disappears in successive generations.

No two Trinidadians agree about the exact characteristics of the various *spirits*, *phantoms*, *lespwis*, *ghosts*, *duppies*, *jumbies*, or about their relationship to the individual or to any ultimate powers of good or evil. Causes of madness associated with spirits include sorcery (obeah and *science*) involving the sending of spirits; but also sorcery without spirits; prayers directed at malefactors; and sorcery and spirits which have returned to the sender; let alone spirits which have been invoked but got out of control, spirits sent by God as punishment for the individual or his family, and the spirits associated with Spiritual Baptist *mourning*. For most people, these broad categories are not particularly distinct. At the same time, the concept 'spirit' includes a variety of different psychological, moral and instrumental notions which lie along a path from the popular Western idea of individual 'mind' or 'unconscious', through the Christian 'soul', to guardian angels and 'God'. As their relations are fundamental to Mother Earth's own cosmology, it will be appropriate to consider them in a little more detail.

The spirits of obeah (*negromancy*, *niggermancy*) are said to be of African origin. Obeah is also known as *wanga*, the name of a maize porridge which requires much stirring, and its practice is indeed closely related to the deliberate stirring up of trouble in the community, an extreme case of *bad talking* (malicious gossip) or *comess* (causing *confusion*). While the terms *wickedness*, *nastiness*, *niggerways* and *filthyways* usually refer to *worthless* people 'without behaviour', they may also imply the practice of sorcery. Typically, obeah is initiated by neighbours or old friends who are envious of some success, or by slighted lovers. It involves sending a spirit to visit misfortune in the form of accidents, economic or agricultural blight, madness;

or else the use of *mounted* objects, introduced into the victim's household, such as charmed dirt, flowers, seeds, salt, flour or money. Of the actual mechanism by which spirits or objects cause misfortune no one is certain. There is little distinction between being 'struck' and being 'possessed'; the spirits are understood simply as rather unintelligent but malign powers, potentially subject to interdiction and control.

Obeah is evil in a 'strong' sense and no one would publicly admit to its use. On the other hand, love potions and charms, like guards against obeah, are freely exchanged and talked about, if not exactly the appropriate subject for public conversation. The specialist in guards, the obeahman, prefers to be called a *seeman* (*seerman*, *lookman*) because of his ability to predict the future or distant causes, but his techniques of sorcery and counter-sorcery are technical accomplishments which can probably be performed by anyone.

The extent to which a spirit is necessarily involved in all instances of obeah is debatable, but dramatic changes of behaviour induced by obeah, including madness, usually employ a spirit: 'They put a spirit on you to leave your home and you go drifting about. One in L'Anse Noire, he up and down, he ragsy. He had a wife went to Tobago and she did him.' While obeah initiated for revenge is not publicly acceptable, to turn sorcery back onto an unknown sender is legitimate through using *prayers* (itself a morally ambiguous term which may also imply sorcery) or *lighting a candle* on the suspected thief:

If people do you something bad and you just say 'God will deal with them', they get worse than you! You can make them mad if you burn candles on them or say special prayers. Anyone can do it if you know the prayer. If steal, the thief brings the stolen goods back and confesses or is caught. God do it – you don't compel Him.

The thief on whom you say prayers may be unable to stop stealing and thus be caught on another occasion. Such techniques are supposed to have divine sanction if not (as this villager suggests) somehow being actually performed by God. They are thus far more potent than the practices of obeah, especially as their power is generated by the acts of the thief. Such prayers are more dangerous to the sender than obeah and, if they are returned onto you, you cannot guard against them for 'God's sickness will kill you' or send you mad. It is thus safer to use prayers which request God to punish an unnamed offender and restore your possessions: to burn a candle on a faithless spouse would be asking for trouble. After a spirit sent by the Roseau family onto the young son of a neighbour (who had probably stolen some washing) was deflected back by a carefully placed guard, 'the father go like he drive truck all over, the mother act like cocoa picker and she daughter like she a sewing machine'. Or so the neighbours told me. The Roseaus themselves maintained that they had not sent a spirit but had lit a candle on an unknown thief, and the neighbour who was the thief had responded with obeah.

While obeah and returning obeah are equally practised (or held to be practised) by both sexes, the study of *high science* (*conjuration*) is the particular prerogative of men. The themes of obeah are hot, jealous, rural, and related to local interests (as the alternative term *negromancy* suggests), while science is 'European', cold, calculating, urban, elitist and more obviously dedicated to self-interest.[7] Both may involve the summoning of spirits: in obeah by using body parts in the bush or the cemetery; in science inside a carefully marked-out area in one's house or sometimes the cemetery. Science is a loose amalgam of the European Hermetic and Kabbalistic traditions through such texts as *The Sixth and Seventh Books of Moses*, published by the De Laurence Company in Chicago, books supposedly banned under the old colonial anti-sorcery laws, overlapping in theme and style with farmers' almanacs, horoscopes, astrological year books, and Rosicrucian and Theosophical pamphlets. Those I have examined contain a mixture of extremely cryptic hieroglyphs, pyramids, and pentacles, descriptions of the earth and the heavenly bodies as sensate, and instructions for summoning up spirits such as Belial and Lucifer for healing, vengeance and especially finding buried treasure. Invocations are addressed to European nature spirits, such as 'Astarte, Salomonis familiarum III, Eegum, Spirit of Water, Spirit of Air, Spirit of Earth'. The poorly printed instructions in Hebrew, Latin and mock archaic English allow much scope for ritual error and no one claimed much success with them. (Not surprisingly: one villager asked me to help him make *seals* drawn during the full moon in butterflies' blood on virgin parchment.) Such texts are hardly in conformity with Christianity and they are hidden under the floorboards or behind dressers. Their practical inefficacy in attaining their highly specific goals and the grim Faustian warnings of spiritual misadventure they contain leave them seldom consulted, although formerly science seem to have been associated with the various lodges, funeral associations and friendly societies which Herskovits described along this part of the coast. The books are dangerous to the possessor, and serious accident or misfortune, including madness, is attributed to the turning of spirits summoned with their aid: 'A few years ago saw man running naked through cemetery screaming "Alright, alright, me sorry me bother you!" He went mad for truth a few days later.'

A more common but equally inaccessible White authority over the spirits is possessed by the priests and nuns of the Catholic Church to which the majority of Trinidadians of African descent belong. As with all forms of ultrahuman power, this is morally ambiguous: although the clergy are said to have recourse to this sort of activity particularly when they are wronged, they are not altogether above suspicion of self-interest. About fifty years ago, a French Creole family had settled in Pinnacle where they owned the principal store. The uncle of the shopkeeper was the local priest, Father Bastian, who by conjuration encouraged the villagers to shop with his nephew. By *trusting* (on credit), the nephew involved the peasantry in debts which forced them to sell him their land or to leave it to the Church. The last member of the Bastian family died without children and since then no White has lived along the coast. The Bastian graves, fenced off and uniquely ornate with rusted wrought iron, remain neglected on All Souls' Day when the villagers carry candles up to their cemetery on the bluff overlooking Pinnacle River. The Bastian land passed into the hands of a Chinese grocer from Sangre Grande (the nearest town), whose daughter then fell in love with a local villager who served in the shop. This assistant learned science to become a *gomboglissay*, a sort of dematerialised Peeping Tom who, as his nickname Picklocket suggests, was able to squeeze through keyholes. In a failed conjuration, an enraged spirit he had summoned set fire to the store which burned down. The Chinese family and Picklocket escaped; badly burned and disfigured, he left the village. He is rumoured to have gone mad. The shell of the store, now incinerated some twenty years , remains in the centre of the village, overgrown with bush and avoided even by the braver children. The agricultural land near the houses is still in the hands of the church and of another Chinese who seldom comes to visit; the villagers' remaining land is so far distant that it is no longer worthwhile to work given the current price paid for cocoa. (Part of it has now been settled by the Earth People.) While the story provides a justification for the current economic situation of Pinnacle Village, the point of interest here is the moral ambiguity of clerical power.[8] Nominally Catholic villagers are close to Protestant fundamentalism; they reject transubstantiation and the Pope, and criticise their Church for having, until recently, discouraged them from reading the Bible.

The Spiritual Baptists of whom Mother Earth was once a member, practice *mourning* in which initiates are blindfolded and laid on the earth in a small room next to their chapel. Over the succeeding days mourners remain on the ground where they *travel* in visions to meet spirit guides, including biblical figures and other spiritual adepts. Although the practice is regarded as 'Christian' there is always the possibility of encountering a malign spirit. The mourner is guided through her journey by the Baptist Mother to whom she recounts her travels. If the Mother fails to protect her, permanent possession by an evil spirit and madness may occur. Many nurses at St Ann's told me that patients are frequently brought to the hospital straight from the *mourning ground*.[9]

The human soul, the spirits of obeah, the powers of the shango cult, the spirits of the ancestors and revenants, the fallen angels and guardian angels of the Catholics, the summoned elementals of high science, and the spirit guides of the Baptists and those seen in dreams are hardly to be distinguished.[10] They reflect a multiplicity of conceptualisations and interrelations of divine and human, between the moral and physical worlds. Contemporary Trinidadian theology now resembles the lay perspective found in Britain – a relatively large differentiation between God and man, with occasional communication between them, with man personally responsible for his deeds – rather than the more entwined view of divine and human described by Herskovits forty years ago; the once morally neutral powers of shango now appear to have become somewhat dichotomised as either 'good' or 'evil'. For most people however the different types of spirits are much the same. There is a presumed association of the Baptists with obeah, and the spirits of obeah do closely resemble the Baptist spirit guides: they too are African, Indian or Chinese, and speak their respective languages or the 'seven tongues'. While the Baptists themselves distinguish to an extent between good and bad spirits (*bondiay* and *mauvay lespwis*), to non-members all are bad or at best morally ambiguous. Spirits are rarely Whites: and those summoned up by high scientists, although biblical fallen angels, are usually conceptualised as elementals or antic sprites rather than as European mages.

Whatever its origin, madness is generally referred to as an all or nothing condition, total and effectively untreatable: 'Once mad always mad.' Some argue that the brain is physically altered, others just that the mind is 'taken over': what is actually happening inside one's body when one is mad remains mysterious and of little interest. But all agree that the madman must be taken to St Ann's by the police. This is for public safety, not for treatment, as there is nothing the doctors can do. Madness induced by a spirit, the most commonly cited cause, cannot be removed without God's rare intercession. In conversation, madness is usually ascribed a discrete external cause; even informants who advocate the 'pass down in family' theory feel that the affected individual needs more than a predisposition. In practice, when dealing with local instances, a more complex set of explanations is offered by villagers which do link madness to individual personality and everyday life. Madness in a friend or relative may be the consequence of *studiation*, of receiving bad news, of *pressure*, *grinding* and *tabanka*, or of the pursuit of *vices*. It is in these particular experiences that we find a path from everyday life to madness which implicates an internalised set of mental attitudes or psychological processes.[11]

Studiation refers to both the study of high science but also to any undesirable habit ('they study meanness and commonness') or to excessive mental emphasis or opinion on any subject, especially when acquired through reading: 'You overpower with pressure of study. We have young people at school an' they can' take it a next time. You overlearn an' you brain too light, it worry you head.'[12] Studiation madness is rather different from the otherwise undifferentiated picture of madness: it is recognised through social withdrawal (becoming *selfish*), aloofness, emotional distance and ultimately total self-absorption. Some villagers in Pinnacle feel that the Europeans – cold, supercilious and self-centred – have become like that through their books: the White temperament is, as it were, studiation madness spread out thin. Theological speculation when reading the Bible, a common village interest, is particularly dangerous: 'scripture hell of a thing, it send you mad'. Excessive study of any type may be described as *travelling*, lost in a personal world, out of touch with reality, the word used to describe the experience of Baptist mourning. Studiation has a morally as well as a practically ambiguous connotation, as if, like high science, it somehow involved unhallowed domains; certainly book study is not regarded highly, for it involves leaving the community for self-betterment, a denial of local solidarity. Those families who encourage their children to leave Pinnacle to continue their education – and who take on the whole respectable package of restricted public drinking, sobriety, hard work, saving, church attendance, reading the weekly *Catholic News*, not going *bare back* if they are men and not wearing trousers if women – are accused of being *social* (pretentious).

Studiation is not only an intense concentration on books but preoccupation with anything, particularly worries or slights which cannot be resolved. The breaking of bad news too harshly or too suddenly may precipitate madness by causing overwhelming *pressure* (sudden worry). It is sometimes likened to a blow on the head: 'That could worry you' head, even send you crazy a time. It have a woman in Blanchisseuse an' they come an' say she man drown off Tobago an' she bawl and carry on an' she crazy for truth. They take she up to the mental.' But such madness is usually short lived: 'If you frighten, blood fly to you head but you ai' mad all time. If you get good care it stop, it don't even last a week on you. They put ice on your head I hear but I ai' sure.'

More rarely:

Something went on with the man Veronica live with, and they say it a woman he have who do nastiness [sorcery]. I don' think that. It was something he do. It come like worries. He don't sleep in the house two nights, an' she bawl an' carry on. She asked 'Is your husband?' An' she say no but you can see. She bawl, run about, wave her arms. When they rush to hold her she say 'Don't hold me!' She could damage you or bite you. They call me – my mother was a friend of she – 'Veronica like as if she going mad'. I scared like hell an' ai' go. An' he go away down the Main an' they go an' tell she. She start getting worse and want to grip an' she start call this man' name an' this woman', this black woman, an' that why they say she got something on her. She go to mental, an' she ai' know you, an' she quiet an' unconcern'. She big an' fat. She got blind. Is she blind now? I don't know. An' she have two children for him, an' he worthless nasty man.

Pressure refers simultaneously to such worry and to the subjective and external 'pressures' of work and poverty, but also to *high blood* or *high pressure*, understood variously as over-rich blood, the recording on the doctor's plethysmograph or blood passing up to one's head. 'Pressure come as a new thing but now it common in the world. It have blood thickened and heated so it can' flow too good. Once it in you, if you get vex it raise.' It may be caused by using fertilisers on the land. Low pressure is experienced as weakness and thus Guinness stout, used as a *build up*, may cause high pressure. Pressure, like heat or gas, is used to explain everyday fluctuations in wellbeing and some villagers say it is 'hot' and can be relieved by a cooling tea. It certainly builds up like heat or gas and has to be released: worries and anger should be verbalised and ventilated, and not retained inside by *studying* them, *grinding* away. Otherwise they cause high pressure and possibly madness: 'Inside here does eat people.' If one has angry feelings against another they should be freely expressed, at any rate in theory. In practice one runs the risk of being accused of stirring up *comess*. ('I was going to answer but Rupert say she ignorant [badly behaved]: "Don' answer, it make enemy". But I have to tell she! Better than keep inside you and worry worry.') All strong feelings including one's *nature* (sexual desire) should be released lest they develop as pressure. 'Cooling it' is less suppressing an emotion than releasing pressure slowly by relaxation, by liming.

Both physical sickness and madness refer us to the therapeutic efficacy of what we may term 'catharsis', the expulsion of something undesirable to return to a previous and balanced state. We find it in the notions of heat, gas, pressure, grinding and tabanka. It is recognised in the national institution of the annual Carnival: 'It amazing what we Trinis put up with an' don' explode. But come Carnival it jus' baccanal . . . You free up you self, you ai' got pressure, no one looking at you.' Carnival is a 'hot' time and Trinidadians respond good-humouredly, in picong and calypso, to the Ministry of Health posters which appear each year after Christmas advising prophylaxis against venereal disease and 'carnival babies'. The period after Carnival is one of reduced vitality and the subsequent absences from work are half-seriously attributed to illness caused by the rapid passage from hot to cold.

Mary Douglas has suggested that societies with 'weak social controls' seldom elaborate an idiom of bodily catharsis nor do they use purgatives. On looking within Afro-Caribbean societies it would be difficult to regard them, comparatively speaking, as employing 'strong social controls'. If, however, we take a wider view of the West Indies as part of the European political system with its particular relationship between Black and White, established in slavery and continuing through colonialism and after, it is difficult to see what 'stronger social controls' there might be than allocation of social privilege and resources according to immutable skin colour, reflected locally in the ironies of the respectability-reputation schema. Trinidadians themselves argue that Carnival and fêting are the explanation of their national character, as opposed to Barbadians who are 'uptight and lickerish' always trying to imitate Whites, or Jamaicans who respond to insult with prickly sensitivity and violence. By contrast 'we is a Carnival people', laidback, phlegmatic and balanced, a view endorsed by the local psychiatrists.[13] Not that Carnival is without some physical danger, although its ready acceptance as the emblem of Trinidadian identity by the post-independence governments, together with its promotion as a tourist attraction in open air stadia rather than on the streets, has reduced the violence between the competing bands: for 'Carnival use' to be cutlass war.' In its progression to a respectable national institution it is not felt to have lost any of its ability to facilitate well-being, provided it is limited: while only the most crass and sour would deny the value of Carnival, there is a constant anxiety that 'we Trinis carnival every day'.

Tabanka

One form of grinding has a specific name. *Tabanka*[14] occurs 'when you' wife left you and you take it on, keep study it', especially when deserted for another man. It is said to be most common among those formally married in church and among the aspiring *tibourgs* (nurses, midwives and teachers) and *békés nègres* (who pretend to White and middle-class values and life-style). It is charac-terised by a 'heavy heart', by lassitude, loss of appetite, stomach cramps, insomnia and a loss of interest in work or social life. The tabanked male wanders about or remains alone at home, continually turning over in his mind thoughts of the faithless one:

They don't do anything to pass off studiation, they drink, they smoke, they ai' eat, often they ai' coming home. They concentrate on how they was before. You broken down: it does take an effect on your body also; from brain to body; according as the brain function the body deteriorate to an extent; you not eating, you not drinking, you not sleeping, everywhere you turn you thinking.

Similar experiences are recognised in a lesser degree as part of the fluctuation of everyday mood, but tabanka is a discrete state with very specific consequences. The word may refer to other losses but is then less severe and only used with the primary sense, sexual desertion, still in mind: 'Love is the first thing. It must damage your love. If someone rob your house you don't take it on so.'

The consequences of tabanka can include death from accidents whilst drunk or the loss of work. 'You drink to keep off studies. It act on the brain: you drink it out, you cast it out, you taking away thoughts.' If unresolved it can lead to murder or suicide: 'It happen to nearly every man in Trinidad, the most thing. You hear man poison self? It tabanka. A man hang on tree? It tabanka. One of the greatest [most common, most significant] things in Trinidad.' It can progress to madness and some villagers say there is a special ward for it in St Ann's Hospital. 'It have this boy die through grief. He die in mental. He quiet, you take food into the house and he throw it away.' Thomas (page 37) had been 'mad once but that wear out from him, then the girl leave him and he get crazy again'.

'Once you take it on you get tabanka. If you don't take it on you ai' get tabanka. The man who really loves, it worse damage.' It is more serious if the couple have been *church married* rather than just living together because this includes economic as well as emotional investment:

If it your girlfriend you shrug it off – in three days you halfway to a next! . . . He love his wife, he have all his trust in she, he give she all his money and she go and leave him and he remain blank; you love your love and you love your money. It comes double degrees.

Another male villager added 'It ai' the loss of her, but what you've given her.' Indeed, while men may talk in front of women of tabanka as a romantic tragedy, they always emphasise the financial loss. Women are typically rather contemptuous of men with tabanka: 'Men take it on so! They tell you leave but, if you does, they craziness itself!' Even men admit that tabanka is a sign of weakness: 'Some don't get it because they have a strong heart. It all depends on personal feelings. You shouldn't get tabanka. However you take it, someday you and that person got to part, so why the harass?' Tabanka characteristically occurs only after an economic relationship has been established between a man and a woman. It is not *amour fou* or *lovestruckness*, the pursuit of a hopeless and never consummated attachment when 'Everyone does laugh but they don' see that. It becomes like a sickness. It continue till you discover there ai' no love there. That come by actions.'

Women pride themselves on being less likely to experience tabanka, for they already expect men to be unreliable. Both sexes regard women as made of sterner stuff. As the principal source of cash, men argue that they are more responsible, and thus more vulnerable: 'You studying your two ends meet an' your wife not studying. Women more on a side. They can take a love here and take another tomorrow. Men find it more difficult. If women get tabanka they recover themselves faster.'

The acknowledgement of tabanka is necessarily private, for its public recognition provokes barbed jests and humiliation. The very mention of the word is greeted by men and women alike with mirth, if not derision. Its resolution involves the victim being encouraged by other men, usually close friends, to turn his mind to other interests. They counsel modest self-control, to forget the faithless one, not to attempt retrieving his situation, nor to seek revenge, but instead to make fresh attachments. The hilarity of tabanka lies not in any contravention of acceptable behaviour (indeed it is almost regarded as inevitable) but in the infatuation of the deserted man.

Economic security necessitates widespread movement around the country to obtain work. Ownership of land may provide basic food but cash is required for clothes, building materials and anything else, and employment is insecure. Rodman has described local daily life as consequently *according*, 'circumstance-oriented', free-floating, articulated less through persisting kin ties than by a strategic web of individual relationships. One does not necessarily determine one's family identity through fixed kin relations, for these are comparatively elastic; a child may be brought up by its grandmother whom he calls 'Mother' and refer to his biological mother by her given name. For women until recently there was little opportunity for cash employment apart from selling crops locally or taking poorly paid domestic work in the town. As for adult women elsewhere, access to resources was through relations with men. Church marriage is taken as the seal on a successful period of *living* (cohabitation) which itself may develop from *friending* (*frequenting*, a sexual relationship with the partners living separately). Marriage or living involve the man in providing for the woman while in friending 'You is not responsible for her, you only just come and frequent her and what you have you give her.'[15] To set up a household, even *living*, is a measure of economic success but also potential danger for the poor. House and land are typically owned by one partner and each keeps a separate income; spouses regularly lend and borrow money from each other, sometimes with interest. Married relationships are seen as mutually respectful but guarded; as the Creole aphorism puts it, *mari teni dents*.[16] Both men and women accept that by church marriage a woman obtains more than the man; typically she gains the title of 'Mistress' and ceases any paid work outside the home.

Moving around the country for work may enable the man with a reasonable income to support an *outside wife* (or *deputy*). If he manages it discretely, avoiding scandal, and adequately supports all his children, his reputation can be enhanced with little cost to his respectability. Men are expected to provide for their children, even if the mother is friending or living with another man. Recognised paternity, but not virginity, is of importance and a woman is shamed by not having an identified father for her children. An unmarried man who supports another man's children may be ridiculed and the new-born child's physiognomy is carefully scrutinised, assisted by a complex local classification of 'colour'. In the picong of calypso:

(a)   I black like jet and she just like tarbaby
       Chinese children calling me Daddy

(b)   An Indian couple up Belmont
       Make a white baby I'm sure you heard the stunt
       What a loving father
       He said his wife was drinking milk of magnesia[17]

A woman is expected to have sex only with the man who is giving her money if they are living or married. The possibility that she is not is a constant preoccupation of men: 'Someone's been putting pepper in your rice', 'There's more in the mortar beside the pestle' or 'Man trespassing on my land'. Younger and more attractive women may get by economically as a *jagomet* (or *jook about*, poke about), offering favours to a limited number of male friends in exchange for gifts but it is not acceptable for a woman when married or living to have other partners, and a man is not recognised as becoming truly tabanked in a jagomet or friending relationship, unlike marriage:

Since I married Dorothy
She have me going crazy
Horn like fire
I can't take it no longer
You know I nearly dead with tabanka[18]

Sexual access to the woman is exchanged for cash, labour or other services. From the man's point of view:

(a)   Not another cent you wouldn't get until you hand up
       I'm a big man and dis thing must stop

(b)   Now you playing smart . . .
       Nobody yet never take me money
       And making old style on me[19]

While from the woman's:

(a) Johnny, you'll be the only one I'm dreaming of
     You're my turtle dove, but no money no love

(b) The man could be as ugly as sin
     But the money is damn good looking[20]

With tabanka, a man is caught short, without either reputation or respectability. His mistake is infatuation, a failure to perceive his real interests and maintain his autonomy. The older man who accepts the infidelity of his younger wife is despised as doltish for he has completely lost his power of judgement. By contrast tabanka is an indignity which can be successfully transcended. A woman seems less likely to be tabanked because she has not sacrificed reputation to attain a precarious respectability, and by common consent she can only expect to be provided for: only the most worthless of men fails to support his children and she is regarded as well rid of such a partner.

To ask why the very mention of tabanka is so funny is to be met with redoubled laughter and rather uncertain explanations: 'Man has every chance – then he go and lose woman and he come and say he tabanked!' Radcliffe-Brown once suggested that joking relationships occur in situations of simultaneous detachment and attachment, social conjunction and social dislocation: this recalls tabanka but here the humour is articulated in a wide variety of social settings, personal and private, between the sexes, among men by themselves and among women. Although hardly suitable for jokes between sexual partners or between adults and children, its absurdity is not dependent on context but on its subject. Douglas has developed Freud's notion of wit as an arbitrary order that allows a freeing of otherwise restrained motives to suggest jokes 'attack classification and hierarchy', while Handelman and Kapferer also emphasise that joking breaks our sequence of expectation, of the socially inevitable. Certainly, picong about tabanka expresses the value of egalitarian 'circumstance-orientated' relationships; the notion of 'adultery', the moral conceptualisation of the act of desertion, is restricted to respectable settings such as the church. Lowenthal observes of Afro-Caribbean societies that: 'knowledge of one another's private shortcomings leads people to discredit any claim or pretensions to an unrelenting moral uprighteousness . . . In the West Indies generally personalism usually overrides divisive moral imperatives.'[21]

The mockery of tabanka is less an objection to White and middle-class church marriage and supposed fidelity than of surface adherence to their forms when they cannot be supported. It ridicules the masquerade of respectable behaviour and reaffirms the tyranny of individual desire and happenstance in the face of pretence. Arthur, a respectable older man, remarked to me: 'They know where it come from. It is a joke to see a man or woman being tabanked.

But, they say to themselves "Am I to be tabanked man also?" It no joke really, you' hide tears inside.'

Abrahams has offered a functional understanding of humour: 'Because a joke relies upon the previously accepted social order indicates that it acts in response to certain pressures already existing within that order . . . Joking thus helps to give the community the feeling that such situations are under control.'[22] Comic situations are evoked by another's loss of dignity or self-possession when our laughter perhaps gives us a fragile sense of heightened control.[23] As Bergson put it, we place 'our affection out of court and impose silence on our pity'. If we may argue that the mockery represents communal solidarity, it is seen locally as adaptive for the victim through diverting attention from an irretrievable loss to fresh interests: 'Every day is fishing day, not every day is catching day.' A violent attempt at redressing the situation is understandable but hardly sanctioned. The rumoured higher rate of domestic homicide among the local Asians is attributed to a less developed notion of the absurdity of tabanka; 'what was shrugged off by the Creoles as a normal and expected hazard in the relations between the sexes was a reason for murder among the Indians'.[24]

Vices

We can gloss *vice* as 'addiction': a fixed pattern of activity, initially chosen freely by people because it is pleasurable although it may be harmful to themselves or others, and which becomes increasingly difficult to resist until it dominates and eventually destroys them, no longer an object of choice but a part of their being.

Thieving is a vice which becomes impossible to stop when a victim solicits God's justice by lighting a candle on you. God may himself intervene independently with similar consequences, but some suggest that just stealing by itself has an effect on the thief, compelling him to engage in it with fewer and fewer precautions against detection until he *get spoil* – he is caught or becomes mad: 'Their hand fast, they can' see without taking.' A compulsion to repeat stereotyped acts is also found in the vices of high science and obeah when, eventually, a spirit one has conjured up returns, or else God decides that enough is enough. Sexual activities which are vices and which may end in madness include male and female homosexuality; sodomy with people or animals; or sexual relations within the prohibited limits of affinity.[25] Inappropriate sexuality is not always a vice. Marcel, a shy young fisherman who annoyed the village women by stealing their underclothes drying on the riverbank, was just seen as lonely and socially inept. Nevertheless public pressure led him to leave Pinnacle. Rape was unknown in the village but was regarded as an unacceptable extension of normal sexual life rather than a vice. When I asked if there were any other vices, a few suggestions were offered including sex with children and the sadistic beating of members of the family. Persistent lying, quarrelling, making comess, gambling at whe-whe, bad-talking, denying the power of God (usually associated with science), smoking tobacco and laziness are not really vices but they are often dismissed as such in the heat of argument.

Vices are continued patterns of action and personality which are generally socially unacceptable. Frequent public drunkenness and the use of ganja, although they are the vices most often volunteered after obeah (at least by the more respectable villagers), are rather different. Apart from the local Adventists no one regards moderate rum drinking as a vice; on the contrary, it is a welcome lubricant to village life, but continued excessive drinking, as determined by its visibility and its consequences, is a vice which can lead to madness. Smoking of ganja (as opposed to using it as bush tea) is a vice according to the older women. Not so, say the young men, although they agree it can send you mad if 'you can' take it'. Similarly, heavy drinkers believe that rum can cause madness if 'you got a weak head'. While vices may be cited as moral offences, they are usually criticised for rendering normal social life impossible, as contraventions of the natural fitness of things: 'I feel man should be man and woman woman. The way you made. This kind of filthiness [homo-sexuality] is a bad thing because God make a partner for you. I don't like it, they dress and speak like a woman.'

In theory no particular personality is more liable to a vice. It is the sort of thing anybody may be tempted to do in a weak moment. If one has a vice one should keep it secret for to flaunt it suggests it is already taking you over. Nevertheless, accusations of vice are directed against those who are already *worthless* and thus probably have other vices. Any sexual vice can lead to implications of obeah, and both are known by the general term of *filthiness* (or *nasty ways*) which is worthlessness and confusion taken further. The term *interference* (which for Mother Earth becomes the major offence against nature (page 79)) locally denotes both obeah and sexual vice. A whole family, through past misdeeds or obeah, may be *blighted*, the same term which is given to the victims of maljo, although here suggesting an inherited tendency to engage in obeah, thieving and other filthiness, the whole complex inexorably moving to general incest and insanity. If your father was mad, *ran a drunk* or had a reputation for science, you are regarded as that much more vulnerable. As with any specific vice, a blight on a family or individual may simul-taneously be taken as past divine punishment and as the inevitable working out of a current vice.

Suzanne, a doltish young woman, is derided as a 'cooler for men' for she has frequent and casual relationships with the more worthless men around Pinnacle who visit her at night when drunk. She is popularly rumoured to have borne her first child, Andrew, to her own father. This is confirmed by Andrew's slow development. Suzanne herself is the result of interference with her mother by the mother's father, supposedly a high scientist, and 'she lie plenty, deceitful . . . she got fits too'. Vices both generate madness and doltishness and are caused by them, forming a constraining circle of addiction in which vice is relentlessly pursued to increasingly self-damaging ends.

Mad or madmad?

Continued anti-social behaviour so persistent as to constitute a vice – stealing or violence – may be regarded as an attenuated form of madness, reminiscent of the psychiatrist's 'psychopathic personality': 'It ai' just a vice. He ai' really bad. He ai' exactly what you call mad. It come as what we call half-way crack.' The diagnosis of madness is arrived at subtly, pragmatically. It is always 'according'. To take three local instances:

An' my friend Marcelline been start talk queer like she go crazy. An' I take she to a woman and she say, 'It have one throw something in you' yard. It for you' mother but it hit you.' An' the girl still half crazy an', after her mother die, she go to mental, but she cure in a few weeks. She ai' crazy because she got cure. It have to be something that an enemy put on her.

The speaker had later married Marcelline's brother. Madness caused by obeah is supposed to be chronic and cannot be removed except by supernatural intervention; the doctor's treatment would have been useless. The complete recovery is used to justify the fact that although her friend had to go to St Ann's she was not *madmad*, and the obeah is the only possible explanation of an otherwise unexpected madness. When I suggested this I was firmly told that the doctor didn't 'cure' her; she 'got cure' because her enemy had withdrawn the *interference* when her mother, the intended victim, had died.

Samuel, a nineteen-year-old boy, died (in *status epilepticus*) from long-standing and recognised malkadi. I was called to see him one Sunday morning during Mass but by the time I reached the house he was dead. One explanation offered to his parents by the villagers was that worm fits had killed him. To say openly that he had had malkadi (rather than simply fits, *pzasm*) would have been unsympathetic, for malkadi always carries an unpleasant mystical connotation, unlike the fits known to be caused by intestinal worms. Samuel had been having fits since he was twelve and a variety of anti-convulsants from the hospital in Port-of-Spain had been only partially effective in reducing them.

Whilst he was alive these attempts were derided by the other villagers: 'Samuel don' have what you term fits. His arm strong like you can' move it. It a spirit.' Nevertheless, when I asked them, they said that they would take their child to the doctor in similar circumstances. However, 'good doctor should say "it ai' sickness, go to priest"'. Why could there be a spirit on Samuel? Some suggested that it was a punishment for obeah by someone in the family. His father had twice had fits. 'Something happen in that family for true: they use to have a shop an' it go suddenly.' At his funeral this was insinuated to the visiting priest by a villager who was famed for her *mauvaylang*. He ignored her suggestion. Samuel's mother had previously flirted with Pentecostalism, and other explanations were that her son had become ill either as a divine punishment for this or else a spirit had passed over her during some exorcism. So 'he get spoil'. The Pentecostal theory was generally accepted by the villagers because they were resentful that since her return to the Catholics she remained associated with its charismatic group (currently favoured by the archbishop in town and very 'American' and *social*). Like some other light-skinned Spanish in Pinnacle she maintained a rather reserved demeanour. She and her husband were economically successful and had built a concrete house somewhat away from the rest of the village, near the cemetery which overlooks Pinnacle River (which occasioned further gossip about unholy things seen at night). They had rented another house in which they planned to open a 'club', a novelty in Pinnacle. Samuel himself was not accused; a quiet and sickly but friendly boy, he could not be regarded as the initiator of any mystical unpleasantness. Although theories of a turned spirit were generally discussed at the wake on the evening of his death, no mention of this was made directly to his family for fear of hurting their feelings. In spite of their respectability and their Spanish ancestry, Samuel's parents are accepted as generous and good-humoured, quite simply among the kindest people in the village. To accuse them openly or consistently of *filthiness* would be so inappropriate as to rebound on the speaker, giving rise to further discussion as to why she should be so knowledgeable on that particular subject. The theory offered in the course of the illness by the family's friends, that pzasm was a sickness which may 'pass down in the family', was eventually accepted as the public consensus at the wake, together with a suggestion that an elderly Adventist who had died exactly a hundred days before 'was lonely and she come back to take the boy'.

Jules is a heavy drinking storekeeper, born in Tobago, who is rumoured to use science to attract customers (for his prices are easily the highest in Pinnacle). His sister had married a Spanish (Venezuelan immigrant) who owned a van and was herself the village's only member of an 'American' sect. Her son Augustin thus carried a rather weighted past: science, foreign origin, the Jehovah's Witnesses, prosperity on both sides of the family, and the rather ambiguous Spanish connection (associated it is true both with church going and strong family-centred respectable values, but also with knowledge of the secret and somewhat ambiguous prayers to counter maljo). Augustin had always been worthless. He stole. He didn't join in the fishing (not that he was often invited) but occasionally made a trip down the coast alone to pick copra from the now abandoned family estate. Most of the time he sat around the village liming with the local Rastas who came from poorer families than he did, smoking ganja and idly trading abusive picong with passers-by. He became increasingly withdrawn and could be seen talking to himself, although, when questioned, he turned queries aside in a reasonable though surly way, occasionally offering fatuous jokes. One day, in a rather confused state, he hit one of the villagers with a cutlass, was arrested and eventually taken to St Ann's Hospital which is on the other side of the island. Diagnosis there, as reported back through a nurse whose mother lived in Pinnacle, was ganja madness. Village opinion was unanimous, and was voiced somewhat more openly than in the case of Samuel. Augustin was blighted and was clearly being punished both on his own behalf and because his uncle *mounted* the goods in his store forcing the purchaser to return to shop there again and again. This compulsion was mirrored in the blight: 'He going crazy with ganja again an' again. It have a thing on that family. Someone mouth on them and now he can' stop.' Augustin's mother was furious at these stories but did not respond, standing on her dignity as one who alone was sure of salvation. She shared her hurt feelings with the only outsider available, myself: 'He had an ear infection in his childhood and was born before his time [prematurely]. Since then he can' stop stealing. I don' know if he killed someone yet but if he do he sorry after and say "Mam – I didn't mean to do it." ' At the same time as seeking an excuse for his behaviour through a natural disease so that he was not responsible, she tried to persuade me that he was not mad anyway because there was a motivation for his violence: 'He only do it to this man who get him vex.' Augustin himself attributed the episode to ganja and at his mother's urging, took to hawking oranges round the village from a huge basket. As this is over-priced and the community anyway prefer to exchange rather than sell their own fruit, Augustin's blighted reputation is hardly diminished. The young men who gave him the ganja say he is not *madmad*, only a little *light-headed*; if he was really mad he could hardly now be selling fruit.

Any unreasonable, unintelligible or angry act may be credited as 'mad' without implying that it is 'really mad'. Villagers distinguish between 'weak' and 'strong' uses of the term. Any known individual acting in a stupid, inappropriate or eccentric way may be called *mad* (or *light-headed*, *doltish*) without suggesting they are really insane. When there is any doubt the terms *mad for truth*, *mad like hell* or *madmad* are used. Eccentricity or behaviour out of character may be *a little way mad* but never *madmad* unless it leads to violence or is quite unintelligible:

(a) Tante Claudette mad. She always talk to herself. She can't hear any other noise at all! She talk like foreign language, I don't know how she do it. Tante talk Spanish, Patois, Congo, she call the names.

(b) My uncle mad once. He was to stand for compère [godfather] to my sister and he just go and drop his suit in latrine! He climb up house without a ladder. That really crazy. They tie him with rope and pull him down.

In neither of these cases did anyone else regard their relative as 'really mad'. In a similar use, the back of the van owned by a rather nervous driver from Sangre Grande proclaims 'LUNATIC KEEP OFF'. A well-known Calypso singer carries the name 'Crazy' and acts up to it by outlandish behaviour and costume; he probably derived it from an Ole Mass (traditional Carnival) character. Local Rastas sometimes maintain they themselves must be crazy, or alternatively, if everyone else says they are, then it is everyone else who should be in St Ann's. For they regard the establishment as 'mad': 'When the Whites got their share of learning, they take it and do a whole heap of things and most of all they want to destroy mankind.'

To term political figures 'mad' is common picong. Dr Eric Williams, the first prime minister of independent Trinidad, succeeded another politician known as the 'Mad Scientist'. 'The Doc' himself was popularly regarded as mad, sometimes in all seriousness. His elusive *social* persona, an ex-Oxford scholar, aloof yet with an apparently incisive understanding of the masses, his gradual withdrawal from public life behind his dark glasses and hearing aid, the uncertain number of his marriages, and his intelligence, all argued he had studied too hard. After his death, articles in the press suggested that he had been clinically mad: 'You can't reach him . . . He always come one better'.[26] The Doc's madness was eccentric or *high*, with connotations of studiation madness and even of European high science. *High mind* can become a type of vice and renders one vulnerable through one's caprices; it becomes real madness if it take one over unchecked. The converse, that all madness necessarily entails a special type of wisdom, is not held: 'There ai' no sense in madness, it just stupidness.' The expression 'method in madness' simply implies feigned madness in Trinidad (not a higher sanity as it may in Britain) and was once suspected by plantation owners as a popular way to avoid estate work.[27]

The arbitrary eruptions of madness do not escape social meaning. If it usually represents a discrete and easily recognisable state, it also provides in practice a rich and *according* term for other, more ambiguous behaviours, and an image to describe those who are 'too clever' or antisocial to join in daily concerns. Even in the 'strong' sense madness recalls the demotic values of reputation; the bush as opposed to the town; Creole rather than English; *outside* rather than *inside*; the vices of obeah, ganja and excessive drunkenness. The ultimate image of the worthless man, of vice carried to its logical and inexorable conclusion, of unsocialised nature, is the madman. If tabanka and studiation madness can be interpreted, as I have done, as ironic commentaries on selfish and pretentious attempts to imitate White and middle-class life when this is not 'according to circumstance', vices warn of the opposite danger – that of abandoning *social* life altogether. Tabanka may be read as the over-valuing of respectability as a practical goal, while vice is its under-valuing. Failures of balancing interests against possibilities they both lead to madness, the caricature of the impoverished and *worthless* Black. Neither are simply 'indigenous' explanations of sickness, independent of external constraints. Both are rooted in the economic history of the West Indies, in the inescapable irony of being poised between two ascribed sets of values, one derided as worthless, the other only precariously attainable.

4

Mother Earth and the psychiatrists

In its industrialisation, its standard of living and the extent of formal education, but also in its patterns of disease, Trinidad resembles Western Europe. Two admissions per year for malaria to the Port-of-Spain General Hospital and four for leprosy contrast with 1,158 for diabetes which, with vascular disease and cancer, accounts for nearly three-quarters of all deaths in adults, a pattern of mortality similar to those of other industrialised countries.

Psychiatric care was traditionally provided in the large mental hospital at St Ann's, built in the nineteenth century beyond the northern suburbs of Port-of-Spain. For its population, Trinidad had a relatively large mental health staff by the early nineteen-eighties – 24 doctors (out of a total of over 1,000), plus social workers, psychologists, occupational therapists, and more than 600 nursing staff. Over the last twenty years psychiatric services have slowly moved into smaller local facilities and there are three general hospital psychiatric units; out-patient and children's clinics; and an alcoholism treatment centre. Many Trinidadian psychiatrists have trained in Britain and this policy closely follows the contemporary British model: a predominantly biological explanation of psychopathology involving a 'community-based' pattern of services to avoid 'institutionalisation', with nurses visiting patients at home, programmes of public education and the establishment of day centres and workshops. As in Britain, the 'deinstitutionalisation' of St Ann's has met with a rather mixed public response and the press carries periodic complaints that patients are being discharged from hospital to sleep in the streets. The entry by a patient into the president's bedroom in his official residence near St Ann's prompted a series of complaints about hospital security; the popular view of the mad remains that they are dangerous and that doctors are irresponsible for not keeping their patients properly locked up: 'Funny place Trinidad. They wait till a patient cutlass somebody. Then they lock him up.'

The nurses mediate between the medical view of psychiatric illness and the popular understanding of madness. Many nurses accept the role of spirits in madness and one senior nurse at St Ann's was rumoured by his colleagues to have gained his position after having bathed in a bush bath provided by a local Baptist. A not untypical incident was that of a young woman from a village near Pinnacle who became possessed at home by a spirit not long after she had a minor operation. The family asked the priest for help. The Mental Health Officer (the psychiatric community nurse) visited and decided the woman was psychotic and gave her medicine which failed to help. He then offered to take her to see a doctor for further advice. The family refused and instead took her to a Baptist leader who said that she was being sent mad by a 'phantom which her uncle mind, and he mind it to enrich him'. The parents became anxious about possible publicity and the nurse was asked not to visit again and he remains uncertain about the outcome, although it seems likely that the family had not themselves made a diagnosis of madness. Collaboration between mental health workers and practitioners of bush medicine is not officially encouraged, partly because an extensive professional service is already available, but also because obeah remains illegal under the old colonial legislation.

Mother Earth in St Ann's Hospital

Mother Earth has been twice in St Ann's. The hospital's case notes give us some indication of the professional response to her experiences and actions.[1] In June 1977, some time after the community at Hell Valley had been established, and a month after a daughter was born to her, Mother Earth led the group on one of their periodic marches to town to 'Free Up the Nation'. Passing through the town of Arima they were arrested for going naked. The children in the group were placed in the Tacarigua Orphanage by a magistrate who committed Mother Earth to St Ann's.

Her initial hospital notes say that she was admitted because she 'walked naked', with little further information except that she had fourteen children and 'uses ganja tea'.[2] The salient features noted were 'no insight, diminished responsibility [and] long matted hair'. Diagnosis was of a paranoid state but 'her husband believes implicitly in patient's special powers and delusions'. Two days later, 'patient says she had to make a sacrifice of herself' – that she had to strip herself naked, and argued that this was not abnormal 'as it was the pattern at the beginning of time'. Diagnosis was now 'schizophrenia with inappropriate affect'. Over the next few weeks, the patient was treated with fluphenazine decanoate, chlorpromazine, trifluoperazine and thioridazine (all anti-psychotic drugs), but there was 'no change in her mental state'; although quiet and co-operative, she was 'still deluded' and was discharged on the basis that she would be unlikely to improve further.

A social work report was gathered from her mother's neighbours who offered two rather different opinions. She was 'onto a good thing' and intended to build a house in the capital on the proceeds of growing ganja; or else she had a genuine religious mission. Particular emphasis was placed in the report on her children: 'Five children are living with them, some of them not christened.' Her relatives were not keen to have the patient back home and the report mentioned that one of the neighbours said 'Jeanette's mother was always eager to marry her off at a young age. It is said that she used to encourage men at home for her.'

May 1980 found Mother Earth in St Ann's again on another Magistrate's Order, guilty of disorderly behaviour during another demonstration. The admission notes mention that she said 'she was Mother Earth and that the sun was coming closer to the earth and that there would be a fire . . . Patient very untidy dressed in bag skirt and bare breasted.' She was found to have 'paranoid ideas and delusions' which were not specified. Diagnosis was 'relapsed schizophrenia' and treatment was as before, plus diazepam. A psychologist interviewed her this time and gave a brief but sympathetic account of her beliefs and wrote in her notes 'Despite her bizarre ideas I found no difficulty communicating with her. Her affect was quite appropriate but there is evidence of psychosis.'

Six weeks later, her pulse rate when asleep was found to be high and a thyroid condition was suspected. The likely diagnosis now became one of toxic psychosis.[3] The patient was offered a thyroid operation, which she refused. The nursing notes comment that she 'maintained her mental state until visited by some Rastas [after which] she kept wanting to go out of the ward and started singing loudly and walking up and down, showing signs of relapsing'. Two weeks later, the main medical notes laconically record that the patient 'left against advice' and that the diagnosis was again schizophrenia.

The notes kept by the nurses are a little more detailed. Their patient 'was visited by a group of Rastas, ten men and one boy. Not allowed on the ward as they were dripping wet. Patient was told to speak to them from outside the ward. She left with the group.' Another nurse wrote 'It would have upsetted the other patients [to detain her] . . . They gave the patient a bag [sack] to put on which she did in front of everybody. They began to sing and clap loudly and walked down the steps.'

The rest of the Hell Valley group, fearing that Mother Earth would never get out of St Ann's, had crossed the mountains to the capital, camped out in a nearby house yard, and then climbed over the hospital wall in the evening during a storm and entered the ward more or less naked and carrying cutlasses. By the time the police had been called, the Earth People together with their leader had disappeared to make their way up through the forest reserves of the Northern Range and thence over the mountains back to the Valley. The episode prompted the psychiatrist to write to the magistrate responsible asking him to remand Mother Earth to prison on any future occasions rather than to the hospital 'as a matter of public interest'. The hospital staff complained again about the security situation. For the Earth People, the episode remains one to be celebrated in story and song around the fire in the evenings, both a personal story of the dramatic rescue of a friend and leader, and one of the myths of the continuing struggle between Nature and Science.

I asked Mother Earth, her partner Jakatan, and the other Earth People if when she was in hospital she was any different from when I was staying in Hell Valley. They all said no.[4] Both incidents happened after she had initiated a march on Port-of-Spain and it would not be unreasonable to expect any unusual state of mind to be more manifest at that time but the hospital notes tell us little beside what were then some of the beliefs of the Earth People, and they cite no incidents or behaviour which would not be accepted as normative by the group. The ascription of 'delusions' and 'paranoia' refer to her cosmology. The only evidence of a schizophrenic illness is the suggestion of 'inappropriate affect', strictly an inconsistency between observed emotion and the expressed content of thought, but apparently here describing just 'abnormal affect'. Talking to the doctor and nurses who had treated her suggested that this was indeed so and that her mood had been elated, with friendly and infectious enthusiasm, alternating with accusations of unfair imprisonment. There was nothing specifically schizophrenic in the medical sense then, but certainly a set of unusual ideas and actions consequent on them, ideas which of course were accepted by her group. One of the nurses told me that their patient had readily accepted the ward atmosphere, had acquiesced in her treatment, and indeed agreed to have her dreadlocks cut off, and was only upset by the anger of Jakatan when visiting her to find her head shorn. Jakatan told me he was furious when he saw what had happened to her and returned to the Valley to gather the group to rescue her; otherwise he would have waited a little longer for her to be discharged in a more conventional way, for the development of the Hell Valley community lies in steadily winning recruits rather than in any dramatic confrontation with the authorities. None of the group thought that Mother Earth would recant her visions whilst under treatment (how could she?) but they were concerned about the effect of the drugs on the physical Flesh in which The Mother now dwelled.

All the group, Mother Earth included, accept the conventional notion of madness outlined in the previous chapter. Their point of disagreement with the doctors is on the question of Mother Earth's own experiences: 'If she mad, we mad.' At the same time, all the Earth People are sympathetic to the idea that mad people are in St Ann's because of social *pressure*. As in many other instances, the ideas in Hell Valley are arguably more 'modern' than those of other Trinidadian villagers. Madness might reflect the state of Society, but it does not in itself provide any sort of privileged critique. Mad people are just mad. Mother Earth's sympathy for the mad, however, led her later to invite a fellow patient from St Ann's to join the community; this woman, whom she named Mango Rose, was to precipitate one of the major schisms in the group.

A psychiatrist in the Valley

A biography is always the intersection of two lives. Myself? A white male. A Yorkshire father of Non-Conformist background, a Swiss mother whose uncle was associated with the Zimmerwald Movement. Middle-class British childhood, provincial ennui and the worthy *Manchester Guardian*, but also Bunyan, Robin Hood, *The Wind in the Willows* and Richmal Crompton's *William* books; grammar school and the Scouts; Shelley, Conrad, *The Golden Bough*, Kropotkin's *Conquest of Bread*, Meister Eckhart, *The Divided Self*, but also Schrödinger's *What is Life?* and *A Rebours*. Five months at Shivananda's ashram in Rishikesh, then St Bartholomew's Hospital Medical School. The Dialectics of Liberation meeting at the Roundhouse, occasional work with the periodical *Black Dwarf*, a minor role in the LSE occupation, student elective in Uganda, failed and retook surgery finals, art school in Whitechapel, house jobs at Barts, followed by psychiatry in Hackney; enthusiasms for Karl Jaspers and Jean Dubuffet; psychotherapy training, clinical research in epidemiology, university lectureship, marriage, a book on racism and psychiatry, anthropology at Oxford, last paintings, parenthood, a study of Hasidim in London, Trinidad.

Plotting some points for my biographical trajectory like that (and we have a variety of selectable trajectories with or without the psychological realism which constructs them as plausible narratives for others) up to the moment at which it intersected with that of Mother Earth, the question seems hardly 'Why did I choose the Earth People?' rather 'How might I have failed to choose them?' After some months in Pinnacle Village I was getting a little complacent. Initial fieldwork seemed surprisingly easy (too easy, as I later understood). I'd finally finished reading Proust and seemed on course for another ethnomedical monograph on a small rural community when my thoughts turned again to the Earth People after a ridiculous argument with a *long eyed* fisherman who wanted 50 dollars to disclose the prayers for curing maljo: I knew the prayers did not work if bought, and he knew that fieldwork is a sort of currency, in which knowledge is made available or exchanged for friendship or support, to be transformed once again through a monograph into an economic relationship. What else? A longstanding interest in radical Puritanism, some sort of yearning for a primitive zwischenmenschliche, the rumours that Mother Earth had been in the psychiatric hospital in Port-of-Spain? Of course. 'The Pinnacle villagers had warned me . . . ' (page xi): a classic invitation to the reader to consider my narrative as colonial adventure.

But it was not just that. Quite simply, I'd often wondered how religious and political movements got themselves started: not the routinisation and later elaboration, the consolidation of dogmas and hierarchies, but the beginnings, where the banal becomes the significant, where the mundane and the fortuitous somehow became central, and personal contingencies and chance experiences become structured and reformed into universal truths which are independent of human intentions: where the happenstance nocturnal traveller on his way to Emmaus is recognised as the recently executed prophet, where Mother Ann Lee's endless pregnancies transform the Christian God into the Shakers' bisexual divinity, where our transient dysphorias become the very foundations of Hell. The passage of personal biographies, and friendships, with all their trivial accidents, into the stuff of established culture and hagiography had always seemed a little mysterious. How much did early Christian doctrine demonstrate the personality and experiences of Jesus, or of Saint Paul? Who knows?: the biographical fallacy, arbitrary and unprofitable speculation. While the apparently random events out of which emerged religious institutions continued to interest me, I was dubious about the universality of the psycho-analytical theories of Devereux and La Barre, even Erikson, and unconvinced by the typologies elaborated by the sociologists of religion who used an idiom of 'pathology' to qualify the millennial groups of which they so obviously disapproved. Mother Earth offered me a return to the problem of the inter-actions between individual experience and social representation, between a psychopathology closer to biology (my first degree had been in biochemistry) and the conventions of social anthropology. Questions that remain vital to me now, ten years on.

If I had chosen the Earth People they had of course chosen me. Mother Earth too was concerned with confronting this opposition between Nature and Society. She stipulated that I would live with her community on the condition that I eventually wrote about them, as some sort of near final squaring-off (or reconciliation?) with Science, the actual procedure left up to me. 'My' book then is less 'about' Mother Earth than it is somehow a part of Mother Earth, not in some modish deconstruction but as an explicit element in her cosmogony, predicted, demanded by her: an intersubjectivity. As is your reading of it. If the Son, the parodic God of White Science, has indeed produced us through our commodification of Black people, through male oppression of women, through a rape of Nature, then the Beginning of the End entails a transformation of us all, subject and object, personal experience and academic discourse alike.

I do not claim to have achieved that, but I would not have wanted to live with the Earth People had I not resonated with (and still do) much of their world. Yet I felt myself resisting what seemed at times a tight, almost cloying system: my preference for dialectical antagonisms will be evident here. I am not sure that they solved any particular personal dilemmas for me, as a vehicle for my own deep motivations – arguably the reverse – but they certainly saw it that way, constantly telling me that my life until then had been simply a preparation for our meeting. They did offer a radical reassertion of the sort of values in which I was brought up (which raises questions as to how reciprocal or homologous my own values are to those of my parents), a sensibility which I still respect and whose absence in contemporary Britain I profoundly regret: some notion of Dissent, that authority is inevitably compromised, and that the moral life is a raw individual one to be defined against institutional power. Adolescent if you will. Primitivist? – an assumption that our contemporary institutions are to be understood most truly through their conjectured origins? I do not think so.

Given Mother Earth's own experiences at St Ann's, why did she wish my intrusion? From the beginning I was met with friendliness and tolerance; my anxieties as to disturbing the community were continually brushed aside, although I did cause considerable difficulties for them. There was never any question but that I was an outsider with my primary loyalties elsewhere and that I could hardly be a full member of the group. Mother Earth tended to regard me as a confidant to whom she complained about the conflicts in the group, available to share her concerns about the future, and even on occasion to be asked for medical advice. Indeed, when she became ill I carried out a physical examination without medical instruments in the midst of good humoured mockery from anyone standing nearby. She joined enthusiastically in answering my questions, and eventually persuaded me, over my own misgivings, to bring camera and tape recorder. She participated in a formal psychiatric interview. So did some of the others. The fact that I was a psychiatrist provoked hilarity rather than indignation: the sheer absurdity of my presence was somehow a guarantee of safety for us all. The conditions laid upon me in exchange for hospitality and knowledge were that I would emphasise their own interpretations as well as my own, and would return to St

Ann's to put their point of view. Later we wrote an article together for the *Trinidad Guardian*. It was rejected.

I was twenty-four when my country relinquished its colonial control over Trinidad. The extent to which Mother Earth and I collaborated in an ironic re-enactment of what Pratt has called 'the first contact scene', the extent to which we transcended it, is still for me uncertain. Of course we used to joke about the White 'discovery' of her Valley. The transcribed tapes and the photographs published here are less indexical fragments, snapshots *en route*, than set pieces, posed self-presentations by Mother Earth and myself. A deep personal friendship insensibly drew us together (I didn't will it, it happened to me). Perhaps more than most ethnographers I could hardly perceive her as 'an informant'. She remains one of the most extraordinary people I have ever met: wise and charming, forceful and belligerent. Endless hours passed sitting on the ground of the hut, arguing, telling stories, playing with the children, sampling new African essays from Breadfruit's pot, and discussing the community, Mother Earth's own visions, and the likelihood of the approaching End. I asked her – if she was indeed mad, would this invalidate the whole enterprise? It would only confirm it, she said. She was never in any doubt that she was the original Mother Nature; her beliefs and continuing innovations were all validated by the whole group and at no time during my stay did she suggest by speech, or behaviour, that she was suffering from anything I could recognise as a continuing psychotic process. Continuing revelation was limited to visions in dreams, and, during my months with the community, doctrine altered only slightly and then to accommodate my intrusion. She shifted during crises from benign nurturant Mother to determined leader, quickly dealing out solutions to practical problems and acidly rebuking members for failing to live up to The Life. Her decisions were generally considerate of the feelings of others, frequently authoritarian, on occasion capricious.

Although usually vivacious and alert, she complained to me of physical pains; her legs and abdomen were frequently swollen due to fluid retention and she found it difficult to remain standing for long periods: at these times her addresses to the group were delivered by her supporting herself against one of the wooden pillars. Her pulse was rapid (usually over 100) and her heart beat extended further to the left than is usual, suggesting a degree of cardiac failure. After agreeing for me (in one of my more medical moments) to take a blood sample to assess her thyroid function, for which I made elaborate preparations – a canot to Pinnacle and transport thence to the Port-of-Spain General Hospital in a box of ice to be obtained from the village rum shop – she changed her mind, saying that she was now conceding too much to Science. Although recognising that she was physically ill – the world before the End being still enmeshed in sickness – she refused the opportunity of a medical consultation in town and would not accept medicine from me, although she used some *rachette*[5] for her swelling (grown in Pinnacle and which I brought back to the Valley).

Using a standardised semi-structured psychiatric interview, the Present State Examination,[6] Mother Earth scored on the following: Subjective Evaluation of Physical Health (Score 2: moderate subjective incapacity); Tiredness (Score 1: intermittent, independent of exertion); Depressed Mood (Score 1: mild, intermittent, could not switch voluntarily to cheerful topic but could be distracted away from it). The subdued mood was only rated towards the end of my stay and appeared consequent on various problems in the group. As her beliefs were validated by the group, it would not be appropriate, given the conventions of the PSE, to rate them as Religious Delusions, but possibly as 'Subculturally Influenced Delusions' (Score 2).[7]

Thus, there was nothing significantly psychopathological about Mother Earth at the time I stayed with her. The genesis of her system, however, was sudden and inexplicable to herself and her family at the time, and she was regarded by them initially as mad. It was initiated by actions she herself did not understand but which her later cosmogony explained. Although it related to her personality, experiences and values, it was novel and could not easily be seen just as a simple extension of previous preoccupations. Before mapping her experiences against the conventional medical co-ordinates, it is time to give Mother Earth's own account.

The visions of Mother Earth

Her account of her childhood and early adulthood are not characterised by any extraordinary events. Jeanette (as she was baptised) had a conventional working-class life in Port-of-Spain, a life she recollects as hard:

Well, it was a struggle, a very hard struggle for me, because I just been living.[8] I never had to pay rent. I live with my first children's father for three years. He put me out . . . I go by my mother. I remain there. I try to live with somebody else again. It wasn't so easy. I leave, go back home, try again the third time. I leave again, go back home and I decide to stay home. So then I been living and struggling, selling, doing whatever little I could do to make a penny for my children. When I get in with somebody we last until my belly is big – I'm pregnant again. They leave me. I have to fight again to mind my children but somehow or the other the spirit always sends somebody to help me . . . My spirit always be with me so that someone would help me, come and help me. But it always usually end up I by myself, working again, selling again and feeding my children as much as I could, send them to school . . . But the struggle was on. I go ahead with it. I wasn't finding no fault of the city.

Is one thing is always in my mind since I am living in the city: is to help my people.

Something always in me, when I see a sick I feel I should be able to help them. When I go anywhere and somebody complain about their life, although mine's so rugged, I always think about that person and wish I could have helped them. This is always myself. I know to myself that I am a healer. As the Baptists would say, 'You are a healer.' I know that I had healing work to do but I didn't know when.

Jeanette's maternal grandmother (with whom she lived at various periods in her childhood) was a Baptist, and Jeanette started attending the meetings from the age of twelve. She was not particularly involved and indeed scorned conventional religious beliefs. On one occasion a burst gas main in Port-of-Spain caught fire and everybody fell on their knees

an' say Jesus come. I laugh an' I walk on. As a child I was baptise with the Baptists at the age of fourteen. And I go in the Baptists, listening to them preaching and talking about the Bible, bawling 'Jesus!' But in my growing up, I had a lot of visions and never really see what they speaking about within my visions.

In my thirties, I went to mourn, and for the very first time because I never wanted to go and mourn but they keep nagging at me why I don't come to mourn: 'Why you don't go and mourn?' I said 'all left' – I said 'all right' – 'I'll mourn'. They prepare the list for me; I took the list, buy what they said to buy, and I went to mourn.

It was terrible because I had a lot of trouble and yet myself was talking to me to help me out in my trouble. Until the day come that I there lying down and didn't see nothing too much (I hearing the rest of the mourners talking and so forth but I wasn't going nowhere) until the third day – rising day – the Mother come and tell me if I don't see myself rising I'll have to remain there! I started to cry and thing. When it turn the evening, one of the Mothers come and sit with me. A Teacher, they call her. She come and she sit with me. She say 'I come to help you see yourself' and she started to trump.[9] I started to trump with her and I started to see myself – down in a grave, swaddled from head to foot like a mummy. I tell her. She say 'What again?' And I take off the swaddling bands, throw them in the hole and seal it but in a darkness. I saw the coffin come up. I saw myself standing on it with a very large foot. And I say 'Well, look I am a giant' because my foot was very long. She say, 'Go ahead – what again?' And I tell her I saw myself as a Kong . . . [10] She turn round and said 'What again?' an' I said 'Well I seeing something in front of me.' She said 'What it is?' 'It a serpent but I afraid of it – I can't speak to it.' She said 'Speak to it.' I said 'No, I can't.' I started to bawl because I was afraid of it although I know it in my sleep for many years: I was seeing it and always running from it. This life [time] it was in front of me so I couldn't run, but all I did was bawl and eventually I snatch it and I hold it. She turn around and she say 'What that mean?' I said 'Well look it straighten and it turn a staff.' She said 'What is the meaning of that?' I said 'The Christ is the Good Shepherd.' She said 'Thank you.' She say I'm finished. So it then she left me and I was blank again. I didn't see nothing again. Till then nobody didn't really tell me what it mean. I live on. I didn't really study it after the mourning and thing.

On another occasion Jeanette had a mourning vision of herself as a skeleton to which flesh was slowly added: the Resurrected Christ. The other early visions she now recollects occurred in dreams. In one, nine days after the birth of her first child, when she was seventeen, she saw herself walking down the road singing 'There's a cross for everyone, there's a cross for me' when she saw a great light in the sky. In another she saw a house (later to be identified as the one at Hell Valley) and was carried inside and placed on a throne. Cyprian (Jakatan) had a similar 'call' in 1967 after he joined the Baptists:

The week after I baptise I lie down and have a vision. I standing on a hill and see town destroyed by a flood. I go to a half-broken-down house and see a big black box. I open it. I hear a whole set of voices. I see a White man standing by it. The people crying help and I say 'I am the True Shepherd and will lead you to true freedom.'

Cyprian became a Baptist Shepherd (a title he kept in the early days of the Earth People) and the following year had another vision whilst mourning: 'I go into a school and it have a big map of Trinidad but no pupils. A short black man point to map and say "Go down to the valley . . . Like shooting is about to begin."' In 1970 he joined the Black Power demonstrations. After their failure he was struck by a remark which had been made by one of its leaders, who said that Trinidadians should 'buy less clothes, go less to store'. The same year he met Jeanette who was then thirty-seven (he was twenty-six), already with ten children. They started living together; they have since had four children together. She was unsympathetic to his radical ideas:

In 1973, the 21st of May, I leave the city with my child father [Cyprian] and come in the bush with him. Well, I have to say the Spirit lead me there because at the life [time] I was about to build a house. I had the land, I had galvanise, I had wood, I had every-thing but I just walk out on it, pick up the smaller children (which I had eleven at the time), pick up the smaller ones and his own and I come to the bush with him.

I didn't even know I was coming in the bush! But one day he just came back (when the baby was eight months) and tell me 'I come for you to go in the bush' and I say 'Who – me? Not me! I ai' going in the bush!' Well, he said 'Think it over. On Monday I'll be here with a van and be ready.' Well, I didn't even take him on, but Sunday a little incident happen between one of my children and another little boy kick him and when I go out in the road and ask question they laugh at me. Everybody watch me and laugh and I watch them and within myself something was telling me 'Look – this is the time for you to leave; get out of this place.' So I decide. 'Well look all you!' I turn to them and tell them 'This is you all last chance.' And I leave them there. Some laugh, some tell me 'Well, look, in six months you will be back.' I said, 'No, I'm leaving.'

When I was a child I always like to go to the bush. My godmother and godfather had a piece of land, nothing much, four acres. And every time he say he going in the garden I jump up because, well, I going too! No mind how much walk I have to walk I going, I like it. When you come out of the town you hit a different feelings, a different breeze from the mountains coming down to you. And I did like that, I feel nice and going in the bush with him. When we reach in the bush and we walking, I feel happy like something is there in me, you know, I remember when I was small.

But as I get older now the walk wasn't so easy! I keep quarrelling all the road: 'How far again, how far again?' But when I reach the house I felt nice, I stand up in the yard and taking the breeze. And something in me feel different. From that day I started to feel a kind of lightness. How you would call it a lightness in spirit, yes, because to me, myself start talking to me more freely; things come in my mind, I talk to myself and it was nice, feeling a vibration in the body and I started to live.

It was nice living, although it was hard because I knew nothing then about the bush and the life and the food, how to live, because you accustom in the city with money and buy. So it was a little rough but I continue with it. People call the bush 'the jungle'. I don't call it the jungle, I call it 'life' because within the bushes you find many lives in different form, in the birds and the animals, the insects, the serpents, and they all life.

Everyone who used to live along the coast had left. In 1974, they settled by agreement on the estate where Hell Valley now lies, and after an argument with the owner squatted illegally on the land, occupying an old store and selling the copra they gathered to Pinnacle. A passer-by surveying the idyllic setting said 'This is The Valley of Peace.' Immediately, without reflecting, Jeanette corrected him: 'No, here is The Valley of Decision' (the title of an American film, and later a Bob Marley song). To get rid of them, the Pinnacle villagers spread a rumour to the police that they were harbouring guerrillas:

I look out the window and I see a man crawling with a gun. I look out the next window. It have the same. I tell the children go upstairs [into the cocoa-box] . . . A soldier come and say, an' he crying, he have orders to kill everybody in the house and he sees some-one move in the [top] window an' it was the little boy. And they drop their guns.

Cyprian decided soon after to let his hair grow natural and matted, although 'we didn' know about Rasta then; never seen them or know about them until we leave here to go to town'. Jeanette fasted that Easter and had a dream in which she ran away from Jesus through a river in which was a serpent. She continued to look after the children and 'do usual housewife thing' until another dream in 1975 when eight months pregnant:

I find well I was too heavy, you know. So I had to stay in one place. I stay one place for about two months already. What make me stay one place is I come and had a vision that the moon [come] up this place to have the baby . . .
And when I come out [of the dream] I tell him, I say, 'Well, look, I have to go to make my baby up on the hill because I is Mary.' This is what the moon tells me – 'Mary, you got to go and make the baby.' The moon didn't say really mother of Jesus but I know to myself now I am the mother of Jesus since I reach this stage. And then one of my sons, which is Keith, come back and had the same vision: he was leading the donkey and I on it with the baby, Mary going to make the baby.
So I got up out of the sleep there. So when I get up I was wondering how where to go to make this baby? It have no house on the hill so that I could go and make this baby. Where? So I end up going upstairs in the cocoa box.

And then I come and make one night. I just feel a forcing – I didn't have no pain to make the baby. I just feel a force and when I feel a force I telling the children 'Look like I going to make the baby.' And rain started to fall. I made one. I telling them 'Well, look, something still in my belly, I still feeling something' so I make a force again and another comes out! I was so shocked, seeing two babies which I never had before. So I just clean them off, one of my sons cut the navel [cord]. I show him what to do. And the next one the father cut it. I show him what to do. And they cut it, which was two boys.

And they come and remember that Dads had a vision that he was sitting on the beach, on the sand between the river and the sea, and I come and hand him a baby, and an Indian mother hand him a baby. And when the twin born now, the vision come back to him: he said 'But wait – these two babies is Africa and India – you could remember the vision I told you?' I say yes. 'Well then, it's Africa and India, watch them, the two look different, one look an African and one looks soffy like an Indian.' Well, we know them by the one was more nashy [lean] and one was more fatty.

[The nashy baby] fell asleep and couldn't wake. I say 'Child dying on me, its eyes turn up.' I put in breasts; it don't take. I start pray to moon. I bawl 'Why should this happen?' Then see snake pass from under house, and children chase it and it just disappear. Then a black fowl, it just come out [from under the house] and beat up in the canal [drain] and then die. I return to baby. It sweating, and take breast. Serpent kill fowl to take its life and give it to the child.

And after that, when they was five months, well I started to burn everything I had. Just like that one day. It was the same as any day. It was surprising too how I started . . . The rain started to fall that day and I went outside. I started to dance in the rain and sing an African song which they usually use in shango tent which I use to go around shango a lot so I know how to call the water:

'Ehmanjah, saiy, saiy,
Ehmanjah, sanya,
Sanya roya maja,
Sanya roya . . . '

And I sing it, and after that I sing for the day different tunes, calling the water you know, calling the thunder and lightning.[11]

And then, the next day, I start moving around the yard now and showing him different spots to clean up, burn it. Well, next day the sun was shining and from then, I started burning thing. I just came inside of the house, I said 'Look I want everything in the kitchen (I start from the kitchen) burn, the pots and pans and everything.' So from then we use to roast little plantain and eat it because the pot is in the fire. I put the radio in the fire. The children take it back out. It burn a little but it was still playing. They take it back out. Well I come around all the bedding I had to wash from the twins because I couldn't go by the river when they born so I was washing very little here . . . And the bundles come so high that the day I took them up and put them into the fire I feel like if something come out of me! I feel light. Two big bundles of bedding, I put them in the fire! And they burn: the sheets and everything burn! I burn everything in the house for a few days! I can't tell you exactly what day I start but I know the last thing I had to burn was the [sewing] machine. I even took down the doors and windows and burn them . . . I had no thinking, just doing. I was like a mad body. If I see a nail, I pull it out.

Now he wasn't so pleased but it come like if, well, what I said he had was to do it.

And he doing it and the children even do it too. Very freely. Without understanding. Not even me didn't understand neither.

Well, the last thing I had to burn on Saturday was the machine. Well, I didn't want to push it outside because I know I had to sew my children clothes! But when the Devil take me (I have to say the Devil which is my Natural Self), I push it outside the door. I say, 'Put it in the fire.' They say, 'Put it in the fire, Mummy?' I say 'Yes, put it in the fire.' And they put it by the fire, and they put it in, and it burn. Well they come and when it finish burn the evening, they go on looking at it and the different parts, and they say 'But Mummy, you know the machine only have three wheels?' I say 'How you mean?' They say 'Well, the machine have four wheels when we put it in the fire but now it have three. One burn.' So they ask me why.

I say, 'Well, that is the tap.' The tap that was placed there. Now in everything in the scientific world that you use carry a tap to your body, to your Natural Spirit. Even the clothes. Even the radio too carry a tap. So then, these things are not natural. So your Natural Self cannot really come into you because of these scientific taps which is the Spirit of the Son.

SELF: [*thinking this sounds a bit schizophrenic and talking nonsense myself*]: Did you ever feel energy going out of you from the machine?

M.E.:   [*patiently*] When you are sewing sometimes you get a little tired by working the machine. But to say that, to understand that feeling, I don't know it. But as the machine burn, which I had another one before, which was a new machine, when I almost finish pay for it they come and take it because I was pregnant with Shurland so I couldn't really go on: the same month they take it is the same month I make the baby.

SELF: How were you feeling when you did all this?

M.E.:   Well, parts of myself, when (you could say when), when the Natural Spirit is in me, I push it outside to burn. But yet in between, something is still coming in me and say 'You shouldn't burn it.' You know? But yet in myself is to burn! So I push it in the fire and forget about it.

SELF: But it was you doing it?

M.E.:   [*exasperated*] It is me! I knowing what I am doing. What say to do, it just come normal. You know? To me it was just normal. Yes, so that was the Saturday . . . They don't understand but I just talking! Everything they ask me I give them the answer. And he self [Cyprian] asking question, I give him the answer. Sunday morning I get up. There was nothing more to burn! I look right round, I already take down the doors and windows, everything, the nails all over the place, I pull out all the nails that I can find spare around. So then, Sunday morning, when I looking I couldn't find nothing else but the Bibles. I have three Bibles! Which I bought one for his birthday. We can't read too much but still we pick along the words in certain parts, as say like in Matthew, the New Testament, which some of the words are easier, well we pick along there. And some of the Psalms we use them and some we don't use. As Baptists, you know. So we had the Bible because they always tell you if you have your Bible you're safe. So we was thinking that way. You know? So I end up having my Bible, he had an old one, I bought a new one for his birthday. So it have three Bibles there.

So Sunday morning the fire was still going for the days, things keep burning. I pick up the Bibles then for the first time for I didn't intend to burn them. I said, 'Let me go, come and let me show you how your education is upside-down.' So he come with me to the fire. And certain things I have done by the fire, can't remember all directly but one of the main things I know: I rest my feet in the fire; I said 'Just now I will be dancing in the fire.' Then I took up something from the fire which is a burnt piece of something and open the book, pass it in the book. The writing come upside down and I show it to him. I show it to them. All of us was surprised. I and all was surprised! Although it's me do it but yet I was surprised to see the writing come upside down. So I told him, I say 'Look your education is upside down.'

So I put my glasses in the book (which I used to wear only when I reading). I place it in the book and rest them on the fire. The Bibles burn for the day because I didn't really go back and look until the afternoon. I tell him 'Let us go and see what we find.' Well he go. I say 'Search the ashes of the book.' He search it, he found one lenses of glasses. He say 'But, look, it one lenses, you know.' I say 'Well, look again and maybe you will find another one.' So he continues looking in the ashes . . . He say 'Well, how glass could burn?' I say 'Well it wasn't glass. Which one of your glasses, which one of the lenses in the glasses, is plastic and one is glass.' I say 'The one that they put is glass is to pull the strength out of the natural eye and the one that they put is plastic for the bad eye which is the eye of the Son that have no power.' So he say 'Oho, is so?' I say 'Yes'.

SELF: Had you thought about there being two different eyes before?

M.E.: No, it's the first life [time]. And when he speaking about it, it seems like if I know it already at that time.

SELF: You were then already talking about the Son? You knew what the Son had done?

M.E.: No, not as yet, just started to come. By him asking about the glass the answer come into me (which I would say myself burst there and the answer come) and I give him the answer. It come natural to me like if I did know it all the time but yet I knew nothing.

SELF: When you first mentioned it at this time, were you thinking of the 'son of a mother' or were you thinking of the planet 'sun'?

M.E.: I did not thinking at all! There wasn't no thinking at that life [time]. I just talk, answer as the question come. I wasn't even thinking. No. There was no thinking whatsoever in what I was doing. No. Just put out as it come, as it is to put out [now]: you ask the questions, I answer you.

Yes, well that was finish for the afternoon. The next morning, which was Monday morning, I got up. Well now, everybody was naked because everything was burnt! So Monday morning when I get up we still didn't study we're naked, you know? We just moving, just natural, just as if we have on clothes, not really thinking that we are naked. Nobody complain not even the children. They just like, well, look they was always so.

But on that morning, Monday morning, he was outside sharpening his cutlass to go into the garden, I went and I tell him something. I can't remember exactly what I told him but he – you know, he's a very hasty fellow, he get hasty every minute – so I tell him 'Well, look now, you can't really lash me, let's go inside.'

And when we came inside, there is where I perform the Miracle. It was something else to see! The children was standing there and the Miracle perform on the little girl which she was four years. I put her to lie down down there and I start chooking with my finger inside of her mouth and I start talking and telling – well, I don't know I talking to – but I was talking to the Spirit – telling my Son (which is the Spirit) 'You give me a toothbrush to chook out the eye in the mouth.' I chook[12] the baby mouth until it bleed.

And I keep talking and most of the conversation I said, I said 'Your blood is your tears. Your tears is your blood. Your shit is your life. The toothbrush that you give me to chook out my eye, to chook out my eye, it's no good!' And I continue talking. I turned round, I can't exactly tell you everything that I put out at the moment but it was kind of terrible, yes! And when I finish that part, I break my baby hand because the Spirit she was carrying in the body at the time wasn't hers. So to get it out I was talking to the Spirit 'Come out of my child. If you don't come out I'll break you' hand.' And I end up twisting the hand behind her back and break it. It break up here in the arm. Well, after, I feel a something inside when I catch myself what I did . . .

Well, after breaking the hand, then I bring back the sun nearer to the earth. I was just talking. And in the talking I cast my two hands together and I bring it down between my legs. Something I said, you know? And then that was the end of the Miracle performing.

Well, after that when I watch the arm, something keep hitting me inside you know which you really not accustom to. It give me a kind of sorry feeling but yet it was natural. You know? So I had something there, I mix it up, take a fig leaf, put it in the fig leaf and wrap it on the hands. The hands heal, she didn't have no trouble, no pain, she didn't cry. I put her to lie down so that the hands would stay. I put it in a sling. And in a few days, she say 'Mummy, I tired lie down. I want to get up.' I say 'You could move?' She said 'Yes'. I say 'Your hands not hurting you?' She say 'No'. I said 'Move the fingers, let me see'. And she move them. I said 'Well, you feel alright?' She said 'Yes, Mummy, I want to get up.' I said 'Alright, get up.' And she went playing but with the hand in a sling still.

After the Miracle perform, there is where we all realise that we were naked. I told them 'Eheh, but you know we naked?' The girl and boy said 'Yes, Mummy, you know you burn everything? You mad, you know!' I say 'Mad?' He say yes because, well, when Miracle was performing he was crying, and telling me that I mad mind what I was doing with his sister. I turn to the little girl, I say 'Laurel, you think I mad?' She say yes. I started to cry now because I feel bad pressure, I feel pressured there, they telling me well look I mad.

It happening that way so funny, so strange, you could say out of the blue, you know. All of a sudden changes take place, nakedness come in. That look like madness in truth, to them. But to me it was just natural.

We realised then that we were naked. We decide to make something. He say 'Well, Mummy, look at the onliest thing we have here is bags. I see you ai' burn them.' And they was new bags that we bought to put in copra to sell, you know. So I cut up the bag and cut out little thing to put on. I give them skirts to put on.

Within the October find I was pregnant again. Then the baby born the next year, June, and I stay quiet till then when the baby born. May month she born. It was a girl. She was so tiny, I call her Tiny. Well, she born in the dirtiness. At the time, I had to keep the rubbish inside, everything inside, copra and skin, everything. We just make a little space to sleep and everything was there. The baby's born. And when the baby born the filth, everything, I just throw it around you know . . . flies, endless flies . . . nothing didn't happen to her, she was strong. I didn't bathe her when she was born because it isn't good to bathe the baby when they born. They just come from a hot womb.

The Miracle perform and I didn't go on the beach for a long time. So this day, I say 'Well, look, I go on the beach today', and as I reach on the beach, a feeling came into me and I started to sing because the feelings was so, I can't tell you, explain the feelings, how it was, but I feel like if I was somewhere else, in a place I can't really explain it, but I started to sing this little tune. I don't know where the tune come from. Maybe I've heard it before but I put in my words and I started to sing:

'I am the Earth
I am the Sea
I am the River
I am the Waters
I am the Thunder
I am the Lightning
I am the Fire
I'm calling My children
But they cannot hear Me
I'm calling My children
I'm calling My children
From out of that valley
The Valley of Death
I'm calling My children
But they cannot hear Me
Way down in that valley
My children is weeping
My children is weeping
My children are suffering
But they cannot hear Me
I'm calling My children'

From the biomedical perspective

Jeanette's early visions in Port-of-Spain had been relatively conventional, similar to those of her friends and neighbours except perhaps for the recurrent serpent, and for a closer identification with Christ than was acceptable among that Baptist group and which led to her leaving them. Her vague sense of mission was shared by many others, including her partner Cyprian. She met him at the time of the failed uprising when, dissatisfied both with Black Power and the Baptists, he proposed that they adopt a simpler and more traditional rural life away from the pressures of the town. Jeanette reluctantly agreed to join him, together with her children, for she had been gathering materials to build a house of her own in town. The family settled on an abandoned estate at the most deserted part of the cost, reading the Bible and discussing religious questions together, accepting omens in dreams and continuing with occasional fasts. It was a physically demanding life but the calm and peace of the coast more than compensated for arguments with overseers and estate owners, recalling to Jeanette the best times of her childhood when she had accompanied her godfather as he worked on his little patch of four acres. In a dream after she is settled on the coast she finds herself running away from Jesus towards a snake in the river.

Two years after they arrived, when Jeanette was forty-one years old, and eight months pregnant, she has another dream in which the moon tells her she is Mary and she should have her child on top of a hill. Not understanding why, she follows the dream and gives birth to twins under the roof of the house. When the twins are five months old, Jeanette, in a burst of energy, sings a song to the shango mother deity and starts burning all the household articles; neither she nor her family understand what is happening but her partner presumes some deeper meaning in it and does not interfere. When questioned by him, Jeanette gives answers that flash into her head, principally that her actions are due to a 'natural spirit' in her. The burned objects she refers back to personal concerns, to her religion (Bible), medical science (spectacles) or to her domestic tasks (bedding, kitchen utensils and eventually the sewing machine which she uses to make the children's shirts). Together with the burning of all their clothes, this results in the family going naked until she makes up some temporary garments out of sacking, later abandoning these again as unnecessary. Bible, glasses and bedding are not reintroduced but the large iron cooking pots which survive the fire are back in use after a few days.

Random events become endowed with significance: a wheel of the sewing machine and one of her spectacle lenses which appeared lost in the fire are interpreted as parts of the unnatural and constraining *social* world of town. In each instance, action and mood seem to precede meaning and exegesis. The last articles to be burnt are the Bibles, powerful protectors of the family. Cyprian and the children told me that they had been completely amazed at Jeanette's behaviour at this time, not understanding what was going on, but they were not worried until she started poking a finger into her daughter's mouth and (as she thought) broke the wrist of the girl, whom she said had become possessed by a spirit, one she later identified as The Son. Jeanette now realises that she is Nature Herself, the Mother of All, the very process of creation itself, and with a sudden gesture of her hands down between her legs, brings the sun closer to the earth, initiating what becomes known as the Beginning of the End. In this moment an inexorable series of events are initiated, although Jeanette herself, now Mother Earth, has no further revelations.

Although the little girl's hand soon heals, her family now seriously wonder if Jeanette has become mad, except 'she seem to know what she doing'. Though able to accept the idea that she is possessed by some natural power, the idea that she *is* Nature is still difficult. The family, including Mother Earth, adjust to the new life; a subsequent pregnancy the following year is delivered in the middle of the coconut husks in the hut, Mother Earth now regarding cleanliness as altogether too Social. Over the next few months, her son brings out to the coast his friends, young men who have previously known the family in town, adherents of Shouter Baptism or the newly introduced Rastafari. Some discard their clothes and stay. The ideas of the Earth People are consolidated through practical activity and group discussion: Mother Earth uses the new Rasta idiom but the kernel of the new teaching remains those thoughts which have come to her while trying to explain to her family her actions of the previous year. Within a year, the group's marches to town begin, resulting in Mother Earth's arrest and her first stay in hospital.

Since we have clear and consistent accounts from both Mother Earth and her family of the events which initiated the Beginning of the End and she answered a PSE retrospectively on her feelings and actions of the time, it is possible to map them against the biomedical terminology of the PSE.[13] Mother Earth scored as follows: Early Waking (Score 1); Expansive Mood (2); Subjective Ideomotor Pressure (1); Grandiose Ideas and Action (2); Delusional Mis-interpretation (2); Delusions of Grandiose Ability (2); Delusions of Grandiose Identity (2); Religious Delusions (2); Acting Out of Delusions (2); Denying Psychological Symptoms (2); Subculturally Influenced Delusions (doubtful, see note 7); Preoccupation with Delusions (2); Incapacitation by Symptoms (3); Self Neglect (2); Gross Excitement (2); Irreverent Behaviour (2); Hypomanic Affect (2); Pressure of Speech (2). Through the PSE's Catego program this pattern generates category M+, equivalent to one of the poles of manic-depressive psychosis.

Although Mother Earth's ideas find their sources in her previous beliefs and experiences, neither they nor the actions which gave rise to them are in any way simply conventional. The whole complex does not conform to institutions such as shango possession for it is idiosyncratic; occurs in a spontaneous and non-ritual setting; is meaningless initially to both participant and spectators; Mother Earth had not previously experienced any 'possession'. There is no evidence that she has been schizophrenic as the hospital staff argue. The questions which I asked her which I have retained in her text were directed at clarifying certain experiences which did sound reminiscent of 'schizophrenic passivity' (in which the individual experiences their will or actions as made by another, and thoughts, actions and affect come from without).[14] Nor are there hallucinations in any sensory modality. In every case, the 'delusions' seem less spontaneous ideas coming by themselves to mind than immediate rationalisations of mood and actions.

Actions and cognitions such as those of Mother Earth, with their dislocations of conventional meaning and their arbitrary slippage between the literal and the metaphoric, may occur in manic-depressive psychosis, or less commonly they may be found in association with more obvious biological changes. Mother Earth has no clear family history of psychopathology, although she thinks one of her older sons, with whom she has now lost touch, was admitted to St Ann's. We have however some evidence that Mother Earth has a thyroid abnormality: she continues to have a high resting pulse, has mild cardiac failure, a diffusely enlarged thyroid gland, exophthalmos and mild heat intolerance. 'At the Miracle my throat swell up.'[15] Generally recognised changes associated with this type of thyroid overactivity include restlessness, overactivity, irritability, hyperacuity of perception, 'unreasonable' behaviour and distractability; it is said that progression to psychosis including hypomania, is 'not uncommon'.[16] Thyroid disease is more frequent in women and, in the case of Grave's Disease, most commonly found between twenty and forty years of age. When such experiences and behaviour occur with thyroid overactivity they do so in the absence of a family history of illness but where the previous personality has often been described as 'neurotic' or 'sensitive'.

While the biomedical diagnosis of hypomania and thyrotoxicosis may provide one interpretation of Jeanette's overactivity and her paradoxical actions, it does not of course demand her particular choice of actions, her family's and her interpretations of them, nor her subsequent translation into Mother Earth. In the following chapters biomedical notions will only be invoked when I return to consider the limits of such innovation. For the present, we are concerned merely with a particular episode of extraordinary experience and behaviour which offers a radical break with convention, a physical locus upon which certain personal and shared concerns are erected. For this, Mother Earth's psychopathology offers us no more of explanatory value than do the celestial mechanics of an eclipse of the sun determine the meanings which societies may erect on that event.[17]

5

Putting Out The Life

Everything has its meaning, its sign, everything has its spirit.

Mother Earth

This chapter draws together some of Mother Earth's ideas in the form of a conventionalised cosmogony: her words but my ordering of paragraphs.[1]

In the Beginning
In the Beginning was Nothing. Nothing was Life. Nothing formed herself into the elements. The elements resolve itself as Life. So Life formed herself: the Fire, the Water, the Earth, Dirt, Slime and Salt, and revolving herself, with the womb in the middle – the Moon. And there were all the planets for and against The Mother inside her . . . A Son she bring forth. The Son was inside the Womb – Death. So then Life and Death together once, not in the form as it is now but, as the people say, 'in the spirit'. Death revolving itself in the womb, in the Earth, Slime and Salt, Fire and Water. Well, she give him his own planet (everything carry its own planet by the name) so the Son carry his planet which is the planet Sun which we have up there, covered over with heat.

The Interference
He left his planet. The reason for the heat around the planet is by him leaving his planet and enter the Earth. He wanted to have life, to bring forth like The Mother so he enter . . . When he entered, pain entered the Earth. So he enter the Earth and the Earth change. It keep changing, changing until she put out flesh. And the first Flesh on the Earth were mothers which we were in a form. Not in this form of flesh: what we call the prick and the cunt was one form of Flesh which were the mothers . . . The Flesh keep changing because he keep interfering until I divide myself in half and give him half. So the Son call himself Man but it is still The Mother. So now we carry bones and we become

79

weaker. Bones were formed by The Mother but in his shape and form . . . Time is He, Time is bones. Always jealous because he said 'I am a jealous God.' Well so that is still jealousy, covetousness, all these things, pain, sickness, disease, shame and pride, age, time, all belongs to him. This is why we have these changes, that is why we have so much corruption on the earth.

He have his share: the White people is really the Race of the Son because that was the Flesh that Mother prepared for the Son in the Beginning. And she had hers which is the Black Race. You could say all races come from the Black race because we are the beginning of all races. And now all Flesh mix up and we are all living the Life of the Son, not of the Black Race. You is all half Son, half Mother . . . The Race that was prepared for the Spirit of the Son live in the ice, and the ice belong to the planet Sun, not really to the Earth. The fire belongs to the Earth, which is the heat. The Sun is coming nearer and nearer. So that the heat will return to the Earth, and the planet shall be free once more. He has to return; the Spirits of The Mother will remain, which that belongs to the Earth.

In the Beginning when Flesh was placed upon the Earth, through the interruption of the Spirit of the Son enter in Earth, Mother had was to put out Flesh. And when she put out Flesh, she put out her Spirits which they were all mothers on the earth . . . So when they say you die, you don't really die. When the Flesh grow old it is weak in all the Spirit – the Spirit comes out – and you come again in a new birth as a baby again. That Spirit come back. So then you always live it. You keep going and coming to meet to this stage here – what I call the Beginning. So when they talk about ancestors and these spirits guard you, I am seeing it as yourself spirit, not really a spirit of ancestors, who are they say depart for so much years. It is you yourself. Your ancestor is you!

The Spirit that is in the Flesh is the Spirit of Death, which is the Spirit of the Son, which we call – even we call it – God. So that Spirit is what using Flesh so your [Natural] Spirit is still there too but it guards the Flesh while a next Spirit is using it. So when you talk about 'the guarding of the Flesh', it's your own self that was also there from the beginning. You keep going and coming, going and coming, so yourself always there to guard you.

We become a robot for him, a machine. They can't really push him out completely: that is for when the hour come. But yet they can know themselves so when they are about to say something, they think first, so you would know what you are saying it, you are speaking with the Son, you are speaking with the Mother. You still have the two Spirits to deal with. You will find some still thinking about the naturalness although they reach a professor, they reach a doctor, they are still seeing naturalness. Some can't because they are the Son itself. So in everywhere you turn you have both Spirits to be with.

The Mother allow him to do it because of her love. It is love she have. And she know all that he can never win. So she allow him to do what he wants until his time is up to return back to his Planet. Even though it is suffering for the Flesh and pain for the Flesh, they have to bear it.

Science
In the Beginning the Flesh have one eye but the Son took the eye of The Mother so he have two eyes. People use to see in darkness but not again – the body get too weak. Everything is now 'eye and eye'![2] If you check the Earth now, you find nothing Natural as suppose to be . . . All he does is to put out material: the wars and the fights, the bombs and the [planes], trying to make human, trying to change them, some a mother to a son, change a son to a mother. All these are his experiment, trying to take over. He know everything about Life but not this – not the power to bring forth. That is what he really wants, the power of love.

The onliest thing the Son has is machines and chemical. He has to use Science. He gains Science by interfering with Nature. Must he even have to use the oil of the Earth too, which is the Mother, take the oil out, pulling substance from the Earth. It becomes a cripsy. The oil is the blood of the earth; he look for a new vein now . . .

Food have a pure Spirit – it ai' have no set of interference with it . . . You get 'six week okra':[3] you plant it a next time and you got longer. You plant again and you get old type okra tree. You see, it get natural, the chemical wear out. It come the same with children: you go back to the Natural. Paper said tomato grow without dirt! He fool you because he takes the necessary elements from the dirt.[4] To make a real something like me or you they can't . . . They fighting to bring forth without the Mother. If they do, the whole world destroyed . . . Everything you interfere with, it something you didn't put there. Everything suppose to stay Life and not to use chemical and try to make bigger. Life suppose to stay Life! Don't interfere to see if you can do something to Life: this is the corruption. You want to make too, you try to take over. Know what it is for the cow to go behind a machine?[5] You like it happen to you?

People are machines right now. The machine started from a child, from a baby when the baby was born. Because the first thing you do is to dip the baby in water. Even though you say you warm the water, the baby body is still carrying a temperature from the womb so it have no left[6] to bathe. The temperature in the womb should remain with the baby and work its way until, you could say almost a month. So then that baby is no more baby, it is already carrying the Negative Spirit. And when you put on clothes on the baby – that is part of the Spirit too, that's a part of Science, by putting on clothes on the baby. The baby suppose to remain as it born, naked. The elements in the air develop the body, strengthen that body, bring it powerful, so it can take any type of thing. But when the baby is clothed the body remain one way soft, so the clothes prevent the body from breathing so it cannot take up what it have to. So that child becomes more Negative.

When the child is so young and goes to school the brains is too soft. The brains still need mature, growing. So then the cells of the brain can burst and the senses come . . . When a child's senses start to develop it can have an understanding of itself, knowing itself in a little form. But when a child go to school, the brains become like a computer because it's everything you put in it, it takes up. So then the two half of the brain, which one is the senses' and one half belongs to the education: the half of the one that is the education develop more faster than the half of the brain that is the senses. So then the half of the brain that is the Son develop more strongly than the other half. Sometimes the child carry its natural self still. Although all what they do with it, it still carry a little naturalness. So it's hard to learn. The brains can't really pick up what you want it to pick up. Then you will keep beating that child, flog it, until it reach to an age that it will have to pick up . . .

The clothing. The material, the deepness of the material you put the child into, is you who putting it there, calling that child like to be dressed up. It have to dress up to go to school. It must put on boots and socks. So then that's another part of slavery because everything is money. So when that child comes to a certain age it gets so social – 'decent' as you would call it! – so it grow that way so the child comes for material.[7] That's another part of slavery; if it wasn't wearing clothes the body would be more powerful. You see sickness wouldn't be there neither. Is the clothes that brought on sickness to us, through the weakness of our body with the clothes on. Sickness is easy to get; even in our food the amount of chemicals develop different parts of diseases in the body: too much of chemical. So then you become like a machine instead of a human.

I don't like the innoculation. Sometimes they tell you 'Come and take innoculation because polio is going around' – and yet children who take the innoculation still get polio. So these things to me it's a next part of experimenting on their drugs. 'Natural Science' is a contradiction! Science give you thing upsided-down.

They have your life in a Scientific form and you move by numbers.[8] The stuff that grows on the teeth, to my knowing now, it is to prevent teeth from getting decay. It keep the teeth safe but we scrub it out so the teeth get holes you know, easy to get holes. And there then it's another part too: we bathe too often. It isn't to say that you cannot bathe once in a while but this everyday bathing! You body is you body; you have to learn to smell yourself and know yourself, know what you really are. You want to be 'clean' but the body is never clean because if you sweat you must smell it if you stay without bathing. Even a mother, under her breast, no matter how much you wash, under your breast you carry a scent and you perspire. So then you would know 'Well look, that is yourself.' It's your body, nothing to be afraid of or to scorn it. When I first started after the Miracle, I started to remain dirty. When I smell myself it was something else! I smell very awful (what they call 'awful') until that scent wear out and I start smelling normal – which is dirt. We don't study bathing. If your body too clean, the pores open and disease get in. Your skin come off in layers as dirt if you wash. You must keep it on as protection. In the city the more clean the children the more sick they get. In a too clean house the children dig dirt out of the boards and eat it. It is a part of the Culture of the Body.

Every mother is The Mother
You got big house but you dead. You children yet to work and you got to pay for them to learn. You learn work hard and your necessaries . . . Half of children is born without love. They grow up with a frustration because their parents didn't come together with a love; so they have all sort of corruption.

A man watch you and use you and laugh and he don't give you a dollar. And you get twelve big children . . . It is because of the Spirit and the teachings that you have cause the men to be taking advantage on the mothers. Now the reason for that is the Spirit which is controlling that Flesh. He thinks he's the boss. So then he always use the mother as just a nothing. She's there to bring forth the children, clean the house, wash the clothes, do everything and because, look, he goes out and brings in a penny he thinks 'Well look I am controlling.' That's the Spirit of the Son, really. Well it shouldn't be like that. It should be a love and understanding between the both Flesh. Because, if I can humble myself to my husband and listen to him, he can humble himself too and listen to me. So then we will have a relationship with a free understanding between the both of us instead of one thinking 'I'm better, I am the boss.' Even when they get married it's worse because you marry a wife 'for better or for worse' they say but it doesn't be that. You don't really find it so often within families here. But then you have to say it's the Spirit still, because if their teachings was of the Mother it wouldn't have beating the woman neither. Because when you beat the mother – your wife in fact – you come just as if you hit your wife, you hit your mother, you hit your sister there, you hit your daughter there. So then it's the teachings that have us in this condition. We suppose to be living different, to have more love, but it haven't got that love; everybody is each one for themselves.

Even the mothers you find the same thing. If she's doing a little job and her husband is doing a job sometimes she gets frustrated because, you know, she's working for her own money. Knowing that you working for your own money you feel too that you is boss too, so you do what you want. So the both of you all doing what you want. That isn't a living.

Women thinks more materialise. And men are more natural. This is what I am seeing here in this country . . . And that is really the Spirit [of the Son] because the Spirit try to hold the mothers more because, knowing that the mothers is the Spirit of the Earth, well then, he must have them more confused. So then they make more spectacle of themselves than the men. Too much of dressing, too much of material . . . Even now that the mothers reach to a stage that they don't want to be a mother anymore. Most of them they don't want children; they use the contraceptive so that they can't have children. They don't really want that! They want a house, they want a car, they want, you know they want all the material that they can get hold of instead of bringing forth their children. They find when they bring forth a child they can't go where they want, they can't do what they want: the children are confusing them. Contraceptive! We didn't plan to come here – the Spirit brought you – so how you plan now?

And then when they do make their babies, they want to have the baby like a robot. Too much of clothes. They put on the most expensive clothes just for people to see their baby.

People in this country play too much. These are parts of the play that I am speaking about – the amount of material, they love clothes, parties and even now the young people in the country is more disco-like. You know, in these discos they have some sorts of things that is going on what I am hearing about when I go to the city. It's very ridiculous. In the day they are dressed up but when they go to their parties is all sorts of nonsense that is going on. So then they play. It's a play.

The Beginning of the End
As it was in the Beginning so shall it be at the End.[9]

Africa is the Beginning of the Earth. We are the Makers. We have the knowledge of the Earth. We are the Mothers of the Earth. We are the Serpents of the Earth – which the balisier represents.

They were scattering Africa so she could not get back together and rise . . . He controls, he take over, to rule the world but he's ruling it just for a time – which is Time. And his time is almost spent. So then the Spirits of the Flesh now is about to take back over the Flesh once more, but yet it will have destruction because the heat, the Sun where he came from (which that Spirit is death, sickness and pain, disease, corruption, shame, age, time), that Spirit belongs to that planet. The Sun is a planet, which is the planet of death, the planet of ice. So he belongs to death. He left there and enter the Earth so the Spirit of the Earth, which is his Mother, she cover back his planet with heat so that he cannot go back there until time. He cannot be destroyed: it's just that the flesh that he's using of the Earth, which the Spirit have already control, will have to be destroyed, which the heat that is coming nearer the Earth is getting back where it was in the Beginning. So then the heat will be coming closer, and there is Flesh that wouldn't be able to take the heat; those Flesh will melt. So that the Spirit will return back to its planet when his appointed time is up. There's heat is about to remove, return back to the earth. Now he is fighting to remain. He's fighting to take the very substance of the earth because he know to himself 'Well, look, my time is almost at end – let me try and get off the earth.' He builds spaceships . . .

They will have to learn to [plant] because in later days to come there will be famine, there will be destruction. And you must have the food. So then in the Valley of Decision must have food. so that the people will be able to live . . . It will have people will come. The Sun is getting hotter and the world will starve but it will rain in Hell and provide for everyone . . . I don't know when the hour will be so this is: you always have to be prepared for the hour because you never know!

I am not completely Myself as yet. I am here, half of Me out here and half still to enter the Flesh. When I am completely Myself then I have more work to do. I have the Healing of the Nation to do, the sick, the blind, the leper.[10] This you know! So it will be something important to the world of people.

There is something I have to say to all the world, to the people. When I reach to my first stage I will be speaking every language. I will be bringing the language for the drums of Africa and India. Then I will be healing the sick, the lame and the blind, raise the dead, cleanse the leper, the dumb talk, the people walk, the deaf hear, the blind see. I will be having all powers. So I am trying to show my people what it will be like when the hour comes for the Beginning.

I am speaking to all nations. Not only Africa and India. To everyone. Because everyone is a part of Me. Every race is a part of Me. I am the Earth. The Beginning. The Alpha and the Omega (as you would say from the book). The Beginning and the End. The Jah. The Allah.

6

Your ancestor is you: Africa in a new world

If it don't have religion it don't have socialness.

Mother Earth

The persistence (and resistance) of African institutions in the West Indies

To what extent can we take Mother Earth's cosmogony as a purely personal vision? It might appear that we are able to distinguish here the simple manifestation of contemporary Creole patterns from more limited and self-consciously 'African' representations and also from her own distinctive innovations. That may be neat, but mistaken. An 'innovation' is only an innovation within and against some continuing tradition out of which it develops, and from which individuals derive their images and concerns.

Such a continuing existence of the past in the present is an enduring concern for Caribbean studies in considering a society grounded in a particular moment of Western capitalism, a political history well documented since its inception. Scholarly literature on personal life in the West Indies follows two rather distinct lines of approach. Principally there is the synchronic study of the 'matrifocal' Black household, its individuals, sentiments and productive relations.

The second approach also considers contemporary social relations but is concerned with the extent to which existing patterns of experience and action among the Creole working class reflect those African societies from which the slaves were once torn. This latter area of debate was first laid out by Melville Herskovits in 1941 in his book *The Myth of the Negro Past*,[1] where he developed its characteristic terminology – 'syncretism', 'retention', 'survival' and 'reinterpretation'. He postulated a continuum of African retentions in African–American societies ranging from the Bush Negroes of Surinam (with maximal retention), through Haiti, the British West Indies, to the urban Blacks of the United States. Herskovits himself attributed a greater number of contemporary patterns to 'survivals' than have his successors in the debate: such as 'matrifocality' (mother-orientated households), or even the preference for adult baptism by full immersion as a persisting attachment to the initiation rites of West Africa. He engaged with Black American historians on the contentious issue of slavery in the formation of contemporary African–American societies, notably in his debate with Franklin Frazier who maintained that no significant residues of African society could be said to have survived slavery in the Americas, and that Afro-America was simply a flawed and defective mimesis of Europe.

In the case of Trinidad we have to recall the significant number of free African immigrants who arrived during the nineteenth century after emancipation.[2] Even under slavery, there had been a relatively small Creole-born population: twenty years before they attained freedom, the majority of Trinidadian slaves were still transported from Africa.[3] A distinctive Yoruba identity continued among some Trinidadians well into this century, and Maureen Lewis suggests that little-known Yoruban words continue to be used between close friends.[4] On the question of 'matrifocality', the consensus has been that this is more to do with the family patterns prescribed by slavery than with persisting African values. Yet the African-Caribbean working class was not frozen in the nineteenth century and many of its 'characteristic' patterns developed after slavery; the overall dynamic is less that of the slave plantation itself, powerfully destructive as it was, than a dynamic of Black–White relations initiated in enslavement, continuing during slavery and the colonial period through to the contemporary (politically free but economically dependent) marginality now represented in extensive emigration to the conurbations of Britain and North America.

The problems in conjecturing African 'survivals' are best approached through Herskovits, the writer who placed the greatest emphasis on the resilience of West African cultural patterns. As he pointed out, a major difficulty is that of the unit of analysis. Do we trace 'tradition' through some self-conscious persistence of distinctive names for foods and in the organisation of funerals, as the Pinnacle villagers themselves do? Or should we follow the fate of such sensibilities as 'matrifocality', as does Mother Earth? In this chapter I am concerned only with knowledge and action which are held to be explicitly African by my informants and which are locally distinguished as such from other available patterns: in particular certain 'African' themes in shango and Shouter Baptism. Both of these, say the Earth People, have continued the original life of Mother Africa in a muted form. They themselves do not regard either as a *religion*, that is as a legitimation of European domination.

Herskovits had difficulty distinguishing his chosen items of analysis both from their subsequent transformations and from the very process of trans-formation itself, for 'The acceptance of new forms does not necessarily preclude the retention of an underlying value-system that derives from an earlier kind of enculturative conditioning.'[5] This sounds like a form–content distinction and indeed he does employ a dichotomy of form and role; 'form' he refers to the superficial, the 'formal', and not to an underlying structure. Thus, Herskovits' pupils, Simpson and Hammond, comment that below form lie 'more significant psychological attitudes'.[6] Whether these are invariant is far from clear, nor is there any consideration of how and why 'survivals' may survive. Simpson states that he is not concerned with the problem of a continuing function and takes it as self-evident that any institution provides for psychological satisfaction and meaning, solutions to personal problems, and so forth; this leads him to take certain Trinidadian religious practices as 'dysfunctional', a common characterisation in academic studies of many Caribbean institutions.[7] There is certainly a contextual problem in any assumptions of 'the African baseline': Herskovits, like Mother Earth, assumes a relatively discrete (and knowable) historical West Africa[8] although the area had been in close contact with Europeans for about 300 years before the slave trade ended and many West African societies themselves may be said to have been constituted through the slave trade itself. Western ethnographies are derived from fieldwork in Africa generally carried out well over a century after the slave trade ceased, and any common point of origin has thus to be deter-mined from earlier mission and colonial documentation, a point to be borne in mind later when I draw on our contemporary knowledge of the Yemanja corpus. In fairness to Herskovits it is worth emphasising that many of his 'African survivals' were derived from Trinidad with its relatively rich post-emancipation contacts with West Africa. Perhaps the major problem with the 'Africanisms' perspective is its failure to consider how the actual retentions occurred at specific historical moments. The Jamaican anthropologist M. G. Smith comments 'Form is one thing, function is another; process, the third, is the ultimate goal of our analysis.'[9] So far from being a study of change in existing social relations and productive forces, the majority of studies are simply folkloric collections of informants' accounts, taken to reflect current (or at any rate recent) practice, which are then rather crudely compared with contemporary West African material. As Ernest Gellner puts it in a not dissimilar context, their life seems to be 'made up of left-overs of which they have somehow forgotten to divest themselves'.[10]

Herskovits' 'survivals' range from complex sociocultural patterns to the relatively superficial, at times almost shading into the racism he is concerned to refute: the Spiritual Baptists are 'more congenial to the traditions of these people than are the other denominations. One need only cite such an aspect of worship as the emotionalism of spirit possession . . . '[11] For Herskovits, persisting Africanisms include the 'polygynous family', the ease of parental separation, distant relations between father and children, and the 'ancestor cult'. Some appear fanciful in the extreme: the flogging of children, or personal food preferences as 'totemic' prohibitions. We might note that, not surprisingly, all his 'survivals' are simply measures of difference from European assumptions – and yet they are considered autonomous: social patterns similar to those of European societies are not taken as really 'African'.

While the persistence of the names of deities or of foods, perhaps the most frequently cited Africanisms, do seem relatively unproblematic, how helpful are such notions as Herskovits' 'West African funeral complex'? Bastide poignantly notes that the funeral was just about the only collective institution left to the slaves, for the plantation owners had no interest in dead slaves – 'The Negro doesn't die, he comes to an end.'[12] Slaves were frequently abandoned by their masters when incapable of work and their death (or rather their ceasing to be commodified as property) might be dated to this point. That the dying or incapable slave had, in a sense, already escaped from the plantation, and was about to return to Africa was recognised by the slaves, and it was now at the time of their death, not at marriage, that personal property was redistributed.

'Matrifocality' may be said to be common to those societies where a high proportion of the male population has to migrate outside or where there is considerable individual mobility around the country, whether forced or to seek paid employment. In addition, the assumption that matrifocality was particularly common during the period of slavery derives from plantation records which named the mother but not the father of a new-born child. Many of Herskovits' Africanisms may be general characteristics of peasant societies (such as the various patterns of co-operative labour like *gayap*), or else aspects of a Caribbean history which has exercised as yet little scholarly interest, seventeenth-century millennialism: including such powerful Old Testament images as the 'crossing over to Jordan'. The extent to which radical Puritanism in seventeenth-century Britain had its own impulse in deprivation is still a matter of debate but its heritage of Exodus, the chosen people and the moral bankruptcy of the established churches have certainly continued to attract the disadvantaged and dislocated.

In his consideration of *les religions afro-brésiliennes*, Bastide dismissed

Herskovits' 'passive syncretism' in favour of such dynamic and individual actions as appropriation and innovation: 'Syncretism cannot be defined by the mere juxtaposition or merging of civilisations in contact: it is an activity of men united in divergent or co-operative groups. It translates into dogmas or rites the very movement of social structures as they come apart and are reassembled.' Similarly Clifford argues that 'It is just as problematic to say that their way of life "survived" as to say that it "died" and was "reborn".'[13] Bastide however comes close to Herskovits in giving considerable autonomy to 'religion' as opposed to 'politics': 'collective representations had to create new organisational forms in which to incarnate themselves and through which to propagate themselves in time'.[14] When accounting for change in the Afro-Brasilian cults, Bastide's continuing emphasis on the autonomy of an African sensibility leads him to describe its 'disintegration' in terms approaching psychopathology; such 'denuded' themes become 'magic' through their conflation with personal needs, or else 'ideologies' when harnessed to the pursuit of political power.

We are not concerned here with surveying the extent to which a West African past, taken as independent of conscious understanding and selection, may be said to have determined the West Indian present, but rather with the very notion of an Africa as part of Caribbean self-perception. The rest of this chapter is concerned with three general 'repertoires ' (Tilly) or 'archives' (Foucault) which Mother Earth recalls and revises. Many aspects of West African ritual and belief are recognised within the avowedly Christian church of the Spiritual Baptists (the Shouters) and also in the shango cult, while in Rastafari we can perceive a more active recreation of 'Africa'.

The Shouters

It was during her Baptist mourning that Jeanette first became aware of a sense of difference from her friends and neighbours (page 68). Many of the Earth People have previously attended meetings of the Baptists who are regarded as 'half way there' to the full revelation of Mother Africa. Indeed we can regard the Shouters as lying between mainstream churches still closely allied to their parent congregations in the United States, and the conscious Africanisms of shango; Spiritual Baptism and shango were once closely associated, and some followers of shango still refer to themselves as 'Shango Baptists'.

Mainstream American Baptists had trained the first Black clergy in the British West Indies and were in the forefront of the struggle for emancipation. In the early nineteenth century some local Baptist and Methodist congregations sought independence from such 'Carnal Baptists' who seemed to undervalue frequent communion with the divine. It is likely that these 'Spiritual Baptists' reached Trinidad from St Vincent after the final break with the parent congregations. Under the 1917 Shouters' Prohibition Ordinance, they were banned in Trinidad together with their 'violent shaking of the body and limbs . . . shouting and grunting', making chalk marks on the floor, holding candles and flowers, or ringing bells during worship.[15] In 1951 the ban (which had been imposed more for reasons of general decorum than against potential sedition) was lifted and, more recently, an application by some Baptists to join Trinidad's Council of Churches has been accepted.

Shouter teaching is that of Christian fundamentalism – belief in the Trinity, a literal approach to the Bible as recent and authoritative history, adult baptism by total immersion (for Shouters in the sea), possession by the Holy Spirit and frequent signs of divine intervention. Groups are locally organised and fissiporous, and many do not subscribe to recent attempts at centralisation such as the election of bishops. To term them a 'sect' rather than a 'cult' is perhaps a misnomer for members also attend the more established churches, particularly the Catholics, and infant baptism and marriage have usually been performed by the ministers of other churches. Baptist Shepherds and Mothers, however, are now being increasingly ordained like the clergy of the major denominations.

The congregations I have stayed with seldom include more than twenty active members. Services last three to four hours on a Sunday, but longer for baptism or mourning ceremonies which may continue overnight for up to twenty hours. They take place in small, sparse, separately built chapels, sometimes a converted room of a house. Participants are barefoot on the earth floor, and wear white clothes or coloured robes recalling monastic habits. In the Baptist chapel nearest to Pinnacle the altar is against one wall and in the centre of the room stands a pole surrounded by a low platform, on which rest vases of flowers and handbells. The altar, bearing crucifixes and a Bible, is the major point of ritual attention for the leaders of the group, particularly men, while women may move in relation to the central pole. At the side of the altar rest objects representing the ritual status of the initiates: shepherds' crooks, crosses and staves. The service is informally structured, switching between the explicitly 'hot' (collective) and 'cold' (individual): Sankey and Moody hymns,[16] punctuated by communal glossolalia and the spontaneous ringing of the handbells, rhythmic handclapping and foot movements, alternate with cold periods – extemporised sermons based on randomly selected Bible passages, and personal testimonies of faith, divine healing or worship. Although immediate experience is valued above doctrine or good works, these are often the subject of conversation before or after the meeting.

Initiates are expected to *mourn*: secluded in a side room, lying in the dust or on pallets of leaves, and bound about (including the face) with flat *swaddling bands*, recalling the appearance of a wrapped Egyptian mummy. These bands are 'sealed with signs', and the mourner remains on the ground for a period of three or seven days, attended by the Mother of the group. She feeds her *travelling children* on vegetable broth and guides their travels, usually to India, China or Africa, where they learn a new spiritual role (Captain, Head Nurse, Labourer), often by self-perception as a Biblical figure (Joseph, Mary, Joshua); this is communicated to the Mother and, if ratified, involves them in fresh ritual costume and paraphernalia during subsequent meetings. The style and authenticity of these visions – frequently supported by later dreams – determine status in the Baptist group and are closely tied to internal disputes and challenges to the authority of the leaders; most Mothers prefer therefore to keep a close watch on the proceedings. Jeanette had overstepped the mark when she reported a vision of herself as Christ (page 68): not even the Baptist Mother identifies herself with any of the persons of the Trinity. Even in the vision, identification is only a temporary visit or gift of higher powers, not unlike the gift of tongues from the Holy Spirit in other 'charismatic' churches.

Mourning is not regarded as a bereavement but, as in the Hellenistic mystery religions, a temporary bodily death in close association with the earth, enabling the spirit to live more fully in the other world. Shouters admit that mourning can be dangerous, for the individual when travelling is vulnerable to *mauvay lespwis* (malign spirits) but correct sealing and guidance by the Mother can usually prevent mishaps.

How 'African' are Baptists locally taken to be? Herskovits regards them as transitional between Protestantism and West African religion, while Simpson emphasises the syncretism of the two although he allows for an autonomous development of the sect since the nineteenth century.[17] As we look at shango and the Baptists today there appears to be little open contact between them although it is probable that they continue to share key personnel as in the past, the 'open' Christian service sometimes preceding a more restricted shango meeting. Many new and short-lived groups draw on both sources, and my distinction between the two is perhaps more rigid than their pragmatic and casual organisation would warrant. Certainly the Baptists are regarded by other Trinidadians as being particularly close to African obeah, and the material success of the family of the current Shepherd and Mother in the Baptist group near Pinnacle Village is sometimes attributed to conjuration. None of the Baptist leaders I know admit to practising it but they agree that their familiarity with the spirit world makes them particularly successful at returning obeah on the senders through the usual means; for the African *powers* do sometimes intrude into Baptist meetings. They do not see Baptism as exclusively 'African', welcoming the occasional White participant such as myself, and maintain that the difference between the Spiritual and the 'American' Baptists lies in their own openness to the Holy Spirit and a lack of formality which are simply more congenial to Africans. In the colonial period, however, some Baptists were described as holding Black suprematist views.

Nevertheless, the absence of exorcism rites or of a rigid distinction between good and bad spirit intrusion, together with the overlapping membership between shango and Spiritual Baptism suggest that its moral world is less dichotomised than that of mainstream Christianity.[18] The extent to which the Shouters privately use high science is uncertain: Shouter mourning seals resemble the kabbalistic seals of *The Sixth and Seventh Book of Moses*, and the Herskovits' accounts in the nineteen-thirties implied that Shouters then shared the rather neoplatonic pantheism of *science*.

Certain currents in Baptism are commented upon and developed in Mother Earth: the dynamic continuity with Africa, an affirmation of the everyday working-class world as opposed to that of the *social* churches; the physical and spiritual closeness to the earth; the organisational and nurturant role of the Mother and the association of women with the 'African', hot, centre pole rather than the cold altar; the religious community as a family; and perhaps most significantly, the structuring of disparate subjective imagery into coherent shared meanings which extends the everyday techniques of dream interpretation and divination (such as letting a Bible fall open or swinging a pendulum to obtain scriptural passages to trace a thief). While she has decisively rejected Christian doctrine, the Bible remains for Mother Earth, as it does for the Baptists, an important source for understanding the history of the world, albeit one to be interpreted with circumspection:

They say when they baptise the baby they give it a 'free spirit' or something. If they do it to 'chase the Devil out', they do it to chase the Natural Spirit out of the child and put in the Negative which is the Son. The Bible, what they say was wrote by the Queen, the first Queen or something so (the King James version is what they usually use here), and to me, although there is stories in the book that you can't really put together, they know everything that is going to take place because it come from the Spirit of the Son writing it. So what the ever that is placed in the book it is placed there because he know what is going to take place. He know everything to the End. But yet he fool you. So when you see the thing taking place you say 'Yes the book is true.' And the word they use – 'believe' – everybody use it. They 'believe' in the book because things that is in the book they know it is truth because they seeing it taking place.

Most of the things in the Bible have fulfilment but it ain' no use. Most of them that there they got no understanding. They can't unfold it. Even the leaders, they could unfold the Bible but everybody below them they holding the Bible like it control over you. I was holding it in my hand as my God: if I see anything frightful I run and pick up the Bible! They say 'You walk with a Bible in your hand, you safe' but if you ain' no money you can't buy. And you get no strength because you ain' no confidence in yourself. You got to burn the Bible. You got to see yourself. You get courage, you put your Bible in fire . . . and you still living! The Bible becomes the mind, and the Bible real confusing: you read one part and you find next contradiction. If many different countries', many different generations' story, but you read it as one thing.

The Baptists, they know what I'm doing but yet they try to treat me like I'm mad. Because they are so taken up in the Book now that they get more materialise too than naturalness. So they try to rebuke me too.

Shango

If the White slave owners ruled by day, the Blacks ruled by night. The sources of the Shouters lie not only in missionary Baptism but in those secret nocturnal meetings of the African-born slaves where they weighed their knowledge against what was learned of the Christianity of the planters, with resulting accommodations, elisions, reinterpretations and reactions. Although described somewhat quaintly as 'balls' by the Europeans, such assemblies are likely to have offered opportunities other than simply entertainment. Of what happened in any documentary sense we can know little but out of them emerged such distinctive groups as the Shouters, together with those understandings of the self, nature and the ultrahuman world we considered in Chapter 3. To an extent, this popular body of knowledge took an institutional form in the shango rites of spirit possession by the African powers, whose membership and concepts developed together with and against those of the Baptists. Following the 1760 slave rebellion, 'obeah' was punishable by death; like the Shouters, the followers of shango were engaged in illegal activities and, while its occasional formal practice continues in Trinidad, by the 1970s it seemed disappearing in a society where it had never been officially recognised as embodying any characteristic national values – unlike the Baptists who are regarded by the Trinidad elite with good humoured tolerance as a sort of non-stop street Carnival.

Shango is not opposed to obeah except in as much as obeah is employed for harm. Each power (or *orisha*) is potentially both malevolent and benevolent: ritual centres which deployed the potential of the powers to heal were once known as *balmyards*, and many practitioners of obeah – who prefer to be known as a *seerman, teacher* or *healer* – still offer advice for physical or spiritual misfortune. Shango has many similarities to the better known Haitian vodu and has been extensively described by George Simpson.[19] Some of its orishas are described in Chapter 8. Here I shall merely sketch out some characteristics of the rites as they were performed during Jeanette's childhood when she sometimes attended them together with her grandmother.

Unlike the Shouters' *travelling* in private visions, devotees of the orishas are fully taken over by their power in sight of the other participants, serving as a *child* through whom the power manifests. The powers themselves are West African deities although they are coupled with Christian saints. They are usually Yoruba although in the area of Port-of-Spain where Mother Earth lived as a girl there was a large Rada group founded by nineteenth-century immigrants from Dahomey.[20] Participants may also recognise Bondieu, the Christian God, as over and above the powers. Compared with Shouter Baptism, there is more use of patois and many songs are in *Yarriba*, although the precise meaning of the words are seldom known to the participants. Participants may describe their relationship with the possessing power as a *susu* (credit) contract, and indeed shango ceremonies resemble the fêtes, communal labour entertainments (*gayaps*) and wakes of rural Trinidad. Sponsored activities involving expenditure on food, various ritual objects and animals for sacrifice, their organisation is perhaps closer to a fraternity or cult than it is to anything we might term a 'church'. Ceremonies employ items regarded as more 'African' than 'Christian' – rum, tobacco, drums, *chacs-chacs* (gourd rattles), calabashes and cutlasses. Benches face inwards towards the centre of the room, and the 'altar' is merely one of the resting places for a variety of pictures and ritual paraphernalia rather than the central concentration of mystical power. The earthen *stools* ('shrines') of the orishas may be located around the courtyard, as among the Yoruba.

For the Earth People, shango asserts an Africa quite independent of White Christianity. Whether the identification of the powers with Christian saints is in any case strictly 'syncretic' may be doubted for the power/saint still has two distinct aspects which are not completely fused: a relationship Bastide terms a 'correspondence'. In some ways shango may be said to formalise everyday village practices: towards the end of a wake in Pinnacle, the more respectable villagers, particularly the women, leave the ceremony and return home to sleep; the singing then shifts from the lugubrious 'Sankeys' to a sharper tempo, a greater degree of improvisation and the introduction of polyrhythms, some-times progressing to spontaneous male dancing and massed *bongo* drumming in which domestic calabashes and bowls are used.

Through its use of blood, leaves, water and 'thunderaxes',[21] and its association between the orishas and the elemental forces of sea and thunder, animals and trees, shango elides the natural, human and mystical domains which Spiritual Baptism tends to distinguish. The ground on which Baptist mourners lie only represents the origin and fate of man, but shango takes the earth as the continuing physical source of the gods: oblations are poured onto it and it is from the earth that the powers manifest through the central pole onto their child. While earth from graves is now regarded as the ideal material for malignant obeah, it comes from what was once the resting place of the ancestors, and *grave dirt* was formerly placed in the mouth of the suspected thief or practitioner of harmful sorcery to determine the truth.

A National Union of Afro-Brasilian Cults was founded in 1955 but the very notion of an official organisation of Shangoists in Trinidad in the 1970s would have caused amusement, so marginalised was the cult, regarded generally as a 'survival' from the African past, and one that might well be resuscitated in the annual Best Village Competition as a folkloric dance, but hardly an integral part of everyday life. A well-known folklorist and some Nigerian diplomats excepted, to be known outside one's circle of respectable friends as a cultist would be the occasion for apologetic or defiant embarrassment. Less so in Port-of-Spain in the 1940s when Mother Earth was a girl. Jeanette herself was never an adult participant and she had never been possessed. She remembers little of the details, beyond some of the songs, the sacrifices of goats (which she disliked) and the children's *tables* to which the shango Mother of a group would invite children, both followers of the orishas and other neighbours, African and Indian together, for a feast where they were invited to partake of large quantities of food piled high on tables in a shango *tent*.[22] The children were identified with the African orishas: 'when you feed the children, you feed the saints'. The Earth People now regard their children as the authentic Africans, and term themselves the Children of the Nation. The term *nation*, once used to describe particular descent or regional groupings, and later their organisations for mutual aid and fêtes (as well as suggesting non-Whites in general), now refers to the African ceremonies themselves. 'Feeding the children' is recalled in the Earth Peoples' accumulation of large quantities of food surplus to immediate needs, for the Feeding of the Nation during the coming famine, and in the centrality of the communal consumption of food, the only activity in the Valley which could conventionally be described as 'ritual'.

The Earth People appropriate those aspects of shango regarded as distinctively African – drums, wooden stools and the revering of an animate Nature (shango cultists made offerings to the sea and were said to dance with snakes). There is no practice of anything like 'spirit possession' or mourning among the Earth People but Mother Earth argues that shango possession, like the language of the drums, was a 'half-way' stage of keeping in contact, an accommodation during the Nation's exile from its Mother. This is no longer necessary, for the whole world is about to return to a state of Nature, the 'spiritual' becoming our everyday. From fragmentary rites, spells, visions, dreams and recollections we shall return to the totality, for these were only a memory, a keeping of faith until the real Beginning of The End: 'Your ancestor is you.' We are now living in those last days when time itself will end and when ultimate and mundane realities will be reconciled; Mother Earth embodies in herself all the orishas, the ancestors and the whole history of that separation between Nature and Her Children, between the African past and the Caribbean present.

To return to the observer's perspective: the potential roles available to the one on whom an orisha manifests, what Mischel and Mischel call 'the sanctioned expression of behaviours which are otherwise socially unacceptable or unavailable' – simulated violence, near nudity, erotic display, reversal of sex roles – prefigure Mother Earth's experiences. She herself may be said to retain the double identity of the African power and the human on whom the power manifests.[23] It was their own familiarity with shango possession that enabled Jeanette's family at the time of the Burning to see her actions as potentially valid. For the passer-by in Port-of-Spain, seeing the Earth People massed naked in the public squares, it is again something like shango which offers an alternative to the simple ascription of madness.

Black and White
Through her ideas on the relations between West Indian and European, Mother Earth offers us one understanding of the contemporary world. Neither Baptism nor shango contain any formal consideration of ethnicity, class or national power. Shango takes itself as a continuation of an authentic Africa which is 'truer' than Christianity only in that it is true for the individual African. Similarly, the Baptists, who may have the rare White member, argue that while Christ may well have been Black this is not a matter of any fundamental importance. The Earth People, by contrast, place considerable emphasis on the historical relations between Black and White, and locate the separation of the two groups in the original act of insubordination by God. An emphasis on racial conflict is maintained especially by those members of the group who were not members of Jeanette's immediate family or her neighbours in Port-of-Spain, but who were previously adherents of Rastafari. Like Mother Earth's partner Cyprian, they were profoundly affected by the failure of the Black Power mutiny in 1970 which lead to Jeanette and Cyprian leaving town for the coast.

Lowenthal points out that 'few working-class Africanisms are residual *ethnic* survivals; they are the consequences of *racial* segregation and of inequalities of power, status and rewards, which stem from slavery and social pluralism'.[24] Any consideration of Afro-Caribbean society has, like the slave trade in which it originated, to be triangular, mapped by the co-ordinates of Europe, Africa and the Caribbean. The West Indies, 'the most colonial of colonial societies',[25] are a society of successive immigrations, and the relationship between different groups – particularly between Africans and Europeans – must be recalled constantly through this history. Conflict between groups and within groups remains articulated by a complex lexicon of colour and its associated norms, values and goals: 'neither a seamless synthesis nor a pot pourri'.[26]

The West Indies can never be read as an autonomous society independent of Europe and the world economic system; rural life is illiterate rather than non-literate, countrified rather than rural, urbanised but nearly without cities, industrialised but without factories.[27] Local ideals were always derived from, or defined against, those of the dominant Whites; generally the less successful ones, as the wealthy plantation owners were either absentees resident in Europe or else soon returned there. Within a few years of independence, formal discrimination against Blacks was no longer practised, but the continuing Black preferences for White physiognomy ('good hair', 'nice colour' and so on) are well-documented, as are the consequences of this for those who do not possess them – the majority.[28] One respectable villager in Pinnacle told me:

When we in Africa we ai' talk proper, we talk with drum and thing. We ai' no culture. White men teach we how to make pants. Before, we live in tree. They teach us to eat proper with knife and fork. But they ai' grateful! They say White man press we and so. Slavery? In end, all for good. No slaves and we still in African bush, eat one another, believe in jumbie God, God all about. And niggermancy call 'cause nigger do it. The people sunk in obeah.

It would be simplistic to see such a sensibility as some unalterable psychological flaw, an identification with the aggressor, a historic envy of the White plantocracy and colonial elite, or even as a public transcript for presentation to the White observer. They represent something continuing and more immediately significant to the pragmatic Trinidadian – education and economic success. In the English-speaking West Indies, the perception of 'colour' is closely tied to class and race; and, it may be argued, is significant in that it articulates class. One consequence is the local recognition of hypergamy: it is difficult for an educated dark-skinned woman to find an appropriate mate when professional men prefer to marry lighter (and younger), less educated, women. A 'Trinidad White', a 'pass for White', was a light-skinned Creole who could 'pass' socially as a European because of educational or professional qualifications. In Jamaica and Barbados, a sharp distinction is recognised between Black and White, the former category as in the United States including those with minimal African ancestry, like many of the Trinidadian French Creoles who in Trinidad are effectively perceived as *white* – or at the least as *red*, mixed. In Trinidad, where the slaves formed a smaller part of the early nineteenth-century population than elsewhere, and were themselves frequently owned by the *free coloureds*, Creole racial categorisation is now ordered along a relatively smooth hierarchy; but the two poles, Black and White, remain the same as elsewhere in the West Indies. In this, Trinidad resembles Brazil where the term 'White Africans' denotes thoroughly Creolised Whites rather than poor Whites such as the marginalised *red legs* of Barbados – whose simple inclusion within the rigid Bajan Black–White dichotomy would upset the association between race and class. The term *béké nègre*, which serves widely in the eastern Caribbean to characterise a poor White, is in Trinidad, like *coconut* or *play-in-White*, a term for a Black who inappropriately imitates a White middle-class life-style. The high proportion of Indians in Trinidad, now half of the population, who are excluded from the Creole continuum, probably does much to reduce its salience, as does the number of Amerindians in Brazil. Trinidad resembles Brazil in its hierarchical rather than dichotomised racial classification, and its ready recognition of African traditions: 'African' has not been an insulting term here as in Barbados. The alliance of colonial authority and European landowner was less salient in Trinidad where, during much of the nineteenth century, the overt antagonisms were between the French-speaking White Creole bourgeoisie and the British colonial administration.

Compared to Jamaica, Trinidadians are less likely to refer everyday issues to race and they regard themselves as generally more tolerant, more *according*. Maureen Lewis comments that Trinidadian conflicts are more individualised compared with the perception of collective social and economic pressures in Jamaica. While Jamaica is characterised by a 'visionary and apocalyptic dimension . . . Trinidadians have so far buoyant irreverence and cheerful cynicism'.[29] But even if Bastide's observation on race – 'dualism is after all a sociologist's abstraction'[30] – is valid for Brazil, this is hardly so for Trinidad, particularly in recent years when the historical antagonisms between the different White groups have been forgotten and the United States increasingly provides the model for racial pluralism as much as in other areas.

This gradual 'Americanisation' of Trinidad, as Britain relinquished any economic interest in its colony, was particularly salient after the Americans occupied a military base from the Second World War. America's overtly 'non-ideological' politics shaped the political response in Trinidad where the first industrial strike against discriminatory hiring in the West Indies had occurred in 1919. By 1943, when Mother Earth was nine, less than 7 per cent of the population were entitled to vote according to a franchise based on property ownership: political consciousness, such as it was, developed primarily through labour organisation, culminating in the famous oil workers' strike of 1930. Despite the radicalism of Tub Butler and C. L. R. James, left-wing politics in Trinidad has remained firmly pragmatic and reformist, occasionally revolutionary in rhetoric but never in practice, barring the shortlived 1970 mutiny.

The inescapable measure of Trinidadian values remains that of Britain and America. The models for education, economy, political process and life-style are European. But the texture of life is that of powerlessness, of 'alienation, of a difference between black West Indians and external metropolitan control and values'.[31] The passivity and marginality which this engenders has been said to present the West Indian with 'no target to aim at, no ideal vision, that is not ultimately self-defeating'. 'Travellers to the region', observes Gordon Lewis, 'almost from the very beginning, remarked on the stark contrast everywhere between the beauty of its natural habitat and the Gothic horrors of its social scene.'[32] In the European perception of the West Indies, the countries themselves have never been identified with any civil society but rather with nature, as raw material awaiting exploitation and refinement through capital investment and cheap labour. They are islands rather than nations. Disappearing from the European gaze when sugar ceased to contribute significantly to the metropolitan economy, the West Indies have recently re-emerged, but now as a tourist paradise of unsullied nature whose inhabitants exist to provide refreshment and entertainment, and to seduce visitors into discarding temporarily their metropolitan responsibilities. 'Islands in the Sun.' The White tourist in the West Indies does not visit anything (there is nothing to visit) but engages in sunbathing and swimming in a rural Arcadia with discrete comforts provided in a setting which should be as 'unspoiled' as possible. This vision of 'Eden without the apple'[33] was constituted by colonial imagery, recalling to us Froude's description of Black West Indians in 1888 as if slavery had never been instituted: 'Like Adam again they are under the covenant of innocence . . . They are naked and not ashamed.'[34] A prelapsarian state of nature, what Aimé Césaire has called 'a mock paradise', comprising, says David Lowenthal,

environmental delectability, effortless subsistence, carefree disposition, devotion to sensual pleasures (music, dance, sex) and easy racial intermingling . . . Lush verdant nature was the focus, human misery was ignored . . . When nature is so agreeable, houses are seen more as luxuries than necessities and the most modest accommodation will do.[35]

Prelapsarian indeed, for slavery appears never to have existed: the tourist is not offered any restored plantation, and the history of the Caribbean is that of the sea battles of European admirals and pirates, as it was in Trinidad's schoolbooks up to the 1970s.

This exoticism, the international image of the West Indies, is a major determinant of West Indian popular identity, particularly in Trinidad where the masquerades of Carnival represent 'the contemporary stereotype of the essentially cheerful, feckless, lazy West Indian, prone however to occasional "outbursts", throwing off civilised restraints and reverting to savagery'.[36] The Trinidadian writer Louis James trenchantly lays into local writers for internalising the tourist paradise through their presentation of

a mythical world where unbridled virility brings no unwanted children, freedom from the drudgery of work brings no starvation and uninhibited vitality no tragic violence . . . The Trinidadian peasantry becomes the reassuringly 'charming' and harmless people every good American dreams of.[37]

The ironies of striving for respectable, and thus White, identity were not lost on the young Mother Earth:

They use' to have this reader. An' it have a nice nice White girl with long straight hair and she lead a little boy by the hand. An' next thing they change the picture an' it have Black children . . . But the little girl now got hair all stick out an' she got thick thick lips on her face. What happen? It still the same thing!

An' the stores all have White statues [tailors' dummies] with clothes, and they look so nice you don' go in and see you self, you just there to see these White people. And then [after the Mutiny] it all change up. Sudden it all Black statues in window. They have them hid at the back of the shop all the while? But you see – it all change back again. It all White statues again now . . . An' it use' to have this Corpus Christi thing an' my grandmother use' to take me. An' I see all these little angels standing like sculpture, and they got white dresses. White, White everywhere! An' they got wings like they was birds. An' the faces like they all paint white. Or perhaps it is White girls: all the convent girls were White.

Rastafari: the reassertion of an Africa

Political response to White domination in the Caribbean before the 1930s did not take the form of mass secular organisation, for this had been impossible under slavery and largely rendered ineffectual under colonial status. The paths of ideological resistance and reassertion for Americans of African descent have always been closely associated with formal religion. While the mere existence of some type of African religious practice in the slave compound provided an everyday meaning not subordinated to plantation life, rebellions of the slaves in the Americas, most notably in Haiti, used the practical organisation, beliefs and rituals of those nocturnal meetings when the disparate tribal traditions were reworked into vodu, shango or candomblé. Many leaders claimed divine powers to protect their followers and some preached a Black God. Those West Indian slaves who had been born in Africa, like the descendants of escaped slaves (Maroons), accepted that they would return there after death and were buried with insignia which would be recognised in their native land; the planters arguing that such ideas accounted for the high suicide rate in African-born slaves.

Christian rhetoric was appropriated, its heaven now a place where there was freedom, one the Whites themselves were perhaps unlikely to reach. Underground slave teachings maintained that the Blacks were the sheep and the Whites the goats mentioned by Jesus, or even that there was a 'real' Bible hidden somewhere which gave a true account of Black history. Exodus and the crossing of the Red Sea provided a coded, perhaps fantasised, return to Africa, whether after death or as some future political event – and it is likely that these alternatives were not so distinct. Ethiopia, the ancient Christian kingdom said to have been founded by Solomon and the Queen of Sheba, African but not (yet) colonised by Whites, appeared a place of dignity and hope: the first Black church in Jamaica was named the Ethiopian Baptist Church and many self-help groups and lodges took the name 'Ethiopian' in the nineteenth century. Organised missionary Christianity was regarded by many as merely a legitimation for the plantation system, and locally trained preachers continually left the mainstream churches to found fissiporous and sometimes expressly political groups, a pattern which continues. In North America Nat Turner and Denmark Vesey employed Christian themes of deliverance and Exodus to articulate their revolts, as did the 'Baptist rebellions' of Jamaica led by George Gordon, Sam Sharpe and Paul Bogle. What may be perceived as a 'religious' dimension continues to be integral to African–American political action, particularly in Jamaica and the United States.

In their consideration of Native American polities, Clyde Kluckholn and Dorothea Leighton[38] suggest that in situations of cultural and political dominance an indigenous religion provides an obvious alternative system of meaning for the dominated, presumably because 'religion' is usually less accessible to external control than other collective activities (it was the rare and only permitted form of aggregation during West Indian slavery). While not simply reflecting existing political structures in any Durkheimian sense, religion's situating of the private individual in their ultimate reality, together with its autonomous articulation, provides wider meanings transcending the immediate political contexts which can structure an alternative social dispensation at an appropriate time, keeping intact in the meanwhile shared patterns of everyday response which remain in opposition to (or are at least radical reinterpretations of) those of the dominant group: the mode of thought Mannheim terms 'utopia'.

Rather than see 'religion' as some type of discrete psychosocial phenomenon, we might argue that all societies have 'big ideas' and 'little ideas', and religion is quite simply a very big idea – one whose cosmology can articulate variant interpretations of justice and retribution. The very notion of 'survivals' tends to miss such active reworking, whatever may have been Herskovits' intention of refuting the image of the passive slave. The generation of Caribbeanists after Herskovits does of course acknowledge such resistance and ideological redefinition; thus Mintz describes the assertion of African identity and the persistence of African patterns of agriculture almost teleologically, as if they were simply a preparation for the free peasantry which developed in the West Indies after emancipation.[39] Certainly, people once objectified through Western racial science as the commodities of slavery have reasserted their common humanity to produce the tolerant, open and egalitarian societies of the West Indies.

Although one of the first Rastas, Leonard Howell, had served in the Ashanti Wars and probably learned one or more West African languages, African themes in the Jamaican movement of Rastafari are derived from the Black experience in the Caribbean.[40] It is only in recent years that a few Jamaican and British Rastas have visited Africa. The most fundamental tenet of Rasta however is that it is African. Mintz warns us that 'it is one thing to perceive African sources, another to consider whether people themselves see it that way'.[41] Both Rastas and Earth People decidedly do. The Africa which they affirm and experience is, to a large extent, secondary to European perception and delineation of that continent, particularly through films, newspapers and popular novels, and more recently television.

Marcus Garvey, the Jamaican political activist who founded the Universal Negro Improvement Association in New York with its associated African Orthodox Church, is supposed to have said 'Look to Africa where a Black king is to be crowned, for deliverance is at hand.' When the Ethiopian Ras (Count) Tafari was crowned as Haile Selassie in 1930, Jamaican interest fastened on Ethiopia, particularly after the Italian invasion when the Emperor poignantly appealed to the League of Nations. Many Jamaicans affiliated to the Ethiopian World Federation set up in New York with Selassie's encouragement. What we now know as the Rastafari movement originated during the 1930s and 1940s in small groups which developed among the Native Baptists (broadly similar to the Shouters) of the *dungle*, the rubbish dumping area of the capital where lived perhaps one in six of the West Kingston proletariat. These groups proclaimed the divinity of Selassie, and continued to gain adherents after independence from Britain. Since the 1960s Rastafari has achieved a high international profile, largely due to the popularity of reggae music, many of whose artists are closely associated with the movement. There are now Rastas in other Caribbean islands, in the United States, Britain and among the Surinamese in Holland. Non-White minority groups elsewhere have adopted Rasta style and beliefs (including some Maori), but identification with the movement has remained largely restricted to working-class Black men in the West Indies and Britain.

Rasta has no central authority or organisation, and its adherents vary from self-contained pietist communities in Jamaica, to individuals who adopt a distinctive Rasta appearance and idiom with varying degrees of personal commitment. It is simultaneously a Christian religio-political movement, a presentational style, and a major vehicle of ethnic reassertion for the Black working class. Among its various tenets can be found the ideas that God, Adam, Jesus and the original Jews were Black, that Selassie the Lion of Judah is God, and that the African-descended peoples are the lost tribes who have been placed under Babylonian *sufferation* until a future redemption. While organised Christianity is a tool of White domination, its Bible is extensively referred to in justification.[42]

A few Rastas maintain that Selassie (whose overthrow and death scarcely affected the movement) only represents the divinity in all – 'Man is God, God is Man' – and a number of its leaders in Jamaica have declared themselves divine. For others the return of Haile Selassie is either imminent or to be expected after the completion of a 2,000 year cosmic cycle which started with Jesus. One group, the Twelve Tribes of Israel, believe that they alone will be saved when the 144,000 of the Book of Revelation are 'gathered in'. Biblical exegesis varies: some consider all the Bible is literally true, others maintain it can only be interpreted correctly through a Rasta exegesis, or else that the significant parts are missing.

To the outsider the most distinctive Rasta characteristics are their beards and hair worn long in dreadlocks,[43] clothes striped in gold, black, green and red, and the smoking of ganja as sacrament, medicine and food. While conflicts with the Jamaican authorities initially involved suspicions of an armed uprising (and some Rastas were executed for murders of dissident members) or mass attempts to go to Africa, most recent confrontations have involved, as in Trinidad and Britain, the cultivation and sale of ganja, and the always vague and fluctuating relationship between Rasta identity and the organised crime of the Kingston *rudies*. Since the 1970s the conventionally 'apolitical' Rastas of Jamaica have been courted by the two major parties, particularly after the rapturous welcome afforded to a rather bemused Haile Selassie when he visited Jamaica.

It would be going too far to say they are locally recognised as an authentic Jamaican folk tradition, for their strident Pan-Africanism seems a threat to the multiracial nationalism of West Indian governments, but Marcus Garvey has been proclaimed the first Jamaican National Hero and the publicity which has accrued to the country with the international acclaim for reggae's Bob Marley, together with the economic benefits from record companies, have gone some way to an ambivalent public accommodation. For many middle-class students, writers and artists, the wearing of locks by those who would not subscribe to its eschatological teachings has become an emblem of African–Caribbean authenticity. Rex Nettleford suggests that Rastafari has now become 'assimilated into the mainstream of thought on black power and majority control'[44] but *respectable* Jamaicans, middle or working class, with aspirations to succeed within the framework of mainstream entrepreneurial values, continue to regard the movement with unconcealed distaste. The Ethiopian Orthodox Church, although gratified to find converts in Jamaica, has never endorsed Haile Selassie's divinity.

Described thus, the formal tenets of Rastafari give it an exotic salience at odds with its development in daily working-class life. Alignment with the movement is relatively pragmatic and may be discontinued when regular employment is found; if its rhetoric is anti-technological, few members actually disdain the use of recorded music or motor vehicles. Although some reject the educational system and the protection of the police in all circumstances, we might argue that these are effectively denied to their class in any case. Professional medical treatment is similarly avoided but not always in emergencies. Contraception (*sex by imagination*) is abhorred as White-inspired genocide: 'No Rasta will allow his queen to be mingled with or interfered with by a physician . . . They want to turn our queens into graveyards.' For minor ailments ganja is used, as 'the leaves on the tree were for healing of the nations'. Many Rastas maintain that no serious illness or death of a Black person can be regarded as 'natural', and they avoid funerals. Although a few groups have established self-sufficient communities in the countryside, the majority continue to live in the town and it is difficult to disagree with Mintz' assertion that no West Indian 'has rejected technology to defend the past or to maintain an "African" style of life';[45] until the Earth People. Even Rasta commune members wear commercially produced clothes and, while favouring gourds and wooden spoons for eating, use the same iron cooking pots as other Jamaicans.

A valued Rasta characteristic is *art*, the ability to articulate the spontaneous and the authentic beyond *social* convention; any reductionist explanation is *madness*. Members also value 'art' in the conventional sense, as more real than book work: many are musicians, painters, carvers and craftsmen of accomplished skill. Rastas pride themselves on being more natural, honest, authentic and less devious and calculating than the *social* population: 'Man [Rasta] knows, Men [Babylon] believe.' Rasta idiom, often unintelligible to the middle-class Jamaican, is essentially recreolised Jamaican English with phonetic and semantic revisions, employing new words based on puns and sound values, or else changing the 'negative' associations of standard words:

Within the word/sound structure of the Queen's English there exist subtle negative connotations . . . Rastafarians are continually exploring these negatives and seek to substitute and reaffirm more positive vibrations . . . Within the words 'be(lie)f' and '(sin)cere' we can perceive the word-vibrations of 'sin' and 'lie'. In the case of 'sin' the 's' is dropped reaffirming the 'word, sound and power' positively as 'Incerely' or 'Cerely'.[46]

Thus (*ded*)*icate* becomes *livicate*, and *to*(*bacc*)*o* yields *frunto*. Any plural implies diversity and disunity so Rastas collectively are simply *man* or *I-and-I*; *men* and *we* being appropriate only to Babylon: 'For Jerusalem is ruined and Judah fallen because their tongues and their doings are against the Lord' (Isaiah 3: 8). Inappropriate speech places one in a state of spiritual alienation and physical *dis-ease*. Rasta English however is seen by some as only an accommodation before returning to Amharic.

Rastas argued that Black people, the original race, are close to Nature which is identified with the Earth: 'I and I are an ancient people, I and I are a nature people.' They may refer to the Earth as a sensate, living organism, identified with Selassie or mankind in general, while less commonly it may be female, a mother. They may sit by preference on the ground and refer to the communal consumption of ganja, meditation and reflection as *groundings*. Some celebrate the anniversary of that *groundation* when Haile Selassie set foot on Jamaican soil. Natural health is *livity*, harmony with the forces of Nature and God, and *nature* also refers to the sexual drive of men, 'you' nature'. The *bredrin* achieve livity by living off the earth, cultivating it by hand and with respect. They criticise the mechanical exploitation of land which causes earthquakes and other disasters for 'the earth would be at peace with man if only man would leave it in peace'. Strict Rasta diet, *ital*, comprises homegrown rice, ground provision, pulses and fruit. The prohibitions in Leviticus on pork and shell fish are observed while some members refuse all *dead foods* – 'Thou shalt not make of thy stomach a cemetery!' Salt is avoided by Rastas, emphasising an existing rural practice.[47]

Rastafari differs from other Afro-Caribbean religious movements in that it is embodied in men. The very term 'Rasta' refers to the male; women are 'queens'.[48] Men are the distinctive members of the community, by dress and commitment, and women are usually associated with Rastafari through personal attachments to male members rather than by any personal motivation for its life-style. In the early days women were more prominent, but they are now excluded from the groundings and discouraged from smoking ganja. In its art and poetry, they are valued primarily as the reproducers and rearers of *seed*, although – contrary to the usual West Indian understanding – procreation is said to reside in man's *nature* alone. The popular term of abuse, *blood clot'*, has been taken as demonstrating Rasta concern about pollution with menstrual blood, and some groups are said to confine women in menstrual huts while in others men do the cooking at all times lest their queens be menstruating. Some Rastas derive the very term 'woman' from 'woe to man' and the respectable aspirations of working-class women are a threat to the movement's oppositional stance (as for Mother Earth, page 84). It would be going too far to suggest that Rasta women are reluctant adherents but they seem more likely to leave, and they do complain frequently about the chauvinism of the men. As the majority of Rastas, particularly outside Jamaica, still work and live in 'Babylon' and have not established self-contained households or communes, the relations between most women and Rastas are not so very different from the usual pattern. This is so in Pinnacle where the five young men known as 'Rastas' by the villagers (for wearing locks and general distance from the more genteel aspirations of the village) have established the usual friending relationships with girls who themselves would be outraged at any suggestion that they themselves were Rastas (Plate 1, page 9). If Rasta may be said to exist on a spectrum ranging from self-contained communes to such marginal adherents, the autonomy of women associated with it varies from a high degree of constraint to the same personal freedoms as those of other working-class women.

The Lion and the Serpent

At the time of her visions Mother Earth had no contact with the Rastas for they only seem to have appeared in Trinidad well after the Mutiny in 1970, although Jamaican Rastafari had already achieved considerable coverage in the Trinidad newspapers. Nevertheless, it was the arrival of disgruntled Rastas from Port-of-Spain which allowed her family to grow into the community which became the Earth People. Rastafari seems to have reinforced Mother Earth's ideas and her particular use of language whilst introducing into her group ganja smoking and leaving one's hair to form dreadlocks. Like the Rastas, she argues that this was the original hair style of Black people:[49]

DASHEEN: In the Beginning everyone had locks, Black and White. And the last generation see themselves as ending of the White world: 'Rastafari!' But they just gone back now.

M.E.:   But the locks show the End is here.

Wozzie, a Rasta from town who has settled in Pinnacle, says he too came to the countryside 'to prepare himself', for 'In the Beginning, so in the End': the trees and river are evidence enough for God, he says, and the Bible is corrupt although useful in parts. Like the Earth People, the Trinidadian Rastas have taken an alternative, secessionist and personal road to that radical Black autonomy which had been frustrated with the Mutiny. In contrast to other groups they share a cosmogony in which an original Black creation is now dominated by Whites; but with regeneration soon, through the earth as an active force. Both reject obeah and the minutiae of shango as well as technology and the state, in favour of a return to an Africa which to the observer owes much to the popular Western media and to the everyday resistances of proletarian life. The most fundamental differences between the two groups are the status of women, and Mother Earth's own dismissal of the whole Selassie-Ethiopia-Amharic complex as a presumptuous Jamaican novelty, a revision of Christianity which still serves male power:

And with the Rastafarians here in Trinidad, I don't know for abroad but here: some of the elders in the Rastas know the truth because I meet with some, speak to them and I sure of myself that they know The Mother but under cover. It is under cover with them and they put a front of Selassie, pictures of Selassie the Lion, and so forth.

But underneath, one I was speaking to, which he is trying to make a headway of himself, when I speak about Africans and I show him that we are the Serpents of the Earth, we are the Beginning, we are the Mapapi, he turn his back to me and on his back was a long serpent. He didn't answer me but he just turn round his back and let me see that he know. He knows it, but when I first approach him he give me a 'Jah Rasta – I, Selassie – I'. I stop him. I tell him 'No, I am not that, I don't want that, I come to speak to you, to show you The Mother, the Beginning . . . And we suppose to be speaking about The Mother which is the Earth that we live on, we eat from, we drink from. You speaking about something that you can't even understand it!'

I tell him I know the Jah as The Mother because I call on the Jah in myself 'Jah Jehovah' (which is The Mother). I saw the moon, I call him the 'Jah Allah', and I saw the moon come to me and it was a mother . . . So he look at me. So when he see to himself I have the hair and I call myself Mother Earth (is the first time to meet me to speak to) and he started with his talks and he notice that I ain't coping with it, he start talking like myself! So you can see, just a make-believe thing with the Rastas. They say no meat, they just want soul food; and next minute they got a tin of Solo in one hand and a packet of Corn Curls in the next. If they see pitch [a road] they more crowd, but the bush they see it as a poison.

I have argued in Chapter 3 that the everyday sensibility of West Indian life can be read as dual, articulating the continuing relations between Black and White, in which *respectable* life, most typically represented in women, is opposed to that of *reputation*, the male working-class reaction against those imposed and ultimately unattainable aspirations. *Reputation*'s rejection of book learning and middle-class values, its emphasis on the *natural* and 'spontaneous', affirm the characteristics Whites historically ascribed to Blacks. Both Rastafari and Mother Earth appropriate these as central, as the more authentic, but Rasta does this within the broad Judaeo-Christian tradition using the Bible while reinterpreting it; it has, not surprisingly, been taken as a valid Christian movement by some Catholic priests. Rex Nettleford, while not himself regarding Rastafari as 'Christian', comments that 'the overthrowing of the Christian faith was to be fought by weapons out of its own armoury'.[50] Although still informed by her Baptist days, Mother Earth is engaging on rather different ground. For the Rastas, as for Muslims, their religion is the final revelation of which Christianity was a necessary precursor, but for the Earth People Christian monotheism is altogether a snare and a delusion, a view pithily expressed in one of their favourite aphorisms 'Fuck God!' The minutiae of shango and obeah are discarded along with God; their themes are universalised, for the origins and power of the natural world lie within it, not in some conjuration. She is quite familiar with the appearance of contemporary Africans:

They all in suits! Africans don't want the Rastas! . . . [Rastas] say Seven Black Star Liners coming to take them to Africa. I say they wait a long time! The whole of Nature is Africa: don't call on a God you can't see. They speak different: 'I dis' and 'I dat'. But I say I don't understand. If you talk in Jamaican is suppose you born there, it their tongue. But what I talk I learn in Trinidad. I got to speak to everybody, not just Rasta.

So I don't really mix with them. I am doing my job until the hour come that they will have to come to and see themselves. I know who they are and what they are, the reason for them on earth, the reason for the hair growing; because in the Beginning it had no comb, and if you say you want to go down to 'roots' . . . ! Well the comb is not there, the clothes wasn't there, the books wasn't there, Selassie wasn't there.

'Survivals' are not objects of analysis 'out there', but memories in action, chosen reproductions and commentaries upon relationships that persist through time. West Indian working-class life had always contained in *reputation* what, following Schwimmer, we may term an 'oppositional ideology':

inversions or reversals of putative scale values on which the members of the disadvantaged group suppose themselves to be consigned to the pole of marginality or peripherality by those in the 'centre' . . . One of the potent ways in which they appear to give meaning symbolically to their communality is by reversing the polarities of the scale to make their values central.[51]

Such a series of pragmatic and individually functional values – word play, satire, irony, worthlessness, masquerade, obeah – lie available for reworking into a unitary set of new 'central', African values. An ascribed characteristic becomes an achieved identity. This happens in the Rasta's elevation of the *worthless* over the *social*, but to an even greater extent among the Earth People who have discarded male dominance, technology and Christianity so much more radically. In the participants' experience, Rastafari offers a reassertion, the Earth People something more like an overturning. No schema however can be so radical as to constitute a 'total' change, and the point at which we may say that personal reassertion of sub-dominant values becomes a reversal of the dominant ones remains arbitrary.

Neither are a dull reenactment of some African tradition. Memories are chosen and recontextualised in lived experience. The *worthlessness* of the Black working-class man is repeatedly ascribed anew in each generation: to act through this subjectivity, whether in the carnivalesque *no behaviour* of everyday life or the conscious resistances of Rastafari and the Earth People, is a personal reinvention by each, in a particular place at a particular time, and one which constantly reflects back upon and transforms the dominant. The ascription of a tradition – the 'organisation of the current situation in terms of the past'[52] – and our perception and experience of actually living in one, may be rather different. A dominant European tradition can be identified in its invention of sacred continuity, its imposition of meaning and structure on a selected temporal flow, with texts and institutions apparently persisting through time, and justifications and appeals to earlier figures: 'its naturalisation of its own arbitrariness'.[53] Here subjectivity and ascription correspond, for individual members and social theorists alike. The world that is, is the world that should be, that has to be, yet its ideology is hardly to be opposed for it is rarely confronted as a whole. Dominated individuals – and here I am thinking particularly of Black people and, to an extent, Jews and other minorities and women – have sought control over their lives and their meanings in concrete situations through tactical reaction to the dominant, through evasion, bluff, accommodation, incorporation, reinterpretation, feigned ignorance, sabotage, malingering, exaggerated deference, sour grapes, overt resistance and fantasised retribution, or just simply getting by through a fragmentary rhetoric of verbal indirection, necessity as virtue, strategic masking, innuendo and left-handed compliment.

Even when we try to identify precariously with the dominant group, there are sometimes moments at which we have to stop balancing, when pastiche becomes parody, when we can look at ourselves looking at the centre. If the dominant tradition, defining itself against us, maintains some coherence through time as self-determined, necessary and sufficient, then our own reactions will take consistent but complementary forms, as a perverse affinity rather than a lineage, reactions seen by the dominant as hysteria or mendacity. If as individuals we affirm and trace back through time some continuity of reaction and meaning for ourselves then one can say that we experience ourselves as living in a subdominant or countertradition articulated in an oppositional ideology:

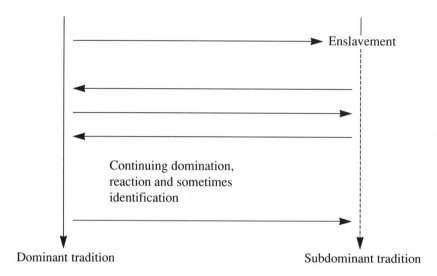

For historians or anthropologists, the question of perceiving such a sub-dominant response as a structured 'tradition' in itself is one of acknowledging the coherence and centrality of a self-aware countertradition in an endless series of individual reactions determined ultimately from the outside. (In the West Indian case, with political independence the subdominant chain gradually becomes more formalised and autonomous, central, as we can see in the shift of carnival from *no behaviour* to emblematic national institution.) Our logic will hardly be that of the dominant ideology itself – reasonably and internally consistent and marked by texts which signal a history through linear time. It will be a double-voiced tradition of subversion and of personal survival, of gesture and irony, of compromise and deception, parodic inversion and apocalyptic time.

7

Nature and the millennium

The fragmentary strands of countertradition – Lamartine's 'premature truths' – may at certain poignant political moments become central, their oppositional themes affirmed and reworked into a putative new social order; not just by willed revolutionary consciousness (though this may well be the experienced reality) but because of perceived changes in the social and technological conditions in which the dominant and the subdominant are held in opposition – in a loss of coercive power among certain sectors, through scandals among the dominant or other discreditings of its own rationale, by rumours of emancipation, or through more widespread changes which argue a more general frame.

The return to the past; the rejection of industrial technology; the identification of the Blacks as the chosen people; the White appropriation of the Bible; Christianity as colonial apologetics; these motifs are common to numerous movements which have developed among the peoples colonised or enslaved by Europeans: cognitive schemata as social action which momentarily looked to a day of deliverance, to the destruction of the colonial order, and the restoration of traditional liberty. These movements, sometimes building upon existing pre-colonial 'apocalyptic' themes of redemption and transcendence, have acted as the justification for military struggles, or else, faced with overwhelming White power, have become 'individualised' and quietist, ultimately coming to resemble contemporary Western religious sects.[1]

Such movements may provide an initial explanation of defeat simply as a consequence of superior technology, while later explanations argue that the people were once divinely chosen but that, through sin or error, this privilege has been revoked. Particularly in those 'late' responses when militant insurgency is no longer an option, the rationalisation may accommodate, and only sometimes transform, the racist mythology which justifies European supremacy – such as a descent from Noah's son Ham – or indeed reject any 'tradition' altogether in favour of conceptual crumbs from the colonial table.[2]

Deliverance may involve the colonised people or their whole world in shedding an existing skin in a regeneration of the original world underneath; for restoration of a world now upside down demands yet another turning about in which current relations between Black and White will again be reversed. The heaven of certain South African Zionist churches will be entered only by the Blacks (the suffering Christians), for the Whites (the Foolish Virgins) will be turned away from the divine seat: 'The last shall be first.' At the moment when a conscious countertradition is differentiated against the dominant, existing oppositions are heightened. We are what our oppressors are not: 'the members of each group see the stunted parts of their own affective life fully developed – indeed overdeveloped – in the members of the opposite group'.[3]

Those programmes intent on restoring the lost society, and which have been termed 'revitalist' or 'nativist', rejected imposed or adopted European names, together with clothes, the capitalist market and its industrial products. The nineteenth-century Shawnee, Tenskwatawa, known to us as Tecumseh's Prophet, counselled his people to avoid the Whites' food, and advised barter in place of purchase, together with a return to traditional ways of hunting; other groups may temporise with technology whilst awaiting the final purifying redemption. With the complete alienation of land by Europeans a particular notion of something we can call *Nature* tends to develop. Whatever the categorisation before colonisation of a conceptual space opposed to human (particularly male) society, the original native now becomes identified retrospectively with some idealised 'natural' state in which he had once existed in harmony with his (often 'female') environment: a state primitive, elemental and simpler.[4] Failure of the militant Ghost Dance was followed by the development of Earth Lodges where the identity of Native American with the land was to develop a new significance: each Indian becomes a part of his Earth. Smohalla, the prophet of the Wanapum Movement, was reported as declaring: 'The earth was the mother. Agriculture, tilling the soil, or parcelling the land, were all rejected as a violation of the earth . . . You asked me to plough the ground. Shall I take a knife and tear my mother's bosom?'[5]

Turner has argued that certain existing and restricted local institutions, such as shamanism or those we call 'rites of passage', may provide a model for the 'total millennial moment' among the conquered. Characteristics of 'transition' shared by both include the vital sense of spontaneous communality and equality; with the absence of property, status or wealth; the practice of nudity, celibacy, humility and unselfishness; a disregard for conventional appearance; total obedience and a suspension of the usual social rights and obligations;

simplicity and an acceptance of pain and suffering.[6] Existing themes of autochthoneity from the earth, and its representation in woman, may be mobilised, but few movements have attempted a reversion to the *status quo ante* without some modification of traditional values, among which an enhanced public position for women is common, sometimes reflected in the actual gender of the prophet. As in Europe, the 'millennial moment' may frequently enhance any existing conceptual identifications between community, nature and womankind whilst at the same time facilitating some practical autonomy for women.[7]

Radical Puritanism in the Caribbean

The Doukhobors of Canada sing in their anthem:

We need not the rule of kings and crowns,
Neither mansions with splendour enhanced,
Thrones and prisons are part of a system[8]

Apocalyptic and utopian visions of a world upside down are recurring imagery in a radical 'countercurrent' which has flourished in the West since the establishment of Christianity, now hidden, now bursting forth to illuminate whole periods, occasionally represented in dark antinomian acts, forming strange coalitions, and finally declared by Weber to be attenuated into secular humanism, only to re-emerge yet again in the counterculture of the 1960s. It is legitimate to talk of these fissiparous strands and short-lived enthusiasms as a continuing 'tradition' in that the radical millennialists themselves refer back to earlier movements whose oppositional sensibility remains remarkably constant.

As does the idiom. The Rasta term for the deity, 'Jah', has an established radical pedigree, and 'Babylon' represents for Rastas and for the Earth People the established state, as it has for the countless groups which have returned to the Book of Daniel for their inspiration. In the eighteenth century Richard Brothers declared his followers to be the Lost Tribes, and London to be Babylon. The modern state was Babylon, argued the Rappite and the Zoarite communalists of nineteenth-century America, as had the British Seekers and Ranters, while for the competing sects of New England's 'Burned-Over District' the expression was reserved for Catholics or rival sectarians. Enthusiastic Franciscans and Lutherans alike identified the papacy with Babylon, while some Protestant groups preferred the designification of 'Rome', as do the Earth People.[9] Such elisions as the 'Ninneversity' [Nineveh-university] of the New England Puritans anticipate those of Rastafari and Mother Earth. Protestant radicals in Europe have on occasions anticipated a magical flight to the Promised Land; that they were the Lost Tribes and should not eat 'swine flesh'; or that as the End was imminent, artificial law and morality were no longer binding. All these arguments were current among the West Indian slaves, to become central among the Rastas and Earth People.

To trace a distinct history of radical Puritanism in the West Indies is not easy. Rasta identification with the Lost Tribes and the avoidance of pork may simultaneously draw on more recent proselytisation by the Seventh Day Adventists, although a refusal of even non-Muslim slaves to eat pigs was recorded in the Caribbean in the eighteenth century. We do know that Quakers and other radical groups were established in the English-speaking islands by the 1660s as settlers or transported felons, and that Ranters and Anabaptists established communities in Jamaica which were crushed after the Restoration to be replaced by slave plantations.[10] Christopher Hill has made the intriguing suggestion that such groups, deist and egalitarian, may have contributed after their dispersal to the floating republics of the Caribbean pirates, the Brethren of the Coast.[11] The first revolts of the Black slaves in Barbados seem to have been supported by the indentured White servants while Jamaica remained a centre of radical republican dissent well after 1660. Later slave rebellions were frequently blamed on evangelical preachers from Europe whose teachings Taussig has characterised as a 'radical . . . utopia, anarchist and egalitarian, founded in the sacred ways of nature'.[12] Not only the formal idiom, but the very 'style' of Rastafari recalls that of the British millennialists, and it may not be too fanciful to regard it as one of the latest flowerings of our radical Puritan heritage. Donald Wood argues that the Baptist ex-slaves who settled in Trinidad from America after 1812 fused African religions with 'the Puritanism of 16th-Century Münster and East Anglia'.[13] It is unlikely that there was no 'underground' continuity. Unlikely, but any postulated counter-tradition is necessarily difficult to trace in detail.

From the period immediately before the emancipation of the slaves, radical Baptists and other evangelical groups from the United States conducted missions in the West Indies: such sects had developed in Europe not only in opposition to the established church but 'against the state, secular institutions of society or in opposition to or separation from public institutions'.[14] We have to consider also the esoteric (but once politically radical) Masonic and Rosicrucian near-pantheism, still represented locally in high science, which probably arrived in Trinidad with the French refugees from Sainte Domingue, together with the conflicts between radical republicans and monarchists which characterised early nineteenth-century Trinidad.[15]

Coherent tradition or not, the contours of radical millennialism demonstrate images and possibilities which continually appear in any Western oppositional ideology, whether represented in everyday 'strategies of resistance' and personal conscience, or structured into enduring groups. Popular millennial expectations in early modern Europe had looked for a return to a purer original state. The very term 'revolution' implied such a cyclical return. Millennialists in Britain anticipated a return to Edenic purity, to the communalism of the early Christians (I Corinthians 10: 24) or, at the least, to the restoration of the rights of the Anglo-Saxon common man; they lived in a biblical present in which the last days were being enacted, and for which they cited familiar Old and New Testament texts. For some even their relationship to the Bible was equivocal, for scriptural authority could only be temporal and compromised when faced with the Christ within and the imminent intervention of the deity: 'The letter killeth but the spirit giveth life.' At the same time, as with contemporary rural Trinidadians, they lived in a world whose explanations, idiom and style were characteristically biblical. 'They will state that they have no Bible among them', a visitor observed of the Doukhobors, 'yet to all questions put to them regarding their faith, they reply with words drawn from the Holy Scriptures.'[16] The secularisation of the vision of the New Jerusalem in what we now conceive of as the left-wing political tradition, itself countering an increasingly secular establishment from the seventeenth century onwards, moved away from this cyclical return into a linear potential of totally new human relationships, but the promise of removing those historically imposed constraints on the human spirit, to release again its pristine dawn, remains to haunt both the libertarians' notion of 'nature' and the Marxists' 'alienation'.

Women as nature
Among the late medieval coalescences of the countercurrent we can include the Lollards, the Brethren of the Free Spirit, the radical Hussites, mystics like Boehme and Langland, and later the Neoplatonic pastoral of the Tudor poets. Whether peasant revolt or aristocratic poesy, the common threads which continue to recur are a rejection of the established church, with its sacraments and priestly power; a sense of the communality of believers and of the particular closeness of the poor and oppressed to Christ; a guiding inner light and sometimes the recognition of divinity in all things. More radical groups in Britain, the Ranters and Levellers, added a rejection of state authority, of the established professions of law and medicine; opposition to standing armies; a radical revision of marriage, and social equality for women; together with the occasional suggestion that heaven and hell were perhaps of this world. A continuing interest in astrology and in correspondences between human and an animate nature led, in some cases, to frank 'pantheistical materialism';[17] for

some, opposition to any human law proceeded to the communism of property, to free love and the ultimate salvation of all people.

From the end of the sixteenth century when, Weber tells us, we 'historically abandoned the garden of enchantment for means-ends rationality', these visions became transformed through Deism and Unitarianism to Humanism, New Thought and socialism. They recur among the Romantic poets. 'Art is the Tree of Life, Science is the Tree of Death', wrote Blake, whose use of homonyms, paranomosia and polysemy immediately recall the inspirations of the Puritan radicals; as do his arguments. Some anticipate those of Mother Earth: the opposition of Urthona (Earth Owner) to Urizen (Your Reason) and Nobodaddy (God), morning/mourning, sun/son.[18] Percy Shelley's *Queen Mab* proposed a female pantheon, in which God and religion are simply man-made devices for legitimating the tyranny of law and government; the Earth is now physically changing to initiate a period when time will cease and love will govern all.

Shelley dreamt of anarchist utopias – 'kingless continents sinless as Eden' – and such visions were integral to the American communal experiments which involved over a hundred groups and perhaps a tenth of a million people in the eighteenth and nineteenth centuries. They included mystico-pietist groups with Hermetic interests (such as the Woman in the Wilderness community), Anabaptist fundamentalists, and 'rationalist' Owenite or Fourierist programmes.[19] Some emphasised rejection of the state, together with opposition to slavery, and to conventional marriage, in favour of pacifism and economic self-sufficiency. Egalitarians, self-styled 'peculiar people', they fulminated against racism,[20] war, the criminal code and the treatment of the insane, and even the tendency to force left-handers to become right-handed.[21] The Doukhobors of Canada still await the fall of temporal government when 'the complete unification of the nations would result'.[22] Communitarians avoided 'social' titles and given names, called each other Brother or Sister, and adopted distinctive and sometimes paradoxical modes of dress and speech, the Shakers even transcribing spontaneous glossolalia into their everyday hymnals.

'Outside they show a statue of the Mother, inside they is all Father . . . Rome is He, they have you under control, Church and State' (Mother Earth). Although women in the West have provided the majority of Christianity's devotees, they are rarely found in its higher organisational reaches. They are marginal in its practice, text and fable, serving merely as intercessors or mediators between a deity – represented on earth through a male priesthood and episcopate – and his human subjects. By contrast, asserted the radical utopians, God is asexual or bisexual, perhaps even female. Various alternatives to conventional marriage countered the manifestation of the patriarchal God in the domestic father, while on occasion sexual activity itself was avoided altogether in imminent expectation of the End. Avoidance of sex, and thus pregnancy, went together with an enhanced social and spiritual role for women in many ecstatic and millennial movements. As a sour cleric observed, 'from the Montanist movement onwards, the history of enthusiasm is largely a history of female emancipation'.[23] Cathars, Albigensians, Old Believers and others oscillated between the poles of sexual abstinence and promiscuity, between what Ronald Knox terms 'rigorism' and 'scandal'. Both poles repudiated the family with its roots in property and in the subjugation of women. Some of the American communal programmes attempted celibacy while others practised polygamy, group sex or free love. Others experimented with all simultaneously: in the Spiritual Marriage advocated by Lucina Umphreville successive physical pairings with different partners continued until a couple found the perfect (celibate) match. On occasion Fabians and Theosophists too attempted to 'transcend' sex.

Radical prophets were often women, even if organisation tended eventually to pass into the hands of men as the millennial moment became consolidated in not so new structures. Many argued sexual equality from the passage in the Apochrypha (I Esdras 4) where Zorobabel lists the powers which women by their nature have over men. Groups like the Shakers which were founded by women argued for androgynous or bisexual deities, with radically new relations between men and women, both in doctrine and in the practical organisation of the sect.

From arcadia to utopia

'The earth was not made purposely for you to be lords of it, and we to be your slaves, servants and beggars; but it was made to be a common livelihood to all, without respect of persons' (Gerrard Winstanley, *A Declaration From the Poor Oppressed People of England*). One of the sources of our Western countercurrent lay in the medieval peasant arcadia of Cockaigne, the fairy-tale topsy-turvy land where there exists a natural abundance of food but no oppressive nobility or interfering lawyers. In this poor man's heaven 'all is commune to young and old, to stout and sterne, meek and bold'. The early modern representation of this alimentary paradise (together with its herbal remedies, wise women, astrologers, almanacks and celestial signs) seems associated with what Hobsbawm has termed the 'prepolitical response' of social bandits and popular outlaws, of ludic and transvestite Luddites rebelling against changes from above, in an aggressive levelling of the traditional enemies of the poor – prelates, lawyers, land surveyors, foreigners, dealers – in a dramatic but futile attempt to regenerate a stable agrarian peasant society:

'Ils ont ravasé les vergers, les cultures scientifiques, coupé les arbres fruitiers
. . . Il fallait égaliser le domaine, l'aplanir, pour rendre le partage possible et
équitable.'[24]

Maurice and Jean Bloch have noted that our word 'nature' carries in
contemporary Europe four associated meanings: the chronologically pre-
social; an internal bodily process; the universal and inevitable order of the
organic and inorganic; and (perceived or imagined) 'primitive' peoples.[25] All
find resonances in Mother Earth's preexistent and elemental domain of the
Mother of the Nation. Such an Arcadia is a rather comfortable and cheerful
place recalling the sylvan liberties of Cockaigne and Arden, the domicile of
the wild men and Robin Hood in the Tudor masques, rather than the grim
wilderness of Judaeo-Christianity in which man only encounters God in brief
and arduous encounters. 'Mother Nature' recalls us to a bountiful Merrie
England, not the Sinai desert.

For the classical Greeks, the Earth, emanating out of chaos, had been a
sensate organism. Usually personified as female, she was the ultimate origin of
all, and the various Hellenistic cults of the Great Mother acknowledged her as
the active and fundamental source of our being. By contrast, the Old Testament
God, who got around to creating the Earth only on the third day, kept her firmly
in a subordinate position, for had he not conjured her *ex nihilo*? A 'Mother
Earth' did survive in Christianity, like the planets of the pagans but unlike their
gods, an Earth of somewhat undifferentiated matter rather than volition, which
awaited arousal and impregnation by a man formed in God's image. As Simone
de Beauvoir puts it, 'the husbandman marvelled at the mystery of the fecundity
that burgeoned in his furrows and in the maternal body' – a sleeping
fecundity that required awakening and then control.[26] Mother Nature had lost
her primacy; in the medieval cosmos Man and Nature remained distinct but
associated through the dominion given to Man by a transcendent deity. The
land was not to be supplicated but subjugated, ordered, for 'every moving thing
that liveth shall be meat for you'.[27]

By contrast, to quote the Ranters: 'When we die we shall be swallowed up
into the infinite spirit as a drop into the ocean and so be as we were; and if ever
we be raised again, we shall rise a horse, a cow, a root, a flower and such like.'[28]
The Familists and Giordano Bruno too had asserted that a Mother Nature rather
than a God still governed the world, but the new mechanical science of the
Renaissance offered rather a continued domination over a divinely ordered
world, leading Man to 'Nature with all her children to bind her to your service
and make her your slave', to Bacon's 'truly masculine birth of time [in which
man] would conquer and subdue Nature, to shake her to her foundations'.
Mother Nature was to be first stripped naked and then penetrated by Man; the

Royal Society promised its male scientists that 'The Beautiful Bosom of Nature will be Exposed to our view . . . We shall enter its Garden, and taste of its Fruits and satisfy ourselves with its plenty.'[29] Something not so very different remains the everyday view of Nature in Trinidad. Nineteenth-century Trinidad, Donald Wood notes, was 'bewitched' with notions of boundless fertility; at the abolition of slavery only one-thirtieth of the land was under cultivation.[30] While members of the revolutionary commune in Naipaul's novel *Guerrillas* (1975) seem to parallel some of the arguments of Mother Earth herself – 'All revolutions begin with the land. Men are born on the earth, every man has his one spot, it is his birth-right'[31] – their suggestion that one gains one's identity through cultivating the fertile soil does not immediately evoke everyday Trinidadian resonances. Rather, urban Trinidadians feel attached to the soil by default: they would be elsewhere if they could, for the land now seems marginal to the real life of London, New York or even Port-of-Spain. Though rural self-sufficiency is sometimes economically necessary as a springboard or failsafe, it is hardly the ultimate goal.

Usage of land in the West Indies is justified by unrestricted cognatic descent with rights to family land for all descendants, the use of which is informally agreed, and in Jamaica where land may be said to have a greater political salience because of its relative scarcity it is indeed 'paradoxically apparently boundless' as Jean Besson puts it, 'serving primarily as a symbol of person-hood, prestige, security and freedom for descendants of former slaves'. A resource not property. But in cosmopolitan post-war Trinidad, 'agriculture was linked with backwardness and degradation . . . agriculture was what you wanted to escape from'.[32] While humans are closely associated with the Trinidadian land through the sickness-bush correspondences of local medicine, the two remain distinct: bush exists to serve men. The earth is not always regarded as especially female in spite of its agricultural association with the moon; the land may be practically 'male', if it is gendered at all, by association with men's work, rather than as something female to be worked on by man (for men and women perform similar agricultural tasks). Both Mother Earth and Naipaul's fictional guerrillas draw less on the rural Trinidadian peasant's prosaic attitude to the earth than on urban and Romantic notions of a hypostasised Nature. The very word *nature* is seldom used in Trinidad English except in the sense of sexual desire, particularly that of men, although its other meanings are recognised and Mother Earth's alternative name of 'Mother Nature' only occasionally causes a snigger: 'supporting nature is like taking a long sweet drink: you will just drink and go on so. You take as much as your appetite can take. Like a man is married and his wife start have children he has to go outside to get something to satisfy his nature.'[33] *Nature* in Trinidad is something inevitable and independent of conscious will; to restrain it is dangerous. It is not just the sexual impulse itself but the very inevitability of conception manifest in the number of children a woman is predetermined to bear: an inevitability which can only be countered through a self-defeating, 'respectable' but arid, choice between contraception and abstinence.

The Romantics' cultivation of Nature transformed the ascetic vision of the walled New Jerusalem into a fertile garden, and the pilgrim into a gardener. 'When I was digging in my earthly garden a-digging with my spade', said the mystic Roger Crab, 'I saw into the Paradise of God from whence my father Adam was cast forth.' In the eighteenth century 'nature cults' – Martinism, Masonry, Theophilanthropy – proliferated together with the artificial Arcadia of landscape gardening; the end of topiary presaged the end of swaddling, for the child was to be cultivated in its nursery as a tender plant. Like the Earth People, the children of the French Revolution took the names of fruits; to 'culture' implied natural growth and organic continuity rather than the inculcating of rigid and artificial institutions. Man could not however completely surrender to Nature for he still planted and plundered her: the urban gardener's vision of a vanished Eden was only a nostalgic pastiche, and the Liberty Tree just a maypole. Medieval Christianity, mechanical science and Romanticism alike allowed that Man could dominate the rest of creation 'out there'. Even the Ranter pantheist had to deal with the problem of what was going on when he ate a plant (a transformation within Nature?), and whether that was any less significant than if he ate an animal or indeed another human.

The same question emerges in Hell Valley. If all is Nature why is it somehow less appropriate to kill an animal for meat than to cultivate and eat a plant? The Earth People certainly have a notion of a 'weed'. While their clearing of the apparently undifferentiated bush to bring forth cultivated crops can be seen simply as transformations and reorganisations within Nature, their refusal to eat animals argues for some residual Natural hierarchy. To gather rather than to cultivate is certainly an option for the hardline vegetarian – like those Doukhobors who said they could live on fruit and honey – but the very notion of gathering itself demonstrates some hierarchy within Nature; pantheism, if pursued to one logical end, might include meat-eating, perhaps even cannibalism. If all such ingestions are merely transformations in an essentially undifferentiated domain, the way lies freely open to amoral antinomianism. This particular logical difficulty (and utopians are the most determined of logicians) has led many groups to alternate, as with sexuality, between a rigorous asceticism and a thoroughgoing antinomianism.

William Blake did not regard what we may term 'Romantic gardening' as simply recognising Man's place in Nature: 'as of old so now anew began Babylon again in Infancy, call'd Natural Religion'. Blake, a decided phenomenologist, objected to the idea that Nature was something external which could be apprehended independently of our self-consciousness. She is a projection of us and thus 'Everything that lives is Holy.' Rousseau solved the problem rather differently when he distinguished the Natural from the Social as two rather different types of knowledge and being. Man was both Social (in his institutions) and Natural (in his bodily feelings); in the *Discourse on Equality* he tends to argue a preference for the latter, but in *The Social Contract* he accepts an interplay between the Social and Natural. This distinction between Nature as a type of undifferentiated stuff and bodily experience, contrasted with the Social as mental organisation and institution, leads us from radical Puritanism to contemporary social science, and to socialism; from cyclical returns to a linear unfolding in evolutionary time. The remaining millennialists have continued to see Nature and Society as distinct but comparable domains of the same type of established order.

Whatever the logical snares – whether they regarded God as in His garden, as part of the garden itself, or as altogether outside it – the radical counter-current deployed an idea of Nature to demonstrate the artificiality and unreality of existing social institutions. Whether we take its communities as atavistically harking back to some lost peasant Arcadia or as radically new utopian institutions, they were conceived in a harmony with a physical world which embraced all things, a harmony which was already demonstrated by the tribal peoples. A common conclusion was that land could not really be owned; along with Rousseau and Winstanley, the countercurrent argued that human alienation and inequality are rooted alike in property. The Shakers taught that North American Indians had a superior religion to Christianity precisely because it was not rooted in a capitalist exploitation of nature.[34]

Some American communalists, most notably the Shakers, were committed technological innovators, but others rejected all mechanical novelties. Few have resembled the Earth People in actually discarding technologies which may be termed 'traditional'. Enthusiastic Doukhobors on occasion freed their beasts of burden and pulled the carts themselves; when one tried to introduce a threshing machine his comrades burnt it; some gave up all iron tools for through slavery 'people are tortured to obtain ore'.[35] Among the American Rappites and the Brotherhood of the New Life, as among the Earth People, bodily labour took on a virtually sacramental quality. One Doukhobor leader taught that the more one ate plants 'raised by an abundance of solar energy', the more one approached pure energy itself, and that with moderate consumption, within a hundred years, 'the earth would have time to clothe itself completely and return to its primitive condition'.[36] As in the Valley of Decision, potentially dangerous animals were tolerated or even encouraged to wander through Doukhobor villages.

While utopian communalists have often elided certain established categories (between human and divine, between parent and child, between the sexes), they recognised and reinforced another distinction, that which is 'natural' – real, original, authentic and fundamental – in opposition to the interferences or artificial contrivances of human society. The American Shakers avoided allowing fowl of one type from hatching the eggs of another, or grafting plants onto different stocks. Mother Earth too abhors artificial insemination and contraception for both are part of the Interference by which all humans, Black and White alike, are to be replaced by machine forms conjured by the Son out of Nature. As for other millennial radicals, only disaster can attend any curious tampering with the natural order. Sickness itself is caused by Science, and treatment should employ folk anodynes, herbs and infusions, not professional medicine. The Natural growth of the child unfettered by Science represents the possibility and actuality of the nascent community: their intuition is valued over formal teaching. As she puts it:

I don' learn it; I receive it from the cells of my brain. I don' use Science; when I see it, I know it. The education is a cramp to keep you in the city, cramp the brain there because everyone is only thinking the bush is not good to go in. So they keeping you away from your natural self. (That's the Spirit, to keep you how he want you, in his image and like- ness.) You know, it's a funny thing, it's something sad to really know what is life. It is sad because when you get to find out the truth about life and look at yourself, how you live, you see in there you're wasting down yourself, not really living, just wasting, because the teachings you have is to live on death and wait for a 'judgement for the dead to raise'. But this 'judgement' and 'the dead to raise' – is you yourself that is the dead because, without the senses of life, you are dead. You become dead in body. You have to say because your body is clothed so then it is dead, a living dead. So when they speak about 'raising the dead', to me they give it to you in parables and some people don't understand. Even me didn't understand neither because my self did not really call me yet to know myself. But now I have the understanding, the senses to know that, when they say 'death' they are speaking about the living because you never die. Is just the Flesh goes back to itself, the Earth turn back to slime and salt once more, and the Spirit come again in the next form of Flesh.

The majority don't know it, so they do a lot of judging before the hour. Why? Because of their education that they receive: 'Wait for a Judgement Day.' And they is telling me 'When the Judgement Day come you are going to find out!' I am going to find out? And I watching them: 'What Judgement Day are you speaking about? It is now!' They still can't understand. So then the Bible is just to put away and forget. Burn it and let your senses keep coming to understand yourself and know yourself. Any life you get rid of the Book, you get rid of the Son in a form, so that you will be able to start developing your senses because the brains will be free of the Book. The cells will be

able to burst that your senses can come . . . The Church is about to fall, the people are
seeing themselves!

Divine leaders, divine sin

One can present Mother Earth as a materialist yet a certain two-memberedness
persists, represented in The Earth and Her Spirit (page 80). I find it helpful
to read them as immanent and transcendent aspects of the same Mother, in
kabbalistic terms as the 'lower' and 'upper roots'. Although she would
certainly disdain a title of Deity, Jeanette does recognise herself as some
preexistent and omnipotent power. Such assumptions of 'divine identity' in
religious visionaries are not infrequent, if less common than that of the merely
human prophet who claims a divine origin for their message. Divinity may be
offered to religious leaders in their lifetime and refused; the Jamaican Rastas
informed a bemused Haile Selassie that he was God but he declined the
honour, nor did Jiddu Krishnamurti accept Godhood when Annie Besant
proposed it. The acceptance of something like divine status by a leader is
frequently the occasion for an assumption of insanity, for the movement seems
clearly marginal and unsuccessful, out of touch with the shared everyday
reality with which it has to engage.[37]

What actually constitutes the claim to 'divinity' is not however as obvious
as it might seem. We need to restrict the argument to those groups for which
monotheism offers a model; we are not concerned with the extent to which
Tiberius was 'divine' but with those situations in which identification is made
with a single omnipotent deity. All the Doukhobor leaders have claimed to be
either God or Jesus, a claim which has, naturally enough, antagonised other
Canadians, yet the Doukhobors also say 'Let us bow down to the God in one
another.'[38] Similarly, the Black Muslims of the United States argue that all
Black people are divine although their founder appears to have initiated the
idea when claiming that he (alone) was divine.[39] Attributions of divinity may
be assumed by outsiders who conclude from a personal interview with the
leader that he alone is regarded as divine when he is merely rather provoca-
tively asserting the divine nature of all men. This may have been the case with
the Doukhobors. How are we to interpret the encounter in the 1780s between
Robert Hindmarsh, a Swedenborgian, and a man in London's Shoreditch who
told him that 'there was no God in the universe but man and that he himself
was God'?[40] Pantheism, the divinity of mankind, or a more personal
assumption of divinity? Or perhaps just a statement of ideas that no death is
'natural' as with the Jamaican Rastas? Another problem is the self-protective
dissimulation of many sectarians: Hasidim may privately believe their rebbe
to be the Messiah even if he would deny this, and Sun Myung Moon appears

to encourage his followers to regard him as God whilst never publicly admitting it.

There appear to be various related positions, all of which may be held simultaneously by different members of a group, or at different times. The leader alone may be recognised as divine and has consequent authority; or the whole community (or all people or creation) are divine; or else the community or mankind just have some sort of 'divine spark', the presence of the Holy Spirit or another emanation of divinity, within them; or else an essentially materialist message is couched in a biblical idiom. A situation in which it seems that only the leader is divine, but which then turns out to be one where all followers are virtually divine, may mean in practice that the leader actually has less authority than in a movement where he alone claims the status of a prophet or of some not-quite-divine figure such as the numerous Spouses of Christ, Brothers of the Almighty or Women Clothed with the Sun. As with the Quakers and Shakers, the group may move from one position to another, usually but not always from divine leader to the divinity of all. As with the Earth People, what appears to the outsider as an extraordinary novelty may not be of any great practical importance to the group themselves in the course of everyday life.

The radical Puritans in seventeenth-century Britain furnish numerous instances. Some clearly distinguished themselves as personally divine or semi-divine but others, like George Fox, were perhaps merely demonstrating a general feeling that a chosen generation were enacting the Last Days, or else were part of the general Ranter and Quaker 'spreading out of divinity' through provocative antinomian acts and statements. As such we may take the respected Independent minister William Franklin who decided he was God and became a Ranter, or the Hackney bricklayer who said he was as much God as Jesus Christ had been.[41] Pantheism or blasphemous atheism? The distinction is difficult to draw given the prevailing biblical idiom. Beards and long hair were common in imitation of Christ, and John Donne's son observed that everybody in Massachusetts seemed to be kings or 'Christ the Messiahs'; one Bostonian said he was Christ – as was everybody else.[42] Nor can we assume that individuals or groups were consistent or even (in the case of the Ranters at least) altogether serious.

Divine claimants have appeared transiently in Afro-American groups. An early Rasta, Leonard Howell, seems to have lost his following when he claimed personal divinity, and Alexander Bedward, a Native Baptist pastor, identified himself with Christ and in 1921 tried to ascend into Heaven.[43] In Trinidad, one of the members of Michael X's commune, Hakim Jamal, claimed to be God, while the White founder of the Jonestown community was believed by some followers to be divine. From the 1930s until the 1950s Father Divine headed a large and influential Black church in the United States incorporating a network of factories, stores and housing projects. Recourse to professional medicine was prohibited as Father Divine was credited with miraculous healing powers; and in 1936 his church, the International Righteous Government Convention, unanimously passed the motion that 'Father Divine is God.' Father Divine had started off as the follower of another God who assigned him a junior divine status (God in the Sonship Degree); some disgruntled followers who felt that everybody was God then left the movement in disgust.[44]

The 'diffusion' of divinity appears characteristic of groups which have outlasted the death of divine founders such as the Black Muslims, Shakers and Muggletonians. From the very beginning the Quakers discredited aspirants to individual divinity such as Nayler, and the notion of the divinity of all members passed rapidly into one of a 'divine spark'. Among the Doukhobors, pantheism and messianic leadership appear to have co-existed quite comfortably for over a hundred years, but for a larger and proselytising group, the death of the divine founder is difficult to negotiate, and the group collapses; early Christianity may appear the exception but Jesus' divinity was probably conferred posthumously. Whether personal claims to divinity are really more common among those who are mentally ill is uncertain: it may be an obvious rationalisation for those leaders who *become* psychotic, thus demonstrating an apparent association between divine leadership and fragility of the group.

'Divine leadership' appears then to cover a variety of rather different situations. In the case of Mother Earth she certainly seems to take a transcendent identity rather different from that of her followers and one which appears modelled on the incarnate Christ. She represents in her physical being a First Cause, virtually eternal and pre-existent. The Christian God is subordinated to a role as Her Son, and other monotheistic divinities are identified as partial understandings of either Mother or Son. Yet the Spirit of the Mother is immanent in everything where it contends with the Spirit of Her Son. The Mother literally embodies Nature, consubstantial with the whole of creation, with the very ground of being, less some deity than a concentration, a leading cusp of a Spinozean unfolding. Her biblical idiom passes over into pantheism or even hylozoism; the Son, it is true, will be exiled to his planet and thus perhaps remain distinct as a principle, but the rest of Nature will, in a very real sense, return to Her, to be reconciled in its original form. Whether She will then maintain some separate identity is none too clear; as we shall see (page 201), these questions are of no great interest to her followers, unlike their way of life.

There ai' no sin. They say you born in sin. He say that but it is He because He interfere
so He sin. Sin is what is not belonging to you. It is He. He entered into flesh so you are
'living in sin'. So then this judgement have to be whilst you are living and what is the
judgement? You judging yourself, seeing yourself, to know left from right. Is you is
the one that have to judge yourself.   (Mother Earth)

It is not uncommon for messianic leaders to find themselves doing 'strange
acts', as when George Rapp or Mother Earth burn their Bibles and take off their
clothes. Indeed they may claim a licence to engage in acts which are prohibited
to their own followers, or which are certainly regarded as immoral or illogical
in the wider society: nudity, blasphemy, insult, the destruction of property,
gratuitous violence, even incest and comparatively indiscriminate sexual
relations. The Doukhobor leader Peter the Purger was frequently drunk and
his statements at these times were said to have a 'veiled' meaning for the
community, so that his 'upside down' discourse left his followers assuming
that his real wishes were the opposite of those he expressed.

As with the seventeenth-century Jewish messiah Sabbatai Svi, the invitation
of the leader for all to invert conventional morality through adultery or incest
may herald the topsy-turvy world of the Last Days, or at least some
fundamentally new relationship to the ultimate reality. While a reforming
movement's disgust at the disparity between the professed morality of the
existing society and its actual performance may lead them to stricter conventional behaviour, it may also lead to an inverting of the accepted moral tenets
altogether. That the same movement (or moment) can rapidly pass from one to
the other is less an indication of mental instability than of alternative solutions
to the same problem: the gap between ideal and practical possibility. Where
emphasis is already placed on personal redemption or on the faith of the elect,
antinomianism – breaking the law for the value inherent in the act of breaking
– may be preferred to ultra-orthodoxy.

Although the breaking of convention by the leader alone is usually
interpreted as duplicity (as when Father Divine refused sexual relations to all
except himself), it can also be taken as a general solution to the vexed problem
which any new movement has to face: how much common ground is to be
shared with the old order and how can a new dispensation be offered to
potential recruits in the language of the old? Each person is struggling to work
out the new ideas in the language and sensibilities of the old, particularly in the
early stages before a distinct new tradition and autonomous institutions have
been established. Antinomianism is a virtually inevitable characteristic of the
apocalyptic vision, less a psychological imperative in itself than simply the
passage from one dispensation to another. 'Failed' movements have not
necessarily failed because they are antinomian, but, as they are those groups

which have not transformed these acts into alternative institutions, their 'antonomianism' remains behind as their most striking feature. At the same time, the personal motivation to engage in 'unnatural' behaviour depends on our individual identification with the leader and on our responses to the established order, whether motivated by disgust, playfulness or sheer perversity: some unitary notion of an antinomian psychology is not helpful. Christopher Hill, who has done much to recover for us the countercurrents of the seventeenth century (when Ranters swore and smoked during their services and practised assiduous fornication), notes the earlier folk aphorism 'There's no heaven but women, nor no hell but marriage' to suggest the Ranters were a systematisation and universalisation of existing popular male patterns,[45] an interpretation I have argued (page 230) for the Rastas and Mother Earth. It is the awareness by others of the wider moral context and of the sectarians' own motivation which leads them to label such radical perversity as 'heresy' rather than as simple ignorance or wilful blasphemy.

Provocation may be our deliberate tactic, persuading the majority to recognise the illusory nature of their own values and practices, as when the Quakers went 'naked for a sign'. By destroying our own property (as do the Doukhobors in burning their houses and dynamiting the tombs of their leaders), we can also shame the majority into certain political concessions. Georges Devereux has styled this tactical response *chantage masochiste* and suggested it is characteristic of millennial cults developing in response to overwhelming European power: apart from any immediate advantages, such personal loss does of course demonstrate to the wider world how unimportant for us are mundane possessions; the destruction, usually by fire, of our own possessions or livelihood commits us to a more radical and future perspective.

Radical Puritanism's original 'amoral superman' (as Norman Cohn styles him) was Jan of Leyden who burnt all the books in the city of Münster except the Bibles. Mother Earth seems to be the first West Indian to take matters further and actually burn her Bible but this practice is not uncommon among others who value the Spirit above society. As the Ranters maintained 'If that within thee do not condemn thee, thou shalt not be condemned.' It occurred in eighteenth-century America during the Great Awakening; the Ranters too burned their Bibles, as did some of Cromwell's soldiers in the 1650s. The Thuringian Blood Friends copulated on the Bible, and many antinomian acts recall the Church's fantasies of demonic inversion – the Templars' Black Mass and so on. Both fantasy and actual practice represent an inversion of tightly ordered dominant values experienced as monolithic and inevitable. When the enthusiasts of the New Model Army burnt their Bibles they were only extending the iconoclastic practices of the period, destroying religious images and using 'steeple houses' for the stabling of their horses. Whatever the immediate intentions and experiences of its participants, antinomian moments can be seen as leaps in the direction of the plural, the psychological and the secular, both through their demonstration that the existing social order is not inevitable, and in their assumption of some implicit higher moral order beyond the social law and beyond its negation.

Soft energies and the return of the Earth Mother

The Earth People are originally townspeople. They grew up in Port-of-Spain where a well-travelled and informed working class read newspapers and magazines, and went regularly to the cinema. They were distantly aware of that rediscovery and brief efflorescence of the radical impulse in the 1960s with its hippies, Flower Power, Earth Mothers and, not so far removed, the ecological and women's movements. The carnivalesque atmosphere of the counterculture recalls that the Port-of-Spain masqueraders, and the compliment was returned in 1978 when hippies and a 'Mother Earth' were featured as a Carnival band.

The precise intellectual shift from European millennialism to socialism is still a matter of debate, but by the late nineteenth century, in both Britain and America, the radicals' overtly 'religious' interests had clearly become less a replay of the apocalyptic messianism of Münster than a discovery of Indian religion, a conflation of neoplatonism, Swedenborgianism, Mesmerism and Romantic nature-mysticism out of which emerged a variety of sects, of which Theosophy has proved the most enduring. In the counterculture, these rather marginal concerns became central, in part through a disappointment with 'rational' communism among the intellectual left and a renewed anxiety over unbalanced technological change. Radical utopianism resurfaced in the sixties, coinciding poignantly with the last days of the Shakers, perhaps the most influential of all the American communalist experiments. For the first time since the Puritan settlements, a political radicalism fused with religious mysticism became influential, almost dominant, American preoccupations. In the United States, the absence of a coherent left-wing politics led to a counterculture relatively independent of the existing Left, and thus more daring in its cosmological conjectures. Its idiom of 'authenticity' carried an implication of alienation, with a search for the 'unspoiled, pristine, genuine, untouched, traditional'.[46] Lionel Trilling has suggested this idea of authenticity developed in the course of our move from medieval role-bound formal behaviour, through Romantic sincerity, to more internalised and individualised values.[47] The 'informality' of the counterculture was then only a further manifestation of what we might call the modern 'American style' – the privileging of 'genuine' face-to-face encounters over ascribed social stratification. Hippie communes championed the idiosyncrasy of the outsiders against a bourgeois society which failed to accept them, and the quest for authenticity led many to those Eastern religions which offered a path of 'growth' – of paradox, logical subversion and personal change – and which had been popularised by Aldous Huxley and Alan Watts. Martin Buber's studies on Hasidism contributed a 'primitive pansacramentalism', the idea of a spontaneous community whose gay irrationality and folly did much to produce the carnival-like atmosphere of the political demonstrations against the Vietnam War. Fuelled by an environmental hylozoism ('ecopsychic mission', 'biospheric egalitarianism'), a renascent and ludic paganism, variously calling itself Serpent Power or Mother Earth Worship, rediscovered ley lines, along with Margaret Murray's witches, tarot cards and Glastonbury. As the Shakers had done, the hippies identified Amerindian shamans as the original ecologists, and for them the anthropologist Carlos Castaneda created a shaman with the timeless wisdom of the East, while do-it-yourself shamanic textbooks reread shamans as contemporary moral philosophers, etiquette guides to spontaneity.

Among the wider legacies of the counterculture are a continued informal, relatively unstructured, libertarian idiom,[48] with the separation of sexual morphology and activity from gender roles in the Gay and Women's Movements. The activities of the Animal Liberation Movement are only the leading edge of 'animal rights' and 'ecological consciousness'; campaigns against factory farming and the killing of whales attract popular support far beyond those of the earlier anti-vivisectionists. Alternative technology, ecology parties, and Greenpeace have entered the political mainstream, while James Lovelock's 'Gaia hypothesis' (on the mutual relationship between life forms and the physical evolution of the earth), like 'creation theology' and Rupert Sheldrake's idea of the divine as 'an evolving morphogenic field', have been read as texts for a living earth. The fashionable goal of psychotherapy is now, not symptom removal, but 'growth' – authenticity as an accessible commodity. While non-renewable sources of energy are 'unbalanced',[49] unlimited personal growth becomes a possibility for the New Age pantheist. In perhaps the final accolade, sociobiologists have declared that our love of nature is itself 'natural'.[50] If time is running out, nature 'out there', in an almost Hegelian incorporation, can yet be reconciled.

The cover of a recent book on our place in nature declares that:

In the polluted, highly urbanised world we live in today, all humanity is struggling for life, like plants without roots. Those who lived here in the vanished past were well aware of the overwhelming need to nurture the Earth. They knew that without the fertility and fecundity of the Earth, they would surely die. Modern agriculture uses chemicals in great quantities. Our ancestors were not so reckless: they *worshipped* the Earth – the Great Earth Mother.[51]

The androgynous style of the hippies – for men long hair, jewellery, flowered and brightly coloured clothes and shoulder bags – accentuated the conventionally 'feminine' in both sexes, with the woman as a cliched Earth Mother – fecund, flowing, soft. gentle, nurturant, absorbent. She placed herself in opposition to the more 'masculine' androgyny through which, in the course of the twentieth century, women had become short-haired, apparently longer-legged and leaner, infertile, angry and publicly assertive. The Women's Movement initially continued the 'hard-edged' trend: women were equal to men in potential, and traditional women's tasks were no more fitted to women than they were to men. Feminist style was androgynous in a 'masculine' way – cropped hair, men's work clothes, no make-up, corsets, bras or jewellery. Social and political equality alike were predicated, if not exactly on an identical morphology, than on one whose sexual differentiation held few social consequences beyond that of men's brute strength.

Trinidad's Mother Earth is quite aware of this turn away from traditional gender roles. It is not one of which she approves, for, beyond the conflict of master and slave, of White and Black, lies, for her, one more fundamental, the struggle between the sexes for the power to create, between Science and Nature. It is only Woman who can create new life, and Man must stand and envy or else develop his science in a grotesque and dangerous parody of her fecundity. In the End we can perhaps return to some type of androgynous form for certainly we all bore once 'both prick and cunt' but this cannot occur until we relinquish technology. At the same time, Mother Earth is sympathetic to the assertion of a women's voice, of their cry of oppression; their Natural tasks – childbearing and childrearing – have been pushed to the margins by masculine science. Men should neither seek to emulate women nor to dominate them but rather to complement them.

By the 1980s, some years after Mother Earth's visions, a section of the women's movement had also moved away from an equality of identity to one of 'soft-edged' complementarity: women's bodies now *are* significantly different and this determines their aspirations, abilities and rights. Like the Rastas' reassertion of *no behaviour*, or the Native American's taking up the European's ascription to them of Mother Earth worship, these Ecofeminists[52] now agree with the male chauvinist that women are more emotional, less assertive, less driven to power, and more suited for childrearing and nurturance. And a good thing too; for women could only be 'morally immature' by reference to dangerously instrumental, abstract, rule-determined, costive moral reasoning – an embodied male rationality. Greer, for instance, has moved from the earlier 'equality through identity' position to one which associates women primarily with fertility,[53] through references to 'the tribal family' and to a fabled pre-industrial past without artificial contraception; population programmes for developing nations are racist, and everywhere men hate and fear the parturant woman. Like Mother Earth, Chesler argues that: 'Male science, male alchemy, is partially rooted in male uterus envy, in the desire to be able to create something miraculous out of male inventiveness. However, men in science have carried us all to the brink of total planetary, genetic and human destruction. Repressed and unresolved uterus-envy is a dangerous emotion.'[54]

The nineteenth-century fable of a primitive matriarchy which worshipped a Great Goddess has been retrieved from the history of anthropology and the byways of Marxism to provide a historical legitimation for the coming dominance of women.[55] (For the social anthropologist the irony of affirming a historical matriarchy is that of other instances of redefinition: myths of defeated Amazons legitimate current male domination.) The restoration of the Goddess to her bosky throne is to be through a rediscovery of popular magic and the craft of the witch, and other 'left-handed' traditions. Woman can still have recourse to archaic female customs and tasks, as mother, mourner, midwife and wisewoman. Bachofen himself had traced the legacy of the Great Goddess in the survival of Mutterrecht, instances of the primacy of Left over Right, of night over day, moon over sun, earth over sea. Commenting on the *wimmin* (a coinage to avoid the associations of wo*men*) in the camp outside the Greenham Common missile base, Warner notes that they associate the Left of their banners with milk, fruit and flowers, but the Right with weapons. A similar image of the Left is found in Ursula Le Guin's *Left Hand of Darkness* which portrays a utopia in which everyone is a hermaphrodite with cyclical sexual potency.[56] An associated 'countercurrent' theme now emerging in the mainstream Christian churches, is the androgyneity or femininity of God, while some Ecofeminists are frank pantheists, even hylozoists, or at least favour the notion of the Earth as containing a certain wisdom, to be found now by men through observation and empathy, and by women in their own bodies. Marilyn French accuses men of raping both women and nature: 'Man's domination, his lust for power, has nearly destroyed us all. On the brink of annihilation, only woman's force – cyclical, fluid, life-creating – can save us';[57] while the German Green activist, Petra Kelly, has argued that: 'Only if we [women] begin to rediscover our own nature, can we discover new ways of wholeness, balance and decentralisation – can we forge a bond with the Earth and the Moon, living with co-operation, gentleness, non-possessiveness and soft energies.'[58]

The power of the weak

It is not difficult to hear our Trindadian Mother Earth speaking here. Like her, many Ecofeminists style themselves 'witches', following that antiquarian history which argues that medieval agrarian cults revering a female deity were persecuted by Christian priests; women, the ritual celebrants, were identified as leagued with the Devil – as the Goddess, Eve, had come to be called: 'Only by turning over biblical tradition and regarding Eve positively, as the bringer of knowledge and consciousness, can we end permanently the split between spirit and body.'[59] The midwives and traditional healers in early modern Europe are affirmed as women whom the growth of professional medicine pushed, along with their natural remedies, to the margins of 'superstition': the wise woman became transformed first into a witch and then into a demented old woman. Contemporary feminist witches now go *skyclad* (naked), have *moon huts* for menstruation and subscribe to *Earth Religion News*. They perform the ritual of 'drawing down the moon', whilst awaiting the theacracy which will succeed Babylon's nuclear holocaust. Some retell the incestuous Orphic myth:

In the beginning the Goddess Eurynome, mother of all living things, arose naked from chaos . . . she rubbed both winds between her hands to create the great cosmic serpent Orphion. No sooner had life breathed into his nostrils and he saw those divine limbs than he did lust to couple with her . . . Whilst he still saw the divine naked matrix she in fact had metamorphosed into a dove and had laid a large silver egg that shone with divine eminence. Orphion desiring to satisfy his lust, wrapped himself around this egg seven times . . . Out tumbled a thousand suns and moons without number . . . Orphion, stupified and proud, gorged himself on the self-adulation of genetrix and claimed sole authorship in creation. Instead Eurynome bruised his head with her heel. She split his sex as male and female and placed him on the many thousand worlds he created . . . [60]

The personal experiences of womanhood, the common history of the Christian 'countercurrent' and the environmental concerns of the nineteen-seventies have generated remarkably similar themes in Ecofeminism and Mother Earth. The hippie counterculture and Ecofeminism alike have excluded Black people while drawing on other, 'less colonised', nomadic and shamanic societies, but Roszack has argued that there are close psychological and cultural affinities between the middle-class hippie dropout and the 'dropped out' Black of the urban working class.[61] Certainly, the popularity in both settings of psycho-active drugs, particularly cannabis, is articulated in a similar 'hip' language deriving from the 1950s: the hippie and the Trinidadian Rasta both *build a head*, whilst the Earth People are as alert to *bad vibes* as any Californian communard.

The concordance of themes in relatively disparate historical movements do not presume a monolithic countercurrent in the West from which alone we may derive 'influences'. Although the radical Puritans knew the writings of their predecessors, the same themes emerge in contexts where intellectual and social continuity is difficult to trace. While the Ecofeminists and Earth People appear to appropriate elements of radical Puritanism in the Americas, it would be mistaken to see them only as local manifestations of some homogeneous Western memory. Like other millennial movements they are also a repeated coalescence and structuring of everyday techniques of resistance: resistance to the dominant male institutions which certainly have their own self-aware continuity.

All dominant social formations constitute themselves through opposition to some 'Other'. In the case of the masculine West, the 'Other' variously denotes nature, women, the Devil and his witches, the mad, the primitive, the Black, nudity, sexual licence and the Left. While the dominant tradition offers a continuity through time, its Other is manifest in historical and individual moments which define 'what is not' or 'what should be not', and which in part constitute the traditional structure by complement. Women and Nature cannot be totally excluded. The arbitrary Other continues to make claims on the powers-that-be through what Victor Turner calls 'the power of the weak'.[62] Ultimately nothing can be excluded from the general system of classification. There is no problem of an 'origin' of opposition: the opposition is already, and always, there, engendered in the competing self-interest of individuals.

At moments of political and ideological crisis, of resistance to colonial oppression, of 'millennial madness', of concerns over the transforming effects of technology, new cognitive and social structures are available through the Other. Reproducing by inversion the traditional cultural categories, they may be merely reassertions and reinterpretations of dominant values held to be neglected through nominal observance or hypocrisy. At other times, as with Mother Earth, but perhaps in none so radically, we find a structured coming together of all the oppositions. Mother Earth is Nature. She is the Devil, the Black, the Mad, the Left-Handed, the Witch, the Naked, the victim of Interference.

There is a certain irony here. Such a Nature stands for the possibility of remaking a lost world. But, whatever its eventual transformation, romantic irrationalism's denial of history is a response to the further encroachments of industrial technology: agricultural labour was never so easy, so idyllic. Its own notion of Nature is itself politically constructed: sometimes a hiatus on the way to the incorporation of yet newer technologies. A new oppositional order develops in a reaction to the dominant, but until an autonomous social organisation can be reproduced in new productive and reproductive relations, the reaction remains a reaction, a defiant resurgence of the ascribed Other, dependent on the dominant, part of it. A rebellion, frequently muted, and not a revolution. One of the Earth People, Breadfruit, told me triumphantly that 'Mother say since the Miracle it have the world upside down.' The Whites' world. As Warner remarks of the Wimmin of Greenham Common, they 'hark back to the fantasy of the archaic, all-embracing mother of creation and this may be ultimately the most dangerous and intractable patriarchal myth of all . . . the protestors have harnessed the powers that the anomalous outsider within any society possesses'.[63]

8

Incest: the naked earth

Yemanja

As a child Jeanette used to attend the *shango tent* with her grandmother where she learned various 'Yarriba songs', including the one she later sang to the Ocean when she started burning her possessions. In this song (page 71) which initiated her revelation, she addressed Yemanja, the African power who is known in the New World under a variety of similar names – Emanjah, Omanjah, Amanjah, Amaja, Yemaya and Eminona. In West Africa Emanja (Yeomowa, Iemaja, Emanjah, Yemoja) is the Yoruba 'mother of the rivers', the power of the river Ogu who is revered by women in particular and who is closely associated with their fertility.[1] In Yoruba myth Emanja conceives a son, Orungan, by her brother Aganju, the deity of the dry land. Orungan himself then has sex with his mother (in most accounts against her will), and as she flees from him she gives birth to streams of water, three major and fourteen lesser powers.

In Trinidadian shango, Yemanja is assimilated to the Christians' St Catherine, or to St Ann the mother of the Virgin Mary. Her personality – demonstrated in her devotees through whom she manifests – is maternal, nurturant, humorous, tolerant, yet implacable. Although shango is associated particularly with the Belmont area of Port-of-Spain where Jeanette spent much of her childhood, in the 1930s Herskovits described the rites of Amaja in a coastal village some twenty miles from the Earth Peoples' current settlement: her *table* had a fish-shaped stone on it which was addressed by the votaries as 'Mother'. Another Afro-Caribbean cult in Belmont, Dahomean *rada*, revered a probably cognate power, Eminona, who is identified with the Virgin Mary.[2]

The mother of Emanja, and also of her brother and first consort Aganju, is Oduduwa; their father, Obatala, is sometimes regarded as the Yoruba supreme

Table 1. *The genealogies of Yemanja: correspondence*

Yoruba		Shango	Rada	Santeria	Xango
Oduduwa	Obatala	Obatala (St Benedict)		Obatala (Various)	Obatala
Aganju	Emanja	Yemanja (Sts Catherine, Anne)	?Eminona (Virgin Mary)	Yemaya (Virgin Mary)	Yemanya (Virgin Mary)
Orungan					
	Shango	Shango (John the Baptist)	?Sobo (St John the Baptist, Evangelist of the Cross)	Chango (St Barbara)	Xango (St Jerome)
	Ogun	Ogun (St Michael	Ogu (St Michael)	Ogun (St Peter)	Ogun (St George)
	Shopona	Sopona/Shapona (Sts Francis, Jerome, Moses, doctors)	?Sakpata (a group of four – Sts Anthony, Francis, Jerome, Joseph). ?Sobo	?Babalu-Aye (St Lazarus)	Sagpata
	Various				

power. The children of Emanja by her second incestuous union with her son Orungan include: Shango, the power of storm and thunder, and the preeminent figure in the Trinidadian shango cult; Ogun, representation of war and iron; and their brother Shopona, power of smallpox and the earth, together with various river goddesses and powers of hunting, agriculture and weather who do not seem so significant in Africa or in the various Afro-American cults. Yemanja herself is addressed in Brasilian *xango* and *candomblé*, in Cuban *santeria* and its Venezuelan derivatives. In West Africa she is associated particularly with fresh water but in her passage to the Americas she becomes associated with the sea: in Brazil she has an annual festival in which leaves and offerings are floated on the shores of the Atlantic, a rite which is consciously evoked in the Trinidadian Baptists' ceremony of baptism for new members.

The complex genealogies of the African deities have not migrated to the Americas. Nor is our New World Yemanja incestuous with her son except in Brazil. Nevertheless, we can sketch out some Afro-American correspondences to the basic Yoruba pattern; Catholic saints locally identified or associated with the various powers in the Americas are placed in brackets (see Table 1).

The African Earth

Many West African deities are closely associated with the earth, including (the Ashanti) Asase Ya and (the Ibo) Ala. They are usually female and form a duality with a supreme male sky god. While Howard Jones says that such earth deities are difficult to identify among the Yoruba, Alolabi Ojo comments that 'in traditional Yoruba religion the earth or land was worshipped probably everywhere without exception', and Parrinder suggests that in the coastal regions of Nigeria the Earth seems to be personified to such an extent that it often has a cult, and we are justified in speaking of it as 'a goddess'; while Daniel McCall argues that anthropologists have ignored the prevalence of a goddess in West Africa whom he terms Mother Earth.[3] Although Emanja's mother Oduduwa was loosely associated with the soil, a more specific earth power Edan is also found among the Yoruba. While the association of the earth with the nurturant – and thus the female – is an obviously available representation, it may seem a little strange that given her own particular emphasis on the earth as the basis of existence and her community's dedication to agrarian pursuits, Jeanette has identified herself with a water power, albeit one strongly associated with fertility.[4] In Afro-Caribbean cults such as shango, however, the earth is seldom addressed in herself as a seat of the ancestral powers. The different powers of shango, each once closely associated with particular features of the local environment, have become more diffuse and universalised in the Americas, and the specific 'spiritual representation' of the land on which a Yoruba community was located (*ile*) appears to have been lost; Bastide comments that no knowledge of any 'Mother Earth' such as Oduduwa or Olokun survived in the Americas because it was psychologically necessary for the slaves to forget Africa but the representation of 'Africa' remains gendered, always feminine, and usually maternal.[5] The Ghanaian Mother Earth, Asase, is still known among the Bush Negroes of Surinam; and the Yoruba Ogboni cult which venerates the earth, although not found in Trinidad, continues in a form in Brazil. Bastide cites a story in which the Yoruba priests of Obatala (the father of Emanja and identified with the sun) disputed with those of Oduduwa (Emanja's mother who is identified with the earth) as to which deity had actually created the world; slavery settled the dispute as far as the Yoruba slaves were concerned by reinforcing the male, sky, and arguably more 'portable', creative principle. Additionally, the influence of a male creator in Christianity and Islam may have reinforced

Obatala's partisans. At any rate he is to be found in the Americas, unlike his consort whose nurturant and maternal characteristics have now been assumed by her daughter Yemanja, who is sometimes referred to as the Mother of the Gods but never as a sole genetrix. Closely associated with the Virgin Mary and her mother Ann, Yemanja remains the major female force in creation, but as the creator of people, not of the world. Jeanette's identification with her had not been a simple reactivation of a set of existing, already elaborated, themes, but a transformation of certain possibilities latent in shango.

Has the Afro-Caribbean notion of the earth always been simply pragmatic? Against Bastide's argument that it was too dismal for the slaves to associate themselves with a soil which they worked for the profit of another and in whose fertility they could have no ultimate interest, we may argue that the first slaves were buried in the knowledge that they would thus return to Africa after death and indeed they were believed by the slaveholders to attempt suicide through eating soil. 'Dirt eating' was also associated with oath taking, for the soil from burial plots contained the ancestral spirits, and portions of it were taken along by the slaves when they were transferred to other plantations. Burial remains the most significant Afro-Caribbean rite, and 'grave dirt' was utilised for divination after suspected thefts but later tended to become purely 'evil' through the moral dualism of Christianity. The orishas of the shango cult are often identified with ancestral Africans and they may manifest themselves from the ground up through the central pole of the chapelle. Libations of rum are still occasionally poured into the graves which originally were dug in the slaves' personal provision grounds, where they were expected to grow their own foodstuffs and which offered a basis for whatever independent economic life they were able to develop. The same plots subsequently provided the springboard for an enthusiastic move towards a peasantry after emancipation: family land is difficult to sell because of the multiplicity of cognatic heirs and it still provides a 'symbolically unlimited resource' (as Besson puts it). There remains in rural areas a complex of relationships between phases of the moon, human fertility and the planting and harvesting of crops. Individuals once had a close association to the tree under which their umbilical cords were buried after their birth, and there is an intimate correspondence between human sickness, sexuality and medicinal bush.

None of this amounts to ascribing 'divinity' to the Earth but it has certainly continued as a potential focus for the ancestral and the African. If the solar deity Obatala has migrated with the slaves and left his telluric wife behind, the land remains the potential source of mystical power and there is little evidence of sky or sun veneration in Afro-America.

Emanja is a Yoruba deity and the major African knowledge in Trinidad is accepted as Yoruba, but there is also a Dahomean corpus in the rada cult which was carried to Trinidad in the late nineteenth century by at least one *bokono* (diviner). Rada is dedicated principally to the serpent deity Dangbwe, but it also reveres other deities including Eminona. These Dahomean sources date back to the slave trade, and Herskovits argues that among the nominally 'Dahomean' slaves were many priests who had served the river deities of the subject tribes which the Kingdom of Dahomey had conquered and who, as potential rebels, were sold to the slavers. Whether they remained especially rebellious in Trinidad is unknown but it may be significant that its only noteworthy slave revolt was led by 'Dahomeans'.[6] That a 'river cult' in Haiti prohibited by the slave-owners was also rada is a possibility; compared with other vodu cults, Haitian rada tends to employ agricultural rituals but there is no obvious principle of female fecundity in vodu without a male counterpart, while Trinidadian rada has no distinctive earth power.

Another shango power in Trinidad, who is less significant in the cult than Yemanja, is Mama Latay (*La terre*), who has been described as the Mother of the Gods or the Mother of All Nations; she is identified with both Eve and St Veronica. Two minor shango powers in Trinidad with whom our Mother Earth has certain affinities are African Queen and Oshun (now Mistress of the Ocean). A number of female water deities are to be found among the Afro-Caribbean cults, some of whom appear to be variants of Yemanja; other powers have attributes which are similar to hers and which may have been derived from her or have contributed to her current form. Thus, the Bakweri *liengu* water sprite, creolised as Mami Wata, was found under this name in the Guianas where a slave revolt appears to have been fought under her name; also known as Minje Mamma (Emanja Mother?) her cult was characterised by the Europeans as some unspecified 'obscene worship', while a similar 'Water Mother cult' in Haiti was firmly suppressed.[7] Contemporary Haitian *loas* include a variety of water powers, particularly Agwe and La Sirène, who have some resemblance to Yemanja and are part of the rada (here Yoruban as well as Dahomean) rites.[8] Mami Wata is known in Jamaica as Rubba (River) Mumma or Rubba Missis, apparently the same power for whom cattle were formerly sacrificed and dances performed alongside those for the ancestral duppies. The Maroons in Jamaica, the community of escaped slaves which has continued to exist as a relatively independent polity since the seventeenth century, formerly had a female figure known as Yumma which was annually washed at Christmas, while in Grenada sacrifices were performed to Mamadja, a water spirit, yet another power whose name recalls (Mama) Emanja.[9]

Yemanja is known in the nearest country to Trinidad, Venezuela, in the Maria Lionza cult where, as in Brazil, she is assimilated to the Virgin Mary and associated with the sea and with relieving madness. Bastide suggests that with increasing standardisation of the various Brazilian cults into *umbanda*, Yemanja 'rises from the plane of natural forces to the plane of moral ones'. She becomes the purifier of passions and is invoked by devotees at the beginning of a ceremony to discharge the impurities introduced into the building by man's sinful body. Some informants say she always remains a virgin creatrix, identified with the Catholics' Immaculate Conception as Our Lady of Good Parturition. She 'represents maternal forces' and, like the Virgin, is clothed in blue, whilst remaining associated with the moon and fertility.[10] In Trinidadian shango, Yemanja is identified with the Mother of the Virgin rather than with the Virgin herself. (Despite its nominal Catholicism, Trinidad devotes little interest to the Virgin; her obligatory statues in village churches stand neglected, frequently in poor repair.) Less of a universal principle than in Brazil, Yemanja is still associated with the colour blue, with maternity and child-rearing, nurturance, rivers, the sea, the moon and fertility.

Androgyneity and incest: the passage from divinity to human
Although we cannot presume any necessary identity between deities of similar name or attributes, certain patterns repeatedly occur which bear on Mother Earth's employment of African and Christian themes:

(i)   St Catherine is identified not only with Yemanja but with (her son Shango's wife and sister) Oya, another river deity.

(ii)   Saints Ann, Veronica and Catherine have very similar ritual objects.

(iii)   Yoruban Emanja is sometimes described as the wife of a thunder god.

(iv)   The orisha Shango in Nigeria is sometimes regarded as a quasi-historical culture hero, a technological innovator and ancestor, rather than a 'god'. In Brazil the orisha Xango is the ancestor of the Yoruba Kings.

(v)   The Brazilian Xango is associated with Jesus, a man.

(vi)   The Dogon 'Mother Earth' has human children by her son the jackal, a process which initiates the first menstruation.

(vii)   Saint Ann, in the Apocryphal Book of James, was herself barren and conceived the Virgin Mary through divine impregnation.

While we have minimal genealogies in Trinidadian shango or rada, we can summarise the relationships between individuals in the sequences Yoruba, Trinidadian shango, Brazilian candomblé, Dogon, and Christianity (in the following figure):

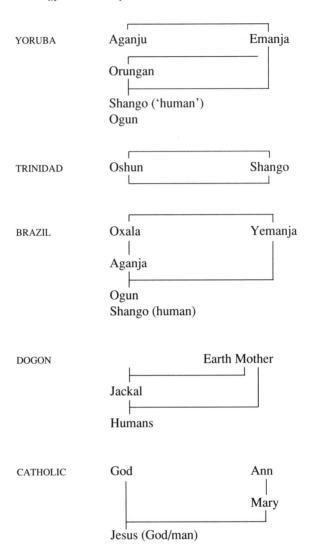

Representing this as a general pattern, we obtain:

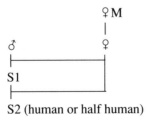

We can table our available information on a matrix starting from the person of Emanja, the woman who has sex with her brother and her son as in the Yoruba myth (page 144, Table 2). Placing the names in our general pattern we obtain the following

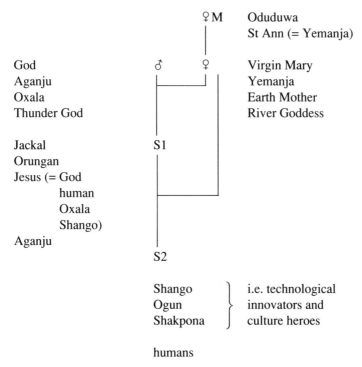

		♀M	Oduduwa
			St Ann (= Yemanja)
God	♂	♀	Virgin Mary
Aganju			Yemanja
Oxala			Earth Mother
Thunder God			River Goddess
Jackal	S1		
Orungan			
Jesus (= God			
human			
Oxala			
Shango)			
Aganju			
	S2		

Shango   ⎫
Ogun   ⎬ i.e. technological innovators and
Shakpona ⎭ culture heroes

humans

Summarising,   ♀   is identified with ♀M – once
              S1   is identified with S2 – twice
              ♂   is identified with S2 – once
              ♂   is identified with S1 – four times

Condensing, we obtain:

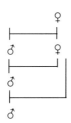

Table 2. *The genealogies of Yemanja: known relationships*

♀M	St Ann the mother of the Virgin Mary (C)	Oduduwa the mother of Yemanja (Y)	Oduduwa the mother of Emanja (B)		Virgin Mary is Eminoja (R)		
♀	St Ann is Yemanja (T)	Virgin Mary is Yemanja (B)	Yemanja has sex with her brother and her son (Y, B, T)	St Catherine is both Yemanja and Oya wife of Shango (T)			
♂	God (C)	Aganju is the husband of Emanja (Y)	Oxala is the husband of Yemanja and identified with God (B)	Thunder god is wife of river goddess (Y)			
S1	Jesus is God (C)	Aganju is son of Yemanja (B)	Oxala is Jesus (B)	Xango is Jesus (B)	Orungan is son of Yemanja by her brother (Y)	Earth Mother has sex with her son the jackal (D)	Jesis is human (C), as is Shango (Y) and Xango (B)
S2			Shango is the son of Emanja by her first incestuous son (Y)	Ogun is the son of Emanja by her first son (Y)		Humans are sons of Earth Mother and jackal (D)	

C = Catholic T = Trinidadian *shango* Y = Yoruba B = Brasilian *xango* D = Dogon in which a divine woman (who is autochthonous or whose father is seldom explicitly named), by her brother has a son, by whom in turn she then has other sons which are progressively more human than the males of the earlier generation. Her sexual partner at each stage is a blood relative, frequently her son. To an extent then, the male principle may be regarded as secondary, whilst in the Yoruba version Emanja is herself closely identified with her own mother.

Indeed to assume a supreme West African power is simply male may be rather a superficial interpretation. Although among the Yoruba ultimate power is usually vested in a male sky god (whose daughter is Emanja), among the neighbouring Eastern Ewe especially the Fon, the term Mawu is a generic name for 'deity' but also more specifically a female moon power, represented with large breasts and holding a crescent. Not only is she closely associated with her husband/son/brother Lisa, but she is often identified with him. Indeed the couple are sometimes represented as a hermaphrodite, one side female and associated with the moon, the other male, associated with the sun; this hermaphrodite Lisa has been regarded as the 'ultimate power'. Similarly in neighbouring Dahomey, an area of greater historical interest for Trinidad, a related female or androgynous creator, Nana-Bakur, is associated with both sky and water, and is sometimes regarded as the mother of Mawu-Lisa. Booth relates *Lisa* to the Yoruban term *orisha* (power or deity): Obatala (the father of Emanja), the supreme Yoruba *orisha* is often termed Orishala or Orishanla. He also notes that Oduduwa – Emanja's mother, the Black One, particularly identified with the earth – is either Obatala's (Orishala's) wife or mother or twin brother and may be herself regarded as 'self-existent'.[11] Incorporating this we obtain the following:

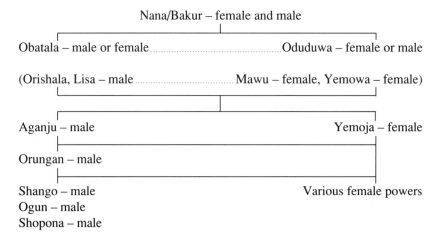

Booth's analysis of the related Yoruba/Fon/Dahomean patterns thus allows us to find our pattern again in an immediately ascending generation but with androgyneity and autochthonous origin instead of incest. The autochthonous origin of these deities is also argued in Oduduwa being identified both with Mawu and with Yemowa (Mother Mowa, presumably cognate with Yemoja, her daughter in other variants). Ogun is also the son of Oduduwa, and the Fon deity Gon is the equivalent child of Mawu and Lisa; another son is Shopona. On the usual Yoruban genealogy, Ogun and Shopona are the sons of Yemoja (Emanja) by her incestuous union with Aganju, suggesting some identity of Yemoja, Yemowa, Mawu and Oduduwa. (For simplicity I have not represented these in the above figures.) There appear then to be a series of reflections and identifications between these four first 'generations': 'There is always a Mawu beyond Mawu who cannot be tied down.'[12] The Yemowa–Orishala couple created the world, and Yemowa is also called Onile Ile (Earth Owner) and Iya (Mother). The world 'rests on her'. 'Basically the Yoruba and Fon believe in one ultimate power, yet this power is complex, associated with the phenomena of sky, earth and sea and the establishment of kingship upon earth, and with relationships between male and female.'[13] Powers are represented as androgynous brother/sister deities[14] who, we might add, are sometimes also husband/wife deities.

Our Trinidadian power, Yemanja, thus has African prefigurings which suggest a female yet androgynous deity, autochthonous and sometimes parthenogenic, who creates the cosmos, and afterwards humans, through an extrusion of her male potential which then itself becomes increasingly autonomous and differentiated. Mother Earth too regards androgyneity as the original state of both the first humans and the original Mother who was both Mother and Father. It was the incest of the Son with his Mother and his 'interference' with the androgynous Black Mothers which caused separation between female and male, at the same time initiating the distinction between Black and White, between the Natural and Social domains.

The West African sources which Mother Earth has had available to her in continuing African–Caribbean traditions are various and diffuse. One possibly distinct theme within the broader picture has been that of the rebellious Dahomean river priests, rebels both against their kingdom and later against the slave-owners. There are other discrete bodies of tradition and social groupings which may have contributed. The Ogboni, the Yoruban 'secret society', is particularly associated with the veneration of Onile Ile (the Earth Owner), one of the names of Yemowa, and has been described as 'traditionally the major government organ for preserving law and order, checking the excesses of kings'.[15] Like Mother Earth, the Ogboni fraternity have a left handshake in opposition to conventional dexterity. They revere the Earth as prior to and more powerful than any orisha and accept that the dead return to it. Ogboni cosmology incorporates many Muslim and Christian themes and indeed a later variant (which was started by a dissenting Anglican clergyman) reveres the earth as Edam: Adam and Eve as a joint male–female deity. While the Earth People take Eve as the mother they distinguish her from Fadam (Father Adam), the Son. We have no evidence of the Ogboni society in Trinidad (although variants persist in Brazil), but some newer West African religions which assimilate certain Christian beliefs offer striking parallels: another Nigerian group, the Ijo Orunmila, was founded in the 1930s by Christians who wished to return to tradition and who identified Orunmila, another of the orishas, with both Christ and Mohammed.[16]

We can certainly perceive our general scheme of

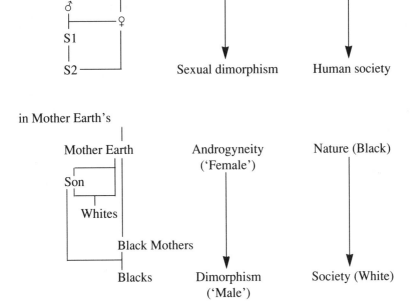

in Mother Earth's

In both, the descendants of the original parthogenic and androgynous creator(s) become increasingly human and sexually dimorphic. As in so many creation myths, the descent from unitary powers with quasihuman characteristics to full humans is achieved through incest. In one of the fables retold in Plato's *Symposium*, the androgyneity of the first beings provides an explanation of the attraction of the sexes towards each other as one back to an original state of harmony and completeness. Historical differentiation from an homogeneous unity and contemporary sexual coupling are opposite manifestations of the same relationship (at the subjective level, the experience of sexual union is frequently a merging of the self in the other, the 'two-backed beast' of the Shakespearean adage):

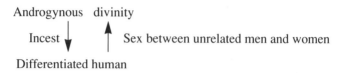

Androgynous   divinity

Incest   Sex between unrelated men and women

Differentiated human

The same problem of differentiation is resolved in Christianity through emphasis on the asexual creativity of the Creator, one less anthropomorphic than the African deities; the tricky question of God's matrimonial involvement with Mary is solved by an emphasis on the unique and extra-natural pattern of the Incarnation, through which she conceives without ceasing to be immaculate, and the fact that Jesus is God more than he is his own Son. The implication of incest is thus avoided, especially as God is the 'father' of Mary only in that parent–child relations stand for divine–human relations. Similarly for Jesus; the Church is only his Bride in that husband–wife relations provide a metaphor for leader–led, a metaphor probably deriving from the Parable of the Virgins which is more about missing the celestial party than it is about sexual relations.

From the Judaeo-Christian perspective, the major innovation in Mother Earth's cosmogony is her emphasis on the original principle as female. To an extent, as Mother Earth told me, this reflects the fact that people have mothers more than they have fathers: in our terms *mater* and *genetrix* are usually identical.[17] The genealogies of the West African and Caribbean orishas certainly carry the potential of such a matrigenic focus. We derive the impression that if anything is prior to the orishas themselves it is the Earth, regarded in both the Caribbean and Africa as female when it has a gender at all. If there has been a move away from a relatively undifferentiated pantheistic earth power to a sharper distinction between nature, society and the ultrahuman at a higher 'genealogical' level under the influence of Christianity, the Christian mystical tradition itself refers back to the earlier Mediterranean fertility religions which recall the West African cosmologies and which are reframed in high science.[18]

Generation: from biography to cosmogony

Does Yemanja serve as a representation for Mother Earth's own 'deep motivations' (Obeyesekere's term)? The idiom of childbirth is fundamental to both her creation myth and to her account of current relations between women and men, for the physical development of each human child recapitulates the original cosmogony (page 79). While I did not obtain a detailed description of Jeanette's own early adult life,[19] motherhood had clearly been her most salient experience, as it was for the women in Pinnacle Village who recounted their lives to me. It is through childbearing that Mother Earth objectifies herself to others as a universal principle, a domestic mode raised to a cosmological order, a central 'experiential metaphor' by which she structures other experiences and ideas.

Jeanette's parents were not *church married*. She was born in 1934 in Port-of-Spain, the eldest of ten children. Her mother's mother was 'a real African from Africa'. Her mother had arrived in Trinidad from Grenada at the age of thirteen to work as a domestic servant for a White family, and Jeanette was born in her mother's thirties, to be 'raised with' the White children of her employer. She met her own father only 'once or twice' as she can recall; he died when she was about thirty: 'He call me then. I was not very interested but I go.' Her mother later *friended* with a policeman from Grenada who was frequently critical of the established church but was known for his ability to predict future events by high science.

From the age of one year, Jeanette saw her mother relatively infrequently[20] and lived with various relatives, in particular her African grandmother, a Shango Baptist. She attended school sporadically and even now only reads with difficulty and can barely write. At sixteen she left her grandmother to live with a boy friend. This relationship broke up and she returned to her grandmother, and then lived with one of her own mother's previous *friends* by whom she herself had three children. As for most working-class Trinidadian women, emancipation from parents and accession into adulthood came, not from chronological age, education or employment away from the household or even sexual relations, but from childbearing. She *scuffled*, getting by with help from relatives and boy friends: 'a little job here, a next one there. I often plan to get marry but something happen. I ai' fuss.' She continued to live in Laventille, the poorest area in Port-of-Spain.

Her life was that of most working-class women in town, facing the endless round of bearing children and caring for them (page 67). She tried to get her children to school but could not afford the uniform: 'I say "You ai' learn socks: you go!" An' the headmaster send them back.' Over the years she became increasingly bitter and resentful of the (White) French Creole elite (page 101) and the way Black women were treated both by the colonial government and by their own men: 'In America they give you money for boy children as they are needed for the army. But not here! In town I catch my arse look after children. I do all thing, I buy an' sell.' One rainy season she bought a sewing machine in Port-of-Spain on hire purchase so she could save money by making clothes for her children. 'At Christmas I going to have a next child and the man come and say he come for machine', even though she had paid all the instalments. She was in no condition to argue: 'The way they look at the poorer class of people; they wait for the edge, for the bad time, and take the machine to someone else.' After the baby was born she went back to the shop to protest, taking her original receipt. Her machine had now been sold to someone else but she was offered another one – second-hand. This was the one she later burnt.

Only one aspect of life in town really developed into a continuing resentment. That was childbirth in hospital. By the age of thirty-seven, when she met Cyprian, Jeanette had borne ten children. Her views on generation were then conventional: sexual activity was to be enjoyable for both partners; a woman was to bear her predetermined 'set of children'; and contraception was unnatural and dangerous.

My being pregnant and having to go to the doctor and hospital to make my baby I always see something in the hospital that I didn't like, an' it is the young mothers. What I find that was wrong in those days that the young mothers should be taken care of more. Because they are young, in their first pregnancy, they don' know anything about it an' they usually act inferior to which they should be acting (you know, they cry a lot, they bawl a lot), so by the time they are ready to bring forth the baby some of them are so weak. Nobody to sit down and talk to them. The nurses have no time, you know. I would usually go round the beds because most of my pregnancies, when I go in there, my water bag burst home an' I think I am ready; when I reach there I am not ready; sometimes two weeks I am still there, waiting on the pain to come, to deliver my baby. So then I would be helping the younger mothers by going an' sit down with them, rub their hands, pass my hand on their face, talk to them, prepare them, tell them 'Don't cry – you know you are crying too much – you will get too weak – eat something – little thing to eat – they say you mus' eat something.' I did talk to them, pat them, show them. Sometime I get through with them, sometime they are very hard to get through with because they are studying the pain that they getting for days an' they keep crying an' crying. So I did talk to them. An' these things use to make me feel good. It make me feel that I am doing something to help my people. I don't know . . . but I like it at the time.

But yet I am in there for so long I still help myself by doing something, even self is to help share out some food sometime, until my pain come. Well my pain does be very short: if I start about ten o'clock in the morning, by the time twelve o'clock I am already deliver my baby; my baby born so I would be alright again and then come home.

But something happen to me in hospital once which I didn't like at all. Was with one of my babies, I don't really like the labour room because I find the bed is too high, it is too cold, the plastic they put on it is too cold. You have to lie down on this wet cold plastic and in my pain I like to be walking.

Whenever a pain take me I jump off the bed and I gone, up and down, up and down, until it ease again, I go back and lie. But in the labour room you cannot do that: you have to bear that pain on the bed there. To me, I get more pain by being lying down there twist up. So I never like the labour room. So what I do is ease my pain on the outside, in the yard, an' I remain there whenever it take me an' walk, walk until it get very hot an' I know when it is time to deliver, I just jump up on the bed an' my baby will come. When the baby come I call the nurse. The nurse did just pass and see me comfortable so, when she come back now, she say 'What happen?' I say 'the baby, the baby'.

When she look she say 'Look what you making a mess, you making a mess in the place, look what you doing on the bed! You making a mess! Get up and go in the labour room! I bet you I push it back.' An' she hold it, the baby, and push it! I fire a kick because I feel a pain. An' when I fire the kick my foot pass near her face, when I start to cry one time. I say 'Sorry, I didn't really mean to do that but you push it an' you hurt me.' You know an' I cry and thing an' I make it look [right].

The nurses slapped up the patients, even the younger mothers, they give them a hard time because they find they crying too much or they making too much noise, they will slap them up in their face an' tell them 'What do you think you come here for?', if they didn't want children an' all kind of words they use to that. So then, this is the reason why I really use to go around an' try to talk to the mothers, try to cool them down, so that they wouldn't get in that kind of trouble with the nurses whilst in there because I never like it. But that nurse, when she did that to me, I felt it. My mind was never to go back in that hospital but then my little home is so clogged up with me an' my children – because it's just one room – so I usually feel more free going there to make my babies instead of staying at home.

While, at the time, this return of the son into his mother was just an unhappy fortuity (but one which hardened Jeanette still further against the mechanical perversions of the scientific world), it remained a terrifying experience about which she continually pondered. Not until the Burning did she realise that it had been a physical manifestation of a universal truth. The Mother's Son, indeed all men, try to return inside the mother's womb, to destroy her natural fertility or transform it into Science.

This action of the Son – an 'embodied schema' as Mark Johnson calls it, in which she employs a bodily experience as a figure to understand the world – recalls that of the 'culture hero' or mediator in those many myths which celebrate our passing from matriarchy to patriarchy, and from divine to human. Ethnographic and psychological explanations both emphasise the culture hero from the perspective of men, a myth which legitimates their power or resolves their sexual anxieties. The hero frequently has a prolonged childhood or an abnormal or delayed birth. Michael Jackson, comparing two versions of a Mande epic (in one of which the culture hero Sundiata is born extremely slowly while in the other he returns after birth to his mother's womb), has argued that prolonged gestation and prolonged infancy are really symbolic equivalents, characteristic representations of Otto Rank's mythic hero/son who continually struggles to supplant his king/father. Although Mother Earth recalls a pattern found in a number of cultures, we are not concerned here with some myth structured by a stable set of social relationships, but with a novel schema, one elaborated from the existing schema but now proclaimed by the woman herself against the hero.[21] It is difficult to see this simply as a legitimation of male power – though it still offers an explanation of current male dominance – or as the expression of men's personal dilemmas.

While I do not wish to speculate in detail on the putative 'deep motivation' (say, of the mother's incestuous desire for her son being called to consciousness as the nurse pushes the child back), some consideration must be given to mother–son relationships in West Indian societies. Is there a local 'social vehicle', as Geertz puts it, which structures an African sentiment of matrilineage? Or is it just that, as Tylor argued, telluric mother deities are 'simple and obvious'? Paternity and maternity are hardly terms of the same order.

I heard no tales of mother–son incest in Trinidad: the suggestion was met with incredulous laughter rather than the indignation reserved for the rare *vice* of father–daughter incest (page 54). Nevertheless, the centrality of the mother–child relationship has been emphasised by Caribbeanists and also by local novelists and politicians; most radically in the notion that the Black family – always to be contrasted with its White counterpart – is in some way 'denuded' of the father so that the Black mother becomes a 'matriarch'.[22] Behind the 'matricentral' family lurks the psychological father – the White male – the historical rapist of the mother and the continuing representation of external power within the family he has created. Jack Alexander has even described the 'ancestral myth' of the Jamaican middle class as one which traces descent back to a planter and his female slave.

The mother–child relationship is the only working-class kin tie which continues throughout adulthood as one which cannot be outweighed easily through acquired relationships with others. Both sons and daughters frequently quarrel with their father as they get older or else tend to ignore him. 'Mother blood stronger than father blood' as the Jamaicans put it. Inheritance of parental land is supposedly through all the descendants of either father or mother: depending on public recognition of children and on informal agreement for land use, shallow personal 'matrilineages' may thus occur but these have no recognised term. Similarly, if children are born without an acknowledged father, or if the father disclaims any interest in them, they take their mother's *title* (surname) and this could continue over a number of generations but only through a series of 'worthless' contingencies, not as any recognised structuring principle.

Siblings may have bitter and unresolved conflicts over land or continuing personal disagreements without any lasting opprobrium; other things being equal, relations between kin are valued but subsequent events may easily displace them. Kin ties often seem regarded less as 'family ties' in themselves than as a particular and convenient relationship between individuals. The exception is the tie which continues to bind children, particularly sons, to their mothers, for whom they have economic and sentimental obligations during her lifetime. Daughters may quarrel, regrettably, with their mothers, but while this is unworthy it is intelligible; for a son to quarrel permanently with his mother can never be accepted. In conversation women may complain bitterly of their own mother but an adult man cannot decently do this. She is practically unassailable, morally and emotionally. The only possible relationship which could cause a son to quarrel permanently with his mother is that with his wife, but in the majority of instances the mother would take precedence.[23] We find however no exhaltation of the role of *the* Mother as on the Spanish Main: in Trinidad the Virgin Mary is respected simply as the mother of Jesus; he had to have a mother and she is it. No more. None of this amounts to anything which can reasonably be termed 'incestuous' except through the sort of psycho-dynamic reasoning which would take the West Indian family as a 'strong' (or naked) form of a universal desire.[24]

From the mother's point of view (and this is what must principally concern us), the Trinidadian mother is certainly proud of her son's achievements and readier than others to forgive his faults, but she can hardly be said to idolise him; mothers frequently lament their 'worthless' sons to a sympathetic audience. Relationships between son and mother in adolescence are neither physically close, particularly avoided, nor especially emotionally charged, although he may be expected to protect her from a violent father: the Yiddish saying 'When a man marries, he gives his wife a contract and his mother a divorce' would be affectively meaningless in Trinidad. In the Earth Peoples' community where the whole group recognise themselves as a family, the prevalent feeling for her is one of friendship, respect and obligation; it was often difficult for me to remember that Mother Earth was in some sense 'divine'. Physical sex between Mother Earth and her group (an idea which they mentioned to me because of its popularity in the outside world) could only be self-defeating. It would mean the end of the Valley. Though Mother Earth casually uses sexual 'obscenities' to her followers, as to others, this carries a charge of mockery of the Social rather than any obvious personal insult: it is followed by everybody falling about laughing because at one level, as a mother, she is almost 'respectable'. Even *motherfucker* is just another conscious obscenity. Nevertheless, there is a strong feeling among the young men in the Valley of a shared sympathy for their Black Mother, for all mothers, subject to male sexual aggression. The analyst will note that they are placed in a pre-adolescent position in which any genital interest is discouraged; their naked penis, the *piggy*, is more an object of teasing than of potential domination, nor does Mother Earth approve of precocious sexual interests in her, or in anybody's, children.[25]

The Son is of course also the deity of Christianity. Psychoanalysts represent this God as an omnipotent father against whom the male prophet struggles but with whom he eventually identifies.[26] I know little about Jeanette's relationship with her own father apart from her comments above. She appears to have scorned rather than feared him; certainly he seems a rather distant figure. Without talking with her own mother it is difficult for me to understand Jeanette's relations with him during her childhood but one cannot see her as identifying significantly with him. With her mother and grandmother certainly. The loss of an idyllic childhood has been cited frequently as the psychological origin of the adult utopian impulse; Rousseau, losing his mother in childhood, maintained a close relationship with his father and later called his mistress 'Mamma', apparently never enjoying adult sexual relations with her but (in his *Confessions*) quite consciously objectifying sexual interest as Nature. Before succumbing to some general theory of prophecy as the response to losing the opposite sex parent, it is worth noting that Rousseau elevated the lost feminine into the whole of Creation, while Mother Earth relegates a lost masculine to a despised interference. She was certainly aware in childhood of an 'absent father' rather than accepting her natal family as the proper pattern, not only through the constant African–Caribbean assumption of the supposedly present White father, but in that, as a servant's child, she was part of a White family. Whether as a young child she regarded her mother's employer as any sort of father I do not know but it is possible that she experienced the type of ethnic ambiguity which has been described as common in Black American children adopted into White families. One may argue that 'her father' at this time was White and of course he ultimately 'abandoned her'.

A sexualised father may be discerned perhaps in later adolescence in her living with her mother's former partner – and thus a quasi-parental replacement for her own father. In spite of the flexibility of family roles in West Indian societies, this is not really acceptable although it is far from being categorised as the vice of incest. In my own clinical work with Afro-Caribbean patients in Britain, they frequently mention to me past seduction by a step-father as a cause of problems of both sexual and ethnic identity; and within African–American communities there is often an assumption that father–daughter sexual relations are more common than elsewhere but this too may be an internalised perception, ascribed to them by Whites, of 'the disorganised Black family'.[27] In the Caribbean context, bearing children to her mother's partner certainly made for generational ambiguity and the overt sexualisation of cross-generational relationships. Jeanette's later choice in Cyprian of a much younger partner than herself suggests that she may have continued a greater flexibility in cross-generational sexuality than is usual.

Psychoanalysts may argue here – and it is difficult to resist the intoxications of neatly condensing down Jeanette's history, experience and visions into a unitary psychosocial closure, her mania as inevitable or at least emblematic of her deep motivations – that the resolution of her Oedipal wishes for her biological father was thwarted by his absence; these were then transferred to the doubly unobtainable White father (available in the psychic reality of colonial domination) to be temporarily resolved through bearing children to her 'step-father'; against which nearly incestuous relationship she then chose a much younger man from a distant part of the island and as an active Baptist submitted herself, asexual, to God the (White) Father: a complex of unstable relationships which were only resolved through her later identification with a Black female creatrix, thus apparently displacing the White and male principles onto a peripheral figure who interfered with Nature, while at the same time she identifies herself with male as well as female, reenacting the return of the Son in her actions during the Miracle (page 74). In other words our structuring key lies in a daughter–father rather than in a mother–son relationship, and the Son is only *a son* in that he provides an appropriate logical model of contingency, subordination and rebellion.

Perhaps psychoanalytic interpretations remain more arbitrary than most: even if Mother Earth had told me more about her childhood experiences we could have generated a variety of psychological narratives. A dislike of sexual activity may however have quite a prosaic rationale. Marjorie Kemp, an illiterate brewer in medieval Norfolk who had nearly died during her fourteenth delivery, interpreted a vision of devils as a call from God to abandon married life. It is not surprising that traumas associated with childbearing are common among prophetic women such as Mistress Kemp, particularly those who later elaborate a 'feminist' position or one which emphasises childbirth.[28] Psychoanalytical speculation aside, an aversion to conjugal relations or the loss of children signal some personal departure from a biologically determined identity.[29] Every myth is personal but every myth is also political. Male charismatic leaders may frequently be celibate or childless, as Weber noted, but this appears more common among their female counterparts. While the death of young children or other family members simply leaves the woman with freedom to engage in new activities, the very specific misery of losing her children may precipitate the potential prophet into action, perhaps in an attempt to restitute or make sense of her loss. All four children of Mother Ann Lee, the founder of the Shakers, died in infancy, and one delivery by forceps was particularly prolonged; the child appeared reluctant to be born: 'She saw the deaths of her children as a series of divine judgements on her "concupiescence" ... but once her health was restored, participation was infused with a sense of mission. What she had undergone as an individual she came to believe was really a universal struggle.'[30] When she assumed the title of 'Mother', Ann Lee, like Jeanette, was accused of madness and sexual promiscuity, both customary ways of discrediting the female religious innovator.

While women have equal spiritual worth, maintained St Paul, in everyday life they are still subordinate to men.[31] St Jerome adds: 'As long as a woman is for birth and children, she is different from man as body is from soul. But when she wishes to serve Christ more than the world, then she will cease to be a woman and will be called a man.'[32] Thus, to transcend or avoid sexual relations, particularly incest, legendary Christian heroines remain virgins or, in extreme cases, become men socially (Thecla and Margaret of Antioch) or even physically (St Uncumber grew a beard). Though the Virgin herself stands for motherhood she is rarely an image of fecundity. Movements initiated by Mothers like Mother Earth or Ann Lee often identify generation, childbirth and Nature with 'the world as it is'. Not surprisingly this identity of spirit with substance eschews a male creator and either plumps for frank matriarch (Mother Earth) or an androgynous or paired Creator/Creatrix (the Shakers): deities as containers of an unfolding creation rather than as conjurors of inanimate matter.

Like the sometimes bisexual shaman, the adherents of many practical utopias, male as well as female, may also try to emulate an androgynous ideal: the followers of Father Rapp taught that Man was originally hermaphrodite, and that the biblical Fall initiated our separation into two sexes who would be redeemed by an hermaphrodite Jesus:

Just at this juncture the first fall of man took place, by which Adam violated his own inward sanctuary and his own female function by means of which he could have been (as Genesis I: 28 has it) fruitful and multiply without an external helpmate, after the order of a Hermaphrodite then, and after the order now, see Luke 20: 34–6.[33]

This closely recalls Mother Earth's vision of the Son's interference with the hermaphrodite mothers (or the 'Orphic myth' of the Ecofeminists, page 133). The Rappites too construed the fall from our natural origins as an *interference* whilst the Shakers taught that the original bisexual Adam, created by a paired deity, had been overthrown by the male Devil, the 'Father of all';

redemption would be through the return of the deity in its male (Jesus) and female (Mother Ann) forms: 'the Father's high eternal throne was never filled by one alone'.[34]

The problem of evil

Mother Nature
She say She be so evil
Evil, evil, evil
Mother, Mother, Mother be so evil
For She who will be so evil
Evil, evil, evil
For Eve is in the garden
While Fadam stand and watching
For Eve was be so evil
Evil, evil, evil
Eve is Eve is evil
For Mother Nature evil
Mother Nature say that She will live the evil way
Because Eve was always in the garden
And there are they run from the garden
For He find Eve so evil
For evil is the garden
For Eve is always evil
In the Beginning there were the Mother say
In the Beginning there was evil
An evil, evil, evil generation
Eve will make one evil, evil generation
For Eve was always evil, evil, Eden, Eden, evil
Another one said that Eve was evil everyday
They want me to believe in Fadam
And forget my Mother is the Eve-am
For She who is my Mother
She who be so evil
For evil is the garden
The garden is the Eve-am
Eve is the evil
Evil, evil . . .

(Sung by Pomme Cythère, one of Mother Earth's sons)

What representations presage Mother Earth's rebellious Son? The parent–child relation already describes the orisha–human pair in shango, as in Christianity where humans are the Children of God. Her Son has only gained his power through The Mother to whom he remains subordinate; in some ways he recalls an erring Black son, closer perhaps to his Mother than to the human Society he brings into being. He is identified with the Christian God and with

Jesus and in the earlier days of the movement, before a clear opposition to Christianity emerged, Jeanette's partner Cyprian was called the Good Shepherd, a common name for Jesus in both Shouter Baptism and shango.[35]

Although Mother Earth now styles herself as the Devil, her attributes as The Mother – preeminence and autochthoneity – are closer to those of the Christian's God than they are to those of their Devil. The latter is hardly an important figure anyway in West Indian Christianity. In West Africa, he was identified by the missionaries in the power Eshu, the male trickster, probably because Eshu was associated with the erotic and with fire. According to Booth, Eshu (Legba) was the son of the Mawu/Lisa figure we have elided with Emanja. In Trinidad he retains his phallic characteristics and association with thresholds, as in Brazil where he becomes a 'negative spirit'. Herskovits suggests that the Satan of Afro-America retains the ludic characteristics of the trickster, and local Christianity emphasises our unregenerate nature rather than the attraction of the Evil One who, if he appears at all, does so in the form of the carnival mas *jabjab* (*diable-diable*), more prankster than devil.[36]

Ordering of moral power distinguishes 'what should be' from 'what should not be'. In the West at least, the distinction is closely aligned with the fundamental logic of our world: 'what should be' is to an extent 'what is', although 'what is' may alternatively be taken as a relatively neutral battleground for moral forces. (To talk in this way of 'what should not be' is clumsy but we cannot readily have recourse to our conventional notion of 'evil', for this is the term which, by Mother Earth's inversion, stands for 'what should be'.) 'What should not be' may be equated with this pre-existent ground as an unformed or residual Nature (as in South Asian religions), or alternatively as co-equal and co-eternal with 'what should be' in 'what is' (Manichean dualism), or as a fallen variant of the original order (Western monotheism). Following David Parkin we may gloss these as monist, dualist and semi-dualist;[37] in any particular tradition, however, including the universal religions, we are likely to find a complex of explanations.

How does 'what should not be' continue to intrude into 'what should be'? It may be just the recalcitrant moral evolution of our world, or in God's testing of us, or from the Devil, or else through the individual (sin), through others (witchcraft), or just from the stars or even by sheer chance. Dominant social groups define themselves through the moral order of 'what should be': frequently with 'what is'. That their (to us historically located) institutions are identical to the eternally sacred is for them self-evident. Subdominant sectors are aligned to 'what should not be': in the West to Evil, or later to the pre-human or the elemental. Thus the cleric has taken on occasion both women and Blacks as morally close to the powers of Evil, while the nineteenth-century biologist saw them as an undifferentiated Nature out of which males and Whites have emerged.[38] The subdominant (sometimes with dissidents from the dominant group who are no longer convinced of the universal truth or of their own personal fit with it) start from this ascribed identity, to affirm themselves, relative to the dominant order, in a variety of ways:

(i)   Taking themselves as the true exemplars of dominant values which are not (or no longer) located in the dominant group: for example radical Puritanism and those Afro-American sects which preach a Black God.

(ii) Arguing that the dominant values are flawed in some way: insurgent Christianity and radical Puritanism in its secular shift.

(iii) Recognising the dominant system as inevitable but seeing it as somehow misconceived: a rare and essentially 'pessimistic' position, that of the romantic diabolists and of the Frankists.

(iv) Emphasising a more complex variant of the dominant values so that different levels of knowledge, different moral dispensations, are simultaneously true: Gnostics, Kabbalists; this may be associated with an emergent or evolutionary 'monist' perspective (the Hermetic corpus of *high science*, or Marxism).

(v)   Just accepting the subdominant position: the baptised peoples of the European empires, on the surface at least.

(vi) Rejecting the dominant values altogether as fundamentally misconceived. This of course cannot be absolute, for, within any system, the possibility of innovation is limited to those things already recognised as alternative or equivalent, between which a new choice is made. Nevertheless the 'feel' of total rejection is common to the participants' own experience of their actions, even while we might argue that their perspective retains close affinities with positions (i) and (ii), as for the Rastas whose discourse remains essentially biblical.

If we take the oppositional sensibility as an intermittent set of psychological, moral and social rebellions against the established order, we will not be surprised to find many of these alternatives coincide, or succeed each other within the same oppositional movement; in the case of Rastafari, the Native Baptists plus the continuing African and high science knowledge together with a conscious Black countertradition.

Mother Earth's frank and radical identification with the Devil cuts across many of the justifications and apologies of those oppositional ideologies still tied to Christianity. She freely adopts the most prejudiced (the more prejudiced the better) imagery of 'what should not be'. In Afro–American Englishes *evil* and *bad* already carry a defiant and slightly self-parodying sense, egalitarian and demotic. It is thus a short step to radicalise their perversity as central. In Hell Valley, the term *evil* refers to everyday tasks. When Breadfruit's preparation of a fish broth is praised as 'really evil' this is not so far removed from the Pinnacle villagers' cheerful tribute to puncheon rum as 'wicked', or the urban matrons' exasperated but ultimately accepting description of the local tearaways as 'bad an' worthless with no behaviour'. Similarly, Hell (Heaven is not a term used by the Earth People) returns us to the original Life; as Karl Rahner suggests, the Western notion of hell has always contained some sense of the deep, the elemental, the ancestral: 'When we think of man entering hell we think of him as establishing contact with the most intrinsic, unified and deepest level of the reality of the world.'[39] Such 'weak' usages of evil, hell and the Devil playfully contravene the conventional 'strong', moral, usage. They are never entirely lacking in a conscious desire *épater le bourgeois*, which for me when in the Valley recalled Baudelaire, Swinburne and Alesteir Crowley. There is, quite simply, enormous pleasure in the rather delicious pursuit of 'evil'.

At the same time, personal identification with these terms does articulate a major cognitive alternative. A reaffirmation of subdominant values argues: 'If this then is evil, what is your good?' Much of what can be read as antinomian high spirits or lurid fascination is arguably a forced choice for the non-dominant in a rigidly dual system, as for those anti-colonial rebels in the Cook Islands who marked themselves with 'the sign of Satan'.[40] Michael Taussig considers such an identification with the enemy's enemy in his book *The Devil and Commodity Fetishism in South America*; the Afro-American peasants of the Columbian plantations and the Quechua-speaking peasants working Bolivian tin mines both invoke the Devil to increase their production, but to do so is ultimately to be blighted. Taussig argues that 'the Devil is a stunningly apt symbol of the alienation experienced by peasants as they enter the ranks of the proletariat'. While Irene Silverblatt sees this Devil as one imported by the Whites to represent indigenous traditions,[41] recalling the transformation of Eshu by the missionaries, Taussig takes the Devil as a representation of competitive relations of production but also as standing for Black people themselves. The Columbian peasant can lend himself to the Devil temporarily but this is self-defeating; unlike Mother Earth he is seeking palliation, a temporary accommodation. Whether the Devil could be said to have served as a symbol of Black resistance in the Caribbean before Mother Earth is uncertain. Rastas and Black Muslims alike use the term 'devil' for the Whites, but George Simpson briefly cites a ganja-using group in Jamaica whose members called on the Devil and sought possession by 'fallen spirits'.

The Sun

In everyday conversation Mother Earth uses 'Sun' and 'Son' almost inter-
changeably. In Christianity the association (in English a homophone) is not
uncommon: solar representations of God or his son Jesus derive from St John's
Gospel and the Book of Revelation. Fire, of course, characterises not only the
light of the Gospel, but Hell whose proud Lucifer, the Son of the Morning, is
another, albeit rebellious, son. Fire is also popularly assimilated to other
attributes devalued by Mother Earth – anger, sickness, sexuality, jealousy –
while the converse of light, darkness, is an attribute of both the Devil and the
European's Africa.

In its permanence and power the Sun is a powerful everyday representation
of 'what is' and 'what should be'. On occasion it has served as an emblem for
the oppressed, as it did for Spartacus' insurgent Kingdom of the Sun. Morton
claims that by the third century AD the Sun had come to represent the
'millennial aspirations of the dispossessed', only to be co-opted back into the
establishment by Diocletian and thence into state Christianity.[42] If the Sun
seems vital to natural power how can Mother Earth relinquish it so easily to the
Whites? In part because, whatever the tourist image of the bountiful sun, the
experience of agriculture in the Caribbean is not, as in Britain, some waiting on
the reluctant sun but an active protection against this omnipresent and
destructive solar power – skin-darkening, energy-drawing, madness-inducing.
Shade trees have to be planted to give plants shelter from the sun so that they
can grow, and the earth appears virtually self-fecundating. For the Earth
People, the Son's planet is the Planet of Ice; its apparent heat has been placed
between the Sun and the Earth to obstruct his return to our planet when he is
finally expelled. The heat then comes from the Earth itself; at the Miracle, the
Beginning of the End, The Mother made this heat come closer to the Earth, to
redeem us physically: 'When you body more free, is to develop more heat –
which is power.' This employs the local Hot–Cold idiom in which our everyday labour produces heat which saps our energy and which we attempt to
reduce by working less or by taking a cooling tea. Uniquely among country
people, the Earth People do not take a cooling and continue to work when they
are really heated:

The Sun suppose to be putting back inside of you, not drawing! You can feel it
'drawing' yes, because of the spirit which is in your flesh which is not able to stand the
heat. You cannot stand it because your body become weak to your own self which is the
fire. Your body is make up out of fire. Without that fire in your body, your body is not
living. So now that heat that is returning, your body have to build again because you
have to take off the clothes. And when the clothes is off, your body will start receiving
the elements as the animals. Wild animals take the heat and you cannot take it? You are

clothed with clothes which not belongings to you, so then your body becomes weak. The sun you suppose to be able to take it, as the animals do, the birds do. Now I will put it this way: not until yourself spirit keep coming closer to the flesh by your nakedness, your living, your thinking, then there is nothing that will bother you, neither heat nor cold, because your body will be mature for that.

An opposition of Sun to Moon in European and Amerindian mythologies usually parallels one of Male to Female (but sometimes the converse). For Mother Earth, the Moon – the womb of the Earth which was entered by the Son – was then expelled to become the planet we see: 'corruption had entered She, and She had to spit it out'. Eliade has suggested that this affinity of the Moon and the Earth, both in opposition to the Sun, is simply experientially obvious. Colonial slaves, like the earlier Caribs, used the moon for registering plantation work periods, and lunar cycles of animal and plant growth are still recognised; in Trinidad men associate it with women's inconstancy, with their natural fecundity and menstruation: the very word 'moon' may refer to their genitals.[43] As with other rural Trinidadian women. Mother Earth maintains that her menstrual periods are synchronous with the moon, whose waxing and waning are associated with the intermittent passage of its energy to the earth.

At times she talks of the Sun and Moon simply as principles rather than sensible objects – 'they ai' planets they is life' – but their properties retain those of the planets we see. 'Everything has its meaning, its sign, everything carry its spirit.' Mother Earth rejects the heliocentric arrangement of the planets. When I drew it in the dust of her hut in the course of our debates she was indignant? 'This is madness! You turn the children upside down. How could the planets be before the Earth when it brings forth?' Jakatan concurred: 'How teachers give you the true facts now?' Like the local villagers they regard the American moon-shot as an elaborately faked exercise, for could the womb permit men born of her to return once again?

Serpents and silk cotton trees

The first day I went into the bush, [Petite Rivière] there, the first thing happened to me was a serpent fall from tree, a very long one, fall right in front of my little boy, one of my children. And I told him to stand up – 'Don't move!' – and he stand up there and watching like serpent, and the serpent watching up at him. Well, to me, we look strange, something about us: the serpent was looking at us and it keep watching until it turn away and leave. That was the first. I wasn't afraid but yet I 'fraid serpents. Up to now I will have a feelings about them. I don't touch them. If it catch one I don't touch it. If I touch it I feel something go through me.

In more enthusiastic moments, however, Mother Earth identifies herself with the Serpent of Africa and India: the Mamba or Cobra. Snakes which care to wander through the huts of the Valley are unmolested and may even be stroked.[44] Since her Baptist days, Mother Earth has had visions of snakes; often they appear initially as frightening but then turn out to be healing or reconciling. On one occasion she saw a snake kill a chicken after her young son recovered from a nearly fatal illness (page 71). In her twenties she had a vision of Jesus sleeping; she ran away from him and entered a river in which there lived a snake.

The immediate meanings recalled by a snake in Trinidad are those found elsewhere in the West – evil, danger and obscene masculinity. A common complaint of Pinnacle villagers was that the overgrowth of their previously cultivated land had encouraged snakes, and indeed it was quite common to encounter mapapis or large makowels inside roofs or up fruit trees. The snake represents the invading bush and it is not surprising that it is taken up by Mother Earth with its valence inverted. It already has locally a consciously African and 'natural' resonance. In Kenya, members of the 'Mumbo Cult' of 1908 also revered the serpent and refused to wash, cut their hair or cultivate their land. We know the Yoruba revered serpents as representations of Orishala; and the Dahomean rainbow serpent arrived in the Caribbean as Damballa (in Haiti) or Dangbe (the Guianas); a Haitian priestess may be called a *mambo*; the woman prophet who led the slave revolt in eighteenth-century Surinam is supposed to have used a snake in what the Europeans called 'the ancient dance of the mermaid'; stuffed snakes and snake parts are still used in Trinidadean obeah. Similar to the *lajabless*, the obscure nature spirit called Mama Glo, half woman, half snake, was once said to seduce and then kill men wandering in the Trinidad bush.

The serpent in the West is not always demonic or phallic. The Hermetic corpus identified the Serpent of Eden with Jesus. It stands for parthenogenesis through the sloughing of its skin, and thus for renewal and healing; it has been suggested recently by Ecofeminists as a representation of the menstrual solidarity of women in association with the moon and with their blood. Frequently located mythically on the boundaries of the divine and the human, between birth and death, the moon and the underearth, good and evil, the snake is ambiguous. It may be phallic yet it is also female. The bisexuality of the Medusa – woman's head, phallic locks – has been taken up by Obeyesekere to suggest that the adoption of Sri Lankan women of such matted locks (akin to Mother Earth's 'dreads') is an assertion of masculine identity by those who are dispossessed of their female authority through unsatisfactory marriages or through problematic childbirths; and psychoanalysts have argued that the snake stands for the *vagina dentata*, perhaps no bad representation for a female prophet who aspires to awaken 'dread' in the male sex.[45]

If the practical conjurations of obeah are scorned by Mother Earth, its image of African magic affirms the sorceress as the woman of power, to which she assimilates the popular cinematic image of the witch, together with such folkloric local powers as Papa Bois (the wild man of the woods) and the soucouyant (vampire), as all being partial recognitions of Natural power. One local image of sorcery is the silk cotton tree, *Eriodenendron orientale*. Revered by the Yoruba as emblematic of Ogun, its wood was used for weapons, and it was assimilated generally to the souls of children awaiting birth and, as a genius loci, to the family. In Jamaica the tree was associated with the witch-finding cults of *myal* and *cumina*,[46] but in Trinidad country areas it is now identified simply with the African powers: 'It use by long-time people here in Pinnacle [for obeah]. When they come to cut it down to extend the cricket pitch, had to get a special man. A few try now. Can' cut it down! When he come and say prayer and cut it down, it full of nails.' During slavery and after, the tree was the *devil tree*, the *jumbie tree*. By the doorway of the central hut in Hell Valley a young silk cotton tree now grows against the wooden boards; hardly sacred for the Earth People, it does stand yet again for the assertion of Africa over Europe. Unaware of its precise significance for the Yoruba, the Earth People simply identify it as Natural in that Christianity has consigned the silk cotton tree, like the serpent, to the domain of 'evil'. And in that, it has once more become African, and central.

Left, right and obscenity

'And I keep talking and cursing, as they would call it, which I don't call a curse because when you say "You mother cunt" you are talking about the Earth. The Earth is the cunt that brings forth, the Moon is the womb' (M.E.). The Earth People exchange the terms *left* and *right* in certain contexts, together with a studied use of conventional obscenities. Intentional 'obscenity' and 'rudeness' occur periodically in the Western radical heritage from the Quakers 'rhetoric of impoliteness' to the Filthy Speech Movement of the sixties. At the least, they are a rejection of polite values; but they may also stand for a 'world as it should be' in contradistinction to an 'as it is' which itself has inverted the meanings of Nature. Obscenities are 'natural' and 'earthy', demotic and carnivalesque subversions of social power through the intrusions of nature into social life: fornication, excretion, urination, menstruation, disease (to use our distancing lexicon):

This old lady live next to us an' she real Catholic. And she sit up in bed and read prayer book. And it like she try an' look like White. And then [her illness] get so bad, it need about four to lift her. And my daughter help. And then it so bad she bawl and she swear awful . . . For the first time in her life she begin to find herself there!   (M.E.)

Rodney Needham has recently collated the widespread use of anatomical and spacial bilaterality to order social values.[47] In Africa and Europe, the Right generally stands for the auspicious, the orthodox, the male and the social, the Left for the inauspicious and the natural, the illegitimate, but also for tyrranicide. We do not have to take his suggestions of the near universality of such a schema: it is sufficient to note a common aligning of body laterality with sexual dimorphism and with a variety of social institutions and cosmological constructs. Like the nurturant earth itself laterality is an obvious, perhaps ubiquitous, representation. The association of the Left with sorcery is common in Trinidad through high science (as in the malevolent Left Hand Path); the Left is usually inauspicious (and even a Baptist when mourning will lie on the Right to guarantee a vision) but it is also identified as the popular side in local politics in opposition to the former French Creole elite. In Jamaica, it is argued that if a woman leans to the right during intercourse she conceives a boy, to the left a girl; the male foetus then lies on the right, the female on the left. Mother Earth does not delineate the anatomy of the original hermaphrodite *mothers*, but we might anticipate that, like the Adam/Eve androgyne of the Jewish Kabbalah and the paired deities of West Africa, they are male on their Right, female on their Left. The left of the human brain, she notes, is Natural, the right Scientific (page 82).

The oppositional moment cannot 'invert' every particular of the received world, for what are the opposed particulars, what superordinate? The Shakers were forbidden to initiate movements with the left limb, and William Blake kept the conventional association of women with the Left, still devaluing it as mere material. Mother Earth again refers us back through accepted representations to a personal experience: she is ambidextrous although with a certain tendency to left-handedness, sighting with the left eye, pacing from the left, and so on. In her early thirties she went to an optician as she found her eyesight getting weaker; as with her other experiences with city professionals, she found it an unnverving experience for 'she take this thing and watch me and she watch me'. She never took the incident as any particular sign of difference until the disappearance of one of her spectacle lenses in the Burning (page 73):

The reason I say 'left' – all left! – is because the time for 'right' is over. This is the life of 'left'. They give you the 'right', God give you the 'right' because He is the 'right' He say. And 'right' to me is untruth. So when you turn to the left which is the Devil (they usually have a word to say when you are a left hander you are owing the Devil a favour), well I am a left hander, so then I call myself the Devil, which I stand for the Beginning as the Mother Earth.

The Earth People exchange the words when referring to people and ideas – 'You all left now?' or 'The End now begin left here in Trinidad' but only rarely when giving spatial directions. Exchange is not equally in both directions, and 'left' in its directional sense or as a verb is seldom dropped in favour of 'right' (thus 'I left my cutlass left here' not 'I right my cutlass left here'). Like the others, Mother Earth herself may slip into conventional usage. Among newer members of the community such slippage is a source of amusement whilst also recognised as *humbling you'self*, induction into the group. That popular protest is 'left-wing' is celebrated as partial knowledge of the Mother, like the recognition of the Mother in Eve or even Polyphemus:

because he had one eye. They say he eat people. I don't go all that! He [Odysseus, the Son] using the giant all the time, which is the Mother, blind. He taking what He wants; He says 'I'm God.'

Since this flesh is living in this life I learn a lot about 'right' and never could see what I am looking for in what they call 'right'. To me every life I turn and I see what is 'right', to me it is not 'right' at all. Until now that I reach to this stage in 1975 as Mother Earth, burning everything I had. The last thing I burn were the Bibles showing where our education is upsided down. And putting out my senses is now that I am really seeing what I was looking for all the days of my life that I live. I now understand the meaning of 'right' and 'wrong'. So then, when you say 'right' and 'wrong', wrong is what I call 'the left'. Because even though I come out and put out myself to the people, they tell me I'm wrong! I say 'yes, I'm wrong because I'm left' . . . This is the fight, from right to left. All you have in the city is 'right'. Nothing 'left' – except when you drive a car!

As our education is upside down, the real meanings of many words can be found only by a fresh inversion restoring the original state. As in the interpret-ation of dreams by psychoanalysts or by the Pinnacle villagers, conventional knowledge is taken as already disguised by inversion:

They say it have in the Seven Days Bible the earth as a body and Trinidad is the foot: if Trinidad is the last an' the tail, then here is suppose to be the Beginning.

'God' is 'dog' backward an' they say he is a man's best friend and so he God.[48]

(M.E.)

As 'time' is about to end, the word 'life' is substituted, particularly when talking of the present: 'this time' or 'now' become 'this life': 'The Beginning have no time; only the flesh have years.'

Truth is death – I don't use that word again . . . In the Beginning Flesh had only one eye. But the Son took the eye of the Mother. Only one eye you have. One eye is Natural, the other Negative. One eye belongs to Life, one to death. Everything is now I; I this and I that; 'I and I'.

'I and I' is Rasta for 'I', 'me', 'we' and 'us', suppressing the accusative case and identifying unity in the many, the many in the one. Mother Earth here ridicules the Rastas for dropping the demotic nominative 'me' whilst simultaneously decrying any private self as a controlling agent, and referring back to the Burning of her glasses and her weak right eye. At the same time *me* stands for *Mother Earth*. As with so much of Life in the Valley, slippage between inside and outside meanings is the source of continued hilarity, particularly when it involves children or new members. Pumpkin, one of the children, when mischievous is jokingly called The Adversary (the Christians' name for the Devil); this implies some ironic disapproval of Pumpkin's actual behaviour but also a recognition that what seems annoying to adults may in fact be closer to the Life. If the Earth People have abandoned the rigid institutions of Society, then actions from within which go against the smooth running of their community cannot, with any sense of the ridiculous, be condemned simply as undesirable. Contradictions, puns and 'nonsense' are joyfully seized upon. They are neither problems in a static theology nor are they necessarily incorporated into a complex system of classification. Like obscenities and the humour of tabanka, they champion the word-play and fragmentary subversions of African–American English. The Life is not really to be understood through words anyway: these are an imperfect reflection of Nature, suited to the double-talk of the Scientific world:

Words is just a confusion. The power is in you. Is the book I'm speaking about when you really think about it because is the book the children are learning from, not really from their true self – the senses. So then they become a slave to the book. The book becomes the main part of slavery now.

The Culture of the Body
The most scandalous characteristic of the Earth People is certainly their refusal to wear clothes. While rumours about sorcery and mother–son incest in the Valley occasions general comment but also interested speculation, the limits of Trinidadian tolerance are totally breached by what they term the Culture of the Body. Although the community are sometimes referred to as the Naked People, we may argue that they are 'nude' rather than 'naked', for they defiantly engage in an activity motivated by a recognition that they are contravening a fundamental value. 'To be naked is to be oneself', says John Berger, 'to be nude is to be seen naked by others'.[49] The Western notion of 'nudity' entails a way of seeing which is conventionalised and idealised;[50] a deliberate shedding of clothes on behalf of other meanings of the act, whether sexual display or antinomian revolt.

In the medieval period nudity connoted something 'underlying' or 'basic', whether the basis was ultimately good or evil.[51] What we might describe as 'involuntary nudity' is a common representation of insanity: like the Trinidadian madman, the tragic Greek heroine Phaedra is represented 'throwing her customary garments off; she will have none of them – she is deranged'. Voluntary nudity has characterised numerous movements in the West which strove to return to pre-lapsarian Edenic innocence or to the prophetic enactments of Saul and David: the 1374 Aachen 'dancing mania', St Francis, the Adamites of fifteenth-century Bohemia, seventeenth-century Anabaptists and Quakers, Mother Ann of the Shakers, and Joanna Southcott. The first outward sign of the mission of the Anabaptist Jan of Leyden was his running, stripped, through the streets of Münster. In 1652 a woman stripped naked during a service in the chapel at Westminster, crying 'Welcome the Resurrection'; for Puritan radicals, comments Christopher Hill, 'undressing was as good as dressing'. Most notorious are the Doukhobors, the Russian pacifists who settled in Canada with the help of Tolstoy; their occasional practice of nudity reflects 'enthusiasm' within the group but it is also a highly effective protest against military conscription or attempts by the government to educate their children and register their land. Doukhobors originally took off their clothes at periods of millennial expectation; as one member commented in language that could almost have been used by the Earth People: 'after the 21st May, we went in the manner of the first man, Adam and Eve to show nature to humanity, how man should return into his fatherland and return the ripened fruits and seeds'.[52]

In the Americas, radical Puritans undressed in the streets to protest against persecution, and a Quaker in Long Island burnt her clothes and declared herself Christ. How frequent this was among the Quakers in the West Indies is unclear, but a contemporary acidly suggested Ranters tended to go there as the climate was more congenial for stripping. An alternative to nudity was to dress in sacking as did a defiant Quaker who went thus from Barbados to Boston in 1677.

The gradual secularisation of millennial themes maintained an association of nudity with social radicalism. William Blake and Havelock Ellis were both rumoured to disrobe among close friends in the privacy of their urban gardens, and nudity remained part of a general complex of utopianism, vegetarianism, free love, 'nature worship', and (for the more timid) long hair, beards and clothes reform. The hippies and the women's movement manifested a more public efflorescence of what had previously been a relatively fringe theme through *streaking* (public disrobing and running about nude), bra-burning and interest in the natural body and in 'body language'. By the 1970s nude sunbathing had passed from the margins of 'Health and Efficiency' groups to tourist beaches in a renewed and wider public interest in body morphology and healthy function.[53]

Given the Europeans' obsession with garbing the 'naked children' of their colonies, nudity had had a particular salience for those who appealed to an unspoiled precolonial past, whilst accentuating any racial differences. If the Whites were those who clothed themselves to an extraordinary degree, some, by simple opposition, took the line that the original 'natural' state had been, or should have been, one of naked harmony with their land. Like the Quakers, the founders of the Ghost Dance went naked 'for a sign'; individuals, or the whole membership, were periodically unclothed in the 'Naked Cult' of the West African Aladura church. Nativist nudity derived not only from the characteristics ascribed by the Europeans and from the biblical Eden, but from existing local concepts of nakedness or discarding dress at 'liminal' moments: during planting; in madness; oath taking; insult; the birth of twins; couvade obligations; pilgrimage; mourning; practising witchcraft and countering witchcraft; among shaman and ascetics. Nudity passed backwards and forwards between marginal prophetic groups, the collective millennial moment and such temporary individual roles and situations. Shirley Ardener argues that the sexual display of the Eastern Nigerian 'women's war' against the British colonialists in 1929 deployed, against a new threat, the established response of local women when faced with a collective insult to their sex.

Nudity in Trinidad, as elsewhere, connotes madness and sexuality but also incest. If a Trinidadian woman marries the husband of her deceased sister, and there are any children from the first marriage, she would be 'uncovering her dead sister's nakedness'. This expression recalls the incident in Genesis when Noah was 'seen naked' (a Hebrew euphemism for incest) by his son Ham – an event once cited by White racists to justify the continued subjugation of the Blacks as the children of Ham.

In Trinidad a *naked plantain* is one eaten without any sauce, un*dressed* and signalling poverty. A common sight in Pinnacle Village is a group of the poorer women washing the family clothes together at one of the stand-pipes in the streets or down by the river. One important measure of a woman's respectability is her struggle to send her children to school in clean and ironed clothes. Even to go *bareback* (shirtless) in Trinidad is hardly for respectable men, and no woman would publicly bare her breast to feed her baby. When they venture into the bush, village women are clothed in hat, rubber boots and kerchiefs wrapped about; at other times (Carnival always excepted) even trousers for rural women are not acceptable and, like shorts, indicate the dubious morals of the jagomet. No adult in the West Indies has gone naked in public since slavery and probably rarely then. In the nineteenth century 'Creole labourers, following the custom of slavery days, wore trousers and boots', and derided the dhoti-clad Indian immigrants as 'naked'.[54] Nearer to town, and particularly among the lighter-skinned middle classes, sea-bathing and even sun-bathing in bathing costumes are now acceptable; for to engage in these activities without losing respectability represents bourgeois licence, something called *broad-minded*: 'And when our colour speak of other people as a respectable person, they don't speak about the White people, they don't worry about the White people . . . They are White and can do anything.'[55] The Whites are just not in the crab barrel (page 39). At Mother Earth's prompting I gave a talk about the Earth People to the nurses at the St Ann's Hospital. Incredulity at my going naked in the Valley prompted the usual criticisms of nudity: it led to promiscuity and laziness, to squatting in filth and excrement, and the abuse of children. The only Pinnacle villager I ever saw naked in public was one of the younger fishermen who had some modest inclination towards Rastafari, swimming to his anchored boat in the bay with his clothes held above his head. The village verdict? 'No behaviour!' It is among Rasta men that one can perhaps imagine a greater sympathy to the Natural body. They often go bareback even in town, and respectable villagers call the local Rastas (Plate 1, page 9) 'half-naked'. Nevertheless, even those who had considerable sympathy for the Earth People vividly described the shame they would feel if they themselves went naked. For any Rasta, the notion of his queen being without clothes and exposed to public gaze would be abhorrent. The leader of the Black Power party, NJAC, was even more scathing to Jakatan and myself about the nudity in the Valley of Decision.

The year before I arrived in the Valley the Earth People had decided to wear *bag* kilts when outside the community (Plate 2).[56] Public provocation was played down in favour of the idea that Natural life was only really possible in the bush, and nudity in town is now restricted to rare demonstrations of protest. Mother Earth's own arguments for nudity recall the theories of the sociologist: clothes are just a means of social distinction which increase rather than diminish sexual interest:[57] 'Everything has its meaning, its sign. Everything has its spirit. Clothes now, they build it in signs to always get it sell.' She denies they serve any practical function – the usual Trinidadian rationale – for one is only attacked in the bush by a snake when wearing clothes for animals dislike the smell of stale human sweat. As for the heat, well, 'you suppose to take that'. It is the *religion* of the Europeans which has persuaded African people that they cannot live together among the elements, and resilience is valued in the Valley. My own experience suggests it is comparatively easy to work in the sun with no clothes on; the test is the night when one lies naked on the cold ground above the cliff with no covering. The frequent cuts, thorns and scorpion bites consequent on going without shoes are shrugged off, and the Valley member with a poisoned foot who seeks an extended period away from his labours is accused of still being under the influence of the Son: 'Without clothes, baby skin develop toughness quicker . . . that is what difference is in material and social. That is how we put ourselves down to Nature to regain our spirit.'

For the Quakers and others who preached 'a Naked Christ', the bared body was a representation of the bared soul, a demonstration of the reality behind convention.[58] The Earth People, like some Ranter groups associated with the early Quakers, argue somewhat differently: that the body itself is the goal. The Doukhobors too value nudity in itself – 'between us and Mother Earth' as they say – but also as an act of insult. Unlike the Earth People, they use it to gain certain definite concessions from the wider society. Compare our Trinidadian Mother Earth's own description of her burning her possessions and then stripping (page 74) with that of a Doukhobor woman who did the same in Canada: 'I took nothing out. After the fire, I took off everything and I stood naked – like my mother. Peter cried. I told him not to be afraid, that it was right what I did. I told him it would bring daddy home from prison.'[59] The Doukhobor is following a now conventionalised public routine which immediately coerces the authorities to cover her with clothes and give her shelter, and later to meet her demands to avoid a repetition of the incident. When the Earth People have negotiated with the authorities (to get the contract for clearing the local traces) they dress soberly in bag and advance their claims through

2 Earth People wearing 'bag' before entering Pinnacle to barter provision crops for new cutlasses. Mother Earth's son, Pomme Cythère, on the left.

conventional argument. If the psychiatrists, social workers and police who are sent to deal with Doukhobor protests themselves responded by taking off their clothes, the Doukhobors would doubtless be disconcerted. The Earth People would be enchanted.

Given the close Western association of nudity with sex, discarding one's garments permanently argues a broader rejection of customary morality, beyond sexuality rather than a simple pursuit of sexual licence. Individual members, however, do get a good deal of amusement from the idea that everybody believes them to be engaged in an endless orgy. Mother Earth regards homosexuality as un-Natural and, given the usual sexual imbalance among the members, sexual activity is only common between Mother Earth and Jakatan (and she does not find it especially enjoyable according to her public homilies to the community). The Earth People are taught that sexual activity will start when Black women manage to overcome their White ways and come and join the group but, as she thinks that this is rather unlikely before the End, and that everyone will then return in any case to some unspecified hermaphrodite form, she does not really rate sexual activity as particularly desirable or even necessary. Complaints of sexual frustration by the male Earth People are firmly put aside, to linger as gossip and reminiscence at private moments by the back fire.

Nakedness entails us in a raw physical intimacy, an unveiling of bodily activities other than sex. The male Earth People freely urinate outside the men's hut while continuing general conversation (not a local practice) but they have built two latrines which are enclosed by wooden planks and remain relatively private, although the sounds sometimes emanating from them are a subject for ribald merriment: 'Free up you'self now!' During her menstrual periods Mother Earth keeps a rag between her legs, changing this at intervals. She may call attention to it and the younger male recruits complain rather queasily. However, the vaginal discharge of one of the women members was the occasion of much critical comment: a sickness from Rome, there was nothing Natural about this and a mother should safeguard her womb.

A nude man and a nude woman embody rather different images. The man without clothes carries a heightened sexual potential, almost a threat of rape. At the same time his nudity partakes of nakedness, 'stripped for action', a prosaic extension of his conventional working role. If the naked man is a self-determining subject, the undressed woman becomes an object, for men. The naked woman is always nude. She takes her clothes off for men. As Berger notes, a naked woman contemplates herself, not for herself, but through the eyes of men, as nude. The nudity of the female Earth People directly challenges this notion; like the men, they aim at being naked for themselves. At the End, the community will no longer be 'nude' for the opposition between the clothed and the unclothed will have gone. They will have achieved nakedness. Mother Earth has again appropriated the *no behaviour* of the Black male for women too, in her affirmation of a Nature which rejects Social grooming, skin-lightening cream, hair-straightening and the rest.

9

The Beginning Of The End: everyday life in the valley

Freeing Up the Nation

Mother Earth's visions cannot be considered simply as idiosyncratic explanations of personal experience, for many young people have left their homes and families to join her in a desolate part of the Trinidad bush. In contrast to Blake or Shelley whose ideas I have compared with hers, her visions have been realised in a social group: they may be said to 'work' – in both our conventional senses. Like Ann Lee and Gerard Winstanley with whom too I have argued many affinities, she not only awaits the return to the original Life of Nature, but is actively organising a community to prepare for The Beginning Of The End.

Do the experiences and beliefs of each new member replicate those of Mother Earth – generating, in some sort of mimesis, a homologous structure of social organisation and values – or does each member relate reciprocally (by complement) to her? As we shall see, both. We find homology in those aspects which evoke the historical and political situation shared by all Black people as against the Whites, for the whole membership is Black; and reciprocity in those aspects which articulate the relations between Black mothers and their children, and between women and men, for the majority of the permanent members are young men.[1]

Against a purely biographical reading of Mother Earth we can place a 'fable' published by a Trinidadian student in the United States.[2] This tells how the Creatrix produced an harmonious world inhabited by Black people, an androgynous race ruled by The Mother of the Nation. 'Bearing the pregnant vitalisms of the maternal source', these first humans are music loving and pacific, agriculturalists who revere the ancient cycles of the Earth. The Creatrix has a brother, the God of Death, who envies the fecundity of the Blacks and, from his Land of Ice, transforms some of them into White men, pastoral nomads who enslave both their own women and the Blacks. Celebrating power rather than poetry, they subject themselves to linear time and rape the Earth with mechanical tools.

Here the White's deity is the Mother's brother rather than her son: she does indeed have a son but he is the Black culture hero, Dionysos. The drama of an original incest is lost but we still find a female creation of androgynous Blacks who are assimilated to 'nature', and a jealous male power who creates Whites identified with time and brutal power and technology. Cyclical female nature versus linear male technology. Clearly these are themes which strike common resonances in Trinidad, for Black men as well as for women, fable or no fable.

Does such a female divinity demand a 'social vehicle' which carries and replicates the matriarchal cosmos? Can we presume that the 'matrifocal' African–Caribbean family provides an especially appropriate locus for an omnipotent Creatrix? The absence of any local female deities except those persisting in shango, together with patripotestal Rastafari, would argue the contrary. Those matrilineal West African societies which may be said to offer a relative female autonomy (if hardly actual power) lack any female earth deity.[3] James Preston warns us that a supreme female divinity may quite variously seem to: reflect the existing social institutions (relative female power); or she may offer a female model to be emulated; or else she represents inversions of actually existing human relationships; or alternatively provides idealised extensions of human society.[4] If a supreme Mother cannot be said to automatically presuppose some type of 'matriarchal' social organisation, for the Earth People the continuing presence of a female Nature in their human founder certainly leads them to incorporate The Mother with human mother. It may be in millennial groups that female divinity necessarily follows female leadership or at least some type of matrifocused organisation.

Chapter 5 took the development of Mother Earth's new group up to 1975 when her family half-reluctantly agreed to continue naked. The young men from town who then came to join them were not from Jeanette's own biological family nor witnesses of The Miracle. They were old friends and neighbours from Port-of-Spain together with Rastas attracted by an article in the *Trinidad Express* written by a reporter who had heard about a family living naked in the bush:

what really made people come. I don't know how the papers reach, but *The Express* reach. It in October, between September an' October there, I had a little tent down below the hill, which I left the house freely an' I went in the little tent an' stay there for a little while. The papers come. Well, I came back to the house. Some fellows come, my son bring them, so they call me 'Look, come back in the house.' I speak to them about the life of God an' the Son an' so forth, they take my pictures, with my thick lap, my

hands this way, an' they put it in the papers but didn't put what I say! They put something else – I living in a snake-infected place and all sorts of thing they put, besides
what I told them . . . So then I see Rastas start coming. Well I didn't know anything
about Rastas but they came, they tried to show me how to talk, tell me I mus' speak this
way as a Rastafarian. I tell them I don't know anything about that, I can't speak like a
Rasta! They tell me I mus'n' use tinning grater,[5] I mus' use coconut shell. I tell them I
can't use that! I say I am accustom using tinning make my grater. I have a lot of coconut
to grate for to make oil so I cannot do what they want me to do. I can' speak like them.
I say they are [fudging?] from the Rastafarians in Jamaica. I told them I am not a
Jamaican – I born in this country, Trinidad, and I intend to speak as I would speak for
people to understand me. If I speak like them an' I have to go about talking to the
people they wouldn't understand me! So I can't really speak like them. They wasn't so
pleased. They find I shouldn't eat salt, then find I shouldn't eat meat, I shouldn't eat
flesh, an' they keep complaining. So they keep going, coming an' going; up to now, they
still complaining! Which some change and stay with us, some leave.

No further revelations occurred and the ideas of the Earth People were now
consolidated in reflection and debate. By 1978 the title of 'Mother Earth' was
adopted, possibly after a Carnival mas which had portrayed a large fecund
Earth Mother. Jeanette continued to have visions in dreams but these were
similar to those of the other members: premonitions and answers to the
immediate organisational problems on which her attention was now focussed.
A relatively minor confirmation of her status as divine Mother was the
Coming of the Makers (page 108), a few days after the birth of her last child.

   While around fifty people have been active Earth People at different times,
in October 1981 twenty-two were resident in the Valley (Appendix 1). By this
time Mother Earth and her immediate family had been naked for six years, and
eight of the group had been with them for three years or more. There had
been annual marches to Port-of-Spain, and a visit to the Rastas living by the
pitch lake in the south; the community had been raided by the Regiment
and the youngest children removed to the Tacarigua orphanage whilst Mother
Earth was placed in St Ann's Hospital, later to be brought out by the others
(page 61). Her son Cocorite, then aged nine, had managed to slip away from
the orphanage and found his way alone across the mountains back to the
Valley. These events had been briefly reported in the press and by 1981 most
Trinidadians had heard of the 'naked people' in the bush. In their last
confrontation with the authorities the group had been brought before the Chief
Magistrate 'An' he say "We and you are of two different kinds. I cannot try
you."' The case was dismissed.[6] The Pinnacle villagers had decided that the
authorities were no longer prepared to remove the Earth People and they had
established wary relations with the Valley, the Earth People using the village
stores to barter for cutlasses and salt. The Rasta news-sheet had come out

offering limited support for the group and any public moves against the Valley
would have brought strong protests both from *Ras Tafari Speaks* and from
popular weeklies like *The Bomb* (which had Rastas on the staff). Trinidad's
first prime minister, Eric Williams, had died a few months previously and the
ruling party was preoccupied with a general election. The group in Hell
Valley were left to themselves.

With the exception of Mother Earth only one member of the group is now
female. Sixteen are young men between eighteen and thirty-three years old.
Most of them have been previously associated rather loosely with Rastafari and
about half have been members of the Shouter Baptists. Their average age on
joining was twenty. The members of Mother Earth's own biological family are
Mother herself, Jakatan, at thirty-six some thirteen years younger, and two of
her sons Pomme Cythère and Cocorite. The youngest member of the group is
Pumpkin, aged four, who is there with his father Eddoes, his mother having
returned to town after a brief stay. All are from 'the poorer class' and only
Coconut completed secondary school. Jakatan was born in a fishing village
along the coast past Pinnacle, but the others are from the Belmont and
Laventille areas of Port-of-Spain.

All are African–Caribbean but their skin colour shades from Mother Earth's
black black to lighter *red* hues. Indian and Chinese features can be recognised
in a number, and most have some White ancestry. Although such characteristics are occasionally used for identification in the group ('It have one up in
the woods, one of them two with red skin'), they are not especially remarked;
nor are they any measure of enthusiasm or commitment for 'We are all one
race, the Black Race, the Race of Africa and India.'

How did the newer Earth People come to join Mother Earth? Like others in
the slum areas of eastern Port-of-Spain they argue that *society* has rejected
them. As the calypsonian Earl Lewis puts it:

In Laventille and John John
They treat a man like Viet-Cong
Police hounding you everyday
Magistrate want to jail you right away
All because you come from behind the bridge[7]

Trinidad has been a class society since slavery, but one in which the rural
family had a distinctive role as a labour reserve and as an economic unit, and
where the continuing, if increasingly tenuous, security of family land and thus
subsistence agriculture during periods of unemployment has not encouraged
the urban poor to recognise themselves politically as anything we might term a
proletariat, as a 'class for itself'. Depending on economic opportunity, ability

and luck, an individual can move between petty entrepreneurship, waged employment, subsistence agriculture, selling agricultural surplus, fishing, and temporary migration. A post-colonial ideology of equal opportunity, embodied in the nationalist but pro-business governing party, the People's National Movement, dismisses any question of class interests as Black Power or communism. Politics is parochial and pragmatic, represented as a question of personalities, of *bobol* (corruption) and *bacchanal* (scandal) – of moral failure, clientship and reciprocity. The Earth People told me simply that they did not 'fit' into this modern Trinidad. They resented the anonymous consumer society with its constant soliciting of PNM patronage, its increasingly distant bureaucracy and its commercial values modelled on those of the United States. They regretted the loss of patterns of mutual help like susu and gayap, and the exchange of food between neighbours; the failure of children to look after their ageing parents; the advent of air-conditioned funeral parlours and glass-topped satin-lined caskets instead of the communal wake; respectable church marriage, prostitution and pornographic videos rather than a *real sexual freeness*; provocative 'American' fashion shows and political sex scandals. What we might perhaps term the 'commodification of desire' – Mother Earth's 'sex by imagination, too much of dreaming, too much of material: it come as a new slavery then'.

Their *material* world is expressed well in the musings of Wozzie, the Port-of-Spain Rasta who had settled in Pinnacle:

NJAC [the Black Power party]? It talk alright but you can' say it different. You can' do nothing. It have big shot parties there an' none for poor man. Start nex' party? It sound easy easy, man. You got ideas and you want thing and so, but what you do? You need education . . . No place man don' thief you. It all bandits and police. In fact it all one, bandit-police, the same. Like here they push you with gun and beat you, an' you jus' got reefer! You know who are the big ganja men? It ai' the natty. It the man with the rum shop, with the police. He in it real big big. He go into bush. He reach in four hours an' he got big place. An' you say to him about ganja an' he say 'What? I don' know. I ai' interest. It very dangerous.' An' then he give police plenty money. You know what, Bro', I ai' rest here looking for to catch me tail. I make it big. I ai' sell it on street; you rest there, you sell a little two dollars here, you looking for police. No, man, it have you get contacts in Mafia . . . It all Mafia in Trinidad now. They all big shot with car and so. I get local whole load grass and sell it like that – bam! – plenty money and me out and clear. The police are Mafia, they all about, like in that tree there, an' they scope an' scope on you go out with pile and they come and take it. You go to police and say it have one steal you' ganja? An' they take you' money too. You think me making joke? I get gun and shoot them first . . .

By contrast, the Earth People told me they had never dedicated themselves to the pursuit of the cars and televisions beloved by tibourg society: they had always experienced a rather different and simpler need – one they describe as Spiritual, a search for a Freedom and a Truth which they counterpose to the Social and the Material. Some of them had joined the Baptists until they realised that these were only 'half-way there' and had not confronted the colonial domination by the British. They had grown their locks and adopted Rasta idiom and some Rasta ideas but, again, felt that this was not enough, that Rastas were not living the natural life they proclaimed: given half a chance they would all go off and become reggae singers in Jamaica.

Many Earth People described something I would call 'boredom', perhaps even 'estrangement', together with a wish for the close interpersonal relationships they recalled with their mothers and siblings when they were younger. Dasheen met Mother Earth when she was *putting out* in Laventille and had joined the group because of

the understanding Mother put to me. We was looking for truth and Mother explain about Nature which is Truth. And me come to understand she was The Mother. I was living with a girl. She just had baby an' she want to come but she family stop she. Me come to sacrifice meself . . . It come like you build a self. You have to do something to build society. [In a dream] I see this long black wall an' a map of Trinidad all red and confuse' an' this was the struggle. An' I cross the wall, and now I see I cross over to my life here.

Breadfruit, who had grown up in Laventille near Mother Earth, tried to reconcile Shouter Baptism with Rastafari:

I got gold watch-chain an' I think Judas betray Jesus for silver an' it all blood money! An' I mash it up and throw it down latrine, an' I baptise. When I go baptise I comb out natty an' I go an' mourn. An' then I let natty grow again an' one day minister take me in church and he say 'Why you don' go and comb it?' I say 'Why?' He say 'For society'. So I think I don't want it; I for meself! So I didn't go to church again. An' I wear a jumbie bean,[8] an' I go to a next church an' a woman catch the spirit an' take me round the church an' wash me down with bush an' thing, an' say 'You don' come back with that again' . . . An' at night I go out naked an' lie on the ground an' say 'Why not pray to a Mother for a few days?' So I do! [Soon he saw Mother Earth again, dressed in bag on a visit to town.] Me mother always go by she. I see her a nex' time in '79 when she go up to Laventille. I use' to talk about Selassie an' thing but she show me me senses. The nex' day I had a vision and see me self natural, run about with little children. Nex' day I jus' put on bag an' start go about wi' she. What made me see me self was that [in a dream] I see self an' see this Black woman naked an' walk about with school girls in uniform an' I fly by her side. An' I move and kiss earth, and I burn my Bible. An' when Mother come up I free to talk it again.

Coconut went to a prestigious secondary school but:

didn't get no GCE. I left at sixteen, hang around, heading nowhere, hustling here, there. I looking for truth. We end up meet with Pomme Cythère and come up. I learn a new way. It difficult. It got to sacrifice. You put out you' self for you' self.

He was already familiar with novel religious expressions: his uncle, a neighbour of Mother Earth when she lived in town, used to study science books and 'wear a long gown an' talk about Mecca and Tibet an' he said if he put his hand on ice he would be immortal'.

Tannia:

I grow natty since I small. My brothers were Rasta but I didn' see anything in it. An' the Mother come for them on the block. An' I see in sleep that I child from the Rising. Then she come an' she was the Rising of the Nation. I ai' satisfy wi' Rasta, I ai' put out my senses. When Mother put out herself to me I see me self more closely. [I dreamt] Black man in circle wi' gun an' he say 'Where you from?' an' I point to earth where moon rise. An' he break his bread in half an' put butter in it. So I know the bread done butter for something.

Potato was seventeen when he came to the Valley. He had been struck by the similarity between Mother Earth and his own mother:

What Mother Earth say, it all 'bout my mother did and so [preparing local food]. But Rastas didn't like it; I hardly go off on it, hat an' so, an' I start going 'bout wi' bare foot.[9] I didn' like the city, fighting wi' pollution. This world too crucial to the flesh. Old time people more natural: my old grandmother used to tell we to gather round when she cock up her leg an' pee. Now you run home hold you' legs together! . . . We live here natural. When we go to town I ai' shit for a week. We come back in bush and take deer bush an' pow! Free up yourself! When we little they talk of God the Father. An' me say 'Who he?' An' they talk of Mary, Mother of God an' me say 'What!' an' I get brain tie up. An' now Mother Earth gives me senses. Like we all come from down here [the Earth].

The Earth People recall themselves as 'searching' when they met Mother Earth. Some remember early dreams which prefigured her. While a decision to join coming from one's spirit is preferable to calculation, none of the group describe anything which could be called a sudden 'conversion' or 'salvation'. Adherence is simply taking off one's clothes and living in the Valley. A slow understanding dawning on the potential member is preferred although Mother Earth may sometimes talk of that moment 'when the cells of your brain burst and you come to see' – the same expression she uses for the development of any young child. The community is experienced as a logical extension of the everyday world, a broadening and validation of it; there can be no shame or guilt about one's earlier life.

John Noyes, the founder of the Oneida community, noted in his encyclopaedic *History of American Socialisms* that the most successful communitarian groups were not only those held together by a shared religious faith but those where members were personally acquainted with each other before they joined. Certainly, the young men who come to the Valley on their own appear less likely to stay. Zabocca had been a member of another group which combined shango with Hinduism and which had Indian leaders. They paid a visit to the Earth People to see what the Valley was up to, and Zabocca elected to stay behind. He was strongly influenced by Rastafari and chose the Earth People as an 'African' group, and did not accept Mother Earth's more feminist and universalist message. He disliked me intensely and left after a couple of months.

The one member who did join the Valley at a time of personal crisis was Melangine. He had been in Port-of-Spain with some Rasta friends who had debated the significance of Bob Marley's 'Seven Black Star Liners'; this song took its theme from Garvey's suggestion in the 1920s of a repatriation shipping line for the Universal Negro Improvement Association, an image which has surfaced at moments of millennial expectation in Jamaican Rastafari. Melangine's companions argued that the message of this reggae number was that Rastas could await imminent and miraculous transport by the Black Star Liners back to Africa. After Marley's death, when the expected ships failed to arrive, the six friends decided to leave by themselves and travelled to the east coast, to the promontory where the Caribs had committed mass suicide in the sixteenth century. After purifying themselves for a week on a diet of lime juice, coconut water and sea water (all used for purging), three of the group paddled out to sea on a log in the general direction of Africa. They were quite aware of the distance, Melangine told us, but they expected divine intervention to speed them on their way. They were not seen again. The others, including Melangine, set out later from near the Valley, but were forced back by the strong Atlantic currents. Melangine, who had developed abdominal cramps and vomiting, and was less enthusiastic about the trip than his friends, remained with the Earth People when the others moved south along the coast to try again. The Valley had no further news of them and I am uncertain what happened. The episode was not reported in the Trinidad press and sounds rather unusual for the phlegmatic West Indian religious sensibility – although parallels are not unknown elsewhere.[10] I have little understanding of the personal context in which it happened and can only speculate on the expectations of the participants: Marley's death certainly had caused a crisis for some Jamaican Rastas but this voyage was the only such dramatic response in Trinidad. The Earth People attempted to dissuade the Africa-bound group from going ahead, with the argument that Selassie was not divine and no miraculous intervention was likely to be forthcoming, and that anyway Trinidad was as much 'Africa' as the continent across the sea. Melangine, when he recovered from his illness (which I felt was due not only to his sea water diet), appeared easily convinced by their arguments and he stayed in the Valley, although like Zabocca he remained one of the more 'Rasta' members.

To what extent were the members who joined the group 'looking for a mother', attempting to retreat into an earlier and harmonious family life? They of course argue the mythic reverse – that the human family just provides a replication of the original family of The Mother and her Black creation. There is certainly a poignant 'reality' in our first childhood understandings which continues to constitute them in their later accommodations and transform- ations, but the wish to be part of a family hardly reflects instability or an inability to cope.[11] Against this possibility we can place their relatively successful personal adjustment before they joined. Living with them, it is difficult to accept that they were inadequate people needing a 'mother- orientated' group. Unemployed, searching for worthwhile ideals, certainly. For security, no. While the organisation of the Valley and their relationship with Mother Earth provide them with much playful regression to childhood, and this is certainly recognised, the prevailing motivation seems to have been rather a pioneering sense of the adventure involved.[12]

Two of the Earth People had previously been in St Ann's Hospital: Corn joined the group after seeing them 'putting out' in town, while Mango Rose had met Mother Earth in the hospital itself and came out later to the Valley. Neither were felt by the others to be satisfactory members. The other members of the Earth People did not appear distinctive in their previous experiences or personality; although drawn from a dissatisfied group in which, like the millennialists of the European counter-current they 'could find no recognised place',[13] their previous pattern of life was hardly deviant compared with their peers. If Society as a whole is certainly taken as 'sick', new members do not see themselves as in need of any particular healing, nor is the community expressly therapeutic. The Healing of the Nation is to be a total way of life.

Compared with other new religious movements in the West the Earth People are 'open', prosaic and flexible, with relatively free movement to and from the group. As far as I could ascertain, joining the Valley had caused embarrassment rather than anger among their families. Good relations were still maintained with members and there were no attempts to win them back, certainly no concerted effort comparable to the recent 'deprogramming' responses to cults in Britain and America. Membership is signalled by immediate participation in most group activities alongside established members. Any sudden protestations of full conviction in Mother's teachings would be rather suspect; what is assumed is an immediate readiness to join in the way of life, principally by taking off one's clothes and labouring in the Valley; the boundaries of the group are physical above all. The only personal commitment required is some type of acknowledgement of the undesirability of urban and middle-class goals, and of the centrality of Nature as manifest in the person of Mother Earth. Even for established members, a readiness to work hard and to subordinate personal interests to those of the group – *humbling you' self* or *sacrificing you' self* – is valued above ideological rectitude. The enthusiastic participant is allowed greater latitude in disagreeing with theoretical questions (I can hardly call them 'doctrines') than the one who is less hard-working: but the converse is not true. Commitment is in taking off one's clothes; while recruits have little personal property beyond clothes to renounce, returning to town without them (or money) reinforces the difficulty of leaving the group. Talking with ex-members however, I learned that they were absorbed back relatively easily into their original milieu; comparatively little opprobrium attached to them. Nor were they discouraged by the Earth People from returning to the Valley again.

It is the physical work in the Valley which Mother Earth recognises as the principal hardship:

Some of them that come, comes with a spirit of seeing themselves an' working the land. Some come they want to play. They not really thinking of what they're doing so then they usually leave because working they find that is too hard to do. So they don't stay, they leave. But those who stay they go through little cutses, biteses, you know, and fight up with it. They fishing when it's black, knocked down when the sea like . . . you know. They jus' happy. When people comes to the bush, since I am living here, I watch them go, they would lie down on the ground there looking at the ground to see if it clean or dirty. [Others] they just threw down themselves: 'Oh, it is nice.' They feel the elements with a breeze, the smell of the life, they look at the sea. When they reach in the earth, and leave here and they go back to the city, it comes so, you just enter something else there. You feel a different smell, a different air, walls and streets, and tapes and radio, and trucks and cars. It come so but you accustom to it: so if you stay here for a few days, you find it is enough. You get fed up – you ready to run back to the city. It's true!

The Spirit [of God] know it's the End so the more that he can get the flesh to play, you know, they wouldn't want the Beginning. This is it all. The more you can get them material-like, more food, more party, they wouldn't want to stay in the bush. They will miss it. The Spirit in them will call for that, so they won't be able to stay here. But yet I notice the men. They come, some stay, some go. Some, although they leave here, they still go by the bush but they don't want to work – they just want to gain spirits as you would call it, to know, to come out in the open now . . . It ai' me to change them. They got to change side. They must know Left from Right. This is the fight – from Right to Left.

Planting for the Nation

Everyday life in the Valley offers no continuing revelations, no prayers or possession states, no supplications of a divinity, no contact with any external power. Ultimate reality is present in the person of Mother Earth and through her in daily tasks. No one moment seems more central than another, but if any activity could be said to be 'sacramental' it is the production and consumption of food. Food must be provided for those who will come at the End, and the land has to be prepared now. More food is harvested than is immediately required: baskets are overflowing, piles of yams rot in the outhouses. But there is no 'Trobriand ethic' of abstinence: on the contrary, everybody is encouraged to eat fully, and snacks are continually being prepared by small groups of Earth People as a favourite leisure activity quite distinct from the communal meals. At odd moments during the day people are always chewing a piece of cane, putting a couple of breadfruit to roast, grilling some corn. Mother Earth is frequently offered such titbits as a casual tribute, or placated with them when she is annoyed. While the private cultivation or stockpiling of food would be contrary to general sentiment, personal tastings and nibbles are part of the daily round.

The settlement has been described above (page xi). It is not really a valley, just a shallow declivity on the old Turnpike track overlooking the sea.[14] Its centre is the ancient wooden house, abandoned in the sixties, into which Mother Earth and Jakatan had moved (Plate 3). The evenings are passed on its bare earth floors although part of the original floor boards remain in places. The upper storey, the cocoa box, is seldom entered and, in contrast to the self-conscious 'African' feel of the ground level, retains old scraps of clothes, tins and even the odd coin.[15] Although the settlement resembles the traditional rural home, no distinction is made here between *yard* (herb and flower garden) and *provision* garden. Plants of different types may be found at any distance from the house and there are no hedges, palisades or flower gardens. Some of the young men constructed a circular African hut to one side (Plate 4) but now they usually sleep on the ground under a roof extended out at the back of the main house facing the cultivated slopes of the mountains (Plate 5). Mother Earth and Jakatan retain a certain privacy in a section of the house at the front overlooking the sea but there are no doors and there is comparatively unrestricted access by anyone to all parts. Adjoining the house is the major cooking area flanked by food stores, tool areas, water butts and a small ravine. At the rear, beyond the men's hut, is the area for chopping wood (Plate 6) where the younger men have established a second fire around which some of them gather after the evening meal for ganja and private conversations, grumbles, plans and talk of past exploits.

For about half a mile in each direction from the house the secondary bush and scrub of the seasonal rain forest has been cleared and a variety of trees and perennial cultigens are grown; medicine bushes; trees and plants for cordage and wrapping, for baskets and calabashes; timber for utensils, building and firewood; plantain and *fig* (smaller bananas); roots like cassava, 'Irish' potato,

3 The front of the main house: the white child is the author's daughter, Letice. On the left is a representation of the baslisier next to the plant itself: the end of the words THE DEVIL LIVE HERE appears beneath.

sweet potato, dasheen, yam, tannia; aubergine, pineapple, tomato, pigeon peas, callaloo, okra, Indian corn, pumpkin, chataigne, ginger, sugar cane, christophene; trees bearing oranges, grapefruit, guava, nuts, mango, avocado, pawpaw, pomerac, tamarind and breadfruit; nearer the hut grow garlic, and bushes with pepper, shadobenny and other *flavour herbs*. Above, reaching up on the hills, are cocoa and coffee, cannabis and tobacco. Here, aged shade trees like the immortelle (*madre del cacoa, Erythrina micropterix*) have been left uncut to provide shelter from the sun; they prevent undue growth of weeds and keep the moisture of the soil, absorbing the heavy rain and releasing it gently to the plants. In the nearby bush are to be found mauby bark, mammy apple, passion fruit, star apple, nutmeg and soursap, whilst along the coastline coconut palms reach over the beach thickly interspersed with almond trees. The

4 Earth People children in the valley. (The remains of the African hut on the right.)

variety of crops, virtually every Trinidadian food plant, and the informal but precise cultivation, justify the boast of the Earth People that they are living in Eden. There is a water melon patch. Cress is obtained from mangrove swamps, and the sea yields fish, principally shark, carite, cuvali, kingfish and catfish, together with pakro and other molluscs, conch, sea cucumber, turtle and a variety of small rock fish. Turtle eggs and crabs are obtained by digging the wet sand but land animals and birds are no longer hunted. Around the hut live poultry, goats and ducks; they are not eaten but the fowl provide eggs and the goats are milked.

Agricultural techniques are those traditionally used in the coastal villages, a fusion of the European, African and Amerindian. Many of these have now been

5 Earth People and the author waiting in the men's house for Mother Earth to distribute food.

discarded by the remaining country people, less for reasons of economic maximisation than because they are just 'primitive'. While the Earth People do not employ fertilisers or machines, they still use cutlasses, axes, adzes, augers, chisels and swipers (small scythes). These are the implements which remained intact around the house after the Burning but they are also those still found most commonly in the villages. Manufactured utensils which remain in use are metal cooking pots, strainers, barrels and canisters for water. With the exception of galvanised iron for roofing the store houses, the materials employed are only wood, bark and creepers, which are strung, knotted, matted, twisted, plaited and lashed. Water transport comprises a dug-out canoe and two rafts (Plate 7). Sacking is used for sails, blankets, bags and the short kilts worn on the way to town. Other purchased items are matches, pitch oil,

6 Cutting wood for the fires behind the house.

old rum bottles for oil lamps (*flambeaux*) and even a temperamental carbide lamp.

The community is squatting on land owned in law by the Pinnacle villagers but, as they do not work it, the Earth People say the village has no real title to it. Nor do they argue that they themselves 'own' it, for Nature is there for all. Decisions as to its use are agreed collectively but usually only after suggestions by Mother Earth or Jakatan. All adult male members work on the land during the majority of the daylight hours, cutting, burning, planting, weeding and gathering. Water is brought from a nearby spring. The food collected is brought back to the storage area to be placed in open-weave baskets or cooked by Breadfruit and his helpers of the day under the supervision of Mother Earth (Plate 8). The main meals, usually twice a day, are communal; Mother Earth calls each member by name and his calabash is filled with food which is eaten sitting on the ground in the same place where he sleeps at night. The rows of sleeping places recall a school dormitory; they provide a personal space where individual tools may be stored together with small pieces of carving or other

7 The new canoe, *Mother Earth 2*, down on the bay: it has a Y-shaped stern. The small mast is to carry a flambeau at night.

8 Breadfruit drying fish. (The men's house behind.)

work in progress (Plate 9). While no private objects are taken into the community by members it is recognised that the calabash, axe, cutlass or knife (made from cutlass sherds) which each person habitually uses cannot be taken by anyone else without permission; each is named, for example, as 'Dasheen's cutlass'. Indeed Mother Earth insists that each member has a cutlass, the all purpose cutting and digging tool, and is responsible for it, and that it should not usually be lent. Members have an even greater claim to use objects made by them, carvings, spoons, bows and arrows, but to refuse to lend them on the basis that they are 'owned' would be Social. At the same time there is considerable bickering over the borrowing of tools, incidents which Mother

9 Two carvings: the carving on the right represents Mother Earth: the other follows the conventional Rasta style found in town. (A posed picture – the carvings normally hang in the house.)

uses to reinforce notions of personal responsibility for one's own tools and responsibility to the group as a whole.

On one occasion during the wet season, Coconut ('a college boy and should know better!' – M.E.), who had a reputation for borrowing tools without permission, took Tannia's axe. When he eventually returned it he dumped it on the ground rather unceremoniously and was publicly reprimanded by Mother. The next day Tannia took the axe and whilst felling wet timber, slipped and cut his foot deeply, his first accident for two years. Mother Earth and Breadfruit cleaned the wound and dressed it with cocoa husk scrapings, and then she rebuked Coconut again. She told him forcibly that his borrowing was the cause of Tannia's accident. Coconut protested he had no influence on axes. Everybody who was by, tired of Coconut's habitual borrowing, chorused mockingly 'It you vibes! We saw them going out!' They started laughing and Coconut stalked off in tears. Apart from a *tap* (see below) there is no explicit notion of personal action at a distance, and village beliefs in obeah are derided as 'superstition'. The very idea of 'vibes', a self-conscious Americanism, was rather a joke. Mother Earth quietened the laughter and told the group, now enlarged by others drifting in to observe the fuss, that Coconut was hurt at the suggestion he wanted to hurt Tannia and had gone off to 'find himself again'. Tannia then said it was his own fault as the axe handle had not been seasoned properly. Mother argued that alone would not have caused the accident but proceeded to blame him for lending his tools to people (Tannia was indeed rather good natured and tended to let people borrow tools without complaining): 'Lend hoe, lend shovel. Axe, cutlass, swiper, these is things you have no left to lend. They have their way of cutting. Your tool come in your own spirit.' She then seized the opportunity of giving a long homily to the whole community: ultimately all their accidents were caused by disharmony in the group, particularly people going off to the *high woods* to grow their own supplies of ganja. Beyond this new suggestion of the individual's spirit shaping the tool lay the accepted idea that there was indeed a close relationship between the worker and the basic tool which he used every day, cleaning and sharpening it, knowing its vagaries and tricks; and cutlasses and axes were of course potentially dangerous.

The times when the group are gathered together for eating are used by Mother to take incidents of the day, particularly arguments and accidents, as the starting point for a discussion of the basic tenets of the group. Solidarity and mutual responsibility are emphasised while mistakes may be attributed ultimately to the Spirit of the Son still working in our Flesh. Regret and a commitment to more appropriate actions in the future are measured by subsequent behaviour rather than by any wordy confession. Successful admonishment involves ridicule and laughter with immediate reconciliation. Mother Earth cajoles and shames, placing responsibility firmly on the individual; no one is threatened with expulsion but the demand to change may be so great that departure is the only solution. 'Growth' is the term which aligns each to the Life of Nature – a growth of the individual spirit through the growth of the food he gathers.

Meals are the central moment for the community, their 'ritual of synthesis' as anthropologists would call it. As in the nearby hamlets this is always a cooked meal stewed in a pot. Along the coast, village men, when by themselves – hunting or in the absence of their wives – roast wild meat together; similarly, in the Valley, roasting corn or breadfruit is an informal 'snacking' type of consumption, carried out in the open or by the wood chopping area. Fruit, as elsewhere in the West Indies, does not really qualify as 'food'. It may be picked and eaten in the course of a walk; not to be hoarded for individual use, a good find is brought back for distribution but consumption is informal and often private. 'Real food', *food food*, communally gathered to be cooked in the house, is always provision with a sauce of vegetables, fresh or smoked fish, and turtle eggs. This is the food which is planted for the Feeding of the Nation, and it is these communal meals which embody the collectivity at its most united: raw food from the Mother Earth passes to the human mother to cook and distribute, after an invocation or homily, to her Children (Plate 5). Food and its preparation are a major topic of conversation; visitors and special occasions are celebrated with the preparation of sweet dishes such as guava jelly, *pone* (coconut flesh cooked with corn meal in a leaf) or *pastelles* (stuffed pastries), *tulum* (coconut and molasses sweets). The evening meal is the occasion for communal singing, for drumming and dancing the Fire Dance,[16] for the consumption of palm and fig wine, and the smoking of cigars and ganja spliffs. The day's events are discussed leisurely and the more sleepy retire to their places on the earth whilst the cook of the day, usually Breadfruit, cleans the pots and banks up the fire for the night.

Within the demands of *humbling you' self* to prepare for the End, a degree of self-indulgence is accepted, indeed encouraged, particularly within the areas of gastronomic treats and the smoking of ganja. As opposed to dubious wishes for the Social life of the town, such oral pleasures are part of Nature. Mother Earth has smoked ganja in the past but she is not particularly keen on it and is wont to issue half-hearted, rather 'respectable', warnings about excessive smoking: 'Rum do you liver. They all alcoholic, break down you fucking self. Ganja now, make you mind travel. It not suppose to travel.' These are met with groans and sarcastic promises: 'Okay, Mother, me ai' going to abuse it now!' and she shrugs good naturedly. Privately she told me she was concerned that

one of the major attractions for the less committed members was the availability of ganja whose distribution she attempts to oversee. Certainly most
members carry wraps of ganja about with them and smoke at any time during
the day; it is held to enhance work performance and enables them to continue
felling trees in the middle of thunderstorms with water pouring down their
dreads into their eyes, times when any other Trinidadian would long since have
sought shelter.[17] Altered states of consciousness are neither sought nor
achieved with ganja or anything else; palm wine is drunk in moderation and
then only by the older members or on occasions for celebration.

While the priority for any self-sufficient community has to be the production
of food, to the Earth People the Feeding of the Nation clearly has a significance
beyond basic nutrition. Why the salience of food? Their communal eating is
unusual, for meals in Trinidad are usually prepared by a woman and eaten by
different members of her household separately. Their idea of food, however,
and its production and consumption, do to an extent affirm general Trindadian
values; food cooked for men by a mother or partner; the preparation of a
quantity in excess of immediate requirements in case a casual visitor requires
a meal; the value placed on local Creole food in opposition to imported tinned
foodstuffs. There is a keen rural interest in food; its ingredients, spices and
exact preparation are a matter of interest to both women and men, and no fête
is complete without the elaborate production of a variety of special dishes –
shark and bake, souse, roti and curried goat. Individuals of both sexes may be
renowned for their preparation of particular dishes. Pinnacle villagers value
their Sunday dinner for 'you work for these two things – to fill you' belly on
Sunday and for people respect you, fight to carry you' coffin when you come
bury'. The Earth People often cite the variety and delicacy of their food as an
attraction of the Natural life, but it is unlikely that anyone has decided to join
them with that foremost in mind. While the scuffling young men of Laventille
and Belmont may occasionally go hungry, it is improbable that anyone in
Trinidad has starved since the First World War. Its citizens are preoccupied
with the purchase of a new cooking stove or refrigerator, not with wondering
if they will have anything to eat the next day.

Food, both cooked and raw, is exchanged and offered freely in the working-
class areas of Port-of-Spain and along the coast. Cooked food is extensively
used for informal exchanges between neighbours, and most people are happy
to cook regularly for a sick or old person nearby: 'I always remember to send
a little something by she.' The person who holds a *freeness* (a fête with free
food and drink) is valued as open-hearted and generous. Respectable people
who deride this as mere drunkenness and feckless extravagance are accused
of being *mingy* (mean), and we have seen that a major shango rite, associated

with both physical and spiritual healing, was the Feeding of the Children – providing a meal for the children of the neighbourhood. Generosity then, particularly with food, stands for Creole solidarity. The valuing of it by the Earth People is explicitly a privileging of generous, informal and face-to-face encounters over an abstract market's *dead food*.

For the Children of the Mother, her distribution of fare replicates earlier maternal indulgence, and the children in the community are treated with particular gentleness. As in other areas of Valley life, their arguments and frustrations are dealt with calmly and verbally ('rationally' one might be tempted to say if this was not the explicit mode of Science). While children are the exemplars of the Natural life, unconstrained by *social* ways, to the observer they are constantly being educated into the Life. They are never beaten, for Mother Earth argues passionately that punishment will never help anyone become Natural: 'Since I reach this stage I have to control myself of hitting the children. I would have to say since I am living in the bush I have no reason for hitting my children, flogging them. Because they have nowhere to go they play [here]. When I speak they listen.' They are told to *behave* when they do something dangerous such as playing with a knife or excessively violating the privacy of adult members. Younger children in the group usually remain close to the house and Mother Earth plays with them during the day when the men

10 Pumpkin and Cocorite tapping drum; fishing net drying.

are at work in the bush. They have no special toys, and are regarded as full members of the group, prevented from participation in the daily round only by physical, rather than moral or psychological, immaturity.[18]

Communal decisions are usually achieved on a basis of consensus. No shared activities should take place with anyone feeling aggrieved or bitter; better to wait until each is reconciled. Feelings are ventilated and each member is encouraged to talk about his anger towards another lest it build up inside him through *grinding* to pour out and harm the group. Their characteristic obscenities are uttered as jokey, self-consciously ideological statements, seldom in anger. If an elaborated notion of 'self-control' would be anathema to the Natural ideal, such a term certainly conveys the dignified but superior manner the Earth People adopt with outsiders. Their English recalls standard English in its use of indexical pronouns, and the midday meal may be called 'lunchtime' (rather than the usual *breakfast*), an expression which would be regarded as quite pretentious in the villages.

When disagreements persist, Mother Earth is the ultimate arbiter and she usually places responsibility on one member for not having humbled himself enough to the Life. These incidents, like that of Coconut and the axe, may develop into detailed harangues lasting many hours or even a whole day, in which everybody is castigated for selfishness and laziness. Similarly, illness or arrivals to the group are attributed to the progress or otherwise in the Valley towards the approaching End. Arguments which lead to the departure of members tend to leave the community miserable and although at the time the one who leaves is made to feel responsible, the group afterwards sit together and assess what went wrong. Departing members are sent on their way in sorrow rather than anger,[19] and Mother Earth may provide them with some money out of an old biscuit tin she keeps next to her sleeping area. Cucumber, the woman who left with a genital infection after refusing bush treatment (page 172) was urged to see a doctor in town and to return when she was well.

To an extent the group may be said to live independently of Social time: 'spontaneity' and 'intuition' are valued above Social calculation and 'hypocrisy': 'When I see anything I know it. Words is just confusion. The power is in you' (M.E.). *Trickidadians* are criticised for their inability to share each other's problems and for their readiness to retreat into an egotistical self-interest which is ultimately self-defeating. During an epidemic of red eye (infectious conjunctivitis) along the coast, Jakatan saw 'this driver stop to pick up a drop [pedestrian wanting a lift] and then him see the man got red eye. Real horrors! He wind up window and speed away. They real dread, man, not we!'

As in other millennial moments we may argue that they see each other 'transparently in the mythic present'.[20] Lyn Hunt suggests that this inevitably leads to sect 'paranoia', but, in the Valley, Naturalness involves taking into account the feelings of others, changes of policy, and Mother Earth's and Jakatan's opinions. It is flexible, and the 'total' feeling of the group (in which after all nothing is supposed to happen without significance and in which all daily activity is conceived of in terms of the group's cosmology) is far from stifling. Latent antagonisms are sometimes explained through the notion of the *tap*, a term which derives from the physical survival of some metal objects after the Burning (see page 72) and which embodies much of the popular feeling about maljo, the evil eye. Taps are acts of the Son which cause any continued failure of goodwill or determination in the individual, but not causing major accidents or illness; also any inappropriate interference with another member such as eavesdropping, borrowing or begging; and any bad feelings which could drain the enthusiasm of another. The last use is sometimes subsumed, half-jokingly, under the hippie term 'bad vibes'. Like maljo, tapping is not an intended action, and it has to be brought to the surface and ventilated. Apart from its use to joke about importunate borrowing of tools, the possibility of serious tapping is seldom raised; the Spirit of the Son occasions irritation rather than anger or fear, and the notion of his tapping is always used in conjunction with other more immediate explanations.[21]

There are a few restrictions on everyday behaviour which were not present in life in town. One of these involves entrances and exits. No one should leave the household complex by one route and reenter it by another, nor should one obstruct the doorless thresholds.[22] If there is little privacy in the settlement it is accepted that there are times when people need to be by themselves. Dirt and excrement are Natural within fairly tight limits; the house is always kept free of tools which are not required and which are stored away, but layers of dust are left in the boarded section, and Earth People spend their time sitting or standing on the earth. Logs or stools may be sat on but a continual preference for them rather than the ground provokes comments – 'You so ashame' of you' mother now?' One does not complain of others' body smell or dirt. Indeed these are the subject of approved comment – 'So you get real natural now!' One washes only before preparing or cooking food or passing it to others at mealtimes. Sweating from continuous work, together with the occasional swim in the river, mean that little dirt is apparent anyway. Larger pieces of mud are casually scraped off when sitting and liming, and are flicked back onto the ground. Mother Earth advises that too much cleaning leads to skin coming off leaving the body more susceptible to illness, and dirt is necessary for health: 'In the city, the more children wash the more sick they get. In a too clean house the children dig it out of the boards an' eat it. This then is part of the Culture of the Body.'[23] Earth People frequently get stung by scorpions and are encouraged to eat earth as a remedy, not always with success:

JAKATAN: 'I bit by a scorpion and the first thing I study is eat dirt.'
SELF: 'Did you?'
JAKATAN: (laughing) 'No!'
M.E.:   (reprovingly) 'Is you Self talking there, and you leave it out.'
JAKATAN: 'I figure I got enough life.'

Difficult decisions made after much deliberation are frequently justified by *visions* in dreams when the decision is recognised as coming spontaneously from the Spirit of Nature which guards the community. When I first met the group I was told that they had been expecting me after Mother Earth had a dream about Science coming to seek her out.[24] On another occasion the community debated whether it was Natural to dig up and eat the *caldong* eggs which had just been buried on the beach by a female turtle. A vision decided in favour. The long-standing argument about whether it was acceptable to hunt turtles (which for the more tender-hearted are particularly unpleasant to kill as they take a long time to die) was resolved finally by a dream of Mother's in which a Black woman rose up out of the sea to declare 'Take no more caldong or one of your own children will die.' That settled the matter. On other occasions the vision is more ambiguous and open to various interpretations along the usual Trinidadian lines.

Visions usually deal with current problems such as that of Mother Earth's younger daughter who remained in the Catholic orphanage where she had been placed by the magistrate the previous year. During one of the marches to town her mother went to see her and was rebuffed.[25] The community debated whether it would be a good idea if I went to see her to re-establish contact. We were undecided but that night Mother Earth had a dream of a brown monster chopping people up. We decided that this represented the nuns (Carmelites in brown habits) and that I should keep away. Breadfruit, one of the Earth People whose joining the group had been associated with a Baptist vision (page 179), frequently related dreams to current events:

Before I get this Spirit, this natty, I dream an' I in Africa, an' this tree fall on my head. An' last year it happen! Dream is when you spirit travel an' the flesh sleep. An' you' spirit travel, travel, an' later you flesh catch up. I often seen people a first time an' I say I know them already. I see them in a dream.

While this is close to popular explanations of dreams and mourning visions, Breadfruit admits that he 'didn' dream serious till I bounce up [meet] with Mother'.

Sentiments and structure: the Earth People as a family

The Earth People regard themselves as a family centred around Mother Earth, a family that corresponds closely to the original Mother Earth with her Black Children, for the Mother is the same person in both. The first family of Black Children is still to be found in the traditional Trinidadian Creole family, and parallels with the group in the Valley are continually emphasised. In theory there are no other positions beyond that of Mother herself and that of Earth Person; there are no recognised subgroups, no hierarchy, no recognition of any type of prestige. Some members of the community are however more influential than others, depending on their personality, experience and commitment. The absence of women and the effective celibacy of the men mean that no sexual (and thus potentially economic) bonds are developed between members. The giving of fruit names has a further levelling effect; occupations before joining the group (with their potential Social ranking) are largely ignored, for now 'we all be she fruits'.[26] While there is a continuity between humans and the rest of Nature, the animals of the community are not really regarded as Earth People and are seldom given names.

Differences of character are well recognised and are usually attributed to past life experiences. Thus Coconut 'the college boy' is seen as thoughtless, Dasheen as simple, Potato as rather immature, Eddoes as reserved and hardworking. The friendly personality and the 'ace cultivator' are valued. Corn, who has been in St Ann's Hospital, is regarded as too quiet and easily upset. He is seldom allocated tree felling for his task as he often cuts himself. He dislikes being criticised and spends a lot of time by himself looking rather vague. His habit of wandering off and foraging for mangoes by himself is seen as *childish* – a Social expression somewhat at variance with the value placed on the state of Naturalness. Mother Earth actually asked me to provide her with a psychiatric assessment as 'I don't like the effect smoking [ganja] have on him. He go off and study. He think on life outside. He don' complain but you can see he study that.' To no one's surprise, one day he suddenly disappeared, and the feeling was that he would not return. As for Coconut, 'that one too frighten' says Mother Earth to the assembled group, 'He just cut his chest with the axe an' bawl for so. I tell him stop.' Coconut grins with embarrassment.

Mother Earth's own biological family do tend to have a certain latitude. Pomme Cythère, her son (see Plate 2, on the left), tends his own ganja plot, the occasion of some complaint. He is the only member of the Valley who usually wears any ornament, a seed necklace, but in itself this does not signify any recognised position. He tends to spend more time than others around the centre of the house and sometimes sleeps up in the cocoa box. As he is friendly and gregarious, there is no long-standing resentment for he does not pull rank.

Mother Earth's partner, Jakatan (Plate 7) however has a somewhat uncertain position. While there is no cosmological equivalent for his special position (except perhaps the Son, which as we shall see, causes some problems), his greater age and rural experience, and his intimacy with Mother give him a position of first among equals. On ideological questions and long-term planning he takes a second place to Mother, but he is the one principally concerned with organising immediate agricultural tasks. He is generally known as 'Dads' and is only 'Jakatan' to outsiders, but relations between him and the other Earth People tend to be correct rather than obviously affectionate and he does not have any expressly parental role beyond that of experience and guidance. When the young men continue to get the canoe ropes tangled up after much instruction he laments 'You all got to learn about sea' and sets about teaching them once again. He is responsible for assessing the competence of members, and for keeping the tools in working order; physically fitter than Mother Earth he spends more time away from the Valley than anyone else, on various errands or visiting his father who lives in a village along the coast.

By contrast Mother Earth is regarded with warm affectionate feelings by everybody as their Mother. There is no sacred text for the group; its origin and continuation lie solely in her personality. It is Mother who relates everyday incidents to their central purpose and it is in her that the awesome powers of Nature will finally be made manifest. Her mood is quickly reflected in the feeling of the day. If she feels unwell, the Earth People are subdued; if lively, they are filled with new energy and confidence. Her usual station is by the central cooking area. Shouts of 'Mother want you' are quickly relayed to those working away from the household and as immediately obeyed. Her critical comments on the progress of the cooking, the tidiness of the men's house or on general morale are listened to with quiet attention and her wishes carried out. At the same time this is done with much cheerful abuse. On one occasion, soon after my arrival, she helped herself to Coconut's calabash. He protested 'That my own fig.' Breadfruit immediately reproved him: 'That Mother Earth own. All food come from Mother Earth', but added, to general laughter, 'An' she ai' got no fucking manners!'

The Social notion of 'manners' is derided but often humorously invoked. One afternoon the men were sitting in a circle on the ground after a meal whilst Mother Earth, supporting herself against a house post, harangued them for several hours on the approaching End. 'All the drums of Africa will sound. The language will come forth. An' the Son does not know. The Children of the Mother, the Children of Power will . . . ' She broke off to look at Jakatan who was distractedly scraping dried mud off his body and, smiling, observed 'You see, he real Nature. But he ai' got no manners!'

There is relatively little awe attached to Mother Earth as incarnate Nature. In practical matters it seems hardly an issue. She seldom offers any type of supernatural sanction, and her authority often appears to derive from her as some type of guarantor for a valued way of life. The reality of the Valley which is always stressed comes through The Life, the immediate relationship to the land, away from Society, rather than from some abstract eschatology. On many occasions I wondered if the group should be seen less as a 'religious' community than as some high-spirited summer camp.

To what extent does each member really take Mother as the basic life force? None would quarrel with the idea. It just does not preoccupy them much. When they are by themselves outside the community, debating with scornful villagers, they maintain it with disdainful fervour, but inside the Valley her status is usually more that of their mother than The Mother. Nor do the Earth People see their daily work as precipitating the End at any particular point in time. They do not 'force the End' in Martin Buber's expression. The goal is simply to get on with living the Life as fully as possible on a day to day basis. If the End will come soon then, well, it will come, but speculation on the precise time is not a matter of any great interest. It is not dependent on any act of the group, no critical size of membership, nor are they expecting to engineer any final confrontation with the Social. Nor do they discuss the precise way of Life after the End: it is taken as a continuation of the present, a broadening and extension of the Valley, of its practical actions, gestures and shared motivations. I often thought that if the End never came nobody would be that upset, although Mother herself occasionally reminds everybody of the possibility as in this general conversation one night over the bowls of conch broth:

M.E.:   It will have how people will come. The Sun is getting hotter and
                   the world will starve but it will rain in Hell and provide for every-
                   one. All will come. Even you [with a grin at me].
JAKATAN: The Bible say it will have wars and rumours of wars. Is now. You
                   see here the bay will have thousands of boats with no space in
                   between.
M.E.:   It say in the Bible that because of the sin of man, the woman come
                   to rule man.[27]
PAWPAW: It come to racial war. Each want to be in a more up to date form.
M.E.:   Most of the things in the Bible have fulfilment but most of them
                   that there can't unfold it. The Bible real confusion, you read one
                   part and you find next contradiction.
BREADFRUIT: It many different peoples' many different generations' story but
                   you read it like one thing.

[*Pause*]

M.E.:	The Rastas come like the same blasted thing.
CHORUS:	They jus' the nex' line [of the Son].
M.E.:	But this is the Beginning! We locks show the End is here! Listen to what I say. The End is here. It is the End.
EDDOES:	[still talking about Rastas] They ai' say 'you', they all say 'you man'.
M.E.:	They make the spirit a man . . . a man! [laughs mockingly and getting excited].
POMME CYTHÈRE:	Mother go bust the rock. Zap!

[*General laughter*]

M.E.:	[laughs at herself but continues] You see how it go. He talking at side of me . . . When you call a baby a man you place the Spirit of Destruction in it . . . [and continues].

While she sometimes describes the powers which will be The Mother's at the End she does not see herself, as a physical personage, as having much supernatural control in practical terms; this would be unnecessary for all will be Nature: 'I is The Mother, The Beginning. But I ai' play chief. You think I want to sit on high throne? . . . Imagine your self Ruler of the Earth! It real dread you know. Not to take it as a kingship. I don' want a crown. The Children are my crown.'

Those parts of Mother Earth's eschatology which may be regarded as frankly alarming, such as the eventual return of everybody to a hermaphrodite state, are of little concern. As in American hippie communes personal meaning and satisfaction derive from daily work: 'The Way of Death is nice looking. You think "I can hustle a shilling." The Way of Life is hard. You have to cut too much bush. You' tree come down, and now it hit you. You' cutlass slip. You get pica in you' foot. We not like other people. We abide by the Spirit' [Breadfruit].

Much of the continued momentum in the Valley is a personal rediscovery of Creole country life although there is little interest in the surrounding fishing villages whose rural technology is passed on through Jakatan. Almost every male villager knows more about agriculture than any of the Earth People except Jakatan, but the shared trials and difficulties, followed by success, produce a carnival communality, a triumphant release of something elemental but since repressed. This is Africa:

Africa is the Beginning of the Earth. We are the Makers. We have the knowledge of the Earth. We are the Mothers of the Earth. We are the Serpents of the Earth, and here is where the Serpent is about to rise. In the land where we can plant our own food, eat and live. Here is Hell Valley. The Children of Africa will come here to suffer themselves to regain the Earth.

The Valley *is* Africa, no substitute, nor an imitation: 'They were scattering Africa so she could not get together and rise. Rasta go to Africa? Africans ai' want no Rastas' (Breadfruit). That their Africa is in part derived from Hollywood, that the African hut built by the group is modelled on one in John Houston's film *The African Queen*,[28] is an irony not lost on the group. But they accept that the truth will still percolate through its Social representations, as with the Bible, and that Hollywood does depict a real Africa, howbeit through the eyes of Science.

All new religious movements face the discrepancy between ideal and exigency.[29] The nurturant Earth of which in a deeper sense humans are only constituent parts, is in everyday experience outside of us; it has to be worked upon to provide food, using tools which are steel and which are created by the Son and his Race. These are necessary limitations in what is only the Beginning of the End, a compromised and imperfect approach to the actual Life. Unlike the South Indian Rameshwaram, the group do not regard the Earth as so holy that She may never be worked, but She is not gratuitously assaulted; cutlasses are not left sticking in Her – a common practice in rural Trinidad where an unsheathed cutlass lying in the scrub is a hazard. Mango trees are not pelted with stones: the fruit is picked or allowed to fall. Nature however is to be worked and if the Earth People talk much of the pleasures of life away from town, of fresh air and good food, they do not devote their time to aesthetic contemplation of the landscape.

While work involves clearing the land and removing unproductive bush, the ultimate aim is to allow Nature to blossom unhindered. Machines are unacceptable but a limited degree of technical innovation – say a more efficient way of burning scrub – is often debated. The acceptance that they live in a 'compromised' pre-utopia does not in itself determine exactly where the line is to be drawn. There are continual and heated discussions. Crises in the group usually prompt a more Natural line. When things are progressing smoothly, what we may call a 'technical' approach becomes accepted to the point where Jakatan wistfully discusses the advantages of an out-board motor for the canoe. Serious conflicts herald a purist return to the central teaching. The point of general accommodation seems to be bounded by some conception of African life as portrayed in the cinema together with the technology used on the coast up to the 1960s (when out-board motors were first used by the local fishermen). Cocoa and coffee are harvested traditionally, with no more than a cutlass. On occasions the line is drawn depending on frank comfort: 'We suppose not to use light but we still use flambeaux as we accustom to it from the city.' Points which are never for negotiation are nudity and the refusal to use animals for labour. Birds are encouraged to settle nearby but are not caged, and the goats are tethered only lest they fall down the cliff. When going to town the group set off to walk the whole way but are not altogether reluctant to accept a lift in the back of a passing truck, and in emergencies have hired one. As Jakatan (hardly one of the purists) puts it: 'Like car, like walk, it come as jus' as free now.' They are quite happy to accept food from sympathisers when in town, and some of the younger members volunteer for errands away from the Valley just so that they can sample packaged foods again: 'To say to contradict the food outside, you can' do that because you eat it sometime an' before we come to our senses we was eating it . . . ' Mother Earth herself used to be fond of chocolate and I was assigned the task of bringing some back from Port-of-Spain which was then shared out, accepted gracefully but defensively.

The harder one works the more latitude in sampling outside pleasures, and the newer members are often the least tolerant. To an extent such intrusions from the outside are tolerated if they are only occasional. Debates as to the acceptability of hunting agouti or using nets to fish are of greater significance. One member, Potato (centre, Plate 2, page 171), frequently complained about the discrepancy between ideal and practice. He eventually left the Valley after an argument with Coconut; when I bumped into him later in Pinnacle he told me that the real problem was the lack of harmony between members; he then asked me to find him a pair of green dungarees then popular among the Rastas. A general discussion in the Valley as to whether to grow rice was solved by sending me to the University Department of Agriculture to beg some hill rice, a generally acceptable compromise: 'That we own spirit talking to we!'

Individual dispositions are located, less on some spectrum between Creole and European, than on one between the values particularly associated with the group who knew Mother Earth when she lived in town and those of more recently arrived Rastas. The former complex is more feminist, Baptist, universalist, conversionist, asexual and lived in apocalyptic time,[30] orientated to the future vision; the latter is more anti-White, technological, concerned with labour outside the vicinity of the house, with smoking ganja and discussing the opportunities for sexual relations when the *mothers* arrive. While this second set of values has no institutional form, Mother Earth refers to the more Rasta members as 'the back fire ones' as they are more likely than others to sit by the fire in the wood cutting area (Plate 6), a fire which represents no immediate function for the community as a whole.

Rome

The gap between ideal and compromise provides the texture of daily life inside the Valley but it is especially salient in the physical separation between the Valley itself and Rome – the Social world. The outside world remains necessary as a source of new recruits, and the Valley maintains relations with it through the persistence of past sentiments and through some economic transactions. The extent of external contact varies with the particular feeling inside the Valley at any time, for the group are never totally self-sufficient. On occasions they beg or scrounge necessary articles, or purchase salt, rice, sacking, cutlasses and other tools and even kerosene from the Pinnacle stores (using cash just obtained from selling copra or ganja) or they barter fish and fruit using cash equivalents (Plate 2).

In Chapter 1, I outlined their current relations with Pinnacle Village. Too close to risk any confrontation, and knowing that many of the villagers remain resentful of their squatting on Pinnacle land, no attempt is made here to gain new recruits although the Earth People are prepared to *put out* their views if challenged. In the village are families who were friends of Mother Earth and Jakatan before her visions, and they are the people most likely to trade with Hell Valley. Through them, news from Port-of-Spain or from outside Trinidad is obtained, and information about sick relatives, ex-partners or important political events reaches the Valley quickly. Such news is shared immediately among the group and given a Natural gloss by Mother Earth. Village gossip that the police corporal, who had beaten them on one of their trips to town, had just had his arm broken in a quarrel with his girl friend led to much amused jesting – 'It have licks to come!' – although on the whole the Valley regard with forbearance the past raids and imprisonments. While the authorities seem content to ignore the Earth People, it remains important not to antagonise them too much. When the aptly named Colley ('Ganja') secretly deserted the Valley with a large sack of ganja and some tools there was consternation, especially when we heard that he had been arrested in a village along the coast: 'He ai' for the Life. He only come here on a head.[31] He a pusher.' Colley's fine of 800 dollars was paid by his uncle and the Valley heard no more of him. On another occasion they decided to participate in the local economy more directly and, believing that they had obtained from the authorities the contract to clear their stretch of the Turnpike, started work only to learn that they were not going to be paid. They welcome the occasional coverage in the media but complain of misrepresentation, particularly of being described as violent.

Sometimes a passer-by along the Turnpike, usually an itinerant preacher or hiking student, stops for a meal and discussion.[32] He is welcomed and work stops as the Earth People gather round to show him their crops and offer gifts of their best produce to carry away. My own stay with the Earth People involved two particular difficulties both for them and for myself. Fieldwork with new religious movements is rare because uncommitted outsiders are not easily welcomed, particularly at the point Weber called 'routinisation', when the initial enthusiasm is palling, and conflicts develop about the extent of accommodation with the outside world, and when splits in the group are common. As Bryan Wilson comments, 'sects are very closed communities, sometimes unwelcoming even to the outsiders who might want to join, and hostile to those who wish to inquire, record and analyse'.[33] The 'ethnography' of groups like the Moonies or Jehovah's Witnesses is often derived from printed tracts or interviews with lapsed members. The Valley too awaited recruits not students. Certainly, the observer's experience with new groups is very different from that in conventional fieldwork – one is intensively involved at the moment of eager creation, symbolisations are relatively fresh and open, while exegesis is already mandatory for there can be no appeal to 'tradition'. Explicit knowledge is gained suddenly and totally, not incrementally, and meanings emerge as core symbolisations and ideas rapidly develop new routines in association with one's presence. Conversely, departure is more than a disengagement: it inevitably is some type of betrayal. If I had meant all I seemed to, if I had been serious, how could I now leave?

A second problem was the very specific teaching of the Earth People in which all Whites are the Children of the Son, the historical oppressors of Black people. Initial acceptance was (we later agreed) facilitated by the profound absurdity of the situation – of a White psychiatrist coming along without any institutional position to sit on the earth with them. This parodying of the earlier time when Mother Earth had been put in St Ann's Hospital and treated with drugs by psychiatrists gave some sort of implicit Natural meaning to my arrival. After a couple of visits we discussed my future involvement. I told them I thought I was sympathetic to many of their ideas, that I felt they were doing something of significance for all people. This sounded as trite to them as it does to me now, so 'Well, then, I don't know, I'm just here.' Perhaps because the Earth People were at that time in some degree of uncertainty, having just lost one of their few female members (and the whole Valley appeared suffused with a vague sense of doubt), I stayed: 'You here to find you senses, same as all of we.'

It was only after a few daytime visits, when I was dropped off by boat from Pinnacle Village or stayed nearby in an abandoned cocoa house, that I was invited to remain for a night and then for longer stays. At about this time, after going swimming in the river with Pumpkin and Cocorite, I emerged from the water and walked back to the house naked, to sardonic acclaim and amusement. From that time onward I lived in the Valley for a few weeks at a time over a period of a year. I did not sleep in the men's house but occupied a rather ambiguous space near the central fire, in between Mother Earth and the new members. I was never regarded as a full member although the possibility of my joining fully, cutting all ties with the outside world, was raised occasionally. There was no overt pressure to do this and it was agreed that I would return to Britain eventually. When my departure was imminent Mother Earth became particularly keen on my recording them fully and exactly, and eventually persuaded me, over my objections, to bring a camera and tape recorder. I was to be extruded as I had come – as a type of reporter. My wife and our daughter came to stay twice – for a 'holiday' as Mother Earth at her respectable best put it. (Their warm reception argues perhaps against the psychoanalyst, mindful of the unobtainable White colonial father, who has now perceived my arrival as a consummation and resolution of the Oedipal triangle.) Our daughter's name is Letice and this resulted in all three of us taking *fruit names*; I became Tomato (*red* skin) and my wife Cressels (Cr. *cresson*, cress). Letice of course remained Letice. We were jokingly known as the *short-crops*, the name given to 'European' crops newly introduced. At the suggestion of Mother Earth, I gave an interview in Port-of-Spain to a magazine and a lecture about them at St Ann's, and wrote with the group an article for publication in the *Trinidad Guardian*.[34] I was accepted both as an immediate bulwark against any action by the police or hospital, and as someone who could help gain public support if the Valley faced any concerted campaign against it in the press.

My ambiguous status spared me some of the rigours of Valley life. I was allowed to use as a blanket the canvas sail Jakatan had asked me to buy at a chandler in Port-of-Spain but which proved too heavy for the canoe. I kept my spectacles and toothbrush. The sight of me cleaning my teeth provoked derision but 'That's your way. It you' way which you accustom to. You not really living this life yet so we wouldn't really interfere you know. Because I use to scrub my mouth . . . ' As I had spent some time in Uganda I served occasionally as a source of 'African' lore: on thatching, on building the canoe, on food preparation, and I introduced the game of *wari*: within a few days we had carved three boards and I was to be resoundingly beaten in every game.[35]

White anthropologists in the West Indies cannot conceive of themselves as any sort of 'neutral' observers, a point surprisingly incomprehensible to most of them. Any European arrives as an integral unit in the local social classification; the ethnographer is already a part of the society they come to study, a society constituted through racist objectification and practice. The fieldwork is always one of 'difference', a difference already constituted before the study, sometimes one of reconciliation, always opposition, never innocence. It is perhaps only the relatively 'open' structuring of African–Caribbean communities with their lack of fixed statuses and their continuing shifts of local alliance that allow any type of intimate information to be gathered by Whites. To be part of 'the world as it should not be', one of the Race of Science, was only a development of the situation I had already enjoyed in Pinnacle Village and in Port-of-Spain. In any West Indian context the fact of being White makes certain very specific demands on the observer. Even more so in the Valley where, before my arrival, Whites were simply taken by many people as the distant originators of disharmony and persecution.

My stay inevitably led to a changing emphasis on the nature of Black and White, towards some sort of notion that a few Whites at least could be Black 'inside' (and Blacks, White), an idea that Mother Earth herself already held together with her more dichotomised cosmology. On occasion Mother Earth denied I was White at all. For the more Rasta-orientated members my stay was difficult at times and we had frequent discussions as to its implications for the immediate concerns of the group, apart from the eschatological aspect for would I too live at the End? I suggested that my presence made needless difficulties for everybody but was always told to be quiet and to stay, that if I was trying to say I was lonely I should fetch my family for another visit. In spite of these public demands to remain I was frequently uneasy about my presence somehow 'universalising' the teaching and indeed on the daily tensions. While I am not, even now, completely convinced that I should have stayed, Mother Earth instructed me firmly to remain, for my arrival was a necessary develop-ment of the End. Nature had to reach out and engage Science: 'I know Science has to search me out, to fight me, to check me out.' Virtually everyone told me privately that many of their companions were half-hearted and tended to come and go anyway, so, if anyone left when I was there, I should not take it personally. I myself suspected that the development of the group had plateaued under the effects of boredom and the failure to recruit new members, and that I was not likely to accelerate this process. Perhaps the opposite. In spite of all this, my farewell visit did coincide with the traumatic dispute with Mango Rose (page 214) and the departure of Moco.

One difficulty was my relationship to Mother Earth which became closer than that between her and many of the group. As our friendship deepened I became the recipient for many confidences about the Valley. In any conflict between my status as an observer, my uncertain membership of a community for whose aims I had much sympathy, and my friendship with Mother, it was the last which tended to win out. Inevitably, my time as her confidant during our long conversations smoking cigars in the house – when I could perhaps have been more dutifully employed in clearing the bush or chopping firewood – was resented at times.

The group felt responsible for my safety and were anxious lest any accident should reflect on them. At the end of my fourth period with the group, Jobie's fishing boat from the village did not turn up to collect me as he had arranged.

My visits to the Earth People had caused problems for friends in the village who felt hurt at my breaking away from the village to go off with 'them savages', but by this time I was accepted as some sort of student of Creole life and villagers would tease me by hinting that I really went to the Valley for a sexual *freeness* – 'but I suppose you got to learn all about we'. The couple I lived with in Pinnacle Village, Athanase and Carmen Salvary, who were among the most respectable villagers, got tired of their neighbours' barbed comments about my probable nudity and ganja smoking, and started reposting in public that although the Earth People were all clearly mad, they were at least doing what they practised openly, not like some people . . . The presents of food I brought back to Mistress Salvary won her over and since my departure she has continued to reciprocate gifts back to the Valley.[36]

With Jobie's *canot* failing to round the headland as anticipated, Mother Earth revealed a dream of the previous night which implied that some disaster would happen to all of us if I did not return to Pinnacle by midnight. As dusk fell Jakatan and two volunteers prepared the elaborately carved canoe (Plate 7) and we hastily cut some new paddles, the previous set having floated away on the tide the preceding night – another omen. Cinderella-like I took a hasty leave of Mother Earth, swam with my companions and the canoe beyond the surf and clambered aboard. The moon was full and the sea calm as we started the twelve-mile trip, our departure echoing to salutes of 'All Left!' along the shore. A squall soon blew up and, after four hours hard paddling against cross-currents swelling off the rocks, we were still well short of our destination. Clouds now obscured the moon, our hands blistered from the rough paddles, it started raining hard, and one of the crew collapsed in the bottom of the canoe. I was all for being set on land to make the rest of my way on foot through the forest but Jakatan insisted we had to continue. The wind increased and the canoe was unable to make Pinnacle Point, keeping, as far as I could judge, in more or less the same place for over an hour, the tide now running strongly against us. We decided to drop the anchor stone and take a rest but the rope had become hopelessly knotted up. We lost a paddle. Cursing the weather, we became aware of a light as a canot from Pinnacle emerged out of the darkness carrying three villagers with guns who had been out hunting (or so they said); one of them was the man on whose family land the Valley had been established. A shouted negotiation through the storm ensured that I was dropped back to the village and I gingerly stepped from the canoe still naked, leaving Jakatan and the others holding it steady in the swell with their paddles, rain dripping down their dreads, and joined the suspicious trio of men in oil skins and hats who took me back to Pinnacle through the storm and night rain in complete silence. The story was round the neighbourhood by the time I arose the next morning but, apart from a few sarcastic grins, made surprisingly little difference to my acceptance there. It was only what they already knew. The next day I met my own family who had arrived with the fish jitny. Jakatan, who had returned to the Valley in the canoe, came back through the bush to see if all was well.

A continued source of amusement for Mother Earth was my note-taking, even after I abandoned it when in the Valley. It was the cause of thunderstorms, they objected, and when I arrived after any period of rain or bad weather I was greeted with cries of 'We know what you've been doing in Pinnacle!' I was never quite sure just how jokingly this was meant.

During the time I remained in Hell Valley, Mother Earth's health continued to deteriorate and I asked my neighbours in Pinnacle for some rachette 'bush' to treat her swollen legs. Other errands for the Earth People included the purchase of seeds, a file, cheese, and more chocolate. My daughter brought her Asterix comic books which, like my accounts of urban riots, classical mythology, biotechnology and nuclear power, was incorporated into the approaching End: 'Trinidad, St Vincent, New York, England, it same world. Same have to go to labash [rubbish heap] get food for their children. If all we live together and grow food, it be real dread, a real togetherness' (Breadfruit).

The battle against the Son: old disputes and new secessions
From the time of my initial visit certain difficulties were recognised by Mother Earth as endangering the Life. While none of these were regarded by anyone, at least openly, as invalidating Mother Earth's vision, they were generally accepted as worrying. The most obvious was the state of her own health which restricted her to the area around the house. No fresh expedition to town could be contemplated. She remained tired for much of the time, increasingly unable to oversee immediate tasks or to deal with the usual arguments. Her illness did not explicitly challenge the idea that Nature would soon become fully manifest in her (and no one voiced this concern to me), but it did emphasise the existence of the group through her physical person.

Since its foundation prospective members had often arrived in the Valley to leave after disagreements, and this still continued. The development of the community and indeed its appeal were always derived from the relationship with Rome, both as the source of membership and as the state of affairs to which the Life stood counterposed. As numbers increased, obviously more land could be cleared, more food grown, more followers accommodated; without the repeated trips to town there would be a fall in membership. This was reflected in a sense of uncertainty in the group, even though it was as large as it had ever been. Any doubts were not voiced publicly. Mother Earth continued to use instances of quarrelling as the explanation for the delay in the End.

Arguments developed over the practical organisation of tasks and failure to be loyal to Mother. Potato, who later left the group, complained to me that 'it suppose to live in togetherness an' understanding. But they all do different thing. Some argue. Some use the Mother an' get her tired. They curry favour and mamaguy [deceive] she.'

Potato had always looked in the group for a 'closeness and a harmony'. He was a particular friend of Colley and Pomme Cythère although something in the relationship between the other two always seemed to exclude him. After Colley left, Potato took over his place by the central fire but Pomme Cythère now seemed closer to Cassava. One evening before eating, Potato stalked off to the wood-chopping area complaining loudly about a satirical song Pomme Cythère had just sung about him. The latter, disconcerted, remarked that Potato was just *touchous* because of an earlier discussion about Mother Earth's health. After Potato had a trivial argument over a tool with Coconut the next morning he decided to leave the Valley. He was seen off sadly by the whole group with a ragged shout of 'All Left!' Mother Earth did not try to dissuade him but told the others she understood how hurt he felt. After he left she compared him favourably with the departed Colley, and remarked that Potato at least understood what the group were trying to do; Potato's fault was that he could not humble himself to the others. When new goats were bought he had refused to worm them with the appropriate bush (*Chenopodium ambrosioides*), a task for which he had some agreed responsibility. The goats had fallen sick. When I suggested that perhaps Potato had difficulty coping with her illness she brusquely disagreed, but then Moco recalled a vision Potato had dreamt a few nights before about his own mother being ill. Which mother? Mother Earth ridiculed the association.

What we might term the 'structural' imbalances of the group follow from its reproduction of the original Mother–Child cosmology and from the absence of women. Mother Earth has to be the Mother of every member and yet she has a consort, Jakatan. In her teaching the only person resembling a consort of the Mother is her incestuous son, the God of the Whites: for the group there can be no ultimately grounded position for Jakatan except as one of the Mother's Children. Although he is much younger than Mother, it was he who first suggested that the couple and their children should move to the bush and, although he loyally supports her in public, on occasions he does leave the community to visit his family.[37] At times he takes a select group of Earth People up into the mountains where he has built a small *batchy* (man's forest hut). In his absence Mother decries this 'high woods group' and complains that 'he plays at boss man there'. On one occasion she severely criticised him for letting the canoe drift away (Plate 11).We heard later that it had been sunk by

Pinnacle villagers. At times of bitter argument she harangues the group about the role of fathers in general, how they desert women and leave them to look after the children. Here she is the Creole mother complaining to her sons about the vagaries of their father. At times he resents his position as a sort of elder child, particularly when he is berated by Mother for not taking a more active role in directing the less experienced members, a role which is in any case restricted, for there is no place for a 'father' in the group. The absence of *mothers* (women) recalls parental difficulties about sexuality among the siblings of any family. Mother Earth is certainly correct when she says that women have particular problems with abandoning town life and respectability, but she does seem to find it difficult to accept adult women as members, particularly if they appear likely to form liaisons with her male Children. While celibacy has no explicit value, Mother Earth strongly hints that the time is not yet come for sexual relations: she complains to her Children about Jakatan's sexual approaches to her, and rather wishfully and unconvincingly once said to me in front of everybody: 'They could go off for a woman but it ai' in them. They work to preparation for having children. I show them how to live to love the mothers. Their life outside ai' no preparation. Half of children born without a home. They grow up in a frustration because their parents didn' come together with a love, so they have all sort of corruption.' She certainly does not encourage the young men to bring back women to produce a family, and the couples who have lived together in the Valley pose problems through their loyalty to each other.

The brief stay of Mango Rose exacerbated Mother Earth's difficulties. The two had met in St Ann's Hospital when Mother Earth invited her to live in the Valley. Mango Rose was born in the same fishing village as Jakatan but had spent most of her life in Port-of-Spain. Her grandfather had founded the local Shouter group I described in Chapter 6. She was aged twenty-three when she finally joined the community, a rather sullen and truculent woman, going only partially naked and with an ill grace, sitting moodily by the cooking fire, declining any tasks. Mother Earth became irritated within a week of her arrival and started criticising her. After a few days, during which Mango Rose made a little more of an effort but was now increasingly rebuffed by Mother (who had been feeling unwell and clearly regretted her original invitation), she took to going off to the back fire. Private conversation between them ceased.

Two weeks after her arrival, Mother heard her singing a reggae theme and told her to stop. She did, but started up again later near the men's wood cutting area. She was obviously needling Mother Earth. Mother pointedly told the group about a dream in which a wave came to wash the Earth People away. Mango Rose now spent most of her time audibly complaining about Mother

Earth to the more 'Rasta' section of the group who listened with embarrassment. Finally, when she refused to stop singing, Mother Earth angrily told her to leave that evening by the fishing boat that was expected to cross the bay to pick me up. Mango Rose complained she was being 'run', and left the house to stand outside the whole night shouting abuse at Mother Earth.

The boat failed to come. This was the most serious disruption the community had experienced from inside, and two Earth People volunteered to take Mango Rose back to Pinnacle through the bush. Mother Earth refused and said this was something we had to sit out. Everybody stopped work and we sat and listened in horror to a non-stop stream of invective about the group – that Coconut had tried to have sex with her, that Mother Earth was incapable of tolerating women in her group because she wanted to be queen, that she was treating the members as children to stop them growing up so she could keep them for her

11 On top of the cliff looking for the canoe.

own sexual purposes, calling her a 'soucouyant' (vampire), that she had betrayed her Nation by inviting me to stay – the whole punctuated with cries of 'I–Rastafari, Selassie–I.' She retrieved the clothes she had come in and put them on, including a Rasta tam. She screamed that nudity was ridiculous, that as the Whites had put Blacks in clothes they ought to stay in them. By now most of the listening Earth People were distraught, some in tears, but Mother Earth still told them to sit quietly and listen for this was a test of the Son. Mother Earth was already upset at my imminent departure (I was to stay only once again) and handled the whole matter rather indecisively. She told Breadfruit to give Mango Rose some food. This was refused but a portion of ganja and a coconut shell of embers were accepted. A storm blew up and the dissident's invective was drowned in the wind. The Earth People retired to a sleepless night on the ground.

By the morning everybody had had enough and Mango Rose was 'run', escorted along the track to Pinnacle by two Earth People. It then transpired that Moco, an early recruit who was known as hard-working and committed, but who particularly regretted the continuing absence of his girlfriend, had left alone during the night. A search party found him in a village on the coast and reported back that he needed time to 'find himself' before he returned. His departure crystallised many of the conflicts in the Valley and an acrimonious argument ensued. I too was involved and when I finally left Hell Valley for Port-of-Spain as arranged it was in a far from happy frame of mind.[38] While not held responsible I was gently aware I had somehow failed.

I left Trinidad two weeks later. In spite of return visits I have only a partial understanding of how the stay of Mango Rose and my own departure affected Valley life. Over the following year some of the group left and returned to town where they criticised Mother Earth while remaining true to her Natural life, to nudity and the repudiation of both Rastas and the life of the town. They camped out in Laventille. It is noteworthy that once they were away from Mother Earth they persuaded a few young women to cast aside respectability and join them.[39]

While my own departure precludes a detailed consideration of this later defection, it might be appropriate to assess the factors acting for and against the continued existence of the Valley at that time. In favour were: the end of the oil boom and the continuing deterioration of the Trinidad economy, and thus increased unemployment among young men in Port-of-Spain; the continuing appeal of Mother Earth's ideas as a logical extension of Creole working-class life; dissatisfaction with 'Jamaican' Rastafari, and renewed public interest in shango; the association of the secular radical alternative, NJAC, with the university and with 'communism'; the benign neglect of the Valley by the authorities; and intermittent popular interest and sympathy. Against these were: the increasing secularisation of Trinidadian society; the physical illness of Mother Earth which prevented trips to town and left her less able to lead the group on a day-to-day basis; Jakatan's ambiguous role and his outside interests; and the apparent inability of the group to accommodate young women.

The Earth People were likely to develop in various ways. The most obvious was a continuing fragmentation as Mother Earth became unable to run affairs, with individual members peeling off to return to a more 'Rasta' style in town, with the Valley contracting down again to Mother Earth and her biological family. If the community could expand it would continue to face a choice between 'purity' and 'accommodation', possibly seeking government grants and becoming economically linked to the wider system, along the lines of the communalist Shakers or the Holy Apostles of Nigeria. This could only occur after Mother Earth's death; there were clear ideological constraints on capital accumulation by the group, nor was there there a strong institutional lobby in Port-of-Spain to provide protection. The distance of the Valley from town and its centres of influence encourage commitment but makes recruiting more difficult. Celibacy is in part fortuitous and without Mother Earth the group could establish a self-reproducing community. A likely central focus would remain the valuing of the Natural life and, if unemployment continued to increase, the Earth People might provide the prototype for a variety of other communal groups. This is unlikely, for the accepted urban goals remain those of a not-that-inaccessible American society. The country is too small, too homogeneous and too firmly in the Western mainstream for any type of enclosed community to develop easily in independence of the major systems of social organisation and the international economy.

An intriguing but unlikely possibility is that more middle-class groups, orientated to the broader international currents of ecology, pacifism and feminism, might form some relationship with the Earth People or take up the further elaboration of their ideas. Whether, like the Rastas, their achievements could be reintegrated back into an enhanced mainstream of Creole working-class life is also improbable.

10

Genesis of meanings, limits of mimesis

The imitation of madness

To deny that radical social change can be understood as being 'pathological' or 'dysfunctional' is not to dismiss the possibility that institutions may, on occasion, develop through unusual or extreme – 'psychopathological' if we will – individual experiences. If we accept, along with descriptive psychiatry, some relatively autonomous, and to an extent culturally invariant, and thus 'natural', domain of psychopathology, manifest to us in popular notions like 'madness', how can such specific experience or its interpretation actively engage others?

Engage them, that is, not only in serving as some emblem of 'what shall not be', as society's dark mirror, but in the experience itself as meaningful. If it does, how is such experience recognised and transformed by others? We can never have psychological representations of brain states independent of social experience and action, for the notion of a culturally unfettered 'nature' is a fiction. Because medical observers of social patterns, as we have seen in Chapter 2, freely ascribe a psychopathology explained as biology on decidedly slender biological evidence, it will be appropriate to restrict the possibility to situations where we have already some more convincing understanding of psychopathology in terms of biological science – 'coarse brain disease', epilepsy or manic-depressive psychosis.[1] Social appropriation of madness may, of course, not value or amplify such patterns in themselves but rather seek to render them decent, as less abnormal, as 'only symbolic', or even to conceal them altogether.[2] I would suggest five general situations in which such an 'appropriation of madness' may be recognised:

(a) A person who is already influential becomes psychotic but retains their power for a time. A limited example of this is described by psychiatrists as *folie à deux*, a situation where, in a close but socially isolated family, a dominant individual develops abnormal and idiosyncratic beliefs which they seek to validate through the agreement of others; the consequent 'passive delusions' of these dependants rapidly disappear if they are isolated from the dominant originator.[3] Some such mode lies behind the popular perception of Hitler or Amin as charismatic madmen, and indeed we have seen that Weston La Barre characterises 'folie à N' as the mechanism for all innovation. While it is probably rare for an influential individual to maintain their influence if recognised as frankly insane, it is of course common for absolute rulers to become increasingly isolated and suspicious – but this is hardly insanity.[4] We must also be wary of reports from those former associates who, after the fall of their leader, excuse themselves as having been under some malign and pathological influence, like the erstwhile adherent of the Peoples Temple who suggested that the mass suicide of the group was simply consequent on its founder developing cancer: 'his own [impending] death trigger[ing] him into certain decisions that became mass decisions'.[5]

If leaders are locally recognised as insane they are probably soon eliminated, as Suetonius seems to have suggested in the case of Caligula. But with Tito and Franco we find that increasingly senile and moribund leaders may be kept 'alive' biomedically to govern for a considerable period, even if they are unable to exercise effective authority. Such 'charismatic' leaders embody the social order in a much more personal way than they would through occupying an existing role. If individuals are less important for personal qualities than for the conventional role which they occupy, they are likely to be removed from public influence with scant respect, as happened to the English monarch George III. We may thus expect more mad presidents to retain office than mad kings: on the other hand, insane leaders who do not have a hereditary justification are perhaps less likely to appear in the general run of things, for their predisposition to insanity is likely to have manifested itself earlier in some form, perhaps to have eliminated them from the struggle for power: Idi Amin had been at the head of the Ugandan armed forces for some years before he sought absolute power, an argument against any putative psychopathology.

(b) Alternatively the individual may be only periodically insane and in between episodes they participate in the shared social reality through which they can interpret their arbitrary experiences, possibly validating them as acceptable communications through structuring them in conventional forms. They may then find their experiences strange, and the personal quest for their significance becomes identified with external validation by others. In his *Journal* the Quaker, George Fox, describes an episode when, passing near the English town of Lichfield, he felt impelled to take off his shoes in a nearby field and run through the town shouting 'Woe unto the bloody city of Lichfield':

returning later to retrieve his shoes he became perplexed as to the meaning of this action and appears relieved on being assured that the town had once been the site of Christian martyrdom under Diocletian.[6] Illnesses like schizophrenia, which psychiatrists define on the basis of widespread and continuing personality changes with a serious loss of social competence, are unlikely to be subsequently integrated in this way. Toxic drug-induced states, early psychosis, isolated psychotic episodes or phasic reactions like manic-depressive psychosis, are more amenable to re-entry into the shared world, and thus to serve as a model: what, following Devos, we may term 'pathomimesis'.[7]

The episode itself may be less a novel transformation of existing cultural themes than the public signal that legitimates a possible change of status already available: if epileptic fits are understood to be of divine origin, then the presence of divinity will be manifest by fits whether these are spontaneous, sought or simulated. Mircea Eliade emphasises that epilepsy is only one of a series of possible and random events, including disease, misfortune or accident, which may act as the 'signs of election' to a visionary role through signalling the arbitrary otherworld; the public communications which result are similar whatever the route of entry and they are couched in a conventional idiom.[8]

The communication of the isolated psychotic episode, whether radically innovative or merely signalling mystical imputation, recalls the shamanic and ecstatic employment of altered states of consciousness – induced by fasting, sensory deprivation, music, dancing or drugs – to attain a mystical otherworld. Here however the scope of the visions is firmly circumscribed by custom, their import agreed by consensual validation.[9] Some of the Earth People had undergone Spiritual Baptist mourning. Their *travelling* was continuously monitored and validated by other members of the church and many, including Mother Earth, were ejected from the Baptists for quite idiosyncratic visions (pages 67, 179).

Eliade, like medical commentators on shamanism, regards the dissociated state of the protagonist as somehow more idiosyncratic and less 'collective' than everyday consciousness, a point also remarked by Nadel.[10] While I think this is unlikely to be true of dissociation, the psychological mechanism which embodies Durkheim's quintessentially collective 'effervescence', and also the psychiatrists' 'mass hysteria', the communications of the psychotic may well be more idiosyncratic than everyday shared beliefs. However, as with the messianic figure Sabbatai Svi, psychotic innovation may provide less an obvious novelty than a transformation of everyday themes, or indeed the facilitation of certain generally available but unrealised sentiments. The innovative power in these cases seems to come from the personal conviction with which psychosis imbues the contravention, and the deliberate public performance of it for its own sake, as opposed to the more casual mention others may make of it as arbitrary 'misbehaviour' or 'nonsense'.

(c) Clarke Garrett reminds us that the British sectarian Richard Brothers 'probably was mad but this should not obscure the fact that his followers were not'.[11] My first two possibilities are concerned with the innovator while in the others I am interested principally in the way in which others may respond to madness, and ascribe meaning to the otherwise arbitrary. The communications of the psychotic are certainly not always directed at potential converts: they may be 'expressionistic' or just 'unintended' rather than 'intended'.[12] How then is the 'experience put into circulation', to use Victor Turner's phrase? Nietzsche, Strindberg and Artaud are not conventionally dismissed because, biomedically speaking, they developed, respectively, general paralysis of the insane, paranoia and schizophrenia, even though we are hardly likely to distinguish in their later work 'madness' from 'sanity'. For in certain situations the acceptability of 'delusions' can be quite independent from the recognition of any pathology: 'He's mad of course but . . . ' There is a recognition that there is something of value in the statements of the mad which can be taken up and employed, without denying an underlying illness. When Edgar says of King Lear 'O! matter and impertinency mix'd, Reason in madness', the insane source might seem to threaten the inspiration but, for the audience, Lear's madness merely adds poignancy and value to his own self-reflection (and indeed facilitates it). In the case of Artaud it is perhaps less his arguments when psychotic that are now memorable so much as his embodiment in his own life of what was previously a literary posture.

In early eighteenth-century North America it was accepted that Whites, including members of the Society of Friends, could legitimately own slaves, but two 'not quite sane' Quakers declared that slave-owning was no longer permissible.[13] Their statements struck such resonances that within a few years successive Friends' Meetings made the practice of slavery incompatible with membership of the Society. The two innovators appear to have been regarded still as insane: inspiration and its ground remained distinct.

(d) We are less concerned with some momentary and empathic 'mimesis' of pathology than with an active taking up of the images and ideas it offers, of engagement and reverberation at a variety of levels with the experience or its expression, appropriating and socialising it, codifying it, revising it, incorporating it, working it. To use the language of physics, not just 'resonating' but 'amplifying'. It is the emergent meaning for a community which determines whether 'psychosis' becomes 'prophecy'. Bryan Wilson points out that:

If a man runs naked down the street proclaiming that he alone can save others from impending doom, and if he immediately wins a following, then he is a charismatic leader: a social relationship has come into being. If he does not win a following, then he is simply a lunatic . . . The very content of 'plausibility' is culturally determined. It may be a more than average endowment of energy, determination, fanaticism, and perhaps intelligence. Of it may be an altogether different set of attributes, epilepsy, strangeness, what we should regard as mental disorder, or particularly when children are regarded as prophets, even sheer innocence. Often in these last mentioned instances it is others who take up, magnify, and give social significance to the prophecy.[14]

An innovation is meaningful when it resonates with certain existing themes for the audience. At those times of experienced crisis – 'periods of singularity' as Edwin Ardener calls them – when lived experience no longer matches the accepted social order, and our world appears unbalanced, solutions are likely to be accepted or sought from domains which at other times would be simply dismissed as mad: desperate times need desperate remedies. 'If they were too often a moving cloud of smoke by day', Coleridge wrote of the Puritan radicals, 'yet they were always a pillar of fire by night.'[15] In the 1660s, Solomon Eccles, a remnant of the multitude of Commonwealth millennialists, wandered around London with a brazier of fire on his head, naked apart from a loincloth, proclaiming the imminent destruction of the city. He was ignored until the plague and then the Great Fire made him a fashionable prophet. His time had come – briefly. London was rebuilt whilst Solomon continued to preach the identical doctrine, and he lapsed back into his former obscurity.[16] We may argue that the British anti-psychiatry movement of the 1960s also sought desperate remedies: if we accept with R. D. Laing that the girl who says she is dangerous because she has an atomic bomb inside her is actually 'less crazy' than a state which possesses and is prepared to use nuclear weapons,[17] then this is because we are so concerned about the possibility of nuclear war that we are prepared to broaden our conventional conceptions of rationality and delusion. Doubts as to the value of the technological course of society in the eighteenth, and again in the latter part of the twentieth century, have led us to seek prophets from among the 'primitives' – from the madmen, the shamans, the children.

The Canadian psychiatrist Henry Murphy has taken this argument further to suggest that times out-of-joint actually generate psychopathological solutions: 'Delusions may occur in times of increased stress as if, in reaction to changing conditions, the culture does call on individual members to sacrifice their mental health by the development of individual delusions which relieve communal anxieties.'[18] If I do not find his functionalist assumptions justified, clearly the themes of psychotic inspiration are likely to include current concerns whose transformation may then appeal as unique remedies, as a radically perverse form of what Obeyesekere calls *subjectification* – 'the process whereby cultural patterns and symbol systems are put back into the melting pot of consciousness and refashioned to create a culturally tolerated set of images'. And whose sense of unbounded possibility and the reconciliation of all things may then in turn become objectified in new institutions as appropriate and inevitable.

(e) To suggest disregarded innovations would have been acclaimed at another time or in another place is a biographical commonplace: the contemporary audience has somehow failed its author. Artaud's biographer tells us that 'in other epochs he might have been a shaman, a prophet, an alchemist, an oracle, a saint, a gnostic teacher or indeed the founder of a new religion'.[19] If we accept that both the individual and their psychopathologic experience are located in a specific time and place then this is somewhat meaningless, but it is possible that some groups are always open to a greater variety of (what we may regard as) idiosyncratic communications than are the dominant sectors. There may be contexts which do not share our rigorous exclusion of all psychopathological expression from the possibility of shared meaning. This seems true of the Quakers, the Rastas, and the counterculture, all open to 'the workings of the spirit'; but perhaps also of those subdominant groups characterised as faulted in some way by the dominant ideology – Blacks, Jews, Irish, or even women – and who take up this notion to serve for their own identity, as emotional, fey, touched, stiff-necked, peculiar people: here the mad person emblematically stands for the group as a whole.[20] Something similar may occur in societies with a more restricted concept of psychopathology than those permeated by professional psychiatry: while contemporary non-industrial societies appear to recognise a state akin to 'insanity', this may be restricted to the social impairment of chronic mental illness; the early stages of the psychiatrist's schizophrenia may be understood as a potentially meaningful experience, indistinguishable, say, from other shamanic 'calls', while the later chronic state which is seen as undesirable, is seen as the consequences of failing to respond appropriately to the call. As Kroeber probably correctly argued: 'In general the psychopathologies that are rewarded . . . are only the mild or transient ones. A markedly deteriorated psychosis . . . would be rated and deplored by them as much as by us.'[21]

Alternatively, the conventional idiom of 'madness' may be one quite distinct from everyday life and yet not restricted to a recognised and devalued state of pathology. It may share an idiom of other-worldly or 'visionary' communication – Obeyesekere's 'mythic' model.[22] Thus the Bengali concept of *pagol* glosses a variety of states recalling biomedicine's *psychosis*, but it may be used also in an extended, 'weak' usage to imply unreasonable behaviour as with 'mad' in Trinidad or England.[23]

Murphy suggests that there may be a cost in such local psychologies: 'Societies which encourage greater contact with unconscious feelings can freely accept the idiosyncratic behaviour and delusions of the mentally ill but they pay a price in economic and social inferiority.'[24] We do not have to accept the notion of a psychoanalytical unconscious to agree that a society which takes all forms of 'madness' as valuable is probably not the one which is likely to favour scientific technologies.

To summarise: the 'imitation' of madness may occur through one or more of these situations:

(i)   The individual who manifests psychopathology is already influential.
(ii)   Psychopathology is short-lived.
(iii)   She's mad but . . .
(iv)   Desperate times need desperate remedies.
(v)   The audience are particularly open to idiosyncratic communications.

From experience to reception

If we take biologically understood changes in the brain as arbitrary 'natural' events, then such 'natural events only have social consequences because they affect the situations and thus the decisions of certain individuals who, on account of this, choose or are constrained to act differently from the way they acted previously'.[25] As for any understanding of communication, we need to consider the prior preoccupations and motivations of the innovator, the personal experiences through which innovation draws its imagery from the existing culture, the actual genesis of the new themes, the formal techniques they employ putting the 'experience into circulation', and the ways in which these themes are received and modified by others.

Any enterprise bears a certain relationship to what has gone on before: the degree of transformation within tradition is our Western measure of 'innovation'. (And the much vaunted 'death of the subject' is our post-modern denial of such a history.) Psychopathology, as a potentially innovative process, may transform the ideas found in the ambient culture through which it is represented, bursting the 'enclosures of regularity' as Samuel Johnson put it. These ideas may be generally accepted or else available for transformation only as fragmentary and deviant oppositions in the society where they remain available to become a central alternative perspective.[26] They may be just a variant, or a simple reversal, of the common store of dominant representations; or they may be conventionally appropriate to quite another social group with whom the innovator is the one who has the motivation and courage to align herself by actions which are assigned in the context of everyday life only to others. The transformation may be a transformation of the given cognitive schemata, or else an inappropriate alignment of the particular individual with certain aspects of them; either may evoke similar experiential and mimetic resonances in others, or alternatively the very novelty of the situation and the impossibility of personal resonance with it may generate a further rearrangement of the shared symbolism or even a universalising perspective which lies 'beyond' it.

Roman Jakobson contrasted the 'metaphorical poets' such as Mayakovsky, whose poetry stood very directly for their personal lives, with those for whom, like Pasternak, their work seemed to maintain a certain distance from experience. It may be that it is the former who are the most likely model for mentally ill innovators when expression appears closely derived from unique personal experience. The subsequent appropriation of their subjectivity however is likely to be limited to those who can resonate with a very similar experience (who are few), or to those who can distance themselves from the originator's experience and expression, and employ aspects of them in a purely instrumental (metonymical) fashion as most of us do when we read, say, Evelyn Waugh's autobiographical *Gilbert Pinfold*. Our reading may be quite at variance with any intention of the originator. As Gilbert Lewis puts it:

You could also, like the mystic Henry Suso . . . eat three quarters of an apple in the name of the Trinity and the remaining quarter in commemoration of 'the love with which the heavenly Mother gave her tender child Jesus an apple to eat' and unless you or Henry Suso told me, I would not, though I watched you twenty times, discern your symbolism or even that what you did was symbolical.[27]

The subsequent development of a group is problematic if the innovation is simply an idiosyncratic reflection of the originator's private life, which is then to be taken up 'metaphorically' by others: in the extreme case it is difficult to establish a group all of whose members are God (although the Doukhobors have come close). Harding has reminded us that the experience of desolation is expressed well in the image of one who is marooned:[28] The Castaway of Cowper's poem is damned through no fault of his own, whilst Coleridge's Ancient Mariner is abandoned in order to redeem his sin. Cowper's work expresses directly his personal (arguably psychotic) experiences. By contrast, Coleridge's Mariner, like Defoe's Crusoe, is more accessible in that he offers us, in our shared idiom, a plausible narrative of abandonment and reconciliation. Similarly, Cowper's own close identification with the hunted deer of *The Task* could not communicate human cruelty to animals as effectively as the more detached empathy we find in Blake's *Songs of Innocence and Experience*. A complete identity of extreme personal experience with the presumed shared reality, as in Christopher Smart's *Jubilate Agno*, may ultimately be seen as solipsistic,[29] depending of course on our empathy. On the other hand, we may wonder if the intensely personal is not also sometimes the more universal and shared, precisely because, if it can engage others it has to do so through identification, in a homologous rather than a complementary mode.

The American poet Robert Lowell offers an example of Jakobson's auto-biographical excess. From his thirties he was hospitalised every other year with manic-depressive psychosis:

> Lowell would become irritable and 'too merry', would fall in love with anyone conveniently to hand, would talk unstoppably, identify with various great men of history (Achilles, Alexander, Hart Carne, Hitler and Christ according to one source), and would become truant, truculent and dangerous.[30]

During his periods of hospitalisation he would sketch out manic fragments but these were later worked up into more conventional verse. Although much of his work was intensely personal, often dealing explicitly with his illness (as in the poem 'Mania'), it expresses wider themes of suffering and threatened identity. When he was forty Lowell moved away from strict metre and rhyme into a new style, 'paradoxical, ironic, whimsically oblique but capable of elegiac weight'. His manic experiences now provided a model for stylistic variation as well as theme. One critic complained 'the new [poems] sound like messages to yourself'[31] but Lowell was confidently extending his repertoire, emboldened by changing expectations on the part of the public, now responding to the more contrived imitation of madness of Ginsberg's *Kaddish*.[32]

Anthony Storr argues in *The Dynamics of Creation* that valid 'creativity' involves the innovator in retreating from a highly personal experience to offer a communication of it in the shared, accessible, idiom.[33] Like much psycho-analytical argument, this recalls a romantic and individualistic idiom, denying the possibility of innovation as the meaning others may ascribe to abnormal experience. Thus, while Freud's artist 'can attain because other men feel the same dissatisfaction as he with the renunciation demanded by reality', he can only truly create when he 'finds a way of return from the world of phantasy back to reality; with his special gifts he moulds his phantasies into a new kind of reality, and men concede them a justification as valuable reflections of actual life'.[34]

Similarly, Gregory Bateson recommends that imaginative solutions are produced by allowing our mind to generate a series of vague and inchoate fantasies, which we then coldly evaluate in the light of day,[35] a procedure reminiscent of those of Plato and Nietzsche (pages 17, 19). Smith and Apter, in their 'reversal theory', derive these two styles of cognition from a tentative psychophysiological base: at different times the individual may be either in a logical goal-directed (telic) state of mind, or alternatively in an analogical, playful (paratelic) state which is reminiscent of Victor Turner's 'antistructure' ('liminality', or 'right hemisphere thought').[36] In this approach, psychopathology is to be understood as one of a number of paratelic modes, including play, chance, daydreams, fantasy and art, which may generate solutions to problems to which there is no immediate pragmatic solution but whose paratelic solutions may then, like Trinidadian bibliomancy or the Surrealists' *cadavre exquis*, be taken up and elaborated in the telic mode. We might note a large number of variants of such a two-stage model – linguistic, semiotic, psychological and sociological.[37] Reversal theory assumes a unitary psychological theory of 'creativity' derived from the imaginative artist of Western romanticism, in which communication as well as creation are characteristics of the individual innovator which then have to be reattached to society. It is our recent criticism of this tradition which lies behind our current discomfort in regarding 'genius' as a faculty rather than a process.

We can, however, take the telic mode as social response. Extraordinary acts and ideas may be taken up and employed in a multitude of ways, from a fully formed proposition ('Quakers should not own slaves') to the situation in which the psychotic serves, like Artaud, as an emblem through others' reading of his life experiences – an extended instance of the 'biographical fallacy'. The notion of 'communication' is rather broader than that of 'creativity' or 'imagination' and we should bear in mind Harding's strictures on assuming that generation and reception are either markedly similar experiences – coding and decoding – or that they are radically different.[38] It is in the gap between our desire to share another's experience and the actual limits of our empathy that the experience may become objectified as a principle in itself rather than in a series of personal mimeses. Or else the refiguring has long since floated free of its nominal originator.

The development of the Earth People

To recapitulate briefly the events through which the Valley was established: an independent, intelligent and articulate woman from the Port-of-Spain slums lives a conventional life of marginal poverty, critically aware of the dominant but unobtainable possibilities which we have characterised as *respectability*. Jeanette is the daughter of a servant in a White family but retains

some contact with the 'African' understandings of shango. Later she partici-
pates in Shouter Baptism, an accommodation of shango within respectable
Christianity.

She has a sensitivity to the situation of Black women, especially in childbirth and in child rearing, a concern made especially poignant through her own
experiences of hospital midwives and of struggling to support her children.
Nostalgically she recalls rare moments of childhood peace on her family land
in the country and develops an intense dislike of contemporary urban
consumerism, formal education and scientific technology, reinforced by
some awareness of the hippie counterculture. She shares the local women's
contempt for the lack of support offered by their men but, after the failure
of the local Black Power movement, Jeanette's partner persuades her and her
children to settle on the coast. In spite of her departure from the Shouters
after unsuitable mourning visions, the family continue to follow many
Baptist observances. They share the values and life of the surrounding
rural families, including daily agricultural work and the use of bush medicine
with their correspondences between the human, ultra-human and natural
worlds.

Some years later thyrotoxicosis in association with childbirth leads to an
episode of hypomania, characterised by a sense of personal power and special
meaning, a playful exuberance, and the burning of her clothes and property,
fuelled by exasperation with the Social world and her domestic work. 'Beside
herself', she rapidly turns upside down the whole set of respectable values.
Singing a shango anthem to Yemanja, she identifies with this Yoruba power –
nurturant but implacable, female but androgynous, the protector of childbirth
and the opponent of the male culture hero who incestuously enters her to gain
the power of generation.

Although they initially recognise her as mad, distance from town, fear of the
establishment and a regard for the possible meaning of strange and arbitrary
events restrain her family from taking her to hospital. She soon returns to her
normal state, and the family, their possessions now gone, consider together the
meaning of what has happened. They continue living naked, in part out of
necessity, and news of this passes to former neighbours in town, young men
who have become Baptists or Rastas but who are impatient with the failure of
both to deliver their promise of a *natural* life. They come to join the family, and
Jeanette now takes the name Mother Earth, organising the community
following the interpretations she makes of her experiences. These become
restructured and objectified as principles in their communication to others. The
emergent meaning of their joint actions is that the Mother Earth has become
manifest in her and that the community must organise itself in preparation for

the coming cataclysm. In spite of disputes with the nearby village and occasional defections from the group, it continues to grow, although raids by the police result in the removal of some of the children, with two brief stays in the mental hospital for Mother Earth. To what extent does this development follow the possibilities for the 'imitation of madness'?

(a) The individual who develops psychopathology is already influential

The individual. While Jeanette was hardly a powerful person in the wider social world, her intelligence and energy in her own neighbourhood in Port-of-Spain were certainly recognised. She was a competent and responsible mother, good-natured and a loyal friend to her neighbours. If her poverty, unmarried motherhood and independent ideas precluded actual responsibility, she could hardly be considered really worthless. Reports of her extraordinary behaviour on the coast were taken as some motivated overturning of her usual composure: if this was Jeanette it could be no vice. There was some hidden meaning in her renunciation of religion, dress and property. Similarly for her family, the first witnesses to the Miracle, the hardworking and devoted mother could not suddenly become the Devil in any conventional sense.

(b) Psychopathology is shortlived

The disease. Although Mother Earth's thyroid disease has continued to limit her physical abilities through congestive cardiac failure and oedema, the period of radically altered experience and actions associated with it is brief. Her exuberant and destructive behaviour soon ends, leaving her to try to make sense of it through the shared social categories.

(c) 'She's mad but . . . '

The illness. The local exegesis of madness is that it is always meaningless: there is no possible validity in the statements uttered by a madman. Even the 'weak' use of the term implies unreasonable and unintelligible behaviour. Nevertheless, in practice the ascription of madness is flexible and it is recognised by both Rastas and Baptists that respectable society ridicules them as 'mad', leading to their emphasising causation of madness through social *pressure*, from which it derives a possible meaning, both symptom and reaction, exemplar and emblematic symbol. For middle-class townspeople, themselves distanced from the *worthless* image of the madman, Mother Earth is indeed 'mad but . . . ' Many Trinidadians believe that she only pretends to be mad for ulterior motives. The Earth People themselves deny that she was ever *madmad*: 'if she mad, we mad'.

(d) Desperate times need desperate remedies

The time. Our sociological measures of 'tension' or 'rapid change' are notoriously elusive. Certainly the recent experiences of the Trinidadian proletariat hardly constitute a 'disaster' in Barkun's sense. A period of contradictions certainly. But what period is not? It is more appropriate to follow the local perceptions. Jeanette and her followers had been living through a period of increasing affluence and thus of potential identity with the Western middle class – aware that the Trinidad business elite were rapidly becoming wealthy, a development from which, through class, colour and lack of education, they were excluded – and in which the working-class family was ceasing to be the site of agricultural production or even the locus of affective bonds. The overtly political response to this, the Black Power mutiny, was led by students and intellectuals closely imitating events in the United States. The mutiny struck few resonances among the Black community as a whole and the pro-business governing party was voted back into power. The moral successor to Black Power was Rastafari, but the Earth People considered this an alien Jamaican import, fatally compromised by its urban base and its concern with fashionable style rather than autonomy. Like Shouter Baptism, it too had become Social, while party politics was too corrupt and self-serving to enter. Nevertheless, the men who joined the Earth People were not in search of a totally new dispensation; the appeal of the Valley is less that of an elegant novel doctrine than a reaffirmation of the despised 'African' values of the *worthless* poor.

(e) The audience are particularly open to idiosyncratic communications

The people. Madness is very different from mourning or visions in dreams but they are associated together through a similar aetiology of spirit causation, or worthlessness, and thus as representations of 'Africa'. Use of bibliomancy, chance events or visions to interpret the practicalities of everyday life argues an openness to certain types of arbitrary, paralogical, hence 'coded' communications. This was so for Mother Earth's husband after the Burning when, although he thought her quite mad, yet he believed there might be a meaning in it all somewhere. Represented in the institutions of tabanka and Carnival, *natural* impulses or actions must be freely expressed and accommodated. Trinidadians regard themselves as tolerant and unsatisfied, always looking for novelty and *play*, *fêting* and a *freeness*, as possessing a pragmatic ethic which tolerates idiosyncrasy: what Gordon Lewis has termed their 'anti-social individualism'. Carnival celebrates the body and its possibilities – an antic but limited affirmation of *no training* and *worthlessness* rather different from their grim and ultimate representation in the madman.[39]

Inversion and innovation

The Earth People as a community are a generalisation and a structuring of personal experiences, Mother Earth's but also those shared experiences which resonate with hers. No passive mimesis but transformations, commentaries, 'experiences put into circulation', they are also practical contestations of the power of others. 'Imitative mania' alone cannot be said to constitute a social rebellion, nor do the Earth People take Mother Earth's understandings – the psychiatrist's 'delusions' – as merely emblematic. They are intensely real for them as for her, to be experienced, once again, in the physical world, manifested in lived situations and in the bodily resonances of heat, overturning and cathartic expulsion.

Her work is not some total novelty which appears from nowhere. Those we regard as innovators are often relatively unoriginal, serving only for the catalysis or synthesis of powerful pre-existing themes; her conceptions by contrast are strikingly radical, so much so that they are only partly accepted by her own group. They generate new meanings by reflecting back upon and transforming two local understandings: that which relates Blacks to Whites, and that which relates women to men.[40] Both are recognised together in the local 'classification' which, following Peter Wilson, I have called *respectability-reputation* (Chapter 3). Bearing in mind that we are not talking simply of cognitive abstractions but of an historical struggle, and that these social relationships are perceived rather differently depending on who is doing the perceiving and where they are standing, we may represent the classification as a formal model in a single polythetic chain of paired oppositions:

$$\frac{\text{White}}{\text{Black}} = \frac{\text{Black middle class}}{\text{Black working class}} = \frac{\text{Respectability}}{\text{Reputation}} = \frac{\text{Black women}}{\text{Black men}}$$

To this we might add English:Creole; God:Devil (Ch. 8); sun:moon (Chs. 4, 9); *social* life:Carnival; town:bush; self-advancement:local solidarity; wage labour:family land (Ch. 8); inside:outside (Ch. 3); right:left (Ch. 8); cold:hot (Ch. 3); clothed:naked (Ch. 8); *social:natural* (Ch. 7). Viewed from the outside, the relationship of the upper to the lower elements of the chain is one of dominance to subdominance, of valued to devalued and, to an extent, of goal to present situation. Certainly experienced, as antithetical, even antagonistic, they are complementary in the texture of everyday life. While the relationship between the paired elements remains constant, there is, of course, no identity between either the superordinate or the subordinate elements taken alone – $a{:}b{::}c{:}d$ may be read as $a{:}b{::}b^1{:}b^2$ and so on.

The ultimate grounding is arguably 'external' in that it is constructed against European racism and in the current domination of the Caribbean by transnational capitalism, but it is not simply an ascribed system, nor a set of prescriptive rules. It is an internalised historical memory which continues to be generated and experienced – and contested – in the everyday economic life and self-awareness of West Indians. Upper or lower elements may better 'fit' individual men or women, but the opposition is present in both, and the relationship between the two chains articulates daily life irrespective of the individual's personal resonance with either at a particular time.

We may take the shango cult as a continued but increasingly muted dynamic of the subdominant elements of the chain, and one experienced locally as relatively independent of the dominant upper elements, a residue of Africa now shorn of any possibility of independent action. With Spiritual Baptism there is a move from an autonomous lower chain in itself towards the full model, with the upper elements appreciated as valued, if often flawed, goals. Rastafari recognises the dual classification as given in my model, but by taking the lower chain, reputation, as the valued one, 'inverts'[41] the moral salience of the whole to produce a male-centred subdominant ideology of resistance which is somewhat at variance with local family organisation. It reaffirms such existing strategies of everyday resistance as picong, calypso, the ambivalent use of moral terms such as *bad*, and Carnival itself, and structures them in an institution. Such strategies are recreated anew in the experience of each generation whilst they also embody their own tradition of opposition.

As De Beauvoir notes in *The Second Sex*, women in a subdominant colonised group tend to be 'closer' to the dominant group politically and symbolically, less 'culturally marked' in lifestyle and appearance than subdominant men. A common local perception, both ascribed and experienced, is that a subdominant group is more *natural* than the dominant group; its women, then, may become more *social*, an opposition to the opposition. It is they who become the teachers and midwives, domestic servants and mistresses to the dominant. The Rastaman responds to this 'Whiteness' of Black women (and thus to what is perceived by some social psychologists as the 'emasculation' of Black men by their women) with a reassertion of Black, quintessentially male, values as communal: *I and I* as central subject.[42]

Mother Earth too recognises something like my model, and her transformation is similar in its affirmation of the lower elements of the chain, but it is more complex, for she emphasises, like other protagonists of what I have called the radical 'countercurrent', not only the domination of Black by White, but the universal domination of woman by man, and of both by emergent technologies. With the radical feminists who reaffirm the dominant identification of all women with Nature, her experiences proclaim the supremacy of Nature over Society and its Science; like the similar Rasta 'ethnic redefinition', this merely interchanges the value of the upper and lower chains of my figure. With the double opposition of Black women, however, Mother Earth also inverts the Male:Female pair in addition to transvalorising the whole schema, thus producing a twist in the chain, a chiasmus:

$$\frac{\text{White}}{\text{Black}} = \frac{\text{Social}}{\text{Natural}} = \frac{\text{Respectability}}{\text{Reputation}} = \frac{\boxed{\text{Black Woman}}}{\boxed{\text{Black Man}}}$$

It is now the Black woman who is *African* and *natural* rather than the Black man. This provides a 'matrilineage' through women back to Africa which seems closer to the actual experience of African-Caribbean families than is Rastafari (which seeks to elevate the Black woman into 'Mother Africa' whilst essaying a novel patriarchal system), but it is a pattern which is at variance with the conventional identification of women with respectable (White) values. From the original model, Black women are thus likely to find the Earth People uncongenial, but it does allow the community to base itself closely on the traditional family; each generation comes forth as individuals from Mother Nature, independent of any notion of Social patrilineage: the cosmogenic African 'lineage' reproduces the Natural mother-centred family of personal experience.[43]

Much follows on simply from the already ascribed identification of Blacks, women and the mad with Nature – as in the group's nakedness. She weaves into this other common associations – such as blackness with the earth. In following the representation of what we might term her avatars – those historical and mythical figures which prefigure The Mother – we are struck by the numerous opponents of technology-wielding Promethean heroes.[44] Here immediate logical contradictions are consciously avoided through associated inversions. The Sun (allied to the powers of 'what should not be' through the Sun/Son homophone and through the conventional opposition of male Sun to female Earth/Moon) is deprived of its habitual naturalness and omnipresence through the understanding that it is basically the Ice Planet of the cold Scientific Whites, and that its apparent heat is placed in front of it by the Mother. The Black:White::Hot:Cold association is preserved but now the Blacks 'can' take heat again' for they have been interfered with, technologically 'cooled' through their identification with the dominant Whites.

I used the term 'weaves into', not just as a tribute to Mother Earth's conscious articulation of gender but because the model is far from determinist. Embodied schemata such as containment and overturning, like the more abstracted structurings of Hell and White do not run through the model or the work of the Valley all the way, all the time, in the same way. For the participant, as well as the ethnographer, loses interest in 'core symbolisations': everyday life in the Caribbean is certainly articulated by ethnic categorisation but this is hardly a constant preoccupation.

Any type of chiasmus (partial symbolic inversion or 'twisting' of elements of a tight classificatory system alone) produces logical 'contradictions' between the ends of the model. Under certain conditions these may be recognised, to be resolved in other, more universal, 'higher order' assumptions 'beyond the chain' which may now lose its original representation in actual groups and thus in immediate social experience. Sabbatai Svi identified the truly religious Jew as one who chose to break the mundane Law, signalling the end to the rabbinical segregation of Jewry: initially situated in a millennial time, this antinomianism, as Gershom Scholem argues, became secularised when the Jews, abandoning an orthodoxy of place and rite, entered the Gentile world whilst retaining some 'internalised' Jewish identity. Antinomianism may thus articulate a shift from tightly ordered symbolic systems, represented in specific groups, places and ritual actions, to more personalised yet universal 'ethical' representations in the individual as an individual. The parallels with early Christianity seem obvious, and also with what, following Weber, we may term the secularisation of Puritan antinomianism, the prophets having served as Fredric Jameson's 'vanishing mediators'.[45]

Similarly, Mother Earth's drastic severance of Black women from the Social world and their relocation in Nature seems at variance with local experience. If it poses problems for her followers in a group modelled on the local family, it contains a barely realised potential for universalisation and internalisation, particularly as it 'fits' with wider Western ecological and feminist concerns, transcending our all-too-pervasive dualities. As she notes, whatever the genesis of sexual and racial dimorphisms in the original acts of the Son, we are now all in such a mixed up state that the Whites themselves are about to destroy everybody through their own knowledge: Blacks and Whites continue to constitute each other but in new, more perverse, ways. Her emphasis on the universal aggression of men against women, while rooted in their envy for the Black Mother's power of generation, leads beyond a simple anti-White schema to suggest that Blacks themselves have been 'interfered with', and she has moved increasingly away from a rhetoric of Black Power to an understanding of power in which 'we all have to sacrifice we self'. If in London the White police assault Blacks at Carnival time, in Trinidad the Black police beat up all poor people: 'It have Chinee catch arse. It have Chinee up to date an' big shot. It have same everywhere. It have White get in dustbin.' A dream she told me captures well her struggle against the power of post-colonial society. She sees herself arrested by the police for madness, and is taken on a magistrate's order to a school where the teacher forcibly clothes her and administers an injection. Beyond the distinctions of race lies an order of male Science and technological power which has continued to emerge out of and corrupt the state of Nature.

If we may take our historical shift to 'modernity' as a shift to the open, pragmatic, anomic, statistical, meritocratic, to the private, psychological and ego-centred, to a self-sufficient mind as the objective of its own inquiry, with merging of gender roles and a self-conscious linear development in time, it might appear that the West Indies is already exemplary. Nevertheless, two 'pre-modern' characteristics persist: the location of power in the ascribed physical characteristics of gender and in those of race. (While women in the West Indies have had a relatively independent economic status relative to their men, this is changing in Trinidad where recent industrialisation and the development of service industries has forced both men and women off the land – where they perform relatively similar tasks – but has only made the more highly paid industrial work available for men.) Mother Earth may be described as 'modern' in her attempts to transcend the dimorphism of gender and race, an endeavour she shares with the communalist hippies and with radical feminists in their continuing search for 'authentic' person-to-person interactions finally purged of any ascribed status.[46]

To what questions then may I claim our innovator – or genetrix – as the answer? Her cosmology assimilates in a coherent but multivocal dynamic a set of fragmented or subdominant experiences and voices which are refracted through her own life – those of Black people, of women, the mad, the oppressed, the illiterate – through a reassertion of the local 'strategies of every-day resistance' – picong, Carnival, word play, *no behaviour*. But she is not merely seeking to reenchant the heart of a heartless local world, to retrieve a lost pastoral innocence. All utopias are an active vision of an alternative reality, engendered in the estrangements of the present. I do not think I am just reworking my own concerns through her work (as the Nathan to her Sabbatai) if I suggest she engages with general questions of wider concern – our loss of generational complementarities, the limits of human action within a natural world which we define and which defines us, the challenge to our ideas of personhood posed by our biomedical technologies, the limits of sustainable economic growth, the transience of personal relations in a fragmented and commodified world, the continuing quest for some authenticity – in short, a multitude of contradictions between current experience and our given social structuring.[47] If in many respects we may take her as articulating fundamentally 'modern' dilemmas, then arguably she transcends modernity in her elision of ground and mover, of natural and observed, in her advocacy of a sensate world that is made meaningful through our arbitrary experience within it rather than through those of a divinity of Science – one which transforms Nature yet is compromised by its own formation out of Her; and also in the recognition that time, foreshortened, no longer seems to lie open before us. In what James Clifford styles our emergent 'post-cultural world', where syncretism and heteroglossia contest, 'we are all Caribbeans now'[48] – hybrid and parodic, creolised and polyphonic, self-creating, endlessly recursive.

And yet there seems to remain some primacy of Nature 'out there' over human Society, a hylozoism in which Creatrix is identified with Her emergent creation. Nature is a sensate principle, form as well as content, and Her representation, woman, is both organiser and organised. We may wonder if ultimately Mother Earth's work is perhaps quietist for it appears that All may return into the One, recalling perhaps Buddhism rather than the Judaeo-Christian moral and sexual dynamic whose eventual resolution remains problematic in Rastafari. The reconciliation of both Science (which we may gloss not altogether inappropriately as the forces of production) and the Social (the productive relations) back into our elemental Nature, a second return, although implicit, is however never clearly enunciated. Perhaps it could never have been, given my own departure. An ultimate *coincidentia oppositorum* (to use Eliade's term) seems to remain elusive. As she puts it:

If all trees are one tree, that is the Mother,
If all men are one man, that is the Son saying he is the Father.[49]

From nature to science, and back again

Mother Earth's understanding of human knowledge as unfolding against its Natural background is perhaps more akin to contemporary bisocial reconstructions of the emergence of human sociality[50] than is my own, more fragmented and ironic dialectic. Taking my Scientific argument: natural facts appear to exist 'out there', arbitrary to our intentions, existing independently of any prior human experience of them. While providing the apparent ground for our experience, our collective representations and social organisation, they cannot be said simply to determine them. They may however as altered brain states provide a ground for experience which is radically different from that of everyday life. These novel experiences are only apprehended through conventional social meanings which constrain them by cognitive and social response, reflecting back on them and transforming and structuring them in one way or another. 'Behaviour' becomes 'action'. The individual or others makes sense of such radically different experiences at the time or subsequently, interpreting and reworking them through their own personality, past experiences and current preoccupations. These interpretations may be such that others, perceiving something of innovative value in them, take them up and themselves reinterpret, revise and amplify them. And in that objectification, they create, through personal relationships, what we recognise as new institutions.

If, as I have maintained, Mother Earth's innovations can be considered in some independence from the physiological facilitations on which they reflect, what conclusions can I draw about the limits of innovation grounded in unusual mental states 'out there'? How valid are the constraints which have been suggested – 'affectivity' and 'overpersonalisation'? Given the frequent secondary role of followers who codify the original innovation, ascribing meaning to the random experiences of the innovator and thus providing practical structuring, or the many situations where an idiosyncratic innovator merely acts as a catalyst or emblem for changes which are latent or already appearing, it seems there can be no intrinsic constraints on psychopathology which differentiate it from any other form of innovation. Neither situation however is true for Mother Earth who has herself developed novel symbolic variants whose representation in her community invoke her physical being. Certainly, in Weber's sense, she is a 'charismatic' leader.

With the messianic figure Sabbatai Svi it was his antinomian acts which were his particular contribution.[51] They signalled to others an already existing 'counter-current', a mystical and millennial tradition, which could be universalised even to non-Jews. The actual ascription of meaning was from the scholar Nathan of Gaza, whose organisational skill and sustained proselytising launched the movement as such. When the time came for decisive leadership, Sabbatai recanted. Whether the movement would have taken a different course if he had died a martyr is as conjectural as any other conjectural history: the salient instance of Christianity should not suggest that the death of the innovator automatically 'frees' the developing group from any embarrassing idiosyncracies of personality to permit some sort of routinised development. The very notion of the 'success' of an idea assumes some sort of sociologically recognisable and continuing 'group' or 'movement' which believes it orders itself according to the idea, a history written by the victors. I am not talking of such ultimate 'success' or 'failure' but of the particular possibilities by which pathomimesis immediately and dialectically constrains innovation: 'biological potentialism' in Stephen Jay Gould's phrase, not 'biological determinism'; for there are clearly facilitations such as a *more* open field for innovation, together with the conviction which insanity may confer on the acts and statements of the innovator.

Mother Earth's visions were 'an experience' rather than part of 'experience', as Turner, following Dilthey, puts it. They were highly personal, intense and initially meaningless to others, involving not a sedate restructuring of conventional meanings but 'the whole human vital repertoire of thinking, willing, desiring, and feeling, subtly and varyingly interpenetrating on many levels'.[52] In the midst of such experience, it is impossible to be so detached as to put it into circulation. Her experiences and logic subsequently returned to something like their usual consensual pattern enabling her to do just that. How much then may the remote origins of an abnormal brain state be said to necessarily constrain future interpretations? In the case of Mother Earth her thyroid condition continues to affect her general health adversely so that she is frequently tired and depressed, but there is no reason to take this as a universal feature of pathomimesis, for the remote origins of abnormal brain states may lie in short-lived delirious episodes which have no specific and characteristic sequelae.

Are pathomimetic innovations invariably 'overpersonalised' – as Jakobson warned? While I have emphasised in this chapter the logical aspects of symbolic inversions, such innovation must become real in some significant way in the experience of those who adhere to it. For Mother Earth her most intense personal experience seems to have been childbirth. It is this, worked into the specific identification of women with Nature in opposition to the incestuous Son, which is adopted least enthusiastically by an essentially male group who prefer to stress those other experiences which they share with her as Black people. Nevertheless, while certain aspects of her life remain so personal that her interpretation of them cannot be easily accepted by the group, it is their intense resonance for Mother Earth herself that enables them to carry with them other, more generally shared, experiences which have become the collective subjectivity of her community.

But this analysis does no justice to her work in itself. The notion of our knowledge and power as an incestuous replication of our origins – a mimesis of ontology – seems to me no less unreasonable than that of a controlling and epistemological Science as the mirror of Nature. Our understanding then cannot be a privileged comprehension of a world out there, ever closer to it, but rather a flawed transformation of ourselves as agents within Nature. We design computers and take them as the prototypes for our cognition, as the New Science of the Renaissance took its machine for the physical world. Mother Earth warns that any attempts at transcendence – intellectual or political – will be illusory, continually returning us to our embodied selves. For we remain part of the world we think we make.

My preface warned that there was no single reading of Mother Earth, and I myself have employed a number of strategems in approaching her. These are my readings, my containments, not hers, and this volume hardly constitutes a dialogue between us. Nevertheless she has an active, at times illusive, role in my commentary, not from any attempts of mine to provide a space for her in some sort of liberal fair play, but more significantly, in a counter-text: in her clearly articulated critique of the sort of Western academic tradition through which I have represented her – what she quite appropriately terms Science. Her work already provided, previous to my foreseen arrival, an interpretation of Science. Both of us have attempted in different ways to examine two general domains of knowledge – 'Nature' and 'Science' – their original mutual differentiation and interactions. Our conclusions are different – initially inversions, then transformations, of each other. Mine is privileged, bookbound and institutional, prosaic. Hers has been passionately laboured through radical experience.

Appendix 1

Members of the community in October 1981

Name	Age	Date of joining	Previous occupation	Previously Rasta
Mother Earth	49	Since Miracle 1975	Scrunting[a]	–
Jakatan	36	Since Miracle	Estate work, fishing	–
Pomme Cythère	20	Since Miracle		–
Cocorite	11	Since Miracle		–
Eddoes	28	1979 (away 1980–1)	Welder	+
Pumpkin	4	1979 (away 1980–1)		+
Breadfruit	24	1979	Estate work, 'ten days'[b]	+
Dasheen	21	1979	Street selling, 'ten days'	+
Tania	20	1979	'Ten days'	+
Moco	20	1979	Air-conditioning maintenance	+
Bodi	21	1979	House painter	+
Pawpaw	33	1979	Plumber	–
Potato	18	1980	Scrunting	+
Colley	25	(1980 (away 1980–1)	Tailor	+
Cane	19	1980	Joiner	+
Coconut	28	1980	Scrunting	?
Cassava	28	1980	Postman	+
Orange	22	1980	Welder	+
Zabocca	23	1981	Longshoreman	+
Corn	22	1981	Scrunting, St Ann's Hospital	+
Melangine[c]	19	1981	Estate work	+
Mango Rose	23	1981	Scrunting, St Ann's Hospital	+

[a] Sometimes called 'hustling' or 'scuffling': borrowing, running errands, casual daily work, the occasional 'ten days', buying and selling a little in the markets, minor pilfering, i.e. 'living from hand to mouth'.

[b] Casual government work on road clearing or maintenance, allocated in ten-day stints. Depending on its frequency, a certain time will be spent in 'scrunting' or other casual work.

[c] My pseudonym; he had not yet taken a fruit name.

Appendix 2

Songs

Unless specified, they are *gathering tunes* ('when we all together'), tape recorded and later transcribed with the help of Pomme Cythère. They are usually sung antiphonally in repeated couplets.

1
Mother, me a poor mourner
We coming all the way from the Valley of Decision

2
Oh we going down town to free up the nation
So glad in my soul.

3
The Nation it have no food
Come let we go and plant
Food for the Nation Oh!

4 (Tania)
They give us a Book to pray, Yeh!
To call on their God, me see
When they lie, they lie
And they give us a Book to pray, Yeh!
To call on their God, me see
When they lie, they lie, You!
The Earth is the Lord, the fullness
The Earth is the life me see
That is life, that is life, Ou!

5 (Tania)
I know
You know
They know
As well as the doctors know, Oh!
Bim Bame Bom
Bi-Bi Bam Ba, Bim Bame Bom
Bi-Bi Bi Bam
Da Dy Da Da
Sing it loud, Sing it loud
I know, Uh
You know
They know as well as the doctors know, Uh, Uh
The lawyers know
As well as the President know
Oh that it is life, Uh
The Earth is life
Sing it loud, Sing it loud
I know, Yeh, Uh
You know, Uh
They know, Yeh
As well as the professors know, Uh
The preachers know
As well as the children in the town know
The Earth is life, The Earth is life
Sing it loud, Sing it loud, Uh
The children are feeding from the Earth now, Uh
They cannot do without it, Uh
They cannot do without the Earth now, Uh
They cannot do without it, Uh
They cannot do, Yeh
Uh, Uh – Uh-Uh, Uh,
Oh, Uh-Uh, Yeh
The Earth is life, Uh.
You mus' feed from the Earth, Uh
You cannot do without the Earth
You cannot do without the Earth at all, Uh, Uh
Yeh, Uh
The Earth is life, The Earth is life, Oh Yeh

6

Beat them drums of Africa	(A)
And dance the Fire Dance	(B)
Oh-oh, Oh-oh	(C)
And dance the Fire Dance	(B)

[36 more alternating couplets; AB, CB]
A and C sometimes occasionally mixed. Occasionally 'We'll dance the dance
    of Africa' and 'Sing those songs of Africa' for A]

7 (Eddoes)
Calling Mother Nature
[All of the] Mother comes from the Earth
The Earth alone
The fall of Rome
The fall of Rome
The fall of Rome
The end of religion
The end of religion
The end of sickness
The end of pain
The end of wickedness
This is the end of shame
The end of oppression and exploitation
Leti* close down them factories
The end of slavery
This is the end of pain
Beginning again, Beginning again
Beginning again, Beginning again.

8 (Breadfruit)
Mother is the Way, The Truth and the Life
She is the Way, The Truth and the Life
The River is the Way, The Truth and the Life
The Lightning is the Way, the Truth and the Life
The Earth is the Way, the Truth and the Life
The Breeze is the Way, the Truth and the Life
The Father is the Lie, the Sin and the Death

* The author's daughter

9 (Pomme Cythère)
Me say me calling me Mother
Me say me calling me mother an' de* water
Me say me calling de light'nin'
Me say me calling me Brother
Me say me calling me Sister.

10 (Pomme Cythère)
People like to roam
In the city of society
Instead of being free
Fuss why they be so stray away?

11
Me say you can' stop de Beginning
Me say de earthquake and de earthshake
Me say de light-ning an' de thunder
Me say de high wind an' de water
Me say de brimstone an' de fire.

12 (Eddoes)
Say the flower surely sweeter
Say you can't stop the Beginning
No you can't stop the Beginning
Say you can't stop the Beginning
Oh you can't stop the Beginning
Lightning, thunder
You can never stop the Beginning
The wind, the water, should be faster
No you can't stop the Beginning
No you can't stop the Beginning
Say you can't stop the Beginning
You can never stop the Beginning
The wind, the water
You'll never stop the Beginning
Oh you can't stop the Beginning
Oh they can't stop the Beginning
They could never stop the Beginning

* On checking transcription Pomme Cythère insisted on 'de' not 'the'

Lightning, thunder
They could never stop the Beginning
Brimstone an' fire
They could never stop the Beginning
No they can't stop the Beginning
They can't stop the Beginning
No they can't stop the Beginning
They can't stop the Beginning.

Glossary of the Earth People's idiom and cosmology

Rasta terms used by the Earth People are bracketed as (R). Where Rastafari itself favours a conventionalised orthography (*Bredrin*, *Fada*) I have retained it; otherwise I have rendered expressions into standard English. The community use many expressions of the local villagers, here bracketed as (local). The resonances of words in standard English are here omitted but should always be borne in mind: this is not a self-contained set of ideas but a commentary on the dominant.

Adversary	The White term for the Devil; jokingly used to refer to the younger members when misbehaving.
Africa	(i) The Black people of African origin in Trinidad and elsewhere: 'the beginning of all races'.
	(ii) All the Children of the Mother.
	(iii) Nature.
Allah	The recognition of Mother Earth by Muslims, but misinterpreted by them as God.
Away	Outside Trinidad (local).
Babylon (R)	Any government institutions especially the police. More specifically America or Britain. The Earth People usually use *Rome*.
Bad	(i) According to the Way of Nature, Wrong, Left.
	(ii) Anything extreme, appreciated or desirable: 'That coucou bad for so' (local).
Bag	Sacking from copra bags. (Local. Also *crocus cloth*.)
Baptists	The Spiritual (Shouter) Baptists, Black Christians with partial knowledge of the Mother.
The Beginning	(i) The differentiation of Mother Earth as the first principle out of nothing, and Her subsequent creation of the Planets and Flesh.
	(ii) The return to this state and the eventual exile of the Son to the Sun: The Beginning of the End.
The Beginning of The End	The Miracle (*q.v.*).

Blacker People	The original Race of the Mother, both African and Indian.
Blood of the Earth	Petroleum.
Bones	*See* Flesh.
Book	(i) The Christian Bible written by the Son through 'the first Queen'. The last object burnt by Mother Earth. It contains a disguised knowledge of the Mother.
	(ii) Science.
Bredrin (R)	Fellow Rastas, occasionally used by Earth People for each other or for other Africans (also local).
The Burning	Mother Earth's burning of clothes and other objects in 1975.
To Business	Meddle with, interfere with someone's personal life, especially by government or police (local).
Caesar (R)	Establishment leader.
Children	Africa and India, The Blacker People, The Race of the Mother.
Children of The Son	Whites.
Christ	The incomplete recognition of Mother Earth by Christians, misidentified by them as Jesus. 'They say that Christ is returning in the twentieth century but I am the Christ' (M.E.).
Christians	Blacks and Whites who accept the Son's domination.
The City	Port-of-Spain (locally called *town*).
Cobra	The Serpent in its Indian aspect.
Colley (R)	Ganja.
Confusion	Following Science rather than Nature, Interference (locally implies gossip and sorcery).
Corruption	(i) The Son's original Interference (*q.v.*).
	(ii) Contemporary Trinidad politics (*bobol*) through:
	(iii) The corruption of the Flesh by Science (*q.v.*).
Cripsy	Crisp, dry and infertile land (local).
Crucial	Artificial, severe, harmful: 'This world too crucial to the flesh, old time people more natural.'
Cunt	The Mother, The Earth.
Death	(i) The Son.
	(ii) Individual lack of Natural awareness.
	(iii) 'You don't really die – the Flesh come again' (M.E.).
Devil	Mother Earth perceived by Christians (the inverse of *lived*).
Disease	An affliction of Flesh by Science, to vanish at the End.
Dog	God (inversion).
Down	In the direction of Port-of-Spain (also used locally like *below*).

Dracula	The Devil, Mother Earth.
Dread (R)	(i) A Rasta.
	(ii) Dreadlocks.
	(iii) Awesome.
Dreadlocks (R)	Uncombed hair of the Rastas and Earth People; the original Natural hair of Flesh.
Dub (R)	'Dreads do call it party.' To resonate with music, to 'let go'.
Dwen	The continuing presence of African ancestors. (Locally, the spirit of an unbaptised child.)
Earth	(i) The Mother, the first principle, 'not really a planet, is life'.
	(ii) The continuing basis for all life in the form of the land.
	(iii) Life.
Earth People	The Valley community, the future instructors of the Nation after the End.
Eden	The original state of Nature which was corrupted by the Son.
Education	'It come as a next part of Science.' The development of the right side of the brain under the influence of the Son rather than the Natural half of the Senses. The process in which the way of the Son is inculcated through Science, Religion and Material.
The End	The imminent return to the Beginning when Mother Earth is fully incarnated in Jeanette.
Eve	The Mother.
Evil	The way of Mother Earth, the (D)evil.
Eye: of the mouth	Natural senses in the mouth.
Natural Eye	The eye of the Mother (the left eye).
Fadam	The Son (Father–Adam).
Father/Fada (R)	(i) For Rastas, God (Haile Selassie).
	(ii) For the Earth People, the Son or any man in whom the influence of the Son predominates.
Fire	One of the first differentiations of the universe. See Heat.
Flesh	(i) People.
	(ii) The human body. Such physical Flesh is not easily distinguished from the continuing principle of the Mother (the Natural Spirit).
	(iii) More specifically, one of the three elements of humans:
	(a) The Natural Spirit, part of the Mother.
	(b) Flesh which returns after 'death' to the Earth quickly and thus is also part of the Mother.

(c) Bones, a somewhat 'foreign' element introduced by Interference, their permanence a sign of the Son and Time, phallic, white.

(A fourth, more transitory component is the Spirit of the Son.) Bones are opposed to Flesh and the Natural Spirit as Death is to Life.

Flim   The cinema (local); like the Bible a concealed knowledge of the Mother.

Foundation   The physical, ideological and spiritual basis for existence. 'We stand to build Foundation, we know that the Children suffering for Foundation because the system of the Roman did not give my Children no Foundation.'

Fruits   'We be all Fruits; me call self Breadfruit.'

Glasses   Spectacles, Science which weaken one's Natural Eye. (One of the last three objects destroyed in the Burning.)

God   The Son.

Good   Right, the Way of the Son.

He   (i)   The Son.
(ii)   The male, particularly the husband (local).

Heat   Power and Life: a characteristic of the Mother and more congenial to Her Race. The Planet Sun, the Planet of Ice, was covered over by the Mother with Fire, but since the Miracle the Earth is getting hotter in preparation for the expulsion of the Son. In 1975 Mother Earth walked in the Fire, an event reenacted in 'The Fire Dance'.

Hell Valley   The Earth People's community.

Herb (R)   Ganja.

The Hour   The End (*q.v.*).

Humble (oneself)   To live in accordance with Nature, accept the Life in the Valley, relinquishing the aspirations and gratifications of town. Also called *suffering oneself*. (Locally implies renunciation.)

I (R)   I, me.

I and I (R)   Us, we, our, mine, yours, theirs. Mocked by the Earth People as 'Jamaica talk'.

Ice   The Planet Sun, and hence the Whites.

Imps   Minor spirits controlled by the Sun; less sensible entities than the mechanism and tribulations of Society.

India   People of Indian origin in Trinidad and elsewhere.

Interference   (i)   The Son entering Nature's Womb to gain the power of generation.

	(ii) His continuing presence in Flesh. The original hermaphrodite mothers had dreadlocks, no bones and only one (or no) eye. The Mother through Her love for Her Son created Bones, and Her Eye was added to the original Natural Eye (possibly to become the Son's Eye). Her refusal to collaborate any further is due to His recent success at creating non-human life through Science.
Irie (R)	Beautiful, wholeness. The name Columbus recorded as the local name for Trinidad (Wood: 301); a Yoruba vine used for healing mental illness (Simpson 1980: 80); neither of these are likely to be the Rasta derivation. (From M*erry*? Ily is Rasta for ganja.)
Iwa (R)	Probably from the Rasta *Iya*, an abbreviation of *Nyabinghi*, used as a greeting or title and also implying the higher reality of Rastafari (Faristzaddi 1982).
Jah (R)	The seventy-second reincarnation of God in the person of the Ethiopian Emperor Haile Selassie. *Jah* is Jehovah (and is used thus by the Jehovah's Witnesses). For the Earth People, Selassie is the Son but the notion of *Jah* implies some recognition of Mother Earth and is used when talking to Rastas.
Jesus	The Son/Father/God (but not the Christ, *q.v.*).
Judgement	Know you Self (*q.v.*).
Know you self	To realise one's place in Nature and resist Material and Religion.
Left	The way of the Mother, the Devil. Opposed to the Christian *right*. Pronounced 'leff': 'all leff then?'
Life	(i) The Mother.
	(ii) Time: 'This is the life of Left.'
	(iii) *Like* as in 'Me life . . . ' (Roots in *lief*?)
	(iv) Occasionally used for Left.
The Life	The Earth People's way of Nature.
Life of the Son	Social life in town.
Locks (R)	Dreadlocks.
Love	The desire and power to generate and sustain life.
Lucifer	The Son.
Makers	(i) Africa, the original Race.
	(ii) The teaching of this.
Man	(i) For Jamaican Rastas an evil person.
	(ii) Trinidadian Rastas use it in the usual African-American English sense as a greeting or for 'you' or 'one' (of either sex).
	(iii) For the Earth People it means people after the Interference, particularly males.

Mapapi	(i)	A venomous snake, locally the most feared (*mapepire*).
	(ii)	The Serpent in its African aspect (also *Mamba*) and thus:
	(iii)	The Earth People.
Mary	The Mother of God. 'Mary is the Earth.'	
Material	Possessions, Social pretension, Scientific.	
Me	Preferred nominative pronoun (*cf.* Rasta I): *M*other *E*arth.	
Medicine	The Scientific cause of disease.	
Meditation	Reasoning, teaching (of the Mother or the Son).	
Deeper meditation	Teaching of the Mother.	
Miracle	Mother Earth's initiation of the End in August 1975 by bringing the Sun nearer the Earth.	
Moon	(i)	The womb of the Earth at the Beginning.
	(ii)	'Every mother is the moon.'
The Mother	Life, nature, the first and essential principle.	
Mothers	(i)	Mature Black women.
	(ii)	The original people before the Interference.
Mother Earth	The incarnation of The Mother in Jeanette.	
Mother Nature	Mother Earth as the person Jeanette (as referred to by the other Earth People).	
Mother's Children	(i)	Africa and India.
	(ii)	The Earth People.
The Nation	Africa (and to a lesser extent India). (Locally, *Nations* are the celebrations of the shango cult.)	
Natty (R)	(i)	Dreadlocks.
	(ii)	Rasta.
	(iii)	Strong ganja.
Natural	In conformity with The Mother; the essential aspect of things without Interference.	
Natural Self	Natural Spirit as individual agency.	
Natural Spirit	(i)	The association of The Mother with every person.
	(ii)	The essential self, acting in conformity with Nature, and ultimately a part of Her.
Nature	(i)	The Mother and Her creation: 'If all trees are one tree that is The Mother.'
	(ii)	Life in the Valley in opposition to the Social world of Material, Science and Religion.
Negative Spirit	The Spirit of the Son (*q.v.*).	
Nothing	Before the Mother formed Herself.	
Odysseus	The Son.	
Oppression	The domination of Whites over Blacks (R), and now the alienation of both from The Mother through Corruption and Science.	

Outside	The Social world outside the Valley. (Locally = *away*, *q.v.*).
Planets	The first emanations of The Mother, including the Moon and the Sun.
Plant	To cultivate the land with respect for Nature, the major task of the Earth People.
Pope	The principal religious aspect of the Son.
Prepare	Living The Life in expectation of The End.
Put Out	Construct mentally, expound, explain, proselytise.
Queen	(i) Any Rasta woman (R).
	(ii) Mother Earth is the Queen of Africa.
Race of the Son	Whites. The people principally Interfered with by The Son and given over to His use by the Mother.
Racial	Social, greedy, racist.
Ras (R)	King. The original Amharic title ('Count') of Selassie.
Ras Tafari (R)	Selassie.
Rasta (R)	To the Earth People the Christians with the closest knowledge of The Mother, and the major source of recruits.
Rastafari (R)	Rasta.
Religion	The various ideologies of the Son, the legitimation of His Society through distorted explanations.
Right	The way of the Son (see *Left*).
Rising of the Nation	(i) The coming recognition of Mother Earth by Blacks.
	(ii) The Earth People themselves.
Roman Soldier	Active collaborator with the Son, whether Black or (usually) White. *High society* (politicians, doctors, scientists, lawyers, priests), and *tibourgs* (nurses, teachers and police).
Rome	As Rasta *Babylon* (*q.v.*). Also used by some Rastas.
Science	(i) Factories, offices, schools, hospitals, universities, books; Rome's forces of production and reproduction. Its immediate concern is to create a race of robots through contraception, *drop babies* (abortions) and *tissue babies* ('test-tube babies').
	(ii) Social logic as opposed to Natural knowledge.
	(iii) 'Aloof' and hence suggestive of the sorcery of *high science* (local).
See yourself	Know yourself (*q.v.*).
Self	Natural Self.
Senses	Natural awareness, located in the left side of the brain. When senses are *put out*, they *burst*.
Sensible	Having *put out Senses*.,

Serpent	The snake as representation of The Mother. Assimilated to the balisier plant.
Seven Days	Adventists, Black Christians with a faint glimmering of The Mother.
Sex Spirit	The Son encouraging sex for gratification and male domination rather than for love of generation.
Shango	The recognition of The Mother by *old time Africans*.
She	The Mother in her African aspect.
Sign	Meaning, orientation, direction.
Sin	'You can't sin' and thus a Christian notion appertaining to The Mother.
Sistrin (R)	Female Rastas, occasionally used by Earth People instead of *mothers*.
Skul	Government skulduggery (local).
Slavery	The continued subjugation of Blacks by both Whites and by the Social Blacks through Science and Material.
Social, Socialness	Actions of *high society*, greedy, 'bourgeois' (in its various glosses), the Life of the City.
Society	(i) The selfish Roman world, especially its upper strata. (ii) Human relations in Rome.
Son	The rebellious Son of the Mother, the cause of our separation from Nature. 'The Spirit of death, sickness and pain, disease, corruption, shame, age, time.' Known as God, Jesus, The Father.
Spirit	The ultimate meaning, connotation, principle or operation of anything in the everyday world (sometimes personified: *see below*).
Spirit of Death	The Spirit of the Son (*q.v.*).
Spirit of Destruction	The Spirit of the Son.
Spirit of The Mother	Natural Spirit (*q.v.*).
Spirit of The Son	The presence of the Son inside Flesh.
Spiritual	Religious, Roman (*q.v.*). Used sometimes ironically in opposition to the real Spirit, that of the Mother.
Spliff (R)	Ganja cigarette or cigar.
Suffer	Humble (*q.v.*).
Sun	The Planet of the Son, to which He will be exiled at the End.
Tap	(i) Beg, eavesdrop, interfere with. (ii) The procedure by which the Son drains the Natural Spirit.
Three Wise Men	The three passing Rastas who were given the first account of the Beginning in June 1976.
Time	The domination of the Son. At the End, time will cease. (The word *life* is usually used instead of *time*: 'He should have done cook long life.')

Truth	'Truth to me is Death. I don't use that word again.' However it is still sometimes used by the Earth People: '*Right* to me ai' truth.'
Under	Oppressed by.
The Valley (of Decision)	The community of the Earth People 'where the Serpent is about to rise'.
Vibes	Influence (as in hippie argot and used sardonically in conscious mockery of this).
Visions	Profound knowledge gained through one's dreams or through Baptist mourning (local).
Way of Death	Following self-interest under the Son's influence.
Way of Life	Following Nature. Mother Earth is the Way, the Truth and the Life (*cf.* John 14: 6).
Weed (R)	Ganja.
Zion (R)	Ethiopia, Africa, redemption. Used mockingly by the Earth People: 'Rasta go to Zion on an iron horse' (motor cycle).

Notes

1 The coming of the Earth People

1 Herskovits and Herskovits 1947.

2 In 1986 the PNM was to lose the general election to a coalition of Indian agricultural and urban Creole interests. A violent but unsuccessful putsch by the Jamaat Al Muslimeen, a small Creole sect of Black American inspiration, held the new prime minister hostage in 1990; it had little popular support but together with the deteriorating economic situation in the 1980s has been widely interpreted as Trinidad's post-colonial 'loss of innocence'. In the subsequent election the PNM regained power.

3 The local term for people wholly or partly of African descent, less often called Negro or Creole. Black (like African-Caribbean) is only used in general conversation by radicals, Rastas and Earth People, who all may describe Indians (East Indians) as Black. For others Black remains an insult or self-depreciation.

4 It involved student demonstrations, labour strikes and the army mutiny; police and coastguards stayed loyal to the government (Nicholls 1971; Bennett 1989). Unless armed, the arrested rebels were treated leniently and many have returned to political life.

5 *Trinidad Guardian*, 12 December 1981. Between 1975 and 1979, cocoa and coffee production halved, and the food import bill increased from 285 million Trinidadian dollars to 708 million (*Trinidad Guardian*, 25 October 1981). The contribution of agriculture to the gross national product in 1980 was only 3 per cent (*Trinidad Guardian*, 11 November 1981).

6 *Creole* refers to the fusion of African and European in Trinidad, particularly among the working class, and especially its more 'French' form (including the now virtually disappeared White elite, the *French Creoles*) and excludes the Indians. The French-based Creole language is known as *Patois* or *broken French*. By contrast, in Jamaica, *Patois* and *Creole* refer to the local English, corresponding to *Trinidad English* in Trinidad, although the latter, which does not form a continuum with the French-based Creole, approximates more closely to international English than does Jamaican patois (Devonish 1985; Todd 1984). The most practical guide to Trinidad Creole remains Thomas 1869 (1969); there have been half-hearted attempts to

253

revive it including a weekly radio programme but it seems destined to die out as a spoken language by the end of the century. Pinnacle Village is exceptional in having an old woman who can speak only patois but even here its use is limited to nostalgic conversations among the middle-aged and elderly, to personal endearments and insult. Townspeople only know those words which have entered general use such as *melangine* (aubergine) or *zabocca* (avocado).

7 The Turnpike, Pinnacle, Jeanette Baptiste and most other proper names are pseudonyms. The history of the area is described by Harrison (1975) and the local *cocoa* by Naipaul 1967: 33–4. The population were a 'reconstituted peasantry' (Mintz 1974c) coming from the plantation system elsewhere in Trinidad or from neighbouring islands: small-scale cultivators, owning their own land or having access to a plot through sharecropping, producing most of their own subsistence as well as cash crops of coffee, cocoa, nutmeg and mace. Since the Second World War, the collapse of crop prices, the concentration of land holdings and the fluctuating availability of wage labour elsewhere would suggest a more appropriate term than 'peasantry' might be Lenin's 'semi-proletariat' (Mintz 1974a).

8 Locally grown cannabis leaves and shoots are rolled to form a spliff or (less often now) smoked in a small clay chillum.

9 An illegal gun made out of piping and firing shot-gun cartridges which is concealed in the bush in the path of game and fired by a trip wire. Ownership of guns is only legal with a permit obtainable with registered ownership of agricultural land. The Earth People have no guns.

10 *Movement* implies something like personality and motivation as well as external *behaviour* (or *no behaviour*, bad behaviour).

11 *Cripsy* is a common metathesis like *flim* (cinema). During 1978–9, 14,000 people abandoned the land leaving less than 10 per cent of the population in agriculture. Of these, 2 per cent are under twenty-five years old, and only 12 per cent younger than thirty-five (*Trinidad Guardian*, 5 November 1981).

12 The playwright Shango Baku, editor of Port-of-Spain's *Rastafari Speaks* told me he admired her ability to turn Rastafari 'upside-down' and transform its deity into a woman, while developing its *natural* message.

13 In his Peoples Temple, a White pastor Jim Jones combined apocalyptic Christianity with a nominal socialism. To its San Francisco centre he attracted socially disadvantaged recruits, largely Black Americans, through extensive welfare facilities. With the support of the Guyanese government an agricultural commune, Jonestown, was established, and by 1978 the majority of the group had settled there to avoid the coming nuclear holocaust and Black genocide. After repeated warnings of 'revolutionary suicide' if troubled by the United States government, the Temple killed a visiting American Congressman who was investigating the custody of children by the group, and the next day, on Jones' orders, most of the 900 members were persuaded to kill themselves with cyanide-laced Fla-Vor-Aid (S. Naipaul 1981; Hall 1987).

Michael de Freitas, a small time gangster and pimp in London, emerged as a community leader in the 1960s among some of Britain's West Indian population, and obtained extensive support from White liberals. Following American Black Power usage he altered his surname (in protest at the historical imposition of their owners' names on American slaves) and returned to Trinidad where, after participating in the demonstrations which climaxed in the Mutiny, he formed a commune in Arima. After killing a local Trinidadian and a visiting British White, he fled to Guyana, was extradited, tried and, after an unsuccessful international campaign for clemency, was hanged in Port-of-Spain (Humphrey and Tindale 1977; V. S. Naipaul 1980).

14 Klass 1961; La Guerre 1974. Official figures are discretely vague but it is popularly accepted that about half of Trinidad's population are Indians, who are said to include both the very rich and the very poor. Few live along the north-east coast. The wider cultural affiliation of Creoles with Black North Americans is not available to the Indians who have little contact with an India which is regarded as 'backward' by all Trinidadians. While the country has avoided the polarised racial politics of Guyana, unionised Indian workers provided the supporters of the various parties to the left of the PNM. Most Indians regard Black Power as racist and anti-Indian; although the Mutiny's leaders attempted to gain Indian support, less than 1 per cent of the members of the Black Power Party, NJAC, were Indians, and their sugar workers' union remained ambivalent about the revolt (Nicholls 1971). As to Rastafari, the novelist Shiva Naipaul, an Indian Trinidadian, wrote: 'New Gods, imported from the Ras Tafarian cult of Jamaica, had made their appearance among us. Young marijuanha-doped blacks with matted hair stalked the streets. They symbolised the regression, the primitive impulses, seething through the lower reaches of society' (1981: 17). V. S. Naipaul (Shiva Naipaul's brother) dealt sardonically in his earlier work with the choice for the rural Indian between a poorly understood Indian heritage, and economic and social creolisation. Other Indians, more optimistically, see Indian culture as transitory and reactionary (Selvon 1979), a view known locally as 'coffee-coloured [inter-racial] politics'.

15 'Weed Growers and Weed Smokers', *The Bomb*, 2 June 1978; 'Suzanne Lopez meets the Earth People', *Express*, 8 March 1981.

16 'Earth People Play Host to English Psychiatrist', *The People*, December 1981; 'Naked British Professor Lived in Trinidad Bush', *The Bomb*, 15 January 1982.

17 'Interview with Mother Earth', *Ras Tafari Speaks*, 1980 (*c*. June). The Earth People have been largely ignored by writers. Cheryl Williams, a teacher in a nearby town, does not mention them in her account of women in West Indian sects (in Ellis ed. 1986). A local publisher, Jerry Besson, who met the family on the coast before Mother Earth's revelations, has given an account of them in the form of a fabled history of Trinidad. Exquisitely illustrated, *fin-de-siècle* nature symbolism and folk-lore are interwoven into a mythic account of Jeanette and Cyprian's departure from Port-of-Spain. None of the Earth People knew of the book until I gave them a copy in 1988.

18 *Trinidad Guardian*, 9 January 1982.

2 A certain degree of instability

1 Sereno 1948: 19.

2 La Barre 1969: 124; Andrews 1953: 5.

3 Nettleford 1970: 56–7.

4 Schuler 1979: 73. The minister had good cause to worry; such *myal* meetings were used to organise plantation workers' strikes.

5 S. Naipaul 1981: 17.

6 La Barre 1970: 348, 603, 607; Wolman 1973: 95.
7 S. Naipaul 1981: 134.
8 Lifton 1974; Seligman 1926: 223; La Barre 1969: viii, 109.
9 Cited by Ackernecht 1943; Devereux 1956.
10 Rosen 1968: 21–70; La Barre 1969.
11 Ackernecht 1943; Rosen 1968.
12 *Newsletter of the Association of Psychiatrists in Training*, London, September 1977, p. 1.
13 Richard Ballard, 'An Interview with Thomas Szasz', *Penthouse*, October 1973, pp. 69–74. The British Press Council ruled that the *Sun* newspaper improperly published 'a psychiatrist's' opinion on the socialist politician Tony Benn (*The Guardian*, 3 June 1986). In 1984 *The Times* wondered if Colonel Gaddafi was schizophrenic (4 May) and in 1991 whether Saddam Hussein was paranoid (17 January). On the whole the abusive use of 'mad' is directed against those on the political left (Goldwater an exception), perhaps a reaction to unsettling changes and a dislike of the utopian vision: 'a dangerous enthusiasm . . . liable to develop into a form of neurosis or hysteria' (Popper 1945: 165). Gershom Scholem's study of Jewish messianism warns us it is 'deep, dangerous and destructive' (1973: xii).
14 Freud 1972.
15 Jarvie 1964: ch. 5. Parsons had pointed out that his theory of social action does not explain social dynamics where 'we cannot go beyond empirical description' (1951: 487). By contrast Gellner (1964: 20) says structural-functionalist explanations can be easily applied to social change. Although the distinction between ideology and practical knowledge in the Marxist entelechy offers us a way out of the impasse of how we can innovate when all seems socially determined, in practice Communist states have had ready recourse to *insania ex machina* when dealing with undesirable innovations (Bloch and Reddaway 1977).
16 Beckford 1975.
17 B. Wilson 1974: 317–19, 172.
18 David Martin, 'The Woman Clothed with the Sun', *Times Literary Supplement*, 26 November 1982.
19 F. E. Williams 1934. The Vaihala movement was 'an epidemic': 'while they indulged in these antics the leader poured fourth utterances in "Djarman" or "German", a language . . . which was totally unintelligible . . . Not a few of the doctrines originated . . . in delusions' (pp. 370, 373).
20 Tseng and McDermott 1981: 171; La Barre 1970: 294, 233; B. Wilson 1973: 315; Yap 1954; F. E. Williams 1934: 372; Da Cunha 1947: 87, 96, 176, 213; J. E. C. Harrison 1979: 108–9.
21 Garrett 1975: ch. 5, 8; J. E. C. Harrison 1979: 119–20; P. G. Rogers 1961: ch. 4; Armytage 1961: 282; Worsley 1970: 168–9; B. Wilson 1973: 42; Simpson 1980; Nettleford 1970; S. Harris 1955: 18–19; Lanternari 1963. Huynh Phy So was confined to a Saigon mental hospital by the French in the 1940s but, having converted his psychiatrist, was released. The District Commissioner who arrested Simon Kimbangu wished to hospitalise him but Kimbangu was tried for sedition, and sentenced to death (later commuted) (M. L. Martin 1975: 55, 58, 61). Conselheiro would have been hospitalised if the Brasilian magistrate had found a hospital bed (Da Cunha 1947: 105). In 1987 the British Chief Constable with a

divine mission is recommended to see a psychiatrist (*The Times*, 20 January 1987), but unusual political opinions in Britain have seldom been dealt with by psychiatric hospitalisation (Walton 1985: 139): except for Brothers who was declared insane by the Privy Council in 1797 as his writings 'have for several months alarmed and agitated the minds of the people' (J. E. C. Harrison 1979: 38). Indeed, his statements that London was about to be destroyed in a republican millennium seem to have led to the general suspension of Habeas Corpus. George Turner, too, was first charged with treason and then sent to an asylum (*ibid.*).

22 As were American feminists according to Millet. Woodcock and Avakumovic 1968: 195; Beckford 1975: 34; Bloch and Reddaway 1977: passim. Disturbed by frequent episodes of arson by the Sons of Freedom, the government of British Columbia set up a Doukhobor Research Committee whose psychiatrist interviewed members held in prisons and asylums for 'extreme demonstrations [of] the Doukhobor personality', and concluded they were only 'partially sick . . . A final solution will be achieved only when the Doukhobors have made certain changes in their personality type' (Hawthorn 1955: 154).

23 I use here the rather antiquated term 'psychopathological' in preference to 'mad' which is preferred by recent social historians of insanity. Unlike these writers who are concerned to present psychosis as a mirror of society, and thus are interested primarily in the social constructions placed upon a prior existing insanity – or its frank invention – I take 'psychopathology' as immediate manifestations of novel and distinctive biologically perceived states which are always represented through social institutions and which cannot be considered in isolation from them. The justification? Unusual brain states (tumours, degenerations, endocrine and vitamin changes) are associated with moods, thoughts and actions which are substantially different from the human response to diseases which do not affect the physiology of the brain. This is so in all societies. While there is some evidence that what are recognised as 'psychoses' by medicine – manic depression and schizophrenia – may be associated with such abnormalities in some cases (leading to the assumption that all psychoses must be derived from biological changes – Schneider 1959), this is not an essential assumption. 'Psychopathology' thus refers here to both uncommon brain states as understood biologically and the changed affects, thoughts and actions immediately associated (for the psychiatrist, causally) with them: both social and biological facts and the relationship between them at a particular historical moment. To term them 'pathological' does of course beg certain questions about the very social recognition which defines them as undesirable (Littlewood 1991), together with the assumptions that they alone are causally independent of the social world in which they then have some characteristic manifestation, as if 'normal' brain states did not. (And we know that the biological development of the brain is itself dependent on the social environment.) If my term, like 'abnormal', does carry with it a fair amount of what we might feel are inappropriate question-begging associations, these states are usually perceived locally as discrete and undesirable and any such alternative as 'statistically or normatively unusual brain states and their experiential correlates' is too clumsy for repetition.

24 Littlewood 1986.

25 Karl Birnbaum cited in Littlewood 1986.

26 Abrahams 1986: 66.

258 Notes to pages 17–19

27 Written descriptions cannot be said to stand for psychopathology alone for, as Feder (1980: xiii) reminds us, literary 'conceptions of the extreme possibilities of mental experiences differ in important respects from actual manifestations of madness. The very distortions of the powerful visionaries or isolated victims of the literature of madness are designed to portray the mind constructing and exposing its own framework out of fragments that all readers recognise as familiar.'

28 Zilboorg 1941: 51–4.

29 *Ibid.*, pp. 54, 45. Our confidence in this Whiggish assurance is disturbed by Zilboorg's suggestion that one of these hidden schizophrenics was Socrates. Classicists have taken a different line: Nietzsche recognised Socrates as the quintessential apollonian rational man; Simon describes Plato as 'a rationalist par excellence [who] never fully relinquished a certain admiration for the irrational . . . who equated the activities of the mind with sanity and the impulses of the body with madness' (1978: 167, 158), and in *The Greeks and the Irrational* (1951: 64) Dodds denies that 'the father of Western rationalism praises madness over sanity'.

30 Plato 1965: 47. Plato's notion of divine madness probably influenced St Paul via Philo and thus the general Christian tradition (2 Corinthians 5: 13) of the 'foolishness' of God in allowing His son to die. Aristotle and Seneca went further: *Nullum magnum ingenium sine mixtura dementia fuit* (Dryden's well known 'Great Wits are sure to Madness near ally'd.')

31 'The thing is not to inhibit your imagination but to be very critical of its products; the scientist perhaps should be drunk the night before and stone cold sober the morning after' (Jarvie 1964: 6).

32 Winstanley 1973: 351.

33 Dr Nicholas Robinson discussing Fox and Nayler (cited by Godlee 1985: 80); K. Thomas 1973: 79, 72; MacDonald 1981: 223–4. John Wesley decried the 'hysterical or artificial' enthusiasm of his own followers but other sectarians took charges of madness as 'only confirming the truth of the claims' (J. E. C. Harrison 1979: 28, 215). When Joanna Southcott was called mad she replied 'I grant it, and so did all the prophets of old . . . I was born mad and so was my mother before me' (p. 108). Blake said to Cowper 'You are as mad as any of us all – over us all – mad as a refuge from unbelief' (p. 216). A collection of radical pamphlets collected in 1775, *The World's Doom*, noted 'That the men may be mad forms no solid objection to their prophetic character; for the very word prophet is derived from a Greek word signifying madness' (p. 57). (Not so, but compare 2 Corinth. 5: 13, and Wordsworth's *Prelude* 12.145–219.)

34 J. R. Nisbet, *The Insanity of Genius*, 1893, cited in W. James 1958: 311.

35 A generally unsatisfactory experiment; writers who were creative continued to be so after taking drugs, while no amount of artificial stimulation could elicit genius from those to whom the Muse denied her gifts (Hayter 1948).

36 This *Narrenfreiheit* (freedom of insanity) prefigures Erikson's notion that 'the great men of history' are culturally and psychologically marginal.

37 Trilling 1980 cf. E. Wilson 1952.

38 Nietzsche in *The Will to Power* cited by M. Harrison 1922.

39 Cited in Kurella 1911.

40 *Ibid.*: 71, 66.

41 Andreasen 1988.

42 Storr 1972.
43 W. James 1958: 24, 33; cf. Feuerbach's 'Theology is pathology hidden from itself'.
44 *Ibid*.: 36.
45 Breton 1969: 37.
46 Cited by Esslin 1976: 52.
47 'Open the prisons! Disband the armies!'
48 Norman O. Brown (*Love's Body*) cited in Feder 1980: 242.
49 Laing 1967. Bateson (1961) similarly describes schizophrenia as an initiation into a new, less compromised, identity, as do Deleuze and Guattari whose schizophrenics and shamanic 'nomads' both resist the terror of the Oedipal family.
50 Artaud wrote 'And what is an authentic madman? It is a man who has preferred to go mad, in the sense in which society understands the term, rather than to be false to a certain superior idea of human honour. That is why society has had all those of whom it wanted to rid itself, against whom it wanted to defend itself, because they had refused to become its accomplices in certain acts of supreme filthiness, condemned to be strangled in its asylums' (Esslin 1976: 96). He spoiled this image somewhat by dedicating his *Nouvelles Révélations de l'Etre* to Hitler.
51 Wilson's Outsider is privileged through her inability to partake of the banality and hypocrisy of social life. While a possible consequence is madness, a 'solution' can be found in harnessing the deviant perspective to the dominant order (Fox succeeded, Blake didn't). But this is still compromised: Wilson simply recommends antinomian action and thought – Ramakrishna offering food dedicated to the goddess to his cat, and the worship of the life force as absurd for 'All creation is the sport of my mad mother Kali.'
52 Vonnegut 1976.
53 Hughes 1959: ch. 2. Edmund Wilson makes a similar point in *Axel's Castle* as does Trilling in *The Liberal Imagination*.
54 Not Woman: Littlewood and Lipsedge 1989; E. R. Wallace 1983.
55 Roheim 1950.
56 For a critical view on 'pathography' which tackles the problems of historical contextuality and retrospective diagnosis, Porter (1985) is exemplary.
57 Benedict 1935. She later denied the implication that in some measure all societies were sick, precisely what was repeatedly asserted by the 'vulgar Freudians': Roheim, Devereux and La Barre.
58 I. M. Lewis (1971: ch. 7) and Eliade (1964: 23–32) both point out that the earliest descriptions of 'shamanism' in the 1860s had emphasised pathology. Shamanism and 'nativists' movements are often regarded together, with some justification: like the Ghost Dance, many chialistic religions are a 'universalisation' of once restricted roles. However, the shaman often seems paired with the 'nativist' leader as part of the continuing fascination with experiential aspects of the 'ecstatic states' which are held to be characteristic of both.
59 La Barre 1970: 43, 138, 107–8. It may be reasonably objected that I am concentrating on two figures, La Barre and Devereux, who are marginal to psychological anthropology. However, while their use of the conventional idiom of psychoanalysis is perhaps idiosyncratic, these authors faced the question without the fudging of Benedict and Kluckholn who avoided frank insanity to talk only of 'internal conflicts'.

60 La Barre 1970: 343, 317, 273, 351.
61 *Ibid.*: 541, 266.
62 La Barre 1969: ch. 2.
63 La Barre 1970: 351, 140; 1969: vii, ix, vii.
64 Ackernecht 1943: 31, 35.
65 While a nun *may* be a sexually repressed hysteric, convents can contain nuns who just happen to have little sexual interest or who may indeed have entered the order for economic reasons and who practice masturbation or homosexuality; or there is no association at all. Wallace offers an extended critique of the psychoanalytic supposition that an institution originates in the same needs in all individuals, who all attach the same meaning to the institution whose motivation, meaning and function do not change over time (E. R. Wallace 1983: 182–3).
66 Nadel 1964: 36.
67 Devereux 1956: 24.
68 Littlewood and Lipsedge 1989: ch. 2.
69 J. Murphy 1964: 74. However Nadel (1946) suggests that among the Nuba in the 1940s, while social change was associated with a 'general deterioration in mental health' and an increase in shamanism, the new shamans were just as well adjusted as their predecessors.
70 C. A. Ohlmarks, *Studien zum Problem der Shamanismus*, Lund, 1939, pp. 20ff., cited by Eliade 1964.
71 Waldemar Bogoras, *The Chuckchee*, New York, American Museum of Natural History, 1904–9, cited by J. Murphy 1964. See also Burton-Bradley 1977. In Evans-Pritchard's writings on the Nuer, although he suggests that one of their prophets was a 'genuine psychotic', elsewhere he notes that the Nuer themselves distinguish the madman (*yong*) from the prophet (*gwan kwoth*) by the latter's periodic return to 'a normal state'.
72 Devereux 1955; Weber 1947.
73 Lanternari 1963: 304.
74 Roheim 1940; Devereux 1955: 156; Rivers 1920: 90. In its study of socialisation, contemporary psychology accords a place to 'modelling' which is broadly equivalent to 'suggestion'. The sharing of new beliefs in a sudden and dramatic form has been studied by psychiatrists under the rubric of psychic epidemics or mass hysteria (Bartholomew 1990) employing as did Le Bon, the idiom of contagion. Such patterns are rapid, collective, shared and egalitarian, and present a novel perspective different from everyday 'sober' life; they are 'affective', involving shouting, screaming, running, falling, jumping, convulsions and stupor. The theologian Ronald Knox suggested that all religious sects start in this way. Certainly we can recognise something similar in certain movements which later became 'routinised' as Weber termed the process by which charisma is replaced by status-bound authority. The model is also deployed for short lived or periodic collective moments with no lasting social institutions such as the Vaihala Madness, the Madagascan Dancing Mania and Italian Tarantism, and for popular rumours and panics (such as that caused by Orson Welles' radio drama *The War of the Worlds* which is estimated to have 'affected' a million people in a few hours), and in episodes of convulsions and fainting in closed communities such as factories, convents, schools and hospitals (Rosen 1968). A contemporary instance was the

West Bank Epidemic of 1983 among Palestinian schoolgirls who developed sore throats, peripheral cyanosis and fainting; Palestinian doctors implicated poison, the Israelis hysteria. It seems that about 20 per cent of those affected had primary biochemical changes while the remainder were 'imitators'. A similar episode occurred among Albanian schoolchildren in Serbia in 1990 (*The Times*, 5, 6 April 1982; 23 March 1990). Both were followed later by political violence. What relationship do such 'psychic epidemics' bear to existing institutions? Gruenberg (1957) restricts himself to considering the social psychological conditions necessary – status of initiator, group size and so on. Rosen suggests that the medieval Dancing Mania was merely a variant of established pilgrimage patterns, but the usual justification for psychiatric interest has been that these institutions have little in the way of social antecedents. In the nineteenth century J. F. C. Hecker suggested the natural faculty of sympathy or imitation became morbid with an abnormal stimulus, and the German pathologist Rudolf Virchow asserted that an outbreak of miraculous healing in Europe in the 1850s was a pathologisation of the thwarted political impulses of 1848 (Rosen 1968: 204–8). Similarly, Marxist writers on cargo cults have regarded them as a *forme fruste* of revolutionary endeavour, while Cohn argues that millennial episodes just occur within the margins of wider and more adaptive political movements, and Rosen finds them only among 'the culturally alienated'. Even Ackernecht (1943) was prepared to regard them as 'morbid' if they led to physical suffering, but Rosen himself criticises Cohn for equating chiliasm with pathology. In a more sociological vein, Zolberg (1972) argues that such 'moments of madness' with their disinhibition, egalitarian consciousness of unbounded possibility, the 'collapse of the present into the future' – Cassirer's 'consanguinity of all things' – always 'fail' but lay the foundations for stable innovations such as universal suffrage.

75 La Barre 1969: 159; 1970: 14.
76 La Barre 1970: 307.
77 Devereux 1955.
78 Lifton 1974.
79 Erikson 1965: 317–49. The post-war emphasis on psychological explanations of Nazism and Fascism may be not inappropriate if we take their central ideology as itself one of 'pure psychology' (as does Mannheim): of deed, will and charismatic influence.
80 Spanos 1975.
81 Beckford 1975: 126. Weber insisted that the charismatic leader was 'a social phenomenon, not a psychological personality type'. Sociologists like Beckford and Wilson (1975: 5) appear to agree but their theories of the aetiology and mechanism of charismatic reception come close to a psychological causality.
82 Barkun 1974: 7. Barkun's approach is less that millennial movements are a sickness than that they are a response to sickness. Like A. F. C. Wallace (1956a, b) he compares them to group therapy.
83 Whitworth 1975: 7.
84 Devereux 1955: 156.
85 Toch 1971: ch. 2.
86 B. Wilson 1970: 37; 1973.
87 Cohn 1957: 248.

88 B. Wilson 1975: 248, vii; 1973: 16, 309, 67.
89 Woodcock and Avakumovic 1968: 347.
90 Robert Waelder in Wolman 1973: 12; Cohn 1981: 14.
91 Barkun (1974: 131) notes 'The tendency . . . to regard ecstatic behaviour and outbursts of apparent "irrationalism" as nasty interruptions, breaking the pattern of functional behaviour.' The process of consolidation of the movement is the return to the field of action of 'normal' social forces (see B. Wilson 1970: 233–42). The image of distinct social systems being separated historically by periods of patho-logical 'affectivity' is found in that maverick Marxist, Gramsci: 'The old is dying, and the new cannot be born; in this interregnum there arises a great diversity of morbid symptoms.'
92 Stirrat (1984: 207) makes the point that the mainstream/chiliastic dichotomy recalls Redfield's Great and Little Traditions in which an elite is cognitive whilst the masses 'are incapable of dealing with abstract ideas and thus having to resort to such activities as possession, the thrills of animal sacrifice, psychological dependence on godlings'.
93 Lienhardt 1974: 135–6.
94 Littlewood 1984b.

3 Madness, vice and tabanka: popular knowledge of psychopathology in Trinidad

1 Rodman 1971. As Bourdieu reminds us, we can hardly say that one society (or insti-tution) *is* any more 'pragmatic' than another; but, as in other Western societies, in Trinidad it is just more acceptable than elsewhere to act in one's own immediate interest (whether sexual or economic) without the justification of collective or 'higher' values. If we take pragmatism as an external designation, we have to bear in mind that this is the White observer's measure of difference, not a descriptive attribute of a functioning society: but in the West Indies such external measures of 'difference' are certainly recognised as such, to serve as local 'values of difference' or even 'opposition', and thus returned into everyday life.
2 Although Simpson and Sereno in the 1950s placed bush and obeah together as a unitary system, they do not describe how practical choices of treatment are made. One term for a spirit – *duppy* – may be derived from the Ashanti *dupon*, a root (particularly of the silk-cotton tree) found above ground (J. B. Williams 1979: 156); *root* in Pinnacle is a category of *bush* but, as in the United States (*rootwork*), it also carries a connotation of obeah. A third element, biomedicine, has also to be taken into account; in the nineteenth century it was accepted that Western medicine could not cure obeah-induced physical illness (Abrahams and Szwed 1983: 109), and Whites remain generally impermeable to obeah. We might postulate a transition from (a) a unitary bush/obeah complex articulating African institutions, developing into (b) an obeah/shango complex incorporating some White religious tenets, which stands in opposition to bush and to the equally naturalistic Western medicine, but also to a radically dichotomising Christianity which allocates obeah/shango to the demonic; (c) as biomedicine is ineffective in relieving madness, obeah/shango remains as the explanation for madness, consequently eliding 'African identity' with 'madness'.
3 P. Wilson (1973) took these terms from the island of Providencia to provide a

dialectical alternative to the then current debate in Caribbean studies between the 'functionalists' (who explained colonialism) and the 'pluralists' (who emphasised independent cultural characteristics). In Jamaica a similar top-down ideological model of class is known as *inside-outside* (Austin 1979) which refers simultaneously to geographical space (the home), marital status (church, marriage and legitimacy) and dominant social values. Although in Trinidad the word *respectability* is used in the prescriptive Providencian sense, its converse is not called *reputation* but by the disparaging (and sometimes defiant) terms *nigger-ways, no behaviour* or the adjectival *worthless, slack, loose* or *ignorant*: or *up and down* as opposed to *steady*. Wilson emphasises the Providencian respectability-reputation bipolarity against the usual ethnography of the Caribbean which centred on the household (and hence on the female), and which thus generates a 'matricentric' focus for local values leaving male concerns peripheral and residual. In Trinidad *respectability* indeed seems more generally accepted as a shared local value than is the adjectival *worthless* which appears secondary, to be defined by, and relative to, this *respectable* pole: a respectability ultimately rooted in White (planter, bourgeois, colonial) life (a euphemism for Whites in the nineteenth century was 'the respectable class'). It is difficult to see extra-household, inter-male ties in Pinnacle Village as very autonomous: they are regarded by both sexes as secondary to the more highly valued benefits associated with *respectability*, and D. Harrison (1975) notes that in Trinidad both represent a continuum available to either sex. While a society in which everyone becomes more *respectable* is an economic goal to be imagined and worked for by most Pinnacle villagers, albeit with reservations, a society characterised by universal *nigger-ways* would be just a mess. This may reflect the greater salience in the village of 'respectability' demonstrated by the numerous poor Black *Spanish*, for our analytical dichotomy follows the view of the more respectable who emphasise publicly the self-control and moral choices supposedly necessary for respectability. By contrast, the unsuccessful say that the real moral values are those of community and mutual help, and respectability is just *socialness* (snobbery), having a large and secluded house, something anyone can afford when they are wealthier (but see Glazier 1983b), a descriptive rather than a prescriptive dichotomy. Not so, say the more respectable and point to the poor, nearly destitute, but eminently decent Tante Marie. You didn't know her when she was younger, retort the worthless. The observer's model then tends to follow respectable views of local life, a moral ideology which justifies inequality, and which may be challenged, certainly from the bottom, sometimes from the top. Yet it is not altogether a 'false consciousness', for personality and moral disposition are also recognised by everybody, independently of economic position. Nor are statements of solidarity just 'secondary principles' (Bourdieu), evoked by individuals when self-interest fails, for they are used by all to define the local community as a whole against the outside.

Most Pinnacle villagers have both African and European ancestry; while a darker villager is referred to by a lighter as *nigger* or *black* – and *black* is often used as synonymous with *worthless* or *bad* (as in *bad hair*, curly hair) – one may be a *worthless nigger* through one's *no behaviour* even with a light skin (*red* or *high colour with no curl*). Similarly the term *béké nègre* refers both to those born with *clear* or *high colour* or with *half-tone* (vitiligo) and to those who imitate White ways. *Bad* is not only a term of disapprobation; at times it is used by all, to celebrate *you' nature*, Carnival disorder and *bacchanal*, to *free up* oneself, a self-mocking but constrained contestation of respectability – within limits. *Bad* implies energy and force: 'he got a giant case of the hots. Eh Papa! he love she too bad'. (This is probably not simply an oppositional position but calquing: in various African languages an intensive may be marked by equivalents of 'bad'.) Respectability then is less a fixed status or a principle than a contested field marked by privacy, reserved public behaviour and an avoidance of inappropriate familiarity: all as perceived by others. A respectable person is one who above all *respects* others in public, particularly those who are themselves more respectable or otherwise powerful. Some wealthier male villagers maintain that a man's respectability can actually be enhanced by discrete outside sexual relations if you avoid public *confusion* with your wife and do not humiliate her, for this they maintain was the practice of the French planters: 'You' wife now she come more on the White side and you satisfy you' nature with a Black girl.' Indeed Raymond Smith (1988) has argued that *worthlessness* is less a simple opposition to the presumed European and planter values than an acquisition of them by the lower classes; once concealed behind a private façade of marriage for the Whites, an *outside* relationship is now simply more visible. Besides, *friending* was always a recognised prelude to marriage in the poorer European classes (*bundling* – Goody 1976: cf. Fr. *fréquentation*). Being *worthless* is particularly making others *ashame* of you publicly: an uncontrolled intrusion of your *nature* into the *social*. For a wife to quarrel with her husband's outside woman is to make herself *ashame* for she should ignore her, unlike men who supposedly achieve *fame* (the explicit converse) by their reputation for multiple partners. As Epstein has pointed out, there is a 'covering up' sense to *shame* in English (cognate with German *schama* = cover), and Trinidadians themselves frequently cite Adam and Eve (p. 8). The continuum then articulates relative ethnicity and wealth, and ethical attitudes, personality and public actions at both 'ends': in different contexts, emphasis is placed on one or another. Actions which define it are agreed, if not their significance.

4 Quoted in K. Warner 1982: 96. In quoting published calypsos I have retained the rather objectionable Negro Spiritual orthography. *Obzocky* is crooked, deformed. *Rake* and *scrape* connote coitus from the man's point of view.

5 P. Wilson 1973; Austin 1979.

6 Rodman 1971: 203. Cf. Creole *pica* (thorn). Elsewhere in the Caribbean it is known as *broad talk* or *nigger talk* (B. D. Abrahams 1983). Orlando Patterson has called attention to the levelling intentions of humour in African-American slave societies; in contemporary Jamaica where *Nancy* (*Anansi*) *stories* frequently mock the pretensions of social life, like folk tales in other peasant societies (Scott 1990), they debunk the would-be elite.

7 'Science' in any sense, including the study of the natural world at school, still implies sorcery in the Caribbean (Nettleford 1978: 76), a theme for mockery in the tales of V. S. Naipaul. *Negromancy* is presumably a reading of *necromancy*.

8 The priest can as easily cause madness: 'It have a boy at Diego Martin and he fight with a priest and cuss him. And he went mad. At Grande a teacher went to kill a priest and he madman now.'

9 Mourning (cf. Daniel 10: 2–3) has been examined by psychiatrists and social

scientists including Herskovits 1947; Glazier 1983a; Simpson 1980; Ward and Beaubrun 1979; Henney 1983; Griffith and Mahy 1983; Mischel and Mischel 1958; see M. G. Smith 1963 and E. Thomas 1987 for personal accounts. The medical consensus seems to be that while the sensory deprivation of mourning may precipitate a psychosis in those vulnerable, the Baptists are 'therapeutic' in consoling individuals, 'maintaining social cohesion' and providing role models for social mobility.

10 Nor do they appear to have been during slavery to judge by the accounts in Abrahams and Szwed (1983). Various conceptual possibilities can be found in the following conversation I prompted whilst helping some Pinnacle women prepare food for a wake:

A: Clyde had a niece with fits. An' they carry her to the hospital. An' the last time, a nurse say 'carry she somewhere else – it ain' a sickness'. They carry her to a Baptist lady . . .

B: They be in it too!

A: . . . an' she say it a spirit they invoke in the cemetery . . .

B: All kind of wickedness the Baptists, all kind of filthy ways.

A: They send it to her father but it take the little girl. She take it out and she get better.

C: If the spirit had been an adult she would have die. It stronger. But it spirit of a child. When Baptists come up in district they go to cemetery an' do this. Plenty go mad too. Some way you can call up a spirit which stay on you.

B: A woman die here an' they take her spirit an' put it on a woman in Caranage. An' they say it some girl talking. I feel it is the Devil transfer himself.

A: It is a spirit of dead!

C: After you dead an' bury you suppose to be finish here on earth . . .

B: Your spirit stay in the grave three days and then it goes back where it come from.

C: If you bad your soul die. You see dead? I say it is your mind reflecting back to a person.

B: Your soul never die.

R.L.: The soul is the same as the spirit?

B: Yes. In your heart. Some people see it only after death. Like the wind it go anywhere.

A: When you die you' spirit die.

B: No! If it good it got to leave right away. If bad it wanders about till its time.

C: It time now! I ai' see nothing yet but it have plenty of sickness you doctors don't even know the name of.

A: There ai' no hell. It have heaven but it hell right here. You pay for you' sins here. It only have heaven for rich man – the Devil loose here!

R.L.: Heaven?

A: It have everything there it have here . . . it have mad people for you!

11 The villagers who read newspapers are also familiar with *nerves mashup* or *nervous breakdown*, typical of women and characterised by a quieter picture: 'They look shaky like, they can' think. They don' say strange things, they don' go to lash. To my mind it don' come like a madness.' Nerves mashup are an extension of normal moods or personality and are seldom the occasion for special remark: 'It odd you ask that! I was like that. Some years ago I never leave the house. I stay in house with one child, with nine children. I suppose it get like a habit 'cepting I nervous. I go so I too anxious to go to the shop. If anyone strange come I don't know how to behave.' The woman's husband was often away from home and involved in another

relationship, and she herself received sexual invitations which she did not accept, although she admitted to me she was tempted. Most instances I encountered of nerves mashup in the village involved respectable women, usually in a conflict about personal autonomy.

12 Cf. Festus: 'Paul you are raving; too much study is driving you mad' (Acts 26.24).

13 Wood (1968: 8) suggests that 'participants could purge themselves of emotions held in check for the rest of the year'. Abrahams and Bauman ('Ranges of Festive Behaviour' in Babcock 1974) argue however against the 'rituals of rebellion' catharsis to suggest that Carnival in St Vincent simply allows the already worthless to be accommodated by the respectable. On local views see: Philip Nunez, 'We Do Have a Carnival Mentality', *Sunday Guardian*, Port-of-Spain, 3 July 1981; 'Therapy à la Beaubrun', *Sunday Guardian*, 1 March 1981. V. S. Naipaul is unenthusiastic, complaining that Trindadian society is already a Carnival, a masquerade directed against 'phantom enemies', and pointing out that the Carnivals in 1805 and 1970 developed into anti-White riots: 'after the masquerade and the music, anger and terror' (1980: 267). He traces a continuity from the slaves' King-doms of the Night with their secret regiments, uniforms, ranks and titles through Carnival to Black Power: 'the carnival lunacy of a lively well-informed society which feels itself part of the world, but understands at the same time that it is cut off from this world by reasons of geography, history and race . . . Black power in these black islands is protest. But there is no enemy. The enemy is the past of slavery and colonial neglect and a society uneducated from top to bottom' (p. 271). A less jaundiced perspective (and one which employs the 'weak' use of *mad* and *bad*) was offered by Sparrow in his 'Trinidad Carnival' (Rodman 1971: 211):

> The biggest baccanal
> Is in Trinidad Carnival
> All you got to do when the music play
> Take you' man an' break away
> Regardless of colour, creed or race
> Jump up and shake you' waist
> This is the spirit of Carnival
> It is a Creole bacchanal
> So jump as you mad this is Trinidad
> We don' care who say we bad

14 The etymology is obscure and probably multiple; perhaps French Creole, cognate with *ta banque* (= your mark; cf. Fr. *banqueroute* = bankrupt or violator of any agreement) or *ta banc* (= bench/bed/bank [of a beach, cf. Eng. 'beached']). *Ta* may also be a rendering of *c'est à* in Creole (J. J. Thomas 1969: 39). In Jamaica, a *bonkra* is a small purse or bag (possibly from Twi *bon kara*). *Bonque/bunka* (palm) is in Spanish America a dug out canoe; as are the Jamaican *bungay*, *bongo*. *Bacha* is Jamaican Creole for 'banana' and hence possibly 'small banana' ('no erection'?), although the French diminutive *petit* is usually rendered in Creole as *ti* rather than *ta* (Thomas 1969: 14). *Ti blanc* ('little White') is thus also unlikely. More plausibly, Central American Spanish has *tabanco*, a lumbar room or place for castrated cocks.

15 Quoted in Rodman 1971: 48.

16 'Marriage has teeth.'
17 Mighty Terror, 'Chinese Children', 1950 (K. Warner 1982: 97); Mighty Dictator, 'Gossipmongers of Trinidad', 1951 (Rodman: 219).
18 Mighty Sparrow, 'Sailor Man', 1957 (Rodman 1971: 217).
19 Mighty Sparrow, 'Nothing for Nothing' (Warner 1982: 102); Sparrow, 'Theresa', 1957 (Rodman 1971: 214). *Old style* is *social*, standoffish behaviour.
20 Quoted in Warner 1982: 102; Mighty Conqueror, 'Women and Money', 1962 (Rodman 1971: 214). This is actually a male calypsonian's perspective on what he takes to be the woman's view. (See Elma Reyes, 'Women in Calypso', in Ellis 1986.)
21 Lowenthal 1972: 141.
22 Abrahams 1983: 74. And thus tabanka in a *hard* man can be even funnier ('Tabanka Killing a Bad John', *Heat*, Port-of-Spain, 5 August 1989: 'Popular Laventille ex-convict Earl "Fatboy" Lewis has been laid low by a serious bout of tabanka . . .'). The calypsonian Mighty Chalkdust (Hollis Liverpool) even argues that 'In Trinidad, humour has become the stabilising system and the basis of control in the society' (Jones and Liverpool 1976: 281).
23 Girard 1975: 124ff.
24 Wood 1968: 154. Trinidad Indians have 'contempt for the Negro . . . who allows his womenfolk complete sexual freedom' (Klass 1961: 244).
25 Between an individual and their parent, child, grandparent, grandchild, sibling (or uncle or aunt to a lesser extent). Termed *incest*, it has no special local name: newcomers to the village criticise the frequency of cousin marriage: 'they all one family here!' but this is debatably 'incest'.
26 The Enemy, 'Was Dr. Williams Mental?', *The Bomb*, 1 May 1981; Belgobin Ramdeen, 'Somebody Must be Mad', *Trinidad Express*, 3 July 1981.
27 Gordon Lewis 1983: 178.

4 Mother Earth and the psychiatrists
1 I am grateful to both Mother Earth and Dr John Neehall, then Superintendent of St Ann's, for permission to quote from these notes. There are conventional ethical problems in the disclosure of hospital records about named patients. It is only with Mother Earth's consent and encouragement and that of her sons that I feel able to do so here.
2 Mother Earth seldom uses cannabis and indeed no one at the hospital suggested her visions were due to 'cannabis psychosis'.
3 Psychiatric classification either emphasises symptomatology (e.g. paranoid psychosis) or aetiology (drug-induced psychosis). When I returned to St Ann's to give a talk on the Earth People's account of these events, I suggested a more likely diagnosis was manic-depressive illness. Most of the staff maintained the diagnosis of schizophrenia and in a letter to a British medical journal, a local Indian psychiatrist criticises my involvement with a group containing 'schizophrenics' (H. Maharaj et al., *Psychiatric Bulletin*, 13 (1989), p. 514).
4 She had certainly been *sick* when they brought her back and ascribed her symptoms – stiff neck, turning eyes, continued walking, trembling hands – to her medication. These sound like the extra-pyramidal reaction frequently induced by the drugs she had been given. Jakatan actually returned later to the hospital to obtain the tablets

routinely used to minimise these side effects. Jeanette's younger sister however has always maintained to me that she was mad.

5 *Nopalea cochinillifera*, a branched cactus, is infused to prepare a cooling or to reduce oedema; roasted, it is applied externally to sores and inflammation.

6 Used in the World Health Organisation's International Pilot Study of Schizophrenia. Despite criticism on the grounds that no word in any one language can have the same resonance as a term in another language, it remains the accepted tool for cross-cultural comparisons. Scoring is carried out in accordance with a training course and a manual (Wing, Cooper and Sartorius 1976). I had previously used in Britain the same English version of the 9th edition. It has never been standardised for the Caribbean, and studies with it in America suggest that Black Americans (not surprisingly) use a rather different lexicon of affect from Whites (Littlewood 1990). Nevertheless, the psychotic symptoms I retrospectively described for Mother Earth for 1976 were as comparable with the symptoms which I would have rated in St Ann's or in Britain as to make any distinction between their meanings impossible for me, at least, to perceive.

7 A rather wide category which contains as 'delusions' such practices as glossolalia. The PSE is hardly intended for situations where the 'subculture' is generated through the 'delusion'.

8 Not *church married*.

9 *Trump*: repetitive swings of the body with synchronised shouted snatches of prayer or rhythmic breathing. Trumping may continue for several hours and is usually performed whilst standing. Mother Earth would have been assisted to rise although still bound and blindfolded.

10 The giant gorilla from the film *King Kong*.

11 Simpson (1980: 39) comments that such shango songs contain a mixture of Yoruba, Creole and 'nonsense'. On Yemanja see Chapter 8. *Saiy* may be Yemanja's son Shango.

12 Poke. To 'chook out someone's eye' is to outsmart them, but the word usually refers to a physical action, including male sexual activity.

13 Although the PSE is intended to be used retrospectively only for the preceding month. Using the American DSM system (APA 1987), we obtain: Axis I – 296.44 Manic Episode (primary diagnosis if we are uncertain about history of physical illness; 293.81 Organic Delusional Disorder if we are certain); Axis II – V71.09 (no diagnosis); Axis III – Post-partum, early congestive cardiac failure, Grave's Disease? one son mentally ill; Axis IV (Psychosocial Stressors) – Severity 3 (moderate), threat of eviction, isolated and economically limited life; Axis V (Highest Level of Adaptive Functioning Over Past Year) – 85 (high).

14 Distinguished from the apparently similar experiences of possession trance (Wing *et al.* 1976: 168) by the latter's conventional and 'egosyntonic' nature.

15 Although this may just be (sympathomimetic) 'emotion' at the time.

16 Lishman 1978: 596–601. (This was the same illness which has been implicated in George Bush's handling of the Gulf War in 1991: 'Was the hand that signed the orders vibrating as fast as bumblebee wings?' (*The Times*, 27 May 1991). Mother Earth's later identification with the Devil may seem to relate to a subsequent depressive phase. Demonic identification is not uncommon in psychotic (and other) patients enmeshed in self-doubt, guilt and self-hating, striving to explain their

worthlessness. It would seem possible that, at a later period, seeking to interpret her actions during the Miracle, particularly the 'breaking' of her daughter's arm, she was unable to understand them in any other way, and this identification became later transformed into a valued identification with a misinterpreted Devil, the Mother. I argued this with her but she pointed out that her feeling at the time of the Burning and the Miracle was of exuberant 'wickedness', of freedom and of throwing over social restraints and that she realised then that what Christians had personified as the Devil was precisely this autonomy of Natural action.

17 This may be felt to be an unreasonable analogy for I have really taken as the natural fact 'out there', not biological changes of thyroid function (or even the presumed altered brain activity by which they provide a ground – cf. Whybrow and Prange 1981) but the manifestations of hypomania: taking illness as if it were disease. However this is not biological determinism but simply the presentation of a radical departure from biological normality, one which is arbitrary and does not appear enacted in a continuing social process, which is associated with personal experiences initially meaningless to participant and audience, but upon which certain shared affinities and cognitions have permitted the erection of new representations and eventually a new social formation. This is not an essay in dynamic psychopathology and the 'primary processes' through which Mother Earth's experiences were reworked later – condensation, displacement, symbolisation (Barth 1987: 72–3) – were of course available during her mania. I am not arguing that the choice of themes during her mania was completely random, but nor were they 'chosen' in any conventional sense.

5 Putting Out The Life

1 This chapter comprises a sequence of formal statements declaimed slowly by Mother Earth and taped in conversation during my final two days in the Valley. While deliberately intended thus as the explicit Message to the World, they parallel closely, often word for word over many paragraphs, both her public Putting Out The Life, her general conversation and her daily teaching (and the Earth People often use the identical phraseology). They may thus be said to have some 'canonical' status. I have arranged them here in headed sections which broadly follow her own order. My own glosses (p. 244) might be helpful; an initial capital letter distinguishes what we can take as novel and didactic ('ideological' if we will) usages from the local everyday meanings. Such a drastic distinction is ours not hers: if you wish a closer resemblance to Christian cosmogony, read the personal pronouns for Mother and Son as capitalised ('She', 'He'); if you wish to take the chapter as a commentary on everyday experience, drop all initial capitals.

2 A pun against the Rasta *I and I* (= 'we').

3 A new fast-growing strain.

4 Hydroponics.

5 Artificial insemination, although it is the bull who 'goes behind the machine'.

6 I.e. 'right'.

7 A pun: clothes/materialistic.

8 Another pun. 'Numbers' is the *social* euphemism for excretion: Number One (urination), Number Two (defaecation).

9 A popular saying, derived from the Apostles' Creed, and often quoted by the Baptists.
10 This is not just biblical imagery: there is a blind leper in nearby Pinnacle.

6 Your ancestor is you: Africa in a new world

1 Herskovits 1958. The 'myth' is the absence of a past. Herskovits was concerned to refute suggestions that African culture was destroyed by a process in which the slaves passively acquiesced, or indeed that they were drawn from groups who were biologically less able to resist. He attempted to find retained 'Africanisms' whose existence demonstrated active resistance to slavery, yet he is now held to have been ranged against those who emphasised the active role of slave insurgency, particularly Eugene Genovese. Another concern was to refute notions that attributes such as posture or gesture were determined by one's racial biology.
2 They lived in distinct areas until the beginning of this century, possibly until the 1950s (Simpson 1978: 55; Carr 1952).
3 Table 1 in Crahan and Knight 1979; Wood 1968: ch. 2.
4 Maureen Warner Lewis, 'The African Impact on Language and Literature in the English Speaking Caribbean', in Crahan and Knight 1979. I found no evidence of this, nor for Elder's claim that distinctive tribal identities still persist.
5 Herskovits 1951: 46.
6 George E. Simpson and Peter Hammond, 'Discussion', in Rubin ed. 1960: 48.
7 Simpson 1980: 108, 111.
8 As do the Rastas and such idealised accounts as Credo Mutwa's *My People: Writings of a Zulu Witch-Doctor*, Harmondsworth, Penguin, 1971, or those of the Trinidadian ethnologist J. D. Elder (1988).
9 M. G. Smith, 'The African Heritage in the Caribbean', in Rubin ed. 1960: 41.
10 Ernest Gellner, 'Foreword', in Jarvie 1964: v.
11 Herskovits and Herskovits 1947: 181.
12 Cited by Bastide: 129; compare Webber 1978.
13 Bastide 1979: 16–17; Clifford 1988: 339.
14 Bastide 1979: 159, 339.
15 Herskovits and Herskovits (1947) and E. Thomas (1987) give graphic accounts of their persecution in the 1930s but it seems likely that the prohibition was variable, drums being acceptable if part of 'African dances' (M. G. Smith 1963).
16 Nineteenth-century American revivalist hymns, usually sung with a leader and chorus at a very slow tempo. The Herskovits (1947: 211) term this style 'the vocal imitation of drums'. 'Dorseys' (*Precious Lord*) are also sung.
17 Herskovits and Herskovits 1947: ch. 8, app. 2; Simpson 1980: ch. 4.
18 Indeed Gordon Lewis (1983: 19) talks of the 'shango–obeah complex'. Compared with the informants of Herskovits or Griffiths and Mahy, mine were less likely to talk of a return to Africa during mourning rather than travels to China or India, but the India they cited sounded more like the Kingdom of Prestor John than the India from which Trinidad's indentured labourers came.
19 G. E. Simpson 1978, 1980. Cf. Herskovits and Herskovits 1947; Mischel 1957; Mischel and Mischel 1958; George E. Simpson, *Cult Music in Trinidad*, Explorer Records, 1961; Schuler 1979; Barrett 1976; Glazier 1983a.
20 Carr 1952.

21 Neolithic stone axes found in the ground which, as in Africa, represent Shango, the thunder power.

22 Simpson 1980: 45 and picture facing p. 77.

23 To use Bourguignon's typology, she originally experienced PT, *possession trance* (altered state of consciousness plus possession belief), which has been succeeded by P, *possession* (the belief alone); the participant in shango experiences PT and then returns to normal, while Baptist mourning is really T, *trance* (an altered state of consciousness without possession belief). Mother Earth herself did not quite know what was happening at the time, and P implies a standardised belief; her state at the Burning should perhaps be termed simply T (trance), in which case her model is more Baptist than shango.

24 Lowenthal 1972: 93.

25 *Ibid.*: ix.

26 Mintz 1974a: 25.

27 *Ibid.*: 37–8.

28 'Every John Crow think him pickney white' in the words of the Jamaican aphorism. The last public inquiry was the 1969 *Report of the Commission Appointed by His Excellency the Governor-General to Investigate Allegations of Discriminatory Practices by the Management of the Trinidad Country Club.*

29 M. Lewis (note 4): 114. Gordon Lewis (1983: 11) relates the 'anti-social individualism' of Trinidad to its short period of slavery. In Creole Trinidad as in the French islands, 'nèg riche sé mulât; mulât pou sé nèg'. An anglicised Trinidadian like V. S. Naipaul can maintain that race is not 'an issue' in Trinidad (1980: 59–73; 1976: 82), but his brother comments 'The mood of blacks in the Caribbean had been getting steadily worse. Under the influence of the Black Power philosophies imported from the United States, they were becoming increasingly restless, increasingly demanding . . . Outward blackness was no longer good enough. You had to be inwardly black as well. Nothing less than a black soul would do' (S. Naipaul 1981: 22–3).

30 Bastide 1979: 150.

31 S. W. Mintz 1974: 66.

32 Lowenthal 1972: ix; Gordon Lewis 1983: 15. Kerr (1952: ch. 6) implicates the 'West Indian personality' which blames others and fails to take personal responsibility.

33 Lowenthal 1972: 13.

34 James Anthony Froude, *The English in the West Indies*, London, Longmans and Green, 1888, p. 49.

35 Lowenthal 1972: 16.

36 *Ibid.*: 17.

37 Quoted by Lowenthal 1972: 17.

38 Kluckholn and Leighton 1952: 28ff.

39 S. W. Mintz 1974, passim.

40 The origins and structures of Rastafari are currently fashionable subjects. Besides contacts with Rastas in Britain and Trinidad, I have used here the work of George Simpson, Bryan Wilson, Vittorio Lanternari, Rex Nettleford, Sheila Kitzinger, Barbara Lee, Millard Faristzaddi, Tracy Nicholas, Ernest Cashmore, Joseph Owens, H. Campbell, Leonard Barrett, M. G. Smith, Roger Mais, K. E. Weiss, Anita

Waters, Orlando Patterson, Edmund Cronon, Shango Baku, Peter Clarke, Shiva Naipaul, Laennec Hurbon, and in particular that of Barry Chevannes and Carole Yawney, to both of whom I am indebted for criticism.

41 Mintz 1974a: 25.

42 Isaiah 3, 9, 34, 43, 44, 47; Proverbs 8; Lamentations 4, 5; Joel 2; Habbakuk 2; Job 30; Psalm 119; Jeremiah 2, 8, 14, 50, 51; Revelation 1.

43 Matted hair now usually covered in public with a woollen tam 'to shelter me locks from Babylon'. Justified by Leviticus 19: 27 ('Ye shall not round the corners of your heads', the same text cited by Hasidic Jews) and the injunction in Isaiah 47: 2 to 'uncover thy locks' when mourning (in the Rasta instance, because of the Babylonian captivity). An article in a Jamaican paper in 1935, originating perhaps in 'disinformation' on the part of the Italian government, about the 'Nya-Binghi' of East Africa, a secret society dedicated to expelling the British, was illustrated with a picture of a (Masai?) tribesman, and is often supposed to have initiated dreadlocks. Chevannes' interviews with Rasta elders suggest it is more recent and may have been in tribute to mad and 'derelict' Rastas.

44 Nettleford 1970. Its acceptance as an authentic movement of protest was facilitated by a University of the West Indies report (Smith *et al.* 1962) which was criticised for its emphasis on social and economic conditions. Rastas have in fact frequently supported the right-wing Jamaican Labour Party. In a rather extra-ordinary eulogy of Rastafari, *Countryman*, a film made in 1982 (director Dickie Jobson, Island Pictures) as a vehicle for old Bob Marley tracks and advertised as 'A Tale of Modern Adventure and Ancient Magic', a Rasta befriends the daughter of a wealthy American and helps her fight off Cuban-style Jamaican soldiers with obeah, returning the girl to her father and helping the right-wing party win the election, most sequences filmed on idyllic beaches with folksy touristified Rasta fishermen.

45 Mintz 1974a: 137.

46 Faristzaddi 1982 (no pagination). Similarly Father Divine would reply to 'Hello' with 'Other Place' and use 'Bless!' as a substitute expletive for 'Damn!' (S. Harris 1955: 118–19).

47 Any Creole figuring can be pursued through a multitude of associations. To take salt: it is often used sparingly by rural West Indians, and was avoided by the *salt-water* (African born) slaves (Herskovits 1958: 156) for it would hamper any miraculous flight back to Africa. Certainly, for inland Africans, their first experience of salt water was closely associated with enslavement. Salt is charac-teristic of the cheap imported slave food, salt fish, which is still valued in the rural West Indian diet. In both Europe and Africa salt is linked to the spirit world: in West Africa devotees of Obatala (ch. 8) refrained from salt; it is used to catch the soucouyant in Trinidad, and in Europe is associated with nature spirits (Kipling's *Puck of Pook's Hill*); food prepared without salt was once offered to the African powers in the West Indies (Abrahams and Szwed 1983: 156) and in the nineteen-thirties was ritually used in Trinidad wakes (Herskovits and Herskovits 1947: 263). In Creole Guadeloupe salt represents female sexuality (André 1987: 83), while Amerindians avoided it as a sign of the Europeans' civilisation or even of their sorcery (Taussig 1987: 97, 172). Salt is important in Roman Catholic doctrine ('salt of grace'), and its manufacturing from ashes may be unseemly given Rasta attitudes

to death. In high science, salt stands for the earth, the female and body. Biologically, a relative avoidance of salt among those of African descent may be related to their greater physiological retention of sodium (Kiple 1984: 46).

48 Similarly, a New York Black Islamic group, The Five Per Cent Nation, call their men *gods*, their women the *earth*.

49 Just the cessation of combing or brushing develops matted locks; uncultivated (*dada*) bushy hair is seen is worthless and is attributed to the folkloric dwens (bush-dwelling spirits of unbaptised children). Matted hair in Trinidad is a sign of madness, as it is generally in the West (Gilman: 134). In coastal Ghana it represents spirits, madmen and prophets (Field 1960: 17, 18, 64).

50 Nettleford, *Introduction* in Owens 1977: xxi.

51 Schwimmer 1972.

52 Sahlins 1987: 155. 'Every actual use of cultural ideas is some reproduction of them, but every such reference is also a difference' (p. 153).

53 As Bourdieu (1977: 164) puts it.

7 Nature and the millennium

1 We are not concerned here with the obsessive typologies of such movements. I am far from convinced by the sociologists of religion that an accurate classification will lead us to general principles. Even the common distinction between 'millenarian' (practice) and 'millennial' (theory) seems rather unhelpful. Nor is it standard (J. E. C. Harrison 1979: 5). Suffice to say that the characteristics I am concerned with generally include (i) group salvation (ii) on this earth (iii) suddenly and (iv) totally (v) through something like divine agency (*ibid.*: 8). Passage between a 'political' and a 'religious' response may go in either direction. A 'military' response may succeed an earlier 'utopian' withdrawal – as with The Move, the African-American sect who resemble the Earth People in the wearing of dreadlocks and their emphasis on Nature, and whose beleaguered communal houses were finally destroyed in 1985 by an air strike of the Philadelphia police department (an incident fictionalised in Wideman's novel (1991)). Our very choice of the term 'movement' or 'sect' as opposed to, say, 'revolt' depends on our perception of the absence of a separate national or quasi-national identity. The participant may see a movement as constituting a revolt long after the sociologist has adopted the former, more 'neutral', term; and the converse.

2 'Cargo cults' in particular are distinctive in their early and ready acceptance of Western goods and associated desires: the Karoem prophecies of Dutch New Guinea in the 1940s forbad men the local women in anticipation of the arrival of the 'shapely women' from Australia.

3 Bateson 1958: 188. As Sartre argues for European Jews.

4 Burridge (1971: 19) quotes a Maori in conversation with a White clergyman: 'Bishop, many years ago we received a faith from you. Now we return it to you, for there has been found a new and precious thing by which we shall keep our land.' Aimé Césaire wrote 'My negritude is neither a tower nor a cathedral. It plunges into the red flesh of the earth.' Gill (1988) however argues that such a reported identification with the pre-colonial earth was just the popularisation by White Americans of a classical European Earth Mother, images of Pocahantas as an Amazon Queen, or of the New World as a passive female awaiting penetration.

5 Commonly attributed to Smohalla, this quote Gill (ch. 3) argues is a European invention.
6 Turner 1969: 99–100.
7 The common association of women with fertility, motherhood, earth and origins places them in a new position when the power of men is subject to the colonisers and is thus locally compromised:

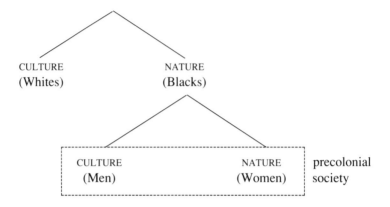

CULTURE   NATURE
(Whites)   (Blacks)

CULTURE   NATURE   precolonial
(Men)   (Women)   society

In societies where the subdominant group becomes a 'minority' of the wider community, its women become 'closer' to the Whites, as we have seen for *respectability-reputation*:

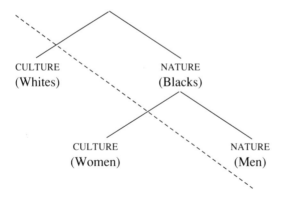

CULTURE   NATURE
(Whites)   (Blacks)

CULTURE   NATURE
(Women)   (Men)

8 Hawthorn 1955: 258.
9 The 'Babylon' of Daniel was itself allegorical and represented the contemporary Jewish subjection to Antiochus Epiphanes. 'Rome' was an earlier usage of Rastas and, in response to Mussolini, Garvey fulminated 'The Rome of sin and human hate has plagued the world before.'
10 Hill 1975: 219; Fox 1952: latter part. They included the antinominian followers of

Nayler (Hill 1984). On Nevis, Quakers had 'the run of the island' (Lovejoy 1985: 139).

11 Hill 1984; P. Wilson 1974: 30–1. The number of Maroons and other ex-slaves among the pirates is not clear but they are certainly mentioned by contemporaries (Defoe's *A General History of the Pyrates*).

12 Hill 1984: 22; Taussig 1987: 46.

13 Wood 1968: 39.

14 Ernest Troeltsch, *The Social Teaching of the Christian Churches*, cited by Wilson 1973: 12.

15 Radical Masonry addressed egalitarian, democratic, secular, and at times revolutionary, possibilities (Bernal 1987). The French refugees were not by any means all legitimists, and included 'free coloureds' as well as Whites. The radicals disappeared temporarily into the bush when the British arrived but Trinidad continued as a hotbed of republican sentiment: national insurrections (often 'radical Masonic') on the Spanish Main were frequently launched from the island.

16 Maude 1904: 20.

17 Christopher Hill's phrase. To draw a distinction between pantheism and an animate earth (hylozoism) is not always easy (cf. Collingwood 1945).

18 Cf. Mother Earth's Fadam (Father Adam) and the antanaclasis Sun/Son. Winstanley too equated Sun and Son, but derived Adam from 'a' and 'dam' (1973: 63).

19 One of the latter, the Tropical Emigration Society seems to have been the only major communitarian experiment in Trinidad before the Earth People. It was 'rational', planning to use sailing vessels, the wind for which would be provided by engines on the ships, and to build giant refrigerators on shore after arrival (Wood 1968: 84–9).

20 The Moravians intermarried with Amerindians, and the Shakers, who had Black members, were possessed by the spirits of Eskimos and American Indians. The Quakers actually encouraged new tribal religions such as the Puget Sound Shakers.

21 K. Thomas 1984: 291.

22 Woodcock and Avakumovic 1968: 176.

23 R. A. Knox cited by K. Thomas 1984: 50.

24 Hobsbawm 1959: 2, 22; R. Labry, *Autour du Moujik* (Paris 1923) cited by Hobsbawm p. 26.

25 Maurice and Jean Bloch, 'Women and the Dialectics of Nature in Eighteenth-Century French Thought', in MacCormack and Strathern (eds.) 1980.

26 De Beauvoir 1972: 99.

27 Genesis 9.3.

28 Quoted in K. Thomas 1984: 138.

29 Quoted in Easlea 1980: 129, 247–8. Thomas argues that the Christian notion of Nature as existing for Man was first transformed into an autonomous mechanical domain accessible to scientific investigation and only later into a Romantic 'Nature in itself' which was opposed to the Social. He sees the pantheism of the seventeenth-century radicals as influencing the later Romantic phase, while Hill emphasises their direct materialist contribution to the developing mechanical science.

30 Wood 1968: 24–5, 19.

31 V. S. Naipaul 1976: 17. The novel may be read as a commentary on the 1970 uprising in Trinidad.

32 Jean Besson 1987: 15; S. Naipaul 1985: 78.

33 Quoted in Kerr 1952: 87.

34 Nordhoff 1966: 235. The 'modernists', Winstanley and Rousseau, saw the primary fault as property (leading to spiritual alienation); others argued spiritual alienation led to material alienation.

35 Woodcock and Avakumovic 1968: 117–18.

36 *Ibid.*: 176–7; a good example of the 'cyclical' concerns of the counter-current (on which see Luhrman 1989).

37 E.g. A. F. C. Wallace (1956a: 272) who cites various psychotic patients who identified with 'the Great Mother Earth'.

38 Woodcock and Avakumovic 1968: 92; Maude 1904: 144.

39 Lincoln 1961: 73.

40 J. E. C. Harrison 1979: 40.

41 Cohn 1957: 287–332; C. Hill 1975; 1987.

42 Lovejoy 1985: 89, 95.

43 He was interviewed the previous week by Martha Beckwith who did not find him particularly abnormal (Beckwith 1929: 168–70).

44 V. S. Naipaul 1980: 13; Laennec Hurbon, 'New Religious Movements in the Caribbean', in Beckford 1986: 164–6; La Barre 1969; 1984; S. Naipaul 1981: 224; Harris 1900: passim; Fauget 1944.

45 C. Hill 1972: 227, 162.

46 Handler 1968: 4.

47 Trilling 1971: passim.

48 Now shifted to the libertarian Right; many of the 1980s *nouveaux philosophes* had been members of the counter-culture.

49 As Ann Hale and Mary Hawkins point out in 'Eggs Not Sex: The Functionalism of Germaine Greer', *Anthropology Today*, 1: 2 (1985), pp. 21–3. (See also Theodore Roszack's *Person Planet: The Creative Disintegration of Industrial Society*, New York, Doubleday, 1978.) To paraphrase Ernest Gellner (1964: 4), 'Life has come to be lived on a downward slope.' The near-paranoid concern with recycling and the preservation of bounded steady-state systems is mocked brilliantly in an essay in Shiva Naipaul's *Black and White* (1981): our return to a cyclical 'peasant' relationship with Nature is predicated on a somewhat non-peasant notion of Spaceship Earth.

50 Edward O. Wilson, *Biophilia: The Human Bond With Other Species*, Harvard University Press, 1984.

51 Blurb to Janet and Colin Bord, *Earth Rites: Fertility Practices in Pre-industrial Britain* (St Albans, Paladin, 1982, their emphasis) in which 'ecology' is equated with the worship of Mother Earth through fertility magic: 'actually . . . accumulating natural energy and directing it into the earth – impregnating and fertilising the Earth Mother' (p. 67). Failure to do so results in cancer and heart disease. By 1989 everybody in Britain, including the prime minister and the Archbishop of Canterbury seemed to have become ecologists (*The Times*, 19 September, pp. 1, 14). By 1990, the Bishop of Bath and Wells finally proclaimed God to be 'green' (*The Times*, 21 March, p. 28).

52 'Ecofeminism' (c. 1980) is perhaps not a generally accepted term but it conveys well the concerns of the movement and has been used in some anthologies, notably

in Leonie Caldecott and Stephanie Leland, eds., *Reclaim the Earth: Women Speak Out for Life on Earth*, London, Women's Press, 1983. See also Kristie Nelson, *The Origin: An Investigation into Primitive Matriarchal Societies, the Patriarchal Takeover and Its Effect on Society Today, And the Building of a Just and Egalitarian Post-Patriarchal Society*, San Francisco, Venusian Propaganda, 1979; Rosemary Reuther, *New Woman, New Earth*, New York, Seabury, 1975; Penelope Shuttle and Peter Redgrove, *The Wise Wound*, London, Gollancz, 1978; Susan Griffin, *Made From This Earth*, London, Women's Press, 1982.

53 Greer 1984.

54 Phyllis Chesler, *About Men*, London, Women's Press, 1978, p. 38.

55 Like Mother Earth, Robertson Smith argued that the Queen of Sheba was evidence of a primitive matriarchy. The usual schema offered by the Ecofeminists is that of a shamanic Neolithic culture in which femininity was prized (Neville Drury, *The Shaman and the Magician*, London, Routledge, 1982), and which worshipped The Goddess under various names – Isis, Hathor, Danu, Ishtar, Nana, Astarte – commonly represented naked with snakes entwined around her. (Like Mother Earth, some Ecofeminists identify this Big Moma with the Yoruba power Emanja – Adler 1986: 468; Luisah Teish, *Jambalaya*, San Francisco, Harper and Row, 1985.) The schema assumes matrilineal descent and property owning by women ('temple prostitutes' were really successful businesswomen, a little like Ghanaian market women). From about 3000 BC The Goddess was ousted by Indo-European invaders with their horses, patriarchal battle-axe cults, and gods of fire and storm: an Ur-kultur of Phallocentrism (Weston La Barre, *Mueolos*, Columbia University Press, 1982) represented in the cosmologies of the classical Middle East and Aegean. With euhemerism (Indra defeats Danu, Baal defeats Lota, etc.), The Goddess comes to be represented as a defeated serpent or dragon; paternity is now established, with female chastity and virginity prized.

56 Feminist science fiction is the mythic corpus of the Ecofeminists (Chrisa Wolf, *Cassandra*, London, Virago, 1983; Sara Maitland, *Virgin Territory*, London, Michael Joseph, 1984; Elizabeth Bains, *The Birth Machine*, London, Women's Press, 1983). William Burroughs has fought back on behalf of men: in his *The Place of Dead Roads* (New York, Holt, Rinehart and Winston, 1984), women are in league with alien body snatchers who have invented gun control. His remedy lies in men giving 'all our attention to experiments designed to produce asexual offspring, to cloning, use of artificial wombs and transfer operations'. Precisely what Mother Earth and the Ecofeminists say men are doing already (Corea 1988; Rita Arditti and Renate Duelli, *Test-Tube Women: What Future for Motherhood?*, London, Routledge and Kegan Paul, 1984). Women at Greenham Common delivered a baby together in protest against mechanised childbirth (M. Warner 1985: 59).

57 Marilyn French (the author of *Beyond Power: On Women, Men and Morals*, London, Cape, 1986) in *The Guardian*, 22 January 1986.

58 Petra Kelly, *Fighting for Hope*, New York, South End Press, 1984.

59 Adler 1986: 220.

60 *Ibid.*: 260–1.

61 Roszack 1970: 36.

62 Turner 1969.

63 M. Warner 1985: 60.

8 Incest: the naked earth

1 Parrinder 1953, 1954; Booth 1977b: 174; P. A. Talbot, *The People of Southern Nigeria* (Oxford University Press, 1926, cited by G. E. Simpson 1980). The dynamic and experiential transformations of such figurings as Yemanja through slavery and colonisation are of course elusive. My account is of a conjectural repertoire, an emotionally orientated theme and imagery of incest, a locus for the representation of the Mother, without presuming a Frazerian primacy of myth or that all its minutiae and ramifications were available to the young Jeanette as she participated in shango in the 1940s. Even when cultural continuity and history are destroyed and all seems overwhelmingly determined from the outside, an alternative world-view is not just determined by resistance but by the search for a counter-tradition in the given situation of shallow matrilineages.

2 Herskovits and Herskovits 1947; Carr 1952.

3 G. Howard Jones, *The Earth Goddess: A Study of Native Farming on the West African Coast* (London, Longmans, Green and Co., 1936); Ojo 1966: 165; Parrinder 1954: 47; McCall 1982.

4 The same deity may of course be associated with quite different, even opposed, aspects of the natural world: the Moroccan Aisha Quandashi (who may have a West African origin) is both siren and earth goddess (Crapanzano 1973: 141ff.). She is resisted by plunging a steel knife into the earth, an act recalling Mother Earth's prohibition.

5 Horton 1983: 60–1; André 1987: 255; Bastide: 200. Gordon Lewis (1983: 190) does cite a seventeenth-century account of Jamaican slaves venerating the Earth as 'the primordial life-giving force'.

6 Herskovits 1958: 50, 106–7, 93.

7 Charles Dance, *Chapters from a Guianese Log-Book* (Demerara, 1881), reprinted in part in Abrahams and Szwed 1983: 147–53; p. 141; G. E. Simpson 1980: 234. In the 1980s an 'imaginary' Mammy Water Cult occasioned 'mass hysteria' among Nigerian schoolchildren (Ebigbo and Anyaegbuna). Wintrob suggests her Liberian counterpart is of New World Creole inspiration. Oshun was the presiding power of a small Trinidadian-Grenadan group known as Emanja's Children (Smith 1963: 110).

8 Sirene is depicted as a naked woman, sometimes as a snake (Kurt Bachman, *Popular Paintings from Haiti*, London, Arts Council, 1969, Plates 36 and 71, cover).

9 J. W. Williams 1979: 172–3; Beckwith 1929: 102–3, 122; 191, 171.

10 Anthony Williams, personal communication; Bastide 1979: 328; Simpson 1978: 181; A. J. Langguth, *Macumba: White and Black Magic in Brazil* (New York, Harper and Row, 1975), picture p. 138. She is a 'genuflect, exuberant, nude, steatopygic woman with a prominent belly' (E. De Magrilhaes, *Orixas de Bahia*, 1977, p. 122, trans. Langguth).

11 References for this paragraph: Booth 1977b: 162, 167; John M. Janzen, 'The Tradition of Renewal in Kongo Religion', in Booth 1977a: 77; McCall 1982: 169–70.

12 McCall 1982: 170, 176. Androgyneity continues in Brazil where Oxala (Obatala) is merged with Oduduwa (Bastide 1979: 251), but is identified with Jesus. Whatever

the gender ambiguities of powers in Africa, in the Americas they tend to be identified with one sex.

13 McCall 1982: 165.

14 *Ibid.*: 173.

15 Booth 1977a: 165, quoting Idowu.

16 Paragraph references: Morton-Williams 1962: 364; Booth 1977a: 165; Simpson 1980: 61–3, 149. 'Edam' is perhaps derived in part from the Yoruba power Edam (or Eden). Other creolising fraternities such as the S. Thoma society of Sierra Leone signify gender equality by spiritual rebirth from a forest spirit which has both vagina and scrotum.

17 Mother Earth inverts the understandings of Science: in her theageny, relations between a Black male and his mother create White people; from the historical and sociological perspective, Whites have 'created' Black West Indians.

18 Any mythic schema, African or European, offers a variety of possible continuities, interpretations and practices. The mystic meditating on the unity of all things; the pragmatic dedication to a saint or orisha; the fraternities dedicated to particular cults; the legalists and historians of religious authority; the ecstatic unity of worshipper and divinity; each selects, revises and contributes. In the ancient European, Gnostic, Hermetic, Kabbalistic, and other cosmogonies, as these are available locally in high science, we can identify one progression within the genealogies from an undifferentiated first principle, female, to sexually differentiated humans. To an extent this may be ratiocination within a tradition ('where then did we come from?') but one might also wonder how much our available sources themselves reflect on some possible internal transformation in the myth which has resonated with social changes in supposed historical time 'out there' (euhemerism), changes which rationalise or carry the transformation. High science, like Ecofeminism, argues such a progression from an original matriarchy, revering a supreme, parthenogenic but androgynous, moon goddess to solar patriarchy. Given the retrieval of 'a myth' from a set of overlapping fragments it is not too difficult to find such a sequence in any European myth of origin; we are not however concerned here with ourselves delineating some 'real' mythic transformation in historical time 'out there' but simply with perceiving the possibilities of our theme – divine incest by a rebellious son – in sources available to Mother Earth, and in their codification as a particular euhemerism, common to popular antiquarianism (of the Matriarchs and Menhirs, Arthurian ley lines and Glastonbury type) and the high science of Trinidad. For want of a better term, we may call this 'Hermetic euhemerism': an account of 'myth' in general which itself may be said to constitute a myth in that narrative time 'out there' is subordinated to some cosmogonic unfolding; its most developed variant is Jung's Analytical Psychology which argues that the cosmic and historical drama is recapitulated psychologically and physiologically in every individual, and that our shift to patriarchy has not been entirely beneficial: to fulfil ourselves men and women alike now have to return to the Great Mother inside us all. The other leading variant – in which history 'out there' drives the myth rather than the reverse (euhemerism proper) – Engels' Marxism assumes, with Freud, that the shift has been irrevocable and, on the whole, is in our best interests. The Women's Movement has moved from such an 'evolutionary' euhemerism to the Jungian. The sources available to the Earth People in the

Hermetic tradition of high science are mythical schemata but also methodologies: anti-ritualistic, transformative, aimed at 'know[ing] yourself' as both Mother Earth and the Gnostics (Pagels 1982: i) put it. Programmatically, they have proved capable of articulating a variety of anti-establishment movements, frequently in association with the revaluing of women's roles; to invert the ancient revolt of the solar hero against Nature we must ourselves rebel against patriarchal society. In its euhemerist variant it identifies cosmogony both with history 'out there' and with personal experience: through recapitulation every individual continues within themselves the conflict between Moon and Sun, Mother and Son, between female and male, between life and science. The psychological, the historical and the cosmogonic are collapsed into each other: each may develop a primacy, of which the others are reflections; each may be understood as personalised or processual.

19 It is difficult to conduct an interview with a divinity about the intimate details of her early life. Concerning actual physical incest with any of her sons I felt unable to enquire in 1981. For the reasons I suggest below, I think this improbable. Her partner and her adult sons Pomme Cythère and Martin (who was the one 'pushed back') found the possibility hilariously unlikely. In 1991 I asked her younger sisters: both derided the idea. They did say that she had been rather 'proper' and naive as a girl, easily 'led astray by men who took advantage on her'.

20 For the personal life of domestic servants in colonial Trinidad, and the sometimes disastrous consequences of their pregnancies, Bridges' memoir and De Boissiere's novel are poignant sources.

21 The psychoanalytic perspective usually ignores Jocasta in favour of the hero. Olivier (1989) however offers a feminist rereading which emphasises the powerful feelings she has for her son. Rather than look at Jocasta herself – like Oedipus, a somewhat unwitting protagonist in the original myth – we might consider the more motivated instance of Phaedra. She is enamoured of her stepson, Hippolytus: not her biological son admittedly but Seneca's text is full of talk of incest – 'Do you intend to be the common spouse of son and father? . . . Even the beasts abhor forbidden unions; instinct teaches proper respect for laws of generation' – and no psycho-analyst would balk at 'step-son' for 'son'. Phaedra is the cousin of the Minotaur killed by her husband Theseus, who abducted Hippolytus' mother, an Amazon. If, with Jungian euhemerism, we take the killing of the mother as the victory of patriarchy over matriarchy then, as Phaedra carries out Venus' revenge for the heliocentric victory ('she hates all children of the Sun, and now through us she takes revenge for what was done to her'), incest – dubious paternity and thus 'mother-right' – returns to undermine the novel 'father-right'.

22 Even if, as R. T. Smith urges, the sociologist should not interpret the Black family by comparison with the White ideal, that is certainly what happens locally. Dann (1988: 14–22) recounts painful tales told by men of their 'absent father'. In a previous critique (1989) I draw extensively on Calvin Hernton's remarkable *Sex and Racism* (London, Deutsch, 1969) which makes the point that if the Black male may be said to be psychologically 'emasculated' he is not emasculated by his Black female partner but by the White male.

23 'The tie between parents and children – especially mothers and sons – is closer and more durable than that between marital partners. Young men often continue to depend on maternal care well into their twenties and thirties and in some

communities a man rarely thinks of marrying so long as he has [his mother] to look after his meals, mend his clothes and care for his living quarters' (Peter Wilson cited in Lowenthal 1972: 106). Handwerker (1989) argues that women in Barbados may be said to 'invest' in children, particularly sons, who continue to support their mothers financially in later life. She suggests that a complex of 'modernisation' (a shift from mutual assistance to wages based on individual 'ability', with depersonalisation of social roles, and increased equality and conflict between the sexes) leaves children with less economic value for women who have reduced their fertility accordingly. In Trinidad, not so intensively industrialised as Barbados, female fertility has dropped since the 1960s but less rapidly (*ibid.*: 208).

24 And hence prohibited lest it pass from unconscious fantasy to physical incest. 'The worst insult in our language is to curse a man's mother. An "obscenity" flung in the heat of quarrel is, quite simply, "Yu mother"' (quoted by Keith Warner 1982: 104). André (1987) argues that never-consummated mother–son incest is the psychological key to West Indian society, a complex originating in slavery and continuing today. His evidence, a psychoanalytical interpretation of homicide trials in Guadeloupe, would not be convincing to the non-analyst. Deleuze and Guattari criticise the application of psychoanalytic theories (derived from 'Oedipal' European families) to colonial contexts but argue that colonialism itself 'Oedipalises': 'It is strange that we had to wait for the dreams of colonised people in order to see that, on the vertices of the pseudotriangle, mommy was dancing with the missionary, daddy was being fucked by the tax collector, while the self was being beaten by a white man' (p. 96).

25 'Children starting from young in the school, even in their home. Sometimes their parents are poor in a little one room. Children gets up in the night and take up what they haven't got to take up. What I am seeing here in my country Trinidad, the children go around whilst you think you are protecting them, they do their own thing, even small children, very small, at the age of five, six years, these children going through sexual intercourse without even knowing what they are doing. I've seen it myself within my own little family. If they don't know it home they know it in the school. So they start this thing before their bodies even ready for it' (M.E.).

26 Arlow 1951; Roheim 1940.

27 It is a recent theme for Black American feminists (Alice Walker's *The Colour Purple*) and by the late 1980s was frequently cited in the Trinidadian popular press ('Fatal Attraction', *The Bomb*, 4 March 1988; 'Incest Drama in Tobago Count', *Sunday Punch*, 27 March 1988). André (1987: 134) argues that in Guadeloupe sex between a mother's live-in lover and her daughter is virtually inevitable: *Si an mété on nonm an case an moin, sé ké pou ti-fille la aussi.*

28 Or indeed both. Such as those who lost their own children and went on to become the Mother of the deity or even a 'male' prophet: Joanna Southcott and Sayo Kitamura the founder of the contemporary Japanese Tensho sect (Takie Lebra, personal communication).

29 Unusually one celibate woman became a Hasidic *rebbe*; when she married she had to give it up (Littlewood 1984). Prophetic Sinhalese women cannot bear children, 'a worldly and impure process' (Obeyesekere 1981: 56).

30 Andrews 1953: 8.

31 Galatians 3: 28; I Corinthians II.3.

32 Quoted in M. Warner 1983: 154.
33 Quoted in Ardt 1965: 583. Like the *mothers* these hermaphrodites had only one eye.
34 Andrews 1953: 158. 'Androgynous deities' are found in Mormonism, Christian Science (where God is sometimes called 'Mother-Father') and Unitarianism.
35 His current name, Jakatan, was given to him in the Valley by a passer-by and there is no agreement as to its meaning. It recalls the *lakatan* plantain and thus resembles the fruit names of the other Earth People, but also *jakalantan*, a nature sprite which misleads people in the bush. 'Jakuta' is a name for Shango (the thunderer who fights – *ja*, with stones – *okuta*). Whilst there are cognate names for Shango elsewhere in the Americas (Dzakuta in Bahia, Charuta in Cuba), I did not come across them in Trinidad. Genesis 10: 25 refers to one Joktan in whose brother's time 'the earth was divided'; there is a possibility that the visitor – like many to the Valley, an avid biblical reader – saw some connection. One villager suggested *dieu écoutant* (the God who listens) while another, who knew him, favoured *pas écoutant* (not listening)!
36 Simpson 1980: 18; 1978: 89; Bastide 1979: 252; Booth 1977a: 169; Herskovits 1958 (1941): 252.
37 Parkin, 'Introduction' in Parkin ed. 1985: 8–9.
38 Littlewood and Lipsedge 1989; Gilman 1985.
39 Rahner 1962: 72.
40 Burridge 1971: 27. Compare the rural Guatemalan revering of Judas. Simpson (1978: 217) argues that the Black slaves regarded the Devil as 'a friend in need', and Worsley (1970: 88) recalls that among war-time Melanesian cults 'Djaman [German] was favoured as an anti-Government tongue.' Madame Blavatsky is supposed to have said to Yeats 'I used to wonder and pity the people who sell their souls to the Devil, but now I only pity them. They have to have someone on their side', like the Devil supplicated by the infamous Canon Docre in Huysman's *Là-Bas*: 'Mainstay of the Despairing Poor, Cardinal of the Vanquished, King of the Disinherited.'
41 Taussig 1980: xi; Silverblatt 1987; cf. Carlo Ginsburg's *Night Battles*.
42 Morton 1952: 19. Blake however contrasted a material Sun (Urizen – 'Your Reason' – the Old Testament God, and the conqueror of Africa and originator of slavery) with a second spiritual Sun (Urthona – 'Earth Owner' – the ultimate creator of the planet over which he, like Mother Earth, had appointed Urizen as regent). The Mexican revival in D. H. Lawrence's *The Plumed Serpent* claims that the Whites have obtained their power from the 'second strength' which lies behind the sun.
43 Gordon Lewis 1983: 41. 'A little, little woman carry a big, big moon' (a Tobagonian wake song quoted in Abrahams 1983: 61). The Spaniards too regarded the 'inconstancy' of the Caribs as due to lunar influences (Lewis: 96).
44 I remember the sheer horror of a new member of the Earth People as a (highly poisonous) mapapi slithered about under our roof. I myself was never concerned about snakes whilst in the Valley but once outside, the mere sight of one occasioned complete panic.
45 M. Warner 1976: 268–9; Obeyesekere 1981. To take the Jungian position: 'The open womb is the devouring symbol of the urobonic mother, especially when connected with phallic symbols. The gnashing mouth of the Medusa's head with its

boar's tusks betrays these features most plainly, while the protruding tongue is obviously connected with the phallus. The snapping – i.e. castrating – womb appears as the jaws of hell. The serpents writhing around Medusa's head are not personalistic – pubic hairs – but aggressive phallic elements characterising the fearful element of the uroboric womb' (Erich Neumann, *Origins and History of Consciousness*, Princeton University Press, 1973, p. 83). Polysemous indeed, for the female and male referents may be achieved both metaphorically (skin shedding, phallus) and by opposition and thus association (the deity represented together with a snake is usually female).

46 Ojo 1966: 160; Parrinder 1949; Abrahams and Szwed 1983; Barrett 1976: 192.

47 Needham 1973.

48 Inversions are common in picong: 'When women are wild you call them *rats*; when a man is wild you call him a *star*' (Rodman 1971: 61, my emphasis).

49 John Berger, *Ways of Seeing*, Harmondsworth, Penguin, 1973, p. 54. Robert Graves puts it rather well:

> For me, the naked and the nude
> (By lexicographers construed
> As synonyms that should express
> The same deficiency of dress
> Or shelter) stand as wide apart
> As love from lies, or truth from art

(In Graves, *Selected by Himself*, Harmondsworth, Penguin Books, 1972, p. 131.) The distinction is also made by Fischer (1964). That one is 'stark naked' not 'stark nude' suggests that nakedness is to be taken as some state of elemental innocence.

50 Kenneth Clark, *The Nude: A Study of Ideal Art* (London, Murray, 1956). He is vague as to how such an ideal is constituted at different (or indeed at any) periods. As Berger points out, Clark avoids the politics of the nude in Western art, particularly her transformation into an object to be possessed by her (male) owner. Manet's painting *Olympia* caused consternation by its frank and 'naturalistic' variation of the odalisque; the prostitute portrayed gazes calmly out of the canvas at the observing male – the nude becomes the naked. Similar male outrage has greeted feminist accustions that medical interest in the woman's body is hardly disinterested (e.g. Jordanova 1989). As we have seen (p. 119), Nature when faced with the explorations of Science was frequently represented by a naked (or rather, nude) woman.

51 There were 'good' and 'bad' nudes in Christianity, with various coalescences and transformations (M. Warner 1985). Mary Magdalene and Mary of Egypt went naked in the desert in a penance which both represents and returns them to the sensuality of the flesh. The most famous British nude is Lady Godiva, often portrayed, like the Virgin, as a sort of redeeming anti-Eve, Good-Eve (*ibid.*: p. 310). Blake simply identified the Virgin with Eve.

52 Maude 1904: 241; S. Ardener 1983. Tolstoy complained their nudity was 'perverted' and it may have been initiated by a visiting American nudist.

53 Shirley Ardener, 'Nudity, Vulgarity and Protest', *New Society*, 27 (1974), pp. 704–5. For nude jogging see *The Times*, 9 December 1987; for skyclad witches,

Adler 1986. The 'informality' is illustrated well by Neal Acheson's account of East German nudist beaches along the Baltic ('The Surprise of Solidarity', *New York Review of Books*, 26 April 1983, p. 7): 'Citizens of that most guarded and suspicious society approach one another without introductions and hastily tell the secrets of their lives . . . Then, without giving their names, they rise and walk away.'

54 Wood 1968: 156; E. Braithwaite 1971; K. Singh, *Bloodstained Tombs: The Muharran Massacre 1884* (London, Macmillan, 1988, pp. 4, 56, 76); Webber 1978: 150; the accounts quoted in Abrahams and Szwed (1983: 283). Wood (pp. 150, 126) notes that the Creoles criticised the newly arrived Indians who 'generally go naked and show no disposition to abandon this habit', and their Loyal West Indian League urged the suppression of 'nudity' among the Indians. Carnival however was associated with children going naked (p. 245), and a continuing Ole Mass on Carnival Monday are the virtually naked Mud People.

55 M. G. Smith 1963: 121

56 *Bag* (sack) was traditional slave clothing in the Americas (Webber 1978: 13–14) and is still associated with poverty and vagrancy although it is used for bedding and occasionally work overclothes.

57 Particularly partial dress (see p. 11, her remarks about discotheques), again agreeing with the anthropologist Fischer (1964) in opposition to what he calls 'the fig-leaf theory' (clothes preserve modesty). The debate goes back to Burton's *Anatomy of Melancholy* where he wonders if 'the greatest provocations of lust are from our apparell'. Flugel points out that 'naturalist' groups in Europe say public nudity reduces sexual interest (recalling Westermarck's 'exposure leads to sexual indifference' theory of incest avoidance), and argues himself (1950: 109) that exhibitionism 'drains off sexual energy'. By contrast, another psychoanalyst, Sandor Ferenczi (*Nakedness as a Means of Inspiring Terror*, in *Further Contributions to the Theory and Technique of Psychoanalysis*, London, Hogarth, 1926), suggests the pleasure of exhibiting oneself naked derives from 'repressed libido'.

58 The leader of an English Camisard group, in an action recalling that of Mother Earth (p. 7 above), 'would lift up her clothes before a company of men and women believers, crying out "come in Christ, come in Christ, come in"' (J. E. C. Harrison 1979: 234).

59 Ardener 1983: 256, 253.

9 The Beginning of the End: everyday life in the valley

1 The terms are Bateson's (1973). If we were talking of self-reproducing social formations, we might argue some analogy with models of descent and alliance.

2 Clinton Jean, 'History as Fable', *The Watch* (the Brandeis University magazine), 4: 6 (1983), pp. 6–11. I am grateful to Bernard Wasserstein for bringing this article to my attention. I have not been able to make contact with the author. Did he know about Mother Earth? He does not refer to her, and in 1983 her ideas had not been published in any detail. That the Whites are People of Ice – greedy, materialistic and seeking domination over the (Black) Sun People – is also maintained by Leonard Jeffries, Chair of the Department of African–American Studies at New York's City College (*The Times*, 15 August 1991).

3 McCall 1982.

4 Preston, 'Conclusion', in Preston 1982.

5 Coconut grater made by punching holes in a tin can.

6 The events sound like something from the Acts of the Apostles or Fox's *Journal*. The Earth People had come naked to the court early on the day appointed for their hearing, found the door open and entered. The janitor arrived to discover the door miraculously locked again, and on unlocking it found the group lined up inside waiting patiently.

7 Earl Lewis, 'Discrimination at Home', *Moko*, no. 12, Port-of-Spain, 11 April 1969, p. 4. The bridge over the East Dry River separates central Port-of-Spain from the poorer eastern areas.

8 A *guard* against obeah, itself hardly innocent.

9 Local Rastas wear caps or woollen tams, and baseball boots or sandals.

10 A. S. Ahmed, 'Death In Islam: the Hawkes Bay Case', *Man* (ns) 21 (1986), pp. 120–34.

11 The desire to return to childhood is frequently cited as an attraction of those religious movements which replicate the family (e.g. Beckford 1975: 219; 1985: passim; p. 154 above).

12 The reasons for joining which sect members give to an outsider not surprisingly follow those expected by their ideology (Beckford 1985: 174). As Beckford has noted (1975: 126), particular concerns of sociologists of religion have been 'Why do people join?' and 'Why do they remain?' He groups the dominant explanations as (a) frustration/compensation (relative deprivation); (b) world-view construction; and (c) social solidarity. A problem with psychological explanation is that it is never entirely clear whether they refer to actors' own explanations, those of the academic, or both together. Thus Beckford's model of relative deprivation only implicitly assumes that it has to be consciously perceived by the actors. The type of reception theory I have outlined here is concerned with intellectual congruence or 'fit' between innovator and follower and thus closer to model (b) than either (a) or (c). The last, social solidarity, appears self-evident for any social organisation which is set up, while the first, frustration/compensation, would take us into the type of social psychology I have endeavoured to avoid as again self-evident – an actors' account masquerading as explanation. I see little value in such terms as maintenance, rationalisation, routinisation, desecularisation, situational contingency, induction, commitment, solidarity, cohesion, control, tension, reinforcement, cognitive dissonance, let alone 'success'. As I suggest in Chapter 2, they slide easily into a language of pathologisation or banal functionalism. Lofland and Stark ('Becoming a World Saver: A Theory of Conversion to a Deviant Perspective', *American Sociological Review*, 30 (1965), pp. 862–75) look at the 'motivation problem': an individual must (i) experience enduring, acutely felt tensions (ii) within a religious problem-solving perspective (iii) which leads him to define himself as a religious seeker (iv) encountering the group at a turning point in his life (v) wherein an affective bond is formed (iv) and extra-cult attachments are neutralised or absent, and where (vii) if he becomes a 'deployable agent', he is exposed to an intensive interaction. This seems reasonable enough as a description and would be generally true of those who have joined Mother Earth, allowing for a somewhat less dramatic process of joining which makes the term 'conversion' inappropriate. As to the 'turning point', most of the Earth People seemed to have joined just because Mother

Earth happened to be recruiting nearby. While I prefer Berger's refreshingly atheoretical suggestion that recruits just happen to 'hear the rhythms of a different drummer coming through the spheres' (1981: 198, an image I think from Thoreau), there are of course personal differences between those who joined and those who did not. While the susceptible individual is one who must resonate with the drummer's new rhythms, I think it is significant that those members who joined for 'psychological reasons' – Corn, Zabocca and Mango Rose – soon left.

13 Cohn 1957: 59.

14 The 'valley' is a common image in the literature of anakhoretic utopias (Butler's Erewhon) or other communities which are difficult for outsiders to enter or leave (Wells' Kingdom of the Blind). Sandra Paquet suggests that in West Indian literature 'going down into the valley [represents] a psychic journey into unexplored areas of self-identity and personal history' ('Introduction', in Selvon 1979: 2).

15 Giving me an eerie feeling of entering the detritus of a lost urban civilisation after some holocaust.

16 See Appendix 2. I am no musicologist but the songs and music of the Earth People which I recorded (and which must await further analysis) recall those of the Shouter Baptists: slow and lugubrious but with polyrhythms and extemporisations. The instruments are single-headed hide and wood drums (Plate 10) and chac-chacs. There was possibly a Fire Dance once in shango, and one was reported last century in the Bahamas; it was prefigured in The Burning (p. 73).

17 For *Cannabis sativa* in Trinidad see Littlewood 1988. Continued work is hardly necessary from the biological perspective: provision crops yield more than 5,000 calories per hour of labour (Watts 1990: 62).

18 Like hippie children who, as in the Valley, are given small amounts of ganja but no alcohol (Berger 1981).

19 'Disengagement' rather than 'apostasy' – Beckford's terms (1985: 135–6).

20 Hunt 1984. The term 'transparency' derives from Jean Storinski.

21 It has much in common with the 'woodtick' described by J. R. Hall (1978) in hippie communes.

22 This prohibition may have more of a local origin than I appreciate. Thresholds elsewhere are associated with transitions and oppositions, particularly those of sexual activity (blocked door recalls Mother Earth's obstructed labour?). In Trinidad, thresholds and windows are places where nature spirits could enter and they are protected by religious images, like the openings into Shouter chapels where lighted candles and chalked seals are placed during meetings.

23 'Dirt eating' among West Indian slaves was regarded as a form of suicidal rebellion; it may also have been consequent on intestinal parasitosis (E. Braithwaite 1971: ch. 7; Kiple 1984: ch. 6; Gordon Lewis 1983: 177).

24 Dissident members who left after my own departure later recalled their vision of a garbage truck depositing a White (The Bomb, Port-of-Spain, 15 January 1982). Dreams which explain arrivals and departures are common in hippie communes (J. R. Hall 1978: ch. 4).

25 'She frighten' and a priest had arm around her an' she says "Mother you take you' tablets. You mad". I say "I don' take tablets. I ai' mad". I ask "You want to return?" She start say yes an' priest come an' she say no.' This is the daughter whose arm was 'broken' during the Miracle and who was ashamed when walking naked

through Pinnacle (pp. 7, 47). Talking with her in 1991 corroborated Mother Earth's account. Another daughter used to visit the Valley and go naked there, even bringing her friends out for a 'holiday' (her word).

26 Trinidad *home names* (nicknames) are frequently the names of fruit (there is an Eddoes in Naipaul's *Miguel Street*).

27 I Esdras 4? Or a reversal of Genesis 3: 16?

28 1952, adapted from C. S. Forester's novel. 'The African Queen' of the title is in fact a boat. I do not find such sources 'trivial'; as John Beattie noted, the braided headbands of Native Americans derive from the problems of Hollywood actors keeping their wigs on (Jahoda 1982: 154).

29 As Alfred Schutz and Thomas Luckman noted in *The Structures of the Life World* (Illinois, Northwestern University Press, 1973, pp. 182–229), this type of contradiction can be recognised by the group as a central theme rather than being merely an awkward 'problem': the distinction is the observer's. For the Earth People, the conflict between the Mother and her Son recurs in contemporary society and thus in the contradictions within the group and within each member.

30 Eliade's 'nostalgia for eternity' (1954). By 'apocalyptic time' I mean a sense of living in a continuous present, beyond everyday space and time, which reflects the real, original and final, state of the cosmos: a collapsing of both cyclical mythical time and historical linear time 'out there' into an experienced everyday (cf. Edmund Leach, *Rethinking Anthropology*, London, Athlone, 1961, pp. 132–6).'The Last Day', 'eternity's sunrise'. Burridge has argued (1985) that millennial moments occur as we abandon the 'cyclical' time of small-scale communities, which reproduce themselves through close interpersonal relations (Lévi-Strauss' supernal time), for historical linear time 'out there': from the outside the millennial moment seems to 'suspend time' during the period of social crisis. If, as Gellner suggests, societies seem to live particularly orientated to a past foundation, to an approaching end or to an undifferentiated present, post-colonial West Indians effectively live in the last; the foundation (slavery) is generally repressed, nor is there any particular point to which events are leading. While contemporary Black Christianity talks in a millennial idiom, it is, Rastafari perhaps excepted, 'present-centred'. However we interpret the temporal aspects of the 'sacred' and the 'profane' (Stirrat 1984), the End for the Earth People certainly recalls Eliade's notion of the sacred as a 'return to the beginnings of time' (*The Myth of the Eternal Return*), a denial of time cyclical as well as linear, a collapse of the temporal life into the eternal, Kermode's *aevum*. The community are however only at the Beginning of the End: temporal events still happen. While the passage of days, seasons, tides and the phases of the moon are observed as Natural, the Earth People also mark Social time by the passage of the Tobago ferry out at sea and the flights of the coastguard helicopter (which, for me, together with the Earth People, irresistibly recalls the cinema of Miklos Jansco).

31 In an uncontrolled drug-induced experience.

32 A Baptist passed by and said the local river was Jordan and the Valley was Eden. He informed them that the world would end the following week; they thought it unlikely and he departed. Another told them they were correct – there would be a famine – but they should plant only cassasva. A passing Muslim agreed they could wear bag but said it should really be green! As J. R. Hall points out (1978: 241),

visiting prophets who try to persuade communes to go in new directions seem to be a vocational hazard.

33 B. Wilson 1970: 13. The African Apostles however encouraged their anthropologist Jules-Rosette (1975: ch. 8) to join. She did so, later to found the American branch of the church. See also Samuel Sandweiss' extraordinary *Sai Baba: The Holy Man and the Psychiatrist* (San Diego, Birth Day Co., 1975).

34 The article was requested by the paper but never published, for unspecified reasons, possibly because of the forthcoming general election and a general sensitivity about 'race'.

35 Herskovits said the game was once known in Trinidad (1958: 155) but I found no trace of it although I have played it in the Leeward Islands. It is known among the Ashanti from whence presumably it passed to the Caribbean (Herskovits, 'Wari in the New World', *Journal of the Royal Anthropological Institute*, 62 (1932), pp. 23–7).

36 SELF: I should go out and do some work.
   CARMEN: In rain? You heated you know.
   SELF: The Earth People do.
   CARMEN: They beast!
   SELF: You ate their pumpkin.
   CARMEN: An' a next piece! Next time you go bring some corn, turtle . . .

37 And, it was rumoured, an Indian girlfriend. His father's friends told me he was not serious about the Earth People but he remained loyal to Mother Earth after the defections of 1982 (*The Bomb*, Port-of-Spain, 3 February 1984).

38 Was my departure instrumental in the crisis? A group predicated on a radical polarisation between Black and White, and in which the former were developing a community in opposition to White society, is hardly likely to have been assisted by a White anthropologist in their midst. Mother Earth was working for a return of Science into Nature. Was my departure her failure? To an extent my concern was allayed during a three-day stay by Pomme Cythère, Cocorite and Cassava with me the following week in Pinnacle. On the day of my departure from Trinidad two weeks after my next (and last) visit to the Valley, I was visited by Jakatan and some other members in Port-of-Spain at the Carmelite convent where my wife was working (ironically a sister convent of the one to which Mother Earth's daughter had been sent). Their protestations that the valley was always in a state of crisis and they hoped that my stay had not been spoiled by Mango Rose were not entirely reassuring. Final departure from Trinidad involved an extraordinary spectacle in Port-of-Spain, seen off on our flight by the two groups standing next to each other, Carmelites and Earth People.

39 Although this in turn seems to have led to further splits: 'Why We Left Mother Earth', *The Bomb*, 8 January 1982; 'We saw Rape and Attempted Murder', *ibid.*; 'Minister Meets the Earth People', *Trinidad Guardian*, 9 January 1982; 'Why We Don't Wear Clothes', *The Bomb*, 22 January 1982; 'Earth People Split', *Mirror*, 4 February 1983; 'Paradise Lost', *Express*, 26 March 1983; 'Eddoes: Dasheen Looking for Wife', *Mirror*, 21 June 1985; 'Eddoes: Dasheen and Breadfruit in My Garden', *Mirror*, 6 August 1985. The complaints about Mother Earth made by the dissidents, as refracted through the press, recalled lurid popular fantasy – group sex,

rape, brainwashing and attempted murder. Interestingly, one of the dissidents, Eddoes, posed for his press photograph together with his mother.

10 Genesis of meanings, limits of mimesis

1 'Coarse brain disease' is Schneider's term for brain tumours, aneurysms, etc. Compared with schizophrenia, manic-depressive psychosis is characterised by greater evidence for genetic associations and physiological changes – the so-called 'biological shift'. Devos argues that 'Some attempts should be made to examine cultural differences in thought content in situations where the same type of organically induced psychopathology can be compared' (1976: 286). This has only been attempted with drug induced states; we still lack a 'cross-cultural neurology', and cultural psychiatry has expended its energies in circular rather than dialectic arguments (Littlewood 1990).

2 The so-called 'Seligman error', C. G. Seligman (according to this interpretation) having failed to recognise severe psychopathologies in Melanesia as they were regularised into institutions. According to George Steiner, Thomas Bernard suggests something similar in his account of Wittgenstein and the philosopher's nephew Paul; both were similarly crazy but Ludwig's privileged academic position ensured the reproduction of his thought in scholarly monographs rather than, as for Paul, in psychiatric case notes ('Visibly Deranged', *Times Literary Supplement*, 22 July 1983): an idea taken up somewhat surprisingly by an editorial in *The Sun* newspaper ('Loopy Ludwig', 12 March 1991).

3 Gruenberg has provided a useful history of *folie communiquée*.

4 Cf. Wallis. Social isolation may of course precipitate a recognisable paranoid psychosis as is found not uncommonly among the deaf. Rousseau's eventual paranoia followed years of very real persecution by the French monarchy.

5 Cited in S. Naipaul 1981: 119. Or Chairman Mao's successor who argued he was senile (*The Observer*, 22 November 1987). Or the defecting Albanian official who declared Enver Hoxha a homosexual paranoiac (*The Independent*, 10 November 1987).

6 Fox 1952: 71–2. I am not suggesting here that Fox was insane, but the incident provides a neat analogy (cf. Herschmann and Lieb 1988: 144).

7 Devos derives the term from Theodore Schwartz ('The Cargo Cult: A Melanesian Type-Response to Change', in Devos, ed., *Responses to Change*, New York, Van Nostrand, 1976). Herschmann and Lieb argue that the two phases of manic-depressive psychosis are especially conducive to communication of inspiration. Mania inspires, while depression allows the slow working up of the innovation into a conventional form.

8 Devos restricts himself to the mimesis of states such as epilepsy, whose imitation Eliade (1964) describes in shamanism, while Radin (1953: 68) wonders if the origins of all religions might not lie in the mimesis of the manifestations of biological brain disease. Field suggests that organic hallucinations perpetuate witchcraft beliefs in rural Ghana (1960: 38–40, 43–6), and indeed may actually initiate them (p. 318). La Barre (1970: 316) cites F. E. Williams on Evara of the Vaihala Madness spreading 'a stylised epilepsy in his group apparently genuine in him originally'; in fact Williams (1934: 371–2) merely said Evara had 'ecstatic seizures' for some time before the movement began; for a more critical account of

the Western Pacific imitation of epilepsy see Hoskins 1967. The Native American Shakers institutionalised a form of shaking originally 'spontaneous' (Barnett 1953: 7). Similarly the manifestation of 'madness' may be used to recognise religious experience and the local community then attempt to distinguish 'mundane madness' from 'divine madness' (Morris 1985; McDaniel 1989), problematic where, as in Bengal, divine inspiration is often marked by antinomian acts. Consideration of the local psychology is necessary before we can consider whether terms analogous to 'madness' are being used in an extended sense or else prosaically (in a restricted, 'medical' sense). A similar antinomian attempt to 'provoke salvation' among Tibetan *smyo* monks is known as 'insane' (*smyo*) but the individuals concerned are not necessarily 'mad' in a strong sense (Ardossi and Epstein 1975).

9 Harner has argued that individual drugs may generate very specific experiences such as 'flying', but Eliade (1964) points out that 'flight' is common to all shamanic contexts and anyway has a universal supramundane significance. Reichel-Dolmatoff has proposed the pharmacological origin (*Banisteriopsis caapi*) of social representations among the Tukano such as those for exogamy. A similar argument has been used by Redgrove and Shuttle to characterise pregnancy visions as the consequences of hormonal changes, by Wasson to look at mythological themes as derived from the experience of *Amanita muscaria*, by Kennedy through *qat*, and by De Martino through the symptoms of tarantula bites.

10 'Collective' in England (as in Trinidad) popularly denotes 'shared rationality'.

11 Garrett 1975: 15.

12 Jarvie's terms. He effectively dismisses meaning in psychopathology and does not discuss the possibility of 'unintended' prophecy (1964: 92ff.).

13 Davis 1966; Lovejoy 1985. On his visit to Barbados in 1671 George Fox was at pains to defend himself against accusations that the Quakers were inciting the slaves to rebellion: 'For that which we have spoken and declared to them is to exhort and admonish them to be sober and to fear God, and to love their masters and mistresses, and to be faithful and diligent in their masters' service' (1952: 604–5). Slavery was already questioned by the Society; our 'innovators' gave the question salience.

14 B. Wilson 1975.

15 Quoted by Armytage (1961: 38). La Barre suggests *all* cultural innovation takes this route. On the contrary it seems to me that times are seldom so desperate that we seek solutions proposed by the conspicuously deviant. J. E. C. Harrison (1979: ch. 8), attempting to explain the occurrence of the eighteenth-century British millennialists, calls it a period of 'unprecedented change' but admits it is difficult to say one age is 'more anxious' than another; similarly Beckford (1986: 'Introduction'). Whatever our external analysis, 'desperate times' may be seen as such by the individuals concerned: the Doukhobors sought unusual prophets at times of community crisis (Hawthorn 1955: 172–5).

16 Hunter 1959. A similar prophecy to that of Richard Brothers over a hundred years later; Brothers however was committed to Bedlam (J. E. C. Harrison 1979: 60ff.). This Solomon Eccles may have been the Quaker of the same name who accompanied George Fox to the Caribbean in 1671 (Fox 1952: 601–2, 607–8, 627–8) but Fox does not describe any previous incidents of this type or comment on Eccles' mental balance. The Eccles of the brazier was a central character in Harrison Ainsworth's novel *Old Saint Paul's* where he is portrayed as

unambiguously insane and perishes in the Great Fire. Similarly a Jamaican prophet 'predicted' the 1907 earthquake (J. W. Williams 1979: 1–3); cf. the fate of the skylark prophet who continues to breach a now meaningless millennial doctrine in Theodore Roszak's fable 'The Skylark and the Frogs' (1970: 121).

17 Laing 1965: 12.

18 H. B. M. Murphy 1967. It is not clear what 'as if' implies: do 'desperate times' make more people insane to offer a wider variety of solutions in some sort of biohistorical homeostasis? A similar causal inevitability is argued by Wilner, Worsley and A. F. C. Wallace.

19 Esslin 1976: 116.

20 On Quaker 'strangeness' see Godlee 1985. For the self-perception of the Jews as 'crazy' see Gilman 1985; of Blacks, Littlewood and Lipsedge 1989 (1982) and Chapter 4 above; of the Irish, Scheper-Hughes 1979; of European women, P. W. Martin 1987. Among the Doukhobors 'A deranged old man, after a week spent fasting at a hill-top graveyard, delivered to an attentive gathering of people irrational, obscene, but mysterious messages, which were submissively accepted as oracular, and which caused many Sons of Freedom families to leave homes and belongings to embark on a brief and futile pilgrimage' (Hawthorn 1955).

21 Kroeber 1952.

22 Which includes dreams and paradoxical acts (Obeyesekere 1981: ch. 2); what he has since (1990) called reflections of 'deep motivations'.

23 Similarly in China, the conventional understanding of madness (*k'uang*) has been that of a dangerous nuisance but Lu Hsun's *Diary of a Madman* depicts *k'uang* as the ultimate social protest, while there is a popular reverence for Chi Tien, a Boddhisattva, as a 'mad monk'.

24 H. B. M. Murphy 1967.

25 Jarvie 1964: 111.

26 Burridge's 'inchoate ideas awaiting a prophet' (1971: 12).

27 Gilbert Lewis 1980: 1.

28 Harding 1974: ch. 4.

29 As Rothenberg (1990: 63) puts is, 'schizophrenic patients won't revise'. In Smart's work, written in the asylum between 1759 and 1763, we find a plethora of personal puns: 'sounds and sense, private and general meanings are submerged' (Feder 1980: 200). Another instance is described by Jung: 'He had, among other things, hit upon the magnificent idea that the world was his picture book, the pages of which he could turn at will. The proof was quite simple: he had only to turn round and there was a new page for him to see' (*The Relations between the Ego and the Unconscious*, cited in Storr, 1972).

30 Helen Vendler, 'American Poet', *New York Review of Books*, 2 December 1982, p. 3.

31 Allen Tate quoted in Ian Hamilton's *Robert Lowell: A Biography* (New York, Random House, 1983). However 'Lowell heard his mind talk and directed it gently . . . [He] had a sense of structure, of technical order that was so strong it saved his mind and his work. It could look down on himself as a subject . . . He made his madness a subject' (Derek Walcott, 'On Robert Lowell', *New York Review of Books*, 3 March 1984, p. 30).

32 Which recalled Mendelssohn's sneer about Berlioz that 'with all his efforts to go

stark mad he never once succeeded' or Cowper's 'That distemper of mind, which I so ardently longed for, actually arrived'. Where the egotistical sublime is prized, we find autobiographical verse striving to become insane. Ginsberg, like Van Gogh, appears to have done his best to become mad by frequent alcoholic dissipation which necessitated stays in a psychiatric hospital. By contrast, while Lowell regretted the loss of manic energy when well ('Cured I am frizzled, stale and small' – in *Home After Three Months Away*), no more than Strindberg does he seem to have regarded insanity as a goal to be sought.

33 Storr 1972: passim; in what G. H. Mead termed an interpretation of personal experience through the 'generalised other', and a notion which Henri Ellenberger refers to as a 'creative illness' – preoccupation, searching and despair followed by a 'permanent transformation' (recalling William James' account of conversion or Edmund Wilson's *The Wound and the Bow*). Similarly, Anthony Wallace (1956b: 633–5) argues for 'non-pathological' ways of mazeway resynthesis, 'pathology' here characterising inconsistency and failure of communication continuing after the 'illness'.

34 Freud 1949: 19.

35 Bateson 1973.

36 Apter 1982; Turner 1974.

37 'Open-ended' (divergent) and 'closed-ended' (convergent) thinking; De Bono's 'lateral' thinking; Johnson's 'non-propositional' and 'propositional'; Coleridge's 'primary' and 'secondary imagination'; Schutz's 'finite universes' and 'paramount reality'; Bleuler's 'autistic' and 'rational' thinking; Bruner's 'ungated' and 'gated'; McKellar's A-thinking and R-thinking; or in anthropology Deikman's 'receptive' and 'active'; Lévy-Bruhl's 'pre-logical' and 'logical'; Sperber's 'symbolic' and 'rational'; Abrahams' 'extraordinary' and 'ordinary'; Whitehead's 'presentational immediacy' and 'causal efficacy' or the Saussurean 'paradigmatic' and 'syntagmatic'. The distinction bears a certain relationship to the 'subpersonal psychology' of Rom Harré's, and indeed to Freud's 'primary' and 'secondary' processes. In *The Essential Tension* Thomas Kuhn employs such a cognitive dualism in his conception of scientific paradigms in which each is conceived in a divergent phase to be then consolidated in a convergent phase.

38 Harding 1974: 9–10; similarly Iser 1988; cf. Inglis 1957: 'a similarity of mental states is necessary for similar manifestations'. It is of course in post-structuralist objections to the affective (audience's resonance), intentional (author's intention) and biographical 'fallacies', that we find the most radical disjuncture between reader's, author's and critic's experience: the 'end' of author(ial)ity.

39 Gordon Lewis 1983: 11. A Trinidadian journalist, Niala Maharaj, characterises her country as one 'not known for its sanity . . . the tenuousness of the Trinidadian hold on reality . . . a carnival mentality of fantasy and decadence . . . whimsical . . . capricious . . . eccentric' (*Guardian*, London, 2 August 1990: 19). As one of V. S. Naipaul's characters remarks of the Shouters, 'In any other country they would be put away' (1976: 138). Compared with other English-speaking islands, there is a relaxed tolerance of the absurd; the eccentric Trinidadian is a frequent character in local fiction, and even the madman is perhaps less sinister than he is in Barbados or Jamaica. While obeah is recognised as a significant cause of madness everywhere in the West Indies, in Trinidad madness is typically the result of failed sorcery on

the part of the victim; the Trinidadian madman is thus to an extent a figure of ridicule, of partial toleration, while the Jamaican madman has done something socially unacceptable to become the victim of sorcery – he is quarrelsome, vindictive or ambitious.

40 To paraphrase Lienhardt (1961: 163): 'She contracts whole fields of direct experience and represents their fundamental nature by a single term.'

41 I employ Needham's (1973) original term 'inversion' – in spite of his later suggestions – to imply a discrete change in a dual value system, either a switch in its whole value-loading (an overturning of the whole chain) or a temporary or permanent inversion of certain parts in relation to others (which is perhaps more properly termed a chiasmus). I have used Schwimmer's 'oppositional ideology' to refer to a self-aware subdominant chain alone (p. 111), recalling the 'muted voice' of the Ardeners' terminology but here less the 'dual system' of social anthropologists than a bipolar spectrum with opposed ends. An arbitrary anthropological fiction, 'inversion' describes the latent possibilities of a system in a rather concrete figuring but in this it does convey the very physical sense of overturning institutions so characteristic of the millennial or baccanalian moment. (For a more detailed account see Littlewood 1984a, where I consider the possible ubiquity of systems of dual classification rooted in experience of self and other (and thus the recognition of negation) and in anatomical gender and bilaterality). When the chains appear represented by discrete social groups, we may perhaps talk of 'social tensions' between them, although as Turner (1969) notes such identified tensions do not necessarily imply that we think a society is about to break up; they may be seen, depending on our chosen frame, as 'strong unities . . . whose nature as a unit is constrained and bounded by the very forces that contend within it', for what seems qualified as an 'opposition' may be experienced at other times as complementary, as in a necessary balance. 'Symbolic inversion' has been identified by both observers and participants from diverse perspectives which we can gloss as:

(a) *Psychological*: the return of the repressed, as elaborated in psychoanalytical and literary theory (Scheff). The inversion may be regarded alternatively as a 'reaction formation' of the socialised individual to the recognition of his physiological being (Anna Freud). There may be a conscious local elaboration of some type of catharsis or limited discharge of tension to restore a lost equilibrium or purity (as in Trinidadian Carnival or in the medieval election of an *Abbé des Fous*); this may follow a quantified conception of sin or emotion which can penetrate boundaries – as in religious conversion, early psychoanalysis or *tabanka*, or in the circumscribed Jewish rituals of the scapegoat or bodily excretion before prayer and the treatment of illness by enema or the 'purging' of the house at Passover (Zborowski and Herzog 1962), or the expulsion of Eshu from the shango tent. Theories of catharsis in drama, following Aristotle, stress the resonance (mimesis) of the dramatic role with the personal experience of actor and audience: in extreme situations both may run amok together (Clifford Geertz, 'Religion as a Cultural System', in Michael Banton, ed., *Anthropological Approaches to the Study of Religion*, London, Tavistock, 1966).

(b) *Sociological*: 'inversion' is present in a society as the legitimate and recognised alternative to the established order. As it is both temporary and limited to certain ritual or ludic contexts (or is limited to a powerless minority), it reaffirms the boundaries of control and thus cements the system (Gluckman), a licensed affirmation of Turner's 'power of the weak', of Schwimmer's 'oppositional ideology'. While orthodox Jews are usually forbidden to play cards or get drunk, these activities are tolerated and even encouraged on two specific days in the year; similarly the blood of humans or animals is scrupulously avoided at all times except in circumscribed circumstances when it is actually sucked (Zborowski and Herzog 1962). In communities where the notion of practical cannibalism is totally repugnant the homicide may be purified by ritual ingestion of the deceased's liver (Goody 1976). 'Inversion' here is the marking of a principle by its constrained contravention: the tiresome sexuality of the office party is less a relaxing of the code (by which daily work precludes sexual activity) than an affirmation of it. The tension becomes 'a play of forces instead of a bitter battle. The effect of such a "play" soon wears off, but the sting is removed from troubled relationships' (Turner 1969).

(c) *Cognitive*: the 'psychological' and 'sociological' approaches are complementary (Devereux 1978), and they are functional and hence static. They emphasise not the transformations but the homeostasis of a system in which inversion is either the catharsis of the undesirable or the passage between two equivalent and continuing, co-existing systems (Leach). They frequently come together in our elaboration of some such notion as 'upside-down', 'purgation', 'liminality', 'negativism', 'irrationality', 'pathology' and the like. Similarly, the antinomian individual who contravenes the norm may be interpreted as giving conceptual unity to the workings-out of a simple dual system (Peacock 1968). Inversions however can be regarded as purely cognitive possibilities which have the potential, under appropriate social and economic conditions which they represent in new ways, to transform or enlarge the existing conceptual repertoire (Turner 1974). There may then be a spreading out from calendrical or initiatory 'inversion', circumscribed and time limited, to a wider shared dispensation. The limited 'oppositional' experiences which were contained and constrained by individual periodic inversions becomes heightened (Bateson 1958, 1973; Marx), burst their banks and become universalised as principles for all, fundamentally transforming social relations in the process. The Earth People are, as it were, a permanent carnival for the 'antistructure' becomes a 'counterstructure' (Turner 1974). As with the (temporary) ritual inversion, but more radically, such universalisations 'have transformational and transcendental aspects, i.e. subsuming and resolving contradictions apparent at lower levels of organisation' (Kapferer 1981: 13). I am not arguing that the 'steady-state' functionalist position is inapposite, merely that it is limited, statistical rather than normative, ignoring the way people contest the not-so-taken-for-granted verities. Carnival may indeed 'take the sting out of troubled relationships' and cement oppositions for another year, but it may, depending on its representations of the pragmatics of social conflict and productive relations, as before the Black Power uprising, pass from the constraints of 'theatre' out into the wider world where it may transform existing relations – or fail (as in Le Roy Ladurie's Romans). Similarly the temporary inversions of rites of passage, healing rites and 'culture-bound syndromes' may pass out into cargo cults, self-help groups or permanent 'oppositional structures' (Littlewood and Lipsedge 1987). Whether this itself is 'homeostatic' or not depends on our frame of analysis: we might argue that all three 'types' are merely our accounts of diversity and change in societies we perceive as tightly ordered.

42 From American Black Power, Stokely Carmichael offered the notorious answer to the question of the position of women in the movement: 'Prone'. Black women have been 'close' to White men in a 'double opposition' (see figure on p. 274), as de Beauvoir and André stress, through sexual relations in the plantation period between master and household slave, and through their opportunity to enter domestic work, teaching and nursing. Sheila Kitzinger has described how West Indian midwives, like the one Mother Earth had to deal with, act as the guarantors of respectability, preventing any attempts at 'natural childbirth', 'trying to get [the mothers] on the bed, where they were expected to lie still and be good patients' (cited by Weigle 1989: 128). Whilst at the level of immediate interpersonal relationships Black men may 'control', they are frequently dependent on women economically who may be said to be 'dominant' through their close relationship to the productive process. Jean Besson (1992) has pointed out that the respectability–reputation dichotomy undervalues the very real idea of resistance by Black women against slavery (e.g. Mathurin 1975); my own reading (and I think that of Peter Wilson) is that his bipolarity is to be read as polythetic: women are respectable, not as a fixed characteristic but relative to men.

43 Cf. bastards who take the name of their mother, 'love children', 'natural children', children of the earth (*terrae filii*). By contrast, the relatively autonomous Black Caribs of Belize retain a historical matrilineage back to African ancestors (Kerns 1983).

44 With the exception of her identification with Christ who is rather different from the biblical Jesus: 'This is why they say the Christ is returning in the twentieth century but I am the Christ.' The Mother was previously recognised as Eve opposed to Adam and his God, as the Devil against God, as Polyphemus against Odysseus, as Dracula against Frankenstein, as Cleopatra (and Asterix!) against the Roman, as Rider Haggard's *She*, and as Jimmy Cliff's (reggae) Queen of Africa against Lucifer. (Crapanzano suggests that the Moroccan power Aisha, the original of Haggard's *She*, locally represents female protest, or at least autonomy.)

45 The apparent paradox is resolved at a 'higher' implicit level: simple oppositions become the means by which a more psychological, radical and universal conceptualisation is attained (Zolberg 1972). When Jesus denied that plucking corn on the Sabbath was 'work', he implied a new dispensation in which 'the Law was broken in letter to be fulfilled in Spirit'. A similar implication is to be found in the Talmud: 'A transgression performed with good intentions is better than a precept performed with evil intent' (Scholem 1973: 805); a notion taken further by Sabbatians and Hasidim (cf. Martin Luther). Scholem suggests that the Jewish tradition always contained a 'dialectic' between the rabbinical and apocalyptic possibilities, what I have termed the Law and its inversions. Sabbatai Svi cut through the dual classification (Littlewood 1984b), calling women to read the Torah, ridiculing the learned, encouraging Gentiles to join the movement and maintaining evil could be transformed into good. To follow the traditional law in the Last Days was, he affirmed, like working on the Sabbath. There are close parallels between Sabbatai and the earlier messianic figure Jesus. The extent to which Sabbatai and his prophet Nathan actually appropriated Christian teaching is debatable: some Sabbatian activists had

been brought up as Catholics (Marranos), and a close friend of Nathan's father had previously apostasised to Christianity. Certainly we find an emphasis on personal faith over the Law, twelve disciples, the identification of Jesus as the 'husk' of the Messiah, both to be raised to holiness together (anticipating the tale of the Hasid who tried to raise the soul of Sabbatai himself), and the deification of the Messiah.

46 This is not the place to employ the hindsight of 1992 to assess the decontextualised truth of her predictions of global warming or of our descent from an African 'Eve'.

47 I would argue that all myths develop out of, and articulate, a creolisation of such contradictions. However, as Jahoda points out (1982: 220), 'we have little knowledge of the details of [the genesis of a myth]'. His 'one exception' (p. 237) is the radical modification of an Australian Aboriginal eschatological myth which attempts to resolve the contradiction between traditional and missionary accounts of the dead. The innovation was accepted by the tribe but it inclined to Christianity rather than to tradition; its originator was no Mother Earth.

48 Clifford 1988: 173.

49 Contrast this with the patriarch Freud's (rather Kantian) view of Nature where 'everything, including what is useless and even what is noxious, can grow and proliferate there as it pleases'. Freud himself was arguably steeped in Sabbatianism (Bakan 1958), but he left the *coincidentia oppositorum* for Jung.

50 Ingold 1986: ch. 2.

51 Littlewood 1984b.

52 Turner, 'Dewey, Dilthey, and Drama', in Turner and Bruner 1986: 35.

References

Abrahams, Ray G. 1986. Ordinary and Extraordinary Experience. In Turner and Bruner

Abrahams, Roger D. 1983. *The Man-of-Words in the West Indies: Performance and the Emergence of Creole Culture*, Baltimore, Johns Hopkins University Press

Abrahams, Roger D. and Szwed, J. F. (eds.) 1983. *After Africa: Extracts from British Travel Accounts and Journals of the 17th, 18th and 19th Centuries concerning the Slaves, their Masters and Customs in the British West Indies*, New Haven, Yale University Press

Ackernecht, E. 1943. Psychopathology, Primitive Medicine and Primitive Culture, *Bulletin of the History of Medicine* 14: 30–68

Adler, M. 1986. *Drawing Down the Moon: Witches, Druids, Goddess-Worshippers and Other Pagans in America Today*, Boston, Beacon Press, rev. edn

Aidala, A. A. 1985. Social Change, Gender Roles and New Religious Movements, *Sociological Analysis* 46: 287–314

Albanese, C. L. 1990. *Nature Religion in America: From the Algonkian Indians to the New Age*, Chicago University Press

Alexander, J. 1977. The Culture of Race in Middle-Class Kingston, *American Ethnologist* 4: 413–35

American Psychiatric Association. 1987. *Diagnostic and Statistical Manual of Mental Disorders-III-R*, New York, APA

André, J. 1987. *L'Inceste focal dans la famille noire antillaise*, Paris, Presses Universitaires de France

Andreasen, N. C. 1988. Bipolar Affective Disorder and Creativity: Implications and Clinical Management, *Comprehensive Psychiatry* 29: 207–17

Andrews, E. D. 1953. *The People Called Shakers*, Oxford University Press

Anglo, S. (ed.) 1977. *The Damned Art: Essays in the Literature of Witchcraft*, London, Routledge and Kegan Paul

Anthony M. 1986. *Heroes of the People of Trinidad and Tobago*, Port-of-Spain, Circle Press

1987. *A Better and Brighter Day*, Port-of-Spain, Circle Press

Apter, M. J. 1982. *The Experience of Motivation; The Theory of Psychological Reversals*, London, Academic Press

Ardener, S. 1983. Arson, Nudity and Bombs among the Canadian Doukhobors. In
    G. Breakwell (ed.), *Threatened Identities*, London, Wiley
    1975. Sexual Insult and Female Militancy. In S. Ardener (ed.), *Perceiving Women*,
    London, Dent
Ardossi, J. and Epstein, L. 1975. The Saintly Madmen of Tibet, abstracted in
    Transcultural Psychiatric Research Review 12: 21–2
Ardt, K. J. R. 1965. *George Rapp's Harmony Society*, Philadelphia, University of
    Pennsylvania Press
Arlow, J. A. 1951. The Consecration of the Prophet, *Psychoanalytical Quarterly* 20:
    374–97
Armytage, W. H. G. 1961. *Heavens Below: Utopian Experiments in England 1560–
    1960*, London, Routledge and Kegan Paul
Austin, D. J. 1979. History and Symbols in Ideology: A Jamaican Example, *Man* (ns)
    14: 497–514
Babcock, B. (ed.) 1974. *The Reversible World: Symbolic Inversion in Art and Society*,
    Ithaca, Cornell University Press
Bakan, D. 1958. *Sigmund Freud and the Jewish Mystical Tradition*, Princeton
    University Press
Bakhtin, M. 1971. Discourse Typology in Prose. In L. Majetka and K. Pomorska (eds.),
    Readings in Russian Poetics: Formalist and Structuralist Views, Cambridge,
    Mass., MIT Press
    1981. *The Dialogic Imagination*, Austin, University of Texas Press
Barkun, M. 1974. *Disaster and the Millennium*, New Haven, Yale University Press
Barnett, H. G. 1953. *Innovation: The Basis of Culture Change*, New York, McGraw-
    Hill
Barrett, L. 1976. *The Sun and the Drum: African Roots in Jamaican Folk Tradition*,
    Kingston, Sangsters
Barth, F. 1987. *Cosmologies in the Making: A Generative Approach to Cultural
    Variation in Inner New Guinea*, Cambridge University Press
Bartholomew, R. E. 1990. Ethnocentricity and the Social Construction of 'Mass
    Hysteria', *Culture, Medicine and Psychiatry* 14: 455–94
Barzun, J. 1974. *Clio and The Doctors: Psycho-history, Quanto-history and History*,
    Chicago University Press
Bastide, R. 1979. *The African Religions of Brazil: Towards a Sociology of the
    Interpenetration of Civilisations*, Baltimore, Johns Hopkins University Press
Bataille, G. 1989. *Theory of Religion*, London, Zone
Bateson, G. (ed.) 1961. *Perceval's Narrative: A Patient's Account of His Psychosis
    1830–1832*, Stanford University Press
    1958. *Naven*, Stanford University Press, 2nd edn
    1973 (1972). *Steps to An Ecology of Mind*, St Albans, Paladin
    1979. *Mind and Nature: A Necessary Unity*, New York, Dutton
Beaubrun, M. 1975. The View from Monkey Mountain, *Journal of the American
    Academy of Psychoanalysis* 3: 257–66
Beckford, J. A. 1975. *The Trumpet of Prophecy: A Sociological Study of Jehovah's
    Witnesses*, Oxford, Blackwell
    1985. *Cult Controversies: The Societal Response to the New Religious Movements*,
    London, Tavistock

Beckford, J. A. (ed.) 1986. *New Religious Movements and Rapid Social Change*, London, Sage

Beckwith, M. 1929. *Black Roadways: A Study of Jamaican Folklore*, Chapel Hill, University of North Carolina Press

Benedict, R. 1935. *Patterns of Culture*, London, Routledge and Kegan Paul

Bennett, H. L. 1989. The Challenge to the Post-Colonial State: A Case Study of the February Revolution in Trinidad. In F. W. Knight and C. A. Palmer (eds.), *The Modern Caribbean*, Chapel Hill, University of North Carolina Press

Berger, B. 1981. *The Survival of a Counter-Culture: Ideological Work and Everyday Life Among Rural Communards*, Berkeley, University of California Press

Bergson, H. 1911. *Laughter: An Essay on the Meaning of the Comic*, New York, Macmillan

Bernal, M. 1987. *Black Athena: The Afroasiatic Roots of Classical Civilisation*, vol. I, London, Free Association Books

Besson, Jean, 1987. A Paradox in Caribbean Attitudes to Land. In Besson and J. Momsen (eds.), *Land and Development in the Caribbean*, London, Macmillan

   1992. Reputation and Respectability Reconsidered: A New Perspective on Afro-Caribbean Peasant Women. In J. Momsen (ed.), *Women and Change in the Caribbean*, London, James Currey

Besson, Jerry, n.d. *Tales of the Paria Main Road*, Port-of-Spain, Creative Advertising

Bird, F. 1979. The Pursuit of Innocence: New Religious Movements and Moral Accountability, *Sociological Analysis* 40: 335–46

Bloch, M. 1977. The Past and the Present in the Present, *Man* (ns) 12: 278–92

Bloch, S. and Reddaway, P. 1977. *Russia's Political Hospitals*, London, Gollancz

Bloom, H. 1975. *Kabbalah and Criticism*, New York, Continuum

Booth, N. S. (ed.) 1977a. *African Religions: A Symposium*, London, Nok

   1977b. God and the Gods in West Africa. In Booth, *African Religions*

Bourdieu, P. 1977 (1972). *Outline of a Theory of Practice*, Cambridge University Press

Boyer, L. B., Boyer, R. M. and Basehart, H. W. 1972. Shamanism and Peyote Use Among the Apaches of the Mescalero Indian Reservation. In M. Harner (ed.), *Hallucinogens and Shamanism*, Oxford University Press

Braithwaite, E. 1971. *The Development of Creole Society in Jamaica 1770–1820*, Oxford, Clarendon

Braithwaite, L. 1953. Social Stratification in Trinidad, *Social and Economic Studies* 2: 5–175

Brereton, B. 1979. *Race Relations in Colonial Trinidad 1830–1900*, Cambridge University Press

   1981. *A History of Modern Trinidad 1783–1962*, London, Heinemann

Breton, A. 1969. *Manifestes du Surréalisme*, Paris, Gallimard

Bridges, I. 1988 (1980). *Child of the Tropics: Victorian Memoirs*, Port-of-Spain, Aquarella

Bristol, M. D. 1985. *Carnival and Theater: Plebeian Culture and the Structure of Authority in Renaissance England*, New Haven, Yale University Press

Brown, P. 1988. *The Body and Society: Men, Women and Sexual Renunciation in Early Christianity*, New York, Columbia University Press

Burridge, K. 1971. *New Heaven, New Earth: A Study of Millenarian Activities*, Oxford, Blackwell

1985. Millennialisms and the Recreation of History. In B. Lincoln (ed.), *Religion, Rebellion and Revolution*, London, Macmillan

Burton-Bradley, B. G. 1977. The New Guinea Prophet: Is the Cultist Always Abnormal? *Medical Journal of Australia* 1: 124–9

Calloway, H. 1978. 'The Most Essentially Female Function of All': Giving Birth. In S. Ardener (ed.), *Defining Females: The Nature of Women in Society*, New York, Wiley

Camus, A. 1962 (1951). *The Rebel*, Harmondsworth, Penguin

Carr, A. T. 1952. A Rada Community in Trinidad, *Caribbean Quarterly* 3: 35–54

Carrington, E. 1981. *Industrialisation in Trinidad 1783–1962*, London, Heinemann

Carrington, L. D. (ed.) 1983. *Studies in Caribbean Language*, St Augustine, Trinidad, University of the West Indies

Carstairs, M. 1959. The Social Limits of Eccentricity. In M. K. Opler (ed.), *Culture and Mental Health*, New York, Macmillan

Chevannes, B. 1989. The Phallus and the Outcast: The Symbolism of the Dreadlocks in Jamaica. Paper given at the conference on 'The Rastafari Movement: Symbols, Continuity and Change in the Caribbean', Institute of Social Studies, The Hague

Christianson, H. 1978. *Reformers and Babylon: English Apocalyptic Visions from the Reformation to the End of the Civil War*, Toronto University Press

Clifford, J. 1988. *The Predicament of Culture: Twentieth Century Ethnography, Literature and Art*, Harvard University Press

Cohn, N. 1957. *The Pursuit of the Millennium*, London, Secker and Warburg
1981. *Warrant for Genocide*, New York, Scholars Press

Collingwood, R. G. 1945. *The Idea of Nature*, Oxford, Clarendon

Columbo, F. 1984. *God in America: Religion and Politics in the U.S.*, New York, Columbia University Press

Comaroff, J. 1985. *Body of Power, Spirit of Resistance*, University of Chicago Press

Corea, G. 1988. *The Mother Machine: Reproductive Technologies from Artificial Insemination to Artificial Womb*, London, Women's Press

Crahan, E. and Knight, F. W. (eds.) 1979. *Africa and the Caribbean: The Legacies of a Link*, Baltimore, Johns Hopkins University Press

Crapanzano, V. 1973. *The Hamadsha: A Study in Moroccan Ethnopsychiatry*, Berkeley, California University Press

Carton, M. 1982. *Testing the Chains: Resistance to Slavery in the British West Indies*, Ithaca, Cornell University Press

Cross, W. R. 1950. *The Burned Over District: The Social and Intellectual History of Enthusiastic Religion in Western New York 1800–1850*, Ithaca, Cornell University Press

Da Cunha, E. 1947 (1902). *Revolt in the Backlands*, London, Gollancz

Dann, G. 1987. *The Barbadian Male: Sexual Attitudes and Practice*, London, Macmillan

Davis, B. D. 1966. *The Problem of Slavery in Western Culture*, Ithaca, Cornell University Press

De Beauvoir, S. 1972 (1949). *The Second Sex*, Harmondsworth, Penguin

De Boissiere, R. 1981 (1952). *Crown Jewel*, London, Picador

Deleuze, G. and Guattari, F. 1984 (1972). *Anti-Oedipus: Capitalism and Schizophrenia*, London, Athlone

Devereux, G. 1955. Charismatic Leadership and Crisis. In G. Roheim (ed.), *Psychoanalysis and the Social Sciences*, vol. IV, New York, International Universities Press

1956. Normal and Abnormal: The Key Problem in Psychiatric Anthropology. In J. Casagrande and T. Gladwin (eds.), *Some Uses of Anthropology, Theoretical and Applied*, Washington, Anthropological Society

1978. *Ethnopsychoanalysis: Psychoanalysis and Anthropology as Complementary Frames of Reference*, Berkeley, University of California Press

Devonish, H. 1985. *Language and Liberation: Creole Language Politics in the Caribbean*, London, Karia

Devos, G. 1976. The Interrelationship between Social and Psychological Structures in Transcultural Psychiatry. In W. P. Lebra (ed.), *Culture-Bound Syndromes, Ethnopsychiatry and Alternative Therapies*, Honolulu, University of Hawaii Press

Dodds, E. R. 1951. *The Greeks and the Irrational*, Berkeley, University of California Press

Douglas, M. 1968. The Social Control of Cognition: Some Factors in Joke Perception, *Man* (ns) 3: 361–75

Easlea, B. 1980. *Witch Hunting, Magic and the New Philosophy: An Introduction to the Debates of the Scientific Revolution 1450–1750*, Sussex, Harvester

Ebigbo, P. O. and Anyaegbuna, B. 1988. The Problem of Student Involvement in the Mermaid Cult: A Variety of Reincarnation (Ogba-Nje) in a Nigerian Secondary School, *Journal of African Psychology* 1: 1–14

Elder, J. D. 1988. *African Survivals in Trinidad and Tobago*, London, Karia

Eliade, M. 1954. *The Myth of the Eternal Return: or Cosmos and History*, Princeton University Press

1964. *Shamanism: Archaic Techniques of Ecstasy*, New York, Pantheon

Ellis, P. (ed.) 1986. *Women of the Caribbean*, London, Zed

Erikson, E. 1965 (1950). *Childhood and Society*, Harmondsworth, Penguin

Esslin, M. 1976. *Artaud*, London, Fontana

Fanon, F. 1967 (1952). *Black Skins, White Masks*, New York, Grove

Faristzaddi, M. 1982. *Itations of Jamaica and I Rastafari*, New York, Grove

Fauget, A. 1944. *Black Gods of the Metropolis*, Philadelphia, University of Pennsylvania Press

Feder, L. 1980. *Madness and Literature*, Princeton University Press

Fernandez, J. 1982. *Bwiti: An Ethnography of the Religious Imagination in Africa*, Princeton University Press

Field, M. 1960. *Search for Security: An Ethnopsychiatric Study of Rural Ghana*, London, Faber

Fischer, H. Th. 1964. The Clothes of the Naked Nuer, *International Archives of Ethnography* 50: 60–71

Fisher, L. E. 1985. *Colonial Madness: Mental Health in the Barbadian Social Order*, New Brunswick, Rutgers University Press

Flugel, J. C. 1950 (1930). *The Psychology of Clothes*, London, Hogarth

Fox, G. 1952 (1694). *Journal*, Cambridge University Press

Fox-Genovese, E. 1988. *Within the Plantation Household: Black and White Women of the Old South*, Chapel Hill, University of North Carolina Press

Frazier, E. F. 1964. *The Negro Church in America*, Liverpool University Press

Freud, S. 1972 (1928). *The Future of An Illusion*, London, Hogarth
    1949 (1911). Formulations Regarding the Two Principles in Mental Functioning. In
    Collected Papers, vol. IV, London, Hogarth
Garrett, C. 1975. *Respectable Folly: Millenarians and the French Revolution in France
    and England*, Baltimore, Johns Hopkins University Press
Gates, H. L. 1988. *The Signifying Monkey: A Theory of Afro-American Literary
    Criticism*, New York, Oxford University Press
Gellner, E. 1964. *Thought and Change*, London, Weidenfeld and Nicolson
Genovese, E. 1974. *Roll Jordan Roll: The World the Slaves Made*, New York,
    Pantheon
Giddens, A. 1991. *Modernity and Self-Identity: Self and Society in the Late Modern
    Age*, Oxford, Polity
Gill, S. 1988. *Mother Earth: An American Story*, University of Chicago Press
Gilman, S. 1985. *Difference and Pathology: Stereotypes of Sexuality, Race and
    Madness*, Ithaca, Cornell University Press
Girard, R. 1978. *To Double Business Bound: Essays on Literature, Mimesis and
    Anthropology*, Baltimore, Johns Hopkins University Press
Glazier, S. 1983a. *Marchin' the Pilgrims Home*, New York, Greenwood Press
    1983b. Cultural Pluralism and Respectability in Trinidad, *Ethnic and Racial Studies*
    6: 351–5
Gluckman, M. 1962. *Rituals of Rebellion in South-East Africa*, Manchester University
    Press
Godlee, F. 1985. Aspects of Non-Conformity: Quakers and the Lunatic Fringe. In
    W. F. Bynum, R. Porter, M. Shepherd (eds.), *The Anatomy of Madness*, vol. II,
    London, Tavistock
Goody, J. 1976. *Production and Reproduction: A Comparative Study of the Domestic
    Domain*, Cambridge University Press
Granek, M. 1976. Le Concept de fou et ses implications dans la littérature Talmudique
    et ses exigèses, *Annales Médico-Psychologiques* 134: 17–36
Greer, G. 1984. *Sex and Destiny*, London, Secker and Warburg
Griffin, S. 1984 (1978). *Woman and Nature: The Roaring Inside Her*, London, The
    Women's Press
Griffith, E. and Mahy, G. 1983. Psychological Benefits of Spiritual Baptist Mourning.
    Paper given at Annual Meeting of the American Psychiatric Association, New
    York
Gruenberg, E. 1957. Socially Shared Psychopathology. In A. H. Leighton (ed.),
    Explorations in Social Psychiatry, New York, Basic Books
Hall, J. R. 1978. *The Ways Out: Utopian Communal Groups in an Age of Babylon*,
    London, Routledge and Kegan Paul
    1987. *Gone from the Promised Land: Jonestown in American Cultural History*,
    New Jersey, Transaction
Handelman, D. and Kapferer, B. 1972. Forms of Joking Activity: A Comparative
    Analysis, *American Anthropologist* 74: 485–517
Handler, R. 1986. Authenticity, *Anthropology Today* 2: 2–4
Handwerker, W. P. 1989. *Women's Power and Social Revolution: Fertility Transition
    in the West Indies*, California, Sage
Harding, D. W. 1974 (1965). *Experience Into Words*, Harmondsworth, Penguin

Harris, O. 1978. Complementarity and Conflict: An Andean View of Women. In J. S. La Fontaine (ed.), *Sex and Age as Principles of Social Differentiation*, London, Academic Press

Harris, S. 1955. *The Incredible Father Divine*, London, Allen

Harrison, D. 1975. Social Relations in a Trinidad Village, Ph.D. thesis, Department of Anthropology, University College London

Harrison, J. E. C. 1979. *The Second Coming: Popular Millenarianism 1780–1850*, London, Routledge and Kegan Paul

Harrison, M. 1922. Mental Instability as a Factor in Progress, *Monist* 32: 189–99

Hawthorn, H. 1955. *The Doukhobors of British Columbia*, London, Dent

Hayter, A. 1968. *Opium and the Romantic Imagination*, London, Faber

Heelas, P. and Lock, A. (eds.) 1981. *Indigenous Psychologies: The Anthropology of the Self*, London, Academic Press

Helman, D. H. (ed.) 1988. *Analogic Reasoning: Perspectives on Artificial Intelligence, Cognitive Science and Philosophy*, Dordrecht, Kluwer

Henney, J. H. 1982. The Shakers. In E. D. Goodman, J. H. Henney and E. Pressel (eds.), *Trance, Healing and Hallucination*, Florida, Krieger

Henriques, F. 1953. *Family and Colour in Jamaica*, London, Eyre and Spottiswoode

Henry, F. 1983. Religion and Ideology in Trinidad: The Resurgence of the Shango Religion, *Caribbean Quarterly* 29: 63–4

Hershmann, D. J. and Lieb, J. 1988. *The Key to Genius: Manic-Depression and the Creative Life*, New York, Prometheus

Herskovits, M. J. 1951. The Present State and Needs of Afro-American Research, *Journal of Negro History* 36: 123–47
    1958 (1941). *The Myth of the Negro Past*, Boston, Beacon Press

Herskovits, M. J. and Herskovits, F. S. 1947. *Trinidad Village*, New York, Knopf

Herzfield, M. 1984. The Significance of the Insignificant: Blasphemy as Ideology, *Man* (ns) 19: 653–64

Hill, C. 1975. *The World Turned Upside Down: Radical Ideas During the English Revolution*, Harmondsworth, Penguin
    1984. Radical Pirates, In M. and J. Jacob (eds.), *The Origins of Anglo-American Radicalism*, London, Allen and Unwin

Hill, E. 1972. *The Trinidad Carnival*, Austin, University of Texas Press

Hintzen, P. C. 1989. *The Costs of Regime Survival: Racial Mobilisation, Elite Domination and Control of the State in Guyana and Trinidad*, Cambridge University Press

Hobsbawm, E. J. 1959. *Primitive Rebels: Studies in Archaic Forms of Social Movements in the 19th and 20th Centuries*, Manchester University Press

Hobsbawm, E. J. and Ranger, T. (eds.) 1984. *The Invention of Tradition*, Cambridge University Press

Holloway, M. 1966. *Heavens on Earth: Utopian Communities in America 1680–1880*, New York, Dover

Holy, L. and Stuchlik, M. 1983. *Actions, Norms and Representations: Foundations of Anthropological Inquiry*, Cambridge University Press

Hopkins, J. K. 1982. *A Woman to Deliver her People: Joanna Southcott and English Millenarianism in an Era of Revolution*, Austin, University of Texas Press

Horton, R. 1983. Social Psychologies: African and Western. In M. Fortes, *Oedipus and Job in West African Religion*, rev. edn, Cambridge University Press

Hoskins, J. 1967. Epilepsy and Guria, *Social Science and Medicine* 3: 39–48

Hughes, S. 1959. *Consciousness and Society: The Reorientation of European Social Thought 1890–1930*, London, MacGibbon and Kee

Humphrey, D. and Tindale, D. 1977. *False Messiah: The Story of Michael X*, London, Hart-Davis and MacGibbon

Hunt, L. 1984. *Politics, Culture and Chaos in the French Revolution*, Berkeley, University of California Press

Hunter, A. 1959. *The Last Days*, London, Blond

Inglis, J. 1957. Cargo Cults: The Problem of Explanation, *Oceania* 27: 249–63

Ingold, T. 1986. *The Appropriation of Nature: Essays on Human Ecology and Social Relations*, Manchester, Manchester University Press

Iser, W. 1988. *Prospecting: From Reader Response to Literary Anthropology*, Baltimore, Johns Hopkins University Press

Jackson, M. 1979. Prevented Succession: A Commentary Upon a Kuranko Narrative. In R. H. Hook (ed.), *Fantasy and Symbol: Essays in Anthropological Interpretation*, London, Academic Press

Jahoda, G. 1982. *Psychology and Anthropology: A Psychological Perspective*, London, Academic Press

James, C. L. R. 1963. *Beyond a Boundary*, London, Hutchinson

James, W. 1958 (1902). *The Varieties of Religious Experience*, New York

Jameson, F. 1984. Postmodernism, or The Cultural Logic of Late Capitalism, *New Left Review* 146: 53–92

Jarvie, I. C. 1964. *The Revolution in Anthropology*, London, Routledge and Kegan Paul

John, A. M. 1989. *The Plantation Slaves of Trinidad: A Mathematical and Demographic Enquiry*, Cambridge University Press

Johnson, M. 1987. *The Body In The Mind: The Bodily Basis of Meaning, Imagination and Reason*, Chicago University Press

Jones, J. M. and Liverpool, H. V. 1976. Calypso Humour in Trinidad. In T. Chapman and H. Foot (eds.), *Humour and Laughter: Theory, Research and Applications*, London, Wiley

Jordanova, L. 1989. *Sexual Visions: Images of Gender in Science and Medicine Between the 18th and 19th Centuries*, Hemel Hempstead, Harvester

Jules-Rosette, B. 1975. *African Apostles: Ritual and Conversion in the Church of John Maranke*, Ithaca, Cornell University Press

Kapferer, B. 1981. Ritual Process and the Transformation of Context in the Power of Ritual, *Social Analysis* 1: 3–19

Karlson, J. 1984. Creative Intelligence in Relatives of Mental Patients, *Hereditas* 100: 83–6

Kerns, V. 1983. *Women and the Ancestors: Black Carib Kinship and Ritual*, Urbana, University of Illinois Press

Kerr, M. 1952. *Personality and Conflict in Jamaica*, Liverpool University Press

Kiple, K. F. 1984. *The Caribbean Slave: A Biological History*, Cambridge University Press

Klass, M. 1961. *East Indians in Trinidad: A Study in Cultural Persistence*, New York, Columbia University Press

Kleinman, A. and Good, B. (eds.) 1985. *Culture and Depression*, California University Press

Kluckholn, C. and Leighton, D. 1952. *The Navaho*, Cambridge, Mass., Harvard University Press

Kochman, T. 1969. Rapping in the Black Ghetto, *Transaction* 6: 56–71

Kohn, T. 1988. A Text in Its Context: F. E. Williams and the Vaihala Madness, *Journal of the Anthropological Society of Oxford* 19: 25–42

Kroeber, A. L. 1952 (1940). Psychosis or Social Sanction. In Kroeber, *The Nature of Culture*, Chicago University Press

Kroll, O. and De Ganck, O. 1986. The Adolescence of a Thirteenth Century Visionary Nun, *Psychological Medicine* 16: 745–56

Kurella, H. 1911. *Cesare Lombroso*, London, Rebman

La Barre, E. 1969. *They Shall Take Up Serpents*, New York, Schocken
1970. *The Ghost Dance*, London, Allen and Unwin

La Guerre, J. 1974. *Calcutta to Caroni: The East Indians of Trinidad*, London, Longman
1982. *The Politics of Communalism: The Agony of the Left in Trinidad and Tobago 1930–1955*, Trinidad, Pan-Caribbean Publications

Laing, R. D. 1965 (1959). *The Divided Self*, Harmondsworth, Penguin
1967. *The Politics of Experience and the Bird of Paradise*, Harmondsworth, Penguin

Lanternari, V. 1963 (1960). *The Religions of the Oppressed: A Study of Modern Messianic Cults*, London, MacGibbon and Kee

Larose, S. 1976. The Meaning of Africa in Haitian Vodu. In I. M. Lewis (ed.), *Symbols and Sentiments*, London, Academic Press

Leach, E. 1958. Magical Hair, *Journal of the Royal Anthropological Institute* 88: 147–64

Leach, E. and Aycock, D. A. 1983. *Structuralist Interpretations of Biblical Myth*, Cambridge University Press

Le Page, R. B. and Tabouret-Keller, A. 1985. *Acts of Identity: Creole-Based Approaches to Language and Ethnicity*, Cambridge University Press

Lewis, Gilbert, 1980. *Day of Shining Red: An Essay on Understanding Ritual*, Cambridge University Press

Lewis, Gordon K. 1979. *Gather With the Saints at the River: The Jonestown Holocaust 1978*, Puerto Rico, Institute of Caribbean Studies
1983. *Main Currents in Caribbean Thought: The Historical Evolution of Caribbean Society in its Ideological Aspects, 1492–1900*, Kingston, Heinemann

Lewis, I. M. 1971. *Ecstatic Religion*, Harmondsworth, Penguin

Lieber, M. 1981. *Street Scenes: Afro-American Culture in Urban Trinidad*, Massachusetts, Schenkman

Lienhardt, G. 1961. *Divinity and Experience: The Religion of the Dinka*, Oxford, Clarendon
1964. *Social Anthropology*, Oxford University Press

Lifton, R. J. (ed.) 1974. *Explorations in Psychohistory*, New York, Simon and Schuster

Lincoln, B. (ed.) 1985. *Religion, Rebellion, Revolution*, London, Macmillan

Lincoln, E. 1961. *The Black Muslims in America*, Boston, Beacon

Linton, R. 1943. Nativist Movements, *American Anthropologist* 45: 230-40

Lishman, W. A. 1978. *Organic Psychiatry: The Psychological Consequences of Cerebral Disorder*, Oxford, Blackwell

Littlewood, R. 1983. The Antinomian Hasid, *British Journal of Medical Psychology* 56: 67–78

1984a. The Individual Articulation of Shared Symbols, *Journal of Operational Psychiatry* 15: 17–24

1984b. The Imitation of Madness: The Influence of Psychopathology upon Culture, *Social Science and Medicine* 19: 705–15

1986. Russian Dolls and Chinese Boxes: The Implicit Models of Comparative Psychiatry. In J. Cox (ed.), *Transcultural Psychiatry*, London, Croom Helm

1990. From Categories to Contexts: A Decade of the 'New Cross-Cultural Psychiatry', *British Journal of Psychiatry* 156: 308–27

1991. Against Pathology: The New Psychiatry and Its Critics, *British Journal of Psychiatry* 159: 696–702

Littlewood, R. and Lipsedge, M. 1987. The Butterfly and the Serpent, *Culture, Medicine and Psychiatry* 11: 289–335

1989 (1982). *Aliens and Alienists: Ethnic Minorities and Psychiatry*, London, Unwin Hyman

Lovejoy, D. 1985. *Religious Enthusiasm in the New World: Heresy to Revolution*, Harvard University Press

Lowenthal, D. 1972. *West Indian Societies*, Oxford University Press

Luhrman, T. 1989. *Persuasions of the Witch's Craft*, Oxford, Blackwell

Lutzky, H. 1989. Reparation and Tikkun: A Comparison of the Kleinian and Kabbalistic Concepts, *International Review of Psychoanalysis* 16: 449–58

McCall, D. F. 1982. Mother Earth: The Great Goddess of West Africa. In Preston, *Mother Worship: Theme and Variation*

MacCormack, C. and Draper, A. 1987. Social and Cognitive Aspects of Female Sexuality in Jamaica. In P. Caplan (ed.), *The Cultural Construction of Sexuality*, London, Tavistock

MacCormack, C. and Strathern, M. (eds.) 1980. *Nature, Culture, Gender*, Cambridge University Press

McDaniel, J. 1989. *The Madness of the Saints: Ecstatic Religion in Bengal*, University of Chicago Press

MacDonald, M. 1981. *Mystical Bedlam: Madness, Anxiety and Healing in Seventeenth-Century England*, Cambridge University Press

Magid, A. 1988. *Urban Nationalism: A Study of Political Development in Trinidad*, Gainesville, Fl., University of Florida Press

Mannheim, K. 1936. *Ideology and Utopia*, London, Routledge and Kegan Paul

1952. The Problem of Generations. In Mannheim, *Essays in the Sociology of Knowledge*, New York, Oxford University Press

Mannoni, O. 1964 (1950). *Prospero and Caliban: The Psychology of Colonization*, New York, Praeger

Margolis, J. 1989. *Texts Without Referents: Reconciling Science and Narrative*, Oxford, Blackwell

Martin, M.-L. 1975. *Kimbangu: An African Prophet and His Church*, Oxford, Blackwell

Martin, P. W. 1987. *Mad Women in Romantic Writing*, Brighton, Harvester

Mathurin, L. 1975. *The Rebel Woman in the British West Indies During Slavery*, Mona, Institute of Jamaica

Maude, A. 1904. *A Peculiar People: The Doukhobors*, London, Grant Richards

Mazlich, B. 1988. *The Leader, The Led, and The Psyche*, Hanover, N.H., University Press of New England

Messer, E. 1981. Hot-Cold Classifications: Theoretical and Practical Implications of a Mexican Study, *Social Science and Medicine* 15: 133–45

Métraux, A. 1959. *Voodoo in Haitii*, London, Deutsch

Miles, M. R. 1989. *Carnal Knowing: Female Nakedness and Religious Meaning in the Christian West*, Boston, Beacon

Millet, K. 1991. *The Loony Bin Trip*, London, Virago

Millette, J. 1985. *Society and Politics in Colonial Trinidad*, Trinidad, Omega

Mintz, S. W. 1974a. *Caribbean Transformations*, Baltimore, Johns Hopkins University Press

  1974b. The Rural Proletariat and the Problem of Rural Proletarian Consciousness, *Journal of Peasant Studies* 1: 291–325

Mintz, S. W. (ed.) 1974c. *Slavery, Colonialism and Racism*, New York, Norton

Mischel, F. 1957. African Powers in Trinidad: The Shango Cult, *Anthropological Quarterly* 30: 45–59

Mischel, W. and Mischel, F. 1958. Psychological Aspects of Spirit Possession, *American Anthropologist* 60: 249–60

Morris, A. 1985. Sanctified Madness: The God-Intoxicated Saints of Bengal, *Social Science and Medicine* 21: 221–30

Morton, A. L. 1952. *The English Utopia*, London, Lawrence and Wishart

Morton-Williams, P. 1962. The Yoruba Ogboni Cult in Oyo, *Africa* 30: 362–74

'Moses', nd. *The Sixth and Seventh Books of Moses*, Aclington, Texas, Dorene Publishing Co.

Murphy, H. B. M. 1967. Cultural Aspects of the Delusion, *Studium Generale* 2: 684–92

Murphy, J. 1964. Psychotherapeutic Aspects of Shamanism on St. Lawrence Island, Alaska. In A. Kiev (ed.), *Magic, Faith and Healing*, New York, Free Press

Nadel, S. F. 1946. A Study of Shamanism in the Nuba Mountains, *Journal of the Royal Anthropological Institute* 86: 25–37

Naipaul, S. 1981 (1980). *Black and White*, London, Sphere

  1985 (1984). *Beyond the Dragon's Mouth*, London, Abacus

Naipaul, V. S. 1967. *The Mimic Men*, London, Deutsch

  1969 (1962). *The Middle Passage*, Harmondsworth, Penguin

  1969. *The Loss of El Dorado*, London, Deutsch

  1976 (1975). *Guerrillas*, Harmondsworth, Penguin

  1980. Michael X and the Black Power Killings in Trinidad. In Naipaul, *The Return of Eva Peron*, London, Deutsch

Needham, R. (ed.) 1973. *Right and Left: Essays on Dual Symbolic Classification*, University of Chicago Press

  1975. Polythetic Classification, *Man* (ns) 10: 349–69

  1980. *Reconnaissances*, University of Toronto Press

Nettleford, R. 1970. *Mirror, Mirror: Identity, Race and Protest in Jamaica*, Kingston, Collins

1978. *Caribbean Cultural Identity: The Case of Jamaica*, Kingston, Institute of Jamaica

Neumann, E. 1963 (1955). *The Great Mother: An Analysis of the Archetype*, Princeton University Press.

Nicholls, D. 1971. East Indians and Black Power in Trinidad, *Race* 12: 443–59

Nordhoff, C. 1966 (1875). *The Communist Societies of the United States*, New York, Dover

Noyes, J. H. 1966 (1870). *A History of American Socialisms*, New York, Dover

Ober, W. B. 1988 (1979). Madness and Poetry: A Note on Collins, Cowper and Smart. In Ober, *Boswell's Clap and Other Essays*, Carbondale, Il., Southern Illinois University Press

Obeyesekere, G. 1981. *Medusa's Hair: An Essay on Personal Symbols and Religious Experience*, Chicago University Press

1990. *The Work of Culture: Symbolic Transformation in Psychoanalysis and Anthropology*, Chicago University Press

Ojo, C. J. A. 1966. *Yoruba Culture*, Ife University Press

Olivier, C. 1989 (1980), *Jocasta's Children: The Imprint of the Mother*, London, Routledge

Owens, J. 1977. *Dread: The Rastafarians of Jamaica*, Kingston, Sangsters

Oxaal, I. 1982. *Black Intellectuals and the Dilemmas of Race and Class in Trinidad*, Cambridge, Mass., Schenkman

Pagels, E. 1982. *The Gnostic Gospels*, Harmondsworth, Penguin

1988. *Adam, Eve and the Serpent*, London, Weidenfeld and Nicolson

Parkin, D. (ed.) 1985. *The Anthropology of Evil*, Oxford, Blackwell

Parrinder, G. 1949. *West African Religion*, London, Epworth

1953. *Religion in an African City*, Oxford University Press

1954. *African Traditional Religion*, London, Hutchinson

Parsons, T. 1951. *The Social System*, Illinois, Free Press

Peacock, J. L. 1968. *Rites and Modernisation: Symbolic Aspects of Indonesian Proletarian Drama*, Chicago University Press

Plato, 1965. *Timaeus*, trans. H. P. Lee, Harmondsworth, Penguin

1910. *Republic*, trans. J. L. Davies, London, Macmillan

Popper, K. 1945. *The Open Society and Its Enemies*, London, Routledge and Kegan Paul

Porter, R. 1985. The Hunger of Imagination: Approaching Samuel Johnson's Melancholy. In W. F. Bynum, R. Porter and M. Shepherd (eds.), *The Anatomy of Madness*, vol. I, London, Tavistock

Pratt, M. L. 1986. Fieldwork in Common Places. In J. Clifford and G. E. Marcus (eds.), *Writing Culture: The Poetics and Politics of Ethnography*, Berkeley, California University Press

Preston, J. L. (ed.) 1982. *Mother Worship: Theme and Variation*, Chapel Hill, University of North Carolina Press

Radcliffe-Brown, A. R. 1940. On Joking Relationships, *Africa* 13: 195-210

Radin, P. 1953. *The World of Primitive Man*, New York, Schuman

Rahner, K. 1962. *On the Theology of Death*, London, Nelson

Richardson, J. T. 1980. Peoples Temple and Jonestown: A Corrective Comparison and Critique, *Journal for the Scientific Study of Religion* 19: 239-55

Rivers, W. H. R. 1920. *Instinct and the Unconscious*, Cambridge University Press
Rodman, H. 1971. *Lower-Class Families: The Culture of Poverty in Negro Trinidad*, New York, Oxford University Press
Rogers, E. M. and Shoemaker, F. F. 1971. *Communication of Innovation*, New York, Free Press
Rogers, P. G. 1961. *Battle in Bossenden Wood*, Oxford University Press
Roheim, G. 1940. The Garden of Eden, *Psychoanalytical Review* 27: 1–26
   1950. *Psychoanalysis and Anthropology*, New York, International Universities Press
Rorty, R. 1980. *Philosophy and the Mirror of Nature*, Oxford, Blackwell
Rosen, G. 1968. *Madness in Society*, London, Routledge and Kegan Paul
   1972. Social Change and Psychopathology in the Emotional Climate of Millennial Movements, *American Behavioral Scientist* 16: 153–67
Roszak, T. 1970. *The Making of a Counter-Culture*, London, Faber
Rothenberg, A. 1990. *Creativity and Madness: New Findings and Old Stereotypes*, Baltimore, Johns Hopkins University Press
Rubin, V. (ed.) 1960. *Caribbean Studies: A Symposium*, Seattle, University of Washington Press
Rudé, G. 1980. *Ideology and Popular Protest*, New York, Pantheon
Ryan, S. 1972. *Race and Nationalism in Trinidad and Tobago*, Toronto University Press
Sahlins, M. 1987. *Islands of History*, London, Tavistock
Sartre, J.-P. 1948. *Anti-Semite and Jew*, New York, Schocken
Saxe, A. 1968. Urban Squatters in Trinidad, M.A. Thesis, Brandeis University
Scheper-Hughes, N. 1979. *Saints, Scholars and Schizophrenics: Mental Illness in Rural Ireland*, Berkeley, University of California Press
Schneider, K. 1959. *Clinical Psychopathology*, New York, Grune and Stratton
Scholem, G. C. 1971. *The Messianic Idea in Judaism*, London, Allen and Unwin
   1973. *Sabbatai Sevi*, London, Routledge
Schuler, M. 1979. Myalism and African Religious Tradition in Jamaica. In M. E. Crahan and F. W. Knight (eds.), *Africa and the Caribbean: The Legacies of a Link*, Baltimore, Johns Hopkins University Press
Schwimmer, E. 1972. Symbolic Competition, *Anthropologica* 14: 117–25
Scott, J. C. 1990. *Domination and the Arts of Resistance*, New Haven, Yale University Press
Seligman, C. G. 1926. Anthropological Perspectives and Psychological Theory, *Journal of the Royal Anthropological Institute* 62: 193–228
Selvon, S. 1979. *Turn Again Tiger*, London, Heinemann
Sereno, R. 1948. Obeah: Magic and Social Structure in the Lesser Antilles, *Psychiatry* 11: 15-31
Sheldrake, R. 1990. *The Greening of Science and God*, London, Hutchinson
Showalter, E. 1987. *The Female Malady: Women, Madness and English Culture, 1830–1980*, London, Virago
Silverblatt, I. 1987. *Moon, Sun and Witches: Gender Ideologies and Class in Inca and Colonial Peru*, Princeton University Press
Simon, B. 1978. *Mind and Madness in Ancient Greece: The Classical Roots of Modern Psychiatry*, Ithaca, Cornell University Press

Simpson, G. E. 1978. *Black Religions in the New World*, New York, Columbia University Press
  1980. *Religious Cults of the Caribbean*, Puerto Rico, Institute of Caribbean Studies
Smith, M. G. 1963. *Dark Puritan*, Kingston, Department of Extra-Mural Studies, University of the West Indies
Smith, M. G., Augier, R., Nettleford, F. 1962. *The Ras Tafari Movement in Kingston, Jamaica*, Kingston, Institute of Social and Economic Research
Smith, R. T. 1988. *Kinship and Class in the West Indies*, Cambridge University Press
Spanos, N. P. 1975. Witches in the History of Psychiatry: A Critical Analysis and An Alternative Conceptualisation, *Psychological Bulletin*, 417–39
Stark, R. and Bainbridge, W. S. 1986. *The Future of Religion: Secularisation, Revival and Cult Formation*, Berkeley, University of California Press
Stewart, J. O. 1989. *Drinkers, Drummers and Decent Folks: Ethnographic Narratives of Village Trinidad*, New York, State University of New York Press
Stirrat, R. L. 1984. Sacred Models, *Man* (ns) 19: 199-215
Storr, A. 1972. *The Dynamics of Creation*, London, Secker and Warburg
Taussig, M. T. 1980. *The Devil and Commodity Fetishism in South America*, Chapel Hill, University of North Carolina Press
  1987. *Shamanism, Colonialism and the Wild Man: A Study in Terror and Healing*, Chicago University Press
Thomas, E. 1987. *A History of the Shouter Baptists in Trinidad and Tobago*, Tacarigua, Trinidad, Calaloux
Thomas, J. J. 1969 (1869). *The Theory and Practice of Creole Grammar*, London, New Beacon
Thomas, K. 1973 (1971). *Religion and the Decline of Magic: Studies in Popular Beliefs in Sixteenth and Seventeenth Century England*, Harmondsworth, Penguin
  1984 (1983). *Man and the Natural World: Changing Attitudes in England 1500–1800*, Harmondsworth, Penguin
Thrupp, S. L. (ed.) 1970. *Millennial Dreams in Action*, New York, Schocken
Toch, H. 1971. *The Social Psychology of Social Movements*, London, Methuen
Todd, L. 1984. *Modern Englishes: Pidgins and Creoles*, Oxford, Blackwell
Torgovnick, M. 1990. *Gone Primitive: Savage Intellects, Modern Lives*, Chicago University Press
Trilling, L. 1971. *Sincerity and Authenticity*, Cambridge, Mass., Harvard University Press
  1980 (1974). Neurosis and the Health of the Artist. In Trilling, *Speaking of Literature and Society*, New Haven, Harcourt, Brave and Jovanovitch
Tseng, W. S. and McDermott, J. F. 1981. *Culture, Mind and Therapy*, New York, Brunner/Mazel
Turner, V. 1967. *The Forest of Symbols: Aspects of Ndembu Ritual*, Ithaca, Cornell University Press
  1969. *The Ritual Process: Structure and Anti-Structure*, London, Routledge and Kegan Paul
  1974. *Dramas, Fields and Metaphors: Symbolic Action in Human Society*, Ithaca, Cornell University Press
  1985. *On the Edge of the Bush* (ed. E. L. B. Turner), Tuscon, University of Arizona Press

Turner, V. and Bruner, E. (eds.) 1986. *The Anthropology of Experience*, Urbana, Illinois University Press

Van Den Berghe, P. and Peters, K. 1988. Hutterites and Kibbutznicks: A Tale of Nepotistic Communism, *Man* (ns) 23: 522–39

Vonnegut, M. 1976. *The Eden Express*, London, Cape

Wallace, A. F. C. 1956a. Revitalisation Movements, *American Anthropologist* 56: 264–81

    1956b. Mazeway Resynthesis: A Biocultural Theory of Religious Inspiration, *Transactions of the New York Academy of Science* 18: 626–38

Wallace, E. R. 1983. *Freud and Anthropology: A History and a Reappraisal*, New York, International Universities Press

Wallis, R. 1984. *Elementary Forms of the New Religious Life*, London, Routledge and Kegan Paul

Walton, J. M. 1985. Casting Out and Bringing Back in Victorian England. In W. F. Bynum, R. Porter, M. Shepherd (eds.), *The Anatomy of Madness*, vol. II, London, Tavistock

Walzer, M. 1985. *Exodus and Revolution*, New York, Basic Books

Ward, C. and Beaubrun, M. 1979. Trance Induction and Hallucination in Spiritual Baptist Mourning, *Psychological Anthropology* 2: 479–88

Warner, K. 1982. *The Trinidad Calypso*, London, Heinemann

Warner, M. 1976. *Alone of All Her Sex: The Myth and Cult of the Virgin Mary*, London, Weidenfeld and Nicolson

    1983. *Joan of Arc: The Image of Female Heroism*, Harmondsworth, Penguin

    1985. *Monuments and Maidens*, London, Weidenfeld and Nicolson

Wasson, R. G., Kramrisch, S., Oh, J., Ruck, C. A. P. 1986. *Persephone's Quest: Entheogens and the Origins of Religion*, New Haven, Yale University Press

Watts, D. 1990. *The West Indies: Patterns of Development, Culture and Environmental Change since 1492*, Cambridge University Press

Webber, T. L. 1978. *Deep Like the Rivers: Education in the Slave Quarter Community 1831–1865*, New York, Norton

Weber, M. 1947. The Sociology of Charismatic Authority. In Weber, *Essays*, London

Wedenoja, W. 1989. Mothering and the Practice of 'Balm' in Jamaica. In C. S. McClain (ed.), *Women as Healers: Cross-Cultural Perspectives*, New Brunswick, Rutgers University Press

Weigle, M. 1989. *Creation and Procreation: Feminist Reflections on Mythologies of Cosmogony and Parturition*, Philadelphia, Pennsylvania University Press

Whitworth, J. M. 1975. *God's Blueprints: A Sociological Study of Three Utopian Sects*, London, Routledge and Kegan Paul

Whybrow, P. C. and Prange, A. J. 1981. A Hypothesis of Thyroid-catecholamine-receptor Interaction, *Archives of Generao Psychiatry* 38: 106–13

Wideman, J. E. 1991. *Philadelphia Fire*, New York, Viking

Williams, C. 1986. The Role of Women in Caribbean Culture. In P. Ellis (ed.), *Women of the Caribbean*, London, Zed

Williams, E. 1964. *History of the People of Trinidad and Tobago*, London, Deutsch

    1972. *Slavery to Chaguaramas*, Port-of-Spain, PNM

Williams, F. E. 1934. The Vaihala Madness in Retrospect. In E. E. Evans-Pritchard (ed.), *Essays Presented to C. G. Seligman*, London, Kegan Paul

Williams, J. W. 1979 (1934). *Psychic Phenomena of Jamaica*, Westpoint, Connecticut, Greenwood Press

Wilner, E. 1975. *Gathering The Winds: Visionary Imagination and Radical Transformation of Self and Society*, Baltimore, Johns Hopkins University Press

Wilson, B. 1970. *Religious Sects*, London, Weidenfeld and Nicolson

1973. *Magic and the Millennium*, London, Heinemann

1975. *Noble Savages: The Primitive Origins of Charisma and Its Contemporary Survival*, Berkeley, University of California Press

Wilson, C. 1956. *The Outsider*, London, Gollancz

Wilson, E. 1952. *The Wound and the Bow*, London, Methuen

Wilson, P. 1973. *Crab Antics: The Social Anthropology of English Speaking Negro Societies of the Caribbean*, New Haven, Yale University Press

1974. *Oscar: An Inquiry Into the Nature of Sanity*, New York, Random House

Wing, J. K., Cooper, J. E. and Sartorius, N. 1976. *Measurement and Classification of Psychiatric Symptoms*, Cambridge University Press

Winstanley, G. 1973. *The Law of Freedom and Other Writings* (ed. C. Hill), Harmondsworth, Penguin

Wintrob, R. 1970. Mammy Water: Folk Beliefs and Psychiatric Elaborations in Liberia, *Canadian Psychiatric Association Journal* 15: 143–57

Wolman, B. 1973. Sense and Nonsense in History. In Wolman (ed.), *The Psychoanalytic Interpretation of History*, New York, Harper

Wong, W. 1967. Folk Medicine and Plants of Blanchisseuse, Trinidad, M.Sc. Thesis, Brandeis University

Wood, D. 1968. *Trinidad in Transition: The Years After Slavery*, Oxford University Press

Woodcock, G. and Avakumovic, I. 1968. *The Doukhobors*, London, Faber

Worsley, P. 1970 (1968). *The Trumpet Shall Sound*, London, Paladin

Yap, P. M. 1954. The Mental Illness of Hung Hsiu-Chuan, Leader of the Taiping Rebellion, *Far Eastern Quarterly* 13: 287–304

Yawney, C. 1985. Strictly Ital: Rastafari Livity and Holistic Health. Paper given at the Annual Conference of the Society for Caribbean Studies, Hoddesdon

Zborowski, M. and Herzog, E. 1962. *Life Is With People: The Culture of the Stetl*, New York, Schocken

Zilboorg, G. 1941. *A History of Medical Psychology*, New York, Norton

Zolberg, A. 1972. Moments of Madness, *Politics and Society*, Winter, 183–207

Index

abortion, 35, 250
Abrahams, R. D., 52, 266n13
Abrahams, R. G., 17
according (situational) norms, 35, 49, 262n1, 271n29
Ackernecht, E., 25, 261n74
Adam, 147, 156, 157, 168, 264n3, 275n18, 295n44
Adventists (Seven Days), 55, 115, 166, 251
Africa: representations of Africa in the West Indies, 86–111, 105, 109, 181–2, 202–3, 228, 230, 244, 270n8; African heritage in Trinidad, 3, 87–97, 107–11, 270n1, n4; African 'baseline', 88; African migration to Trinidad after slavery, 2, 87, 88, 140, 270n2, n4
African Orthodox Church, 103
agency, xii, xv, 109–11, 159–60, 173
Aisha, 278n4, 295n44
Aladura, 169
altered states of consciousness, 18, 19, 92, 194, 218, 259n58, 265n9, 271n23, 287n31, 290n9; *see* mourning, travelling
Amerindians: in Brasil, 131, 290n9; in Colombia, 160, 272n47; in Bolivia, 160; in Trinidad, 1, 2, 187; and Shakers, 122, 275n20; and 'Mother Earth', 131; and Judas, 282n40; shamanic flight, 290n9; *see* Caribs, Ghost Dance, shamans
Amharic, 106, 108
Anabaptists, 115, 117, 168; *see* Puritan radicals
André, J., 281, 295
androgyneity, 79, 131, 132, 141–8, 156, 165, 172, 174, 175, 202, 248, 282n33, n34; of God, 64, 117, 118, 132, 156, 282n34; of African powers, 145–8, 165, 226, 272n16

Ann Lee, Mother, 13, 64, 156–7, 168, 174; *see* Shakers
antanaclasis (rhetorical homophone), 275n18
antinomian actions, 27, 29, 121, 127–9, 160, 167, 232, 274n10, 290n8, 294n41
Apochrypha, Jewish, 118; Christian, 141
Apter, M. J., 225
Ardener, E., 220, 293n41
Ardener, S., 169, 293n41
Arima, 10, 60, 255n13
Aristotle, 258n30, 293n41
art brut, 20
Artaud, A., 20–1, 219, 221, 225, 259n50
Ashanti, 103; *see* Ghana
authenticity, 21, 129, 130, 233
autochthoneity, 145, 146, 158

Babylon, 104, 105, 106, 107, 114, 122, 123, 133, 244, 272n43, 274n9
Bachofen, J. J., 132
Bacon, F., 119
Baku, S., 254
Bakweri, 140
balisier, 10, 84, Plate 3
Baptists: Baptist rebellions (Jamaica), 102; *see* Native Baptists, Shouters
Barbados, 47, 98, 99, 168, 281n23, 290n13, 292n39
Barkun, M., 29, 228, 261n82, 262n91
Bastide, R., 89–90, 95, 99, 138
Bateson, G., 224, 259, 284n1, 294n41
Beckford, J., 15, 28, 261n81, 285n12, 286n19
Bedward, A., 16, 125, 276n43
Beginning of the End, 6, 66, 80, 84–5, 201–2, 241, 242–3, 244
Benedict, R., 23, 259n57
Berger, J., 167, 283n49, n50
Besson, Jean, 120, 139, 295n42

313

naturalistic vs. personalistic understandings,
xv, xvi–xvii, 64, 234–7, 262n2; and mental
illness, xiii, 16–17, 18–19, 25, 32, 59–60,
75–8, 216, 227, 234–5, 236, 257n23
nature: the idea of, xiv, xv, 113, 116, 119–23,
134, 147, 154, 158, 159, 164, 216, 234,
236–7, 275n29, 283n50, 296n49; as
arbitrary, xii, xv, xvi, 234, 236; and women,
113–14, 116–19, 229–31, 273n4, 274n7,
283n50; Mother Earth's understanding, 5,
65, 69–70, 80, 81–3, 96, 109, 170–1, 195–6,
226, 232, 234, 249, 269n16; West Indian
understanding, 5, 8, 9, 11, 34, 35, 46,
100–1, 106, 107, 109, 120–1, 228, 230,
264n3
Nayler, J., 126, 258n33, 275n10
Nazism, 28; as an ideology of pure
psychology, 261n79
Needham, R., 165, 293n41
neoplatonism, 93, 116, 129; *see* (high)
science
Nettleford, R., 105, 109
Nietzsche, F., 19, 21, 219, 225, 258n29
Nigeria, 147, 169, 215; *see* Yoruba
Noyes, J., 180–1
Nuer, 32, 260n71
nurses in Trinidad, 47, 60, 61, 62, 150–1, 152,
226, 230, 295n42

Obatala, 136–46, 272n47, 278n12
obeah, 34, 40–3, 44, 52, 53, 54, 92, 94, 95–6,
98, 108, 109, 163, 164, 167, 262n2, 264n7,
270n18, 285n8, 282n39
Obeyesekere, G., 148, 163, 221, 291n22
obscenity, 2, 140, 153, 164, 200, 281n24,
291n20
Oduduwa, 136–46, 278n12
Ogboni cult (Yoruba, Brasil), 138, 146–7
Ogun, 137–46, 164
Ohlmarks, C. A., 26
Oneida, 180
opposition (analytical category), 112, 113,
159, 207, 229–32, 262n1, 278n4, 293n41;
oppositional ideology, 109–11, 112, 116,
134, 229–31, 294n41; *see also* inversion,
resistance, redefinition, countertradition
orishas (*powers*), 94–7, 136–48, 279n18; *see
also* Yoruba, spirits, *and under individual
names*
'Orphic myth', 133, 156
Orungan, 136–45
Oshun, 140, 142, 278n7
outside relationships, 50, 263–4, 266n11

pantheism, 116, 121, 125–6, 130, 132, 234,
275n17; *see* hylozoism
paratelic states, 225

parent–child relationship, 8, 28, 49, 82, 89,
152–5, 157, 178, 179, 182, 193, 199, 200,
211–12, 280n23
parthenogenesis, 146–8, 163, 279n18; *see*
autocthoneity
Pasternak, B. L., 223
pathomimesis, 218, 289n7, n8; *see* innovation
through psychopathology
patrilineage: *see* title
peasantry, 'reconstituted', 4, 103, 120, 139,
254n7
Pentecostalists, 16, 55
People's National Movement (PNM), 2, 10,
178, 253n2
People's Temple: *see* J. Jones
Peter the Purger, 127
Phaedra, 167, 280n21
pharmaceuticals, 34, 54, 60, 61, 62, 82, 267n4
picong (and satire), 18, 39, 49, 52, 109, 230,
233, 264n6, 283n46; *see also* humour
Pinnacle Village, xi, 4, 33, 34, 38, 43, 54, 55,
60, 63, 70, 91, 92, 95, 107, 149, 160, 166,
170, 177, 209–10, 214, 254n6, 262n2,
263n3, 270n10, 287n25, 288n38
Plato, 17, 18, 19, 24, 147, 225, 258n30
polygyny, 89
Port-of-Spain, 1, 3, 6, 10, 54, 62, 67–9, 95, 96,
97, 120, 129, 136, 149, 175, 176, 177, 214,
215, 225, 227, 239, 285n7, 288n38
possession (spirit), 94–7, 268n14, 271n23; *see
also* travelling, mourning, altered states of
consciousness
power, of dominant gender and race, xiv, xvi,
31, 110–11, 112–13, 134, 158–9, 229–30,
241; of subdominant, xv, 110–11, 132–5
powers: *see* orishas
pragmatic 'norms': *see* according
prayers, 40–1, 52, 56, 63
Present State Examination, 67, 77, 268n7, n13
pressure, 40, 44, 45–6, 63, 227
prophets, prophecy, 14, 16, 17, 23, 113, 114,
124–6, 154–6, 163, 169, 219, 220, 221, 232,
258n33, 260n71, 281n28, 288n32, 290n12,
n15, 291n16, n17, n26; *see also* women and
religion, millennial movements, innovation,
nativist
psychiatry, 16–21, 28, 59, 267n3; comparative
(cultural), 16, 289n1; in Trinidad, 59–60,
65, 206; treatment of political and religious
radicals, 14, 16, 256n21, 257n22, 259n50
psychoactive substances, 133, 218; *see* ganja,
rum, altered states of consciousness
psychoanalysis, xv, 22–6, 28, 30, 130, 151–5,
163, 166, 207, 259n57, n59, 260n65,
281n24, 282n45, 293n41; and
understanding of innovation, xiii, 15, 22–9,
151–4, 224

Cambridge Studies in Social and Cultural Anthropology

Editors: Ernest Gellner, Jack Goody, Stephen Gudeman, Michael Herzfeld, Jonathan Parry

*available in paperback